To Marcus,

With best wishes
and many happy hours
on your birthday.

Fondest wishes

Joseph + Stephen

Sept. '89

Bravo!

Also by John Cargher:

Music for Pleasure
Opera and Ballet in Australia
There's Music in my Madness
How to Enjoy Opera Without Really Trying
How to Enjoy Music Without Really Trying

TWO HUNDRED YEARS OF OPERA IN AUSTRALIA

JOHN CARGHER

M

For Elizabeth, who helped a
self-made man make himself.

First published 1988 by The Macmillan Company of Australia
Pty Ltd in association with the Australian Broadcasting
Corporation

THE MACMILLAN COMPANY OF AUSTRALIA PTY LTD
107 Moray Street South Melbourne 3205
6 Clarke Street, Crows Nest 2065
Associated companies and representatives
throughout the world.

Cargher, John, 1919–
    Bravo! two hundred years of opera in Australia.

    Includes index.
    ISBN 0 333 47867 3.

    1. Opera – Australia – History. I. Title.

782.1'0994

National Library of Australia
cataloguing in publication data

Set in Meridian by Setrite Typesetters Ltd
Printed in Hong Kong
Design by Guy Mirabella

PROGRAMME

AUTHOR'S NOTE

A note for those who already own *Opera and Ballet in Australia*, written in 1975. Most of the old material has been re-written or amplified. The text has doubled! More has happened to raise opera to higher levels of excellence, specially in the smaller states between 1975 and 1987 than in the previous hundred years, and as much as possible of this has been included. You have here a new book, but some early histories of, for example, the Elizabethan Theatre Trust or the two National Theatres have been largely left intact; there was very little which could be added, because what I wrote then was told to me by people who lived through the period in question. Most of the illustrations are also new; in many instances what was first choice in 1975 has been replaced with different pictures of the same production.

The reality that no comprehensive history of the art in this country has ever been written weighed heavily on my mind. I cannot, and will not claim that my facts, or even my theories, will stand the test of time. I have done my best to eliminate inconsistencies. Where two or more interpretations or dates exist, I have often left them out. My positive assertions are based on previously published snippets from sources which I have found not only in Australia, but overseas. Frequently they have been contradictory or out of sequence, so that gaps are waiting to be filled. I have drawn mainly on three sources. Contemporary newspaper accounts, like those in the National Library, Canberra, and La Trobe Collection, Melbourne, and articles published in respected magazines, such as London's *Opera*, *Opera News* in New York and *Opera Australia*, have provided historical background. More important were personal reminiscences and memorabilia.

Like all the best stories, this is a book with a happy ending. While the previous volume left us in doubt as to the future of opera in Australia, that doubt no longer exists today.

ACKNOWLEDGEMENTS

This book could not have been written without the assistance of many people, so many that it would be impossible to separate them in order of their importance to the end result. Many prominent figures in the world of opera have given me hours of their time and I shall always treasure the tapes I made of our conversations. Others have done little more than contribute a single important piece to the jigsaw puzzle of Australian operatic history which led me into paths not previously explored. Sadly, a few of these people have since died. To one and all I offer my thanks for everything they have done to help me in my quest:

Douglas Abbot, William Akers, Claudio Alcorso, Douglas Anders, M. J. Aronsten, Charles J. Berg, Richard Bonynge, David P. Brown, Colin and Jenny Brumby, Frank Callaway, Clio Calodoukas, Sylvia Carr, Anthony Clarke, Marie Collier, Corinne Collins, David Colville, John Copley, Roger Covell, Sally Dawes, Richard Divall, Ronald Dowd, George Dreyfus, Jennifer Eddy, Lauris Elms, George Fairfax, Rosemary Florrimell, Tony Frewin, Robert Gard, Peggy Glanville-Hicks, Heather Grant, Mrs E. M. Gunston, Margaret Haggart, Stephen Hall, Sir Rupert Hamer, Brian Hansford, the Earl of Harewood, William and Laura Harrison, Marvell Hart, Eric Hauff, Karl Helmond, Mirrie Hill, Sir Robert Helpmann, Peter Hemmings, Judith Jacks, Gertrude Johnson, Ian Johnston, Barry Jones, Jeffry Joynton-Smith, Sir Robert Knox, Josephine Landsberg, John D. D. M. Lanigan-O'Keeffe, Glen Lehman, Mary Lewis, Alan Light, Kevin McBeath, Donald B. McDonald, Justin McDonnell, John A. McKenzie, Ken Mackenzie-Forbes, David Macfarlane, Carole McPhee, Jim McPherson, Molly Maddocks, Joan Maslin, Mr O. Miezitis, Harry M. Miller, James Mills, Peter Moore, James Murdoch, Kenneth Myer, Prue Neidorf, Moffat Oxenbould, Josephine Peoples, John Pine, Wendy Pomroy, Joseph Post, Thérèse Radic, Glenda Raymond, William Read, Robert Rosen, Kenneth and Victoria Rowell, Joseph Rush, Alfred Ruskin, Donald Smith, Kerry J. Smith, Leonard Spira, Maurice C. Timbs, Frank van Straten, Denis Vaughan, Terry Vaughan, Patrick Veitch, Miss V. E. Voigt, Neil Warren-Smith, Vincent A. Warrener, Celia Winter-Irving, John Winther, Elizabeth Wood, John Young.

My apologies to anyone I may have accidentally omitted; my quest has been spread over many years. Finally, I would like to thank the staff members of the many opera companies who have at all times been most co-operative in assisting me in every way.

John Cargher

overture

'Opus' is a Latin word meaning work. And this book could be described as Cargher's Opus 6. However, over the years Opus (or Op.) has been commonly identified with music, not books. Therefore I must justify the extravagant claim that you are reading 'an opera'. The reality is that John Cargher has written six opera.

That last sentence is neither a printing error, nor a literary aberration. 'Opera' is the plural of 'opus' and the theatrical spectacle which is the subject of this book, and which is presumably of interest to the reader, is not a single entity but rather a collection (more than one opus) of music, drama, design, scenic construction and much else, which together forms one work of art. Unfortunately, few operas — the musical kind — reach the ideal which caused Wagner to add another German word to the international music language, *Gesamtkunstwerk*; literally translated: a complete work of art. The history of opera in Australia somehow divides itself naturally into acts, scenes and the 'overture' you are reading at this moment, hence my whimsical description. Like modern Australia itself, opera in this country grew from humble beginnings to a multi-faceted and culturally grown-up entity, which justifies the subtitle: *Two Hundred Years of Opera in Australia*.

Australians have always been better at keeping cricket scores than music scores. Every player in every Football Grand Final and the name of the jockey of every horse in every Melbourne Cup is preserved for evermore. I am afraid that we are a race of snobs, real and inverted. This was not always so. Once upon a time we took a naïve pride in the achievements of all Australians. Today we believe that our sportsmen are the greatest in the world but that our artists, in most fields, are sub-standard.

Any history of opera in Australia can only be as good as the sources available to the author. This book, like its predecessor, is a house built of straw because its bricks can not be made without the clay of historical facts and they, as you will see, are often not only non-existent, but held together by contradictory legends created over the years by well-intentioned people. A lot could be done, time and finance permitting, but little has been done. The potential has been proven to exist during the last twelve years with the publication of Harold Love's *The Golden Age of Australian Opera*, which covers only the Lyster opera companies from 1861 to 1880 and, to a lesser extent, by Thérèse Radic's *Melba, the Voice of Australia*, which assembled the facts and legends surrounding the greatest singer of the past produced by this country more accurately than anybody had done previously, including Melba herself.

We have, thus far, only one tenth of the history of opera in this country comprehensively covered in the Harold Love book, and my own reasonably accurate history of the Australian Opera from its inception in 1956 until 1975, together with very superficial surveys of other activities in the field of opera in Australia.

One remnant of the past still haunts us. The very mention of Dame Nellie Melba's name implies that no other singer ever born in this or any other country can possibly equal that greatest of all Australians. In recent years, Joan Sutherland has also attained fame far beyond the confines of the opera house. At the risk of a public lynching, I honestly believe that most of the millions who watched the telecasts of Sutherland in recent years did not greatly enjoy what they heard and saw. It was the thing to say that they had heard Sutherland 'live', just as everybody over eighty claims to have heard Melba in the flesh. Love of singing, let alone love of opera does not come into it.

Melba and Sutherland rank with Phar Lap and Don Bradman as national symbols. Yet, to find one serious music critic who will admit that evenings at the opera in Australia can be as good as anything seen or heard anywhere else in the world, is impossible. It happens to be a fact, though not, admittedly, an everyday occurrence. What has become the norm in recent years is that routine performances by several of our opera companies have an average standard as good or better than most overseas companies. The reality of the capacity audiences for quality opera cannot be denied; people do not spend $40 or $50 to see something they do not enjoy. And they can rest assured that, despite what they may read in the press, their enjoyment is due to the excellence of the singers, the designers, the producers and the managers who assemble the world's most complex art for our benefit.

The invention of 'Surtitles' has brought opera within the reach of all, and the fact that not only here but overseas the critics have fulminated against them in vain should give us food for thought. Far be it from me to say that every Australian performance of opera is faultless. But the same faults can be found all over the world, and what matters in the end is the balance between those faults and the individual virtues of a performance in which so many things can and, by the sheer law of averages, must go wrong. The perfect performance for which we all yearn is rare in even the greatest of the world's opera houses. For every person gaining entry to La Scala in Milan or the Metropolitan Opera House in New York or the Royal Opera House, Covent Garden, there are many hundreds of others who go to see comparatively cheaper and often inferior opera and enjoy its pleasures, as Australians are now doing.

This book is for those who have ignored the acidulous comments of our critics who often know very little more than most of their readers. Newspapers have to print reviews of current happenings and many 'experts' are no more than staff reporters who were thrown into their jobs head first. 'It's only music...' Is it? The great composers did not think so. They set out to entertain, to make money! The fact that some of them were geniuses has nothing to do with it. Who cares if a diminished seventh (whatever that may be) is in the wrong place, as long as we have a good time?

The publishers and I believe that anyone interested in opera who lives in this country would wish to know how we came to be so very good, in spite of the immense distances from the other opera centres of the world. Making a chronological list is not only impossible, but would be dull reading. My prime concern is to keep you reading, to hold your interest, to perhaps enlighten you as to this, that or the other aspect of the domestic article. You will not find here the achievements of Australians abroad, but only their contribution on the home front.

I hope my book will be read — not like a novel, but like a box of chocolates from which you can choose the soft or hard centres, according to taste. It covers a very broad field. What fascinates one reader may bore another. Perhaps I have devoted too much space to the early days of companies which have helped to create the rising stocks of my favourite art. Personally, I always find the beginnings of any career described in a biography the most interesting part. The battle to overcome impossible odds holds a fascination for me. Beginnings are also the most vital stage in the history of an art. On the other hand, some obvious gaps may be found in my coverage of the most recent years. Not only do you and I remember them, but they can be found in the newspaper files of your local library. Nobody knows whether they may not one day prove to have made a lasting contribution to Australian culture. 'Culture' is not a word I like, nor do I find 'education' particularly edifying. This is not a cultural or educational book, but something which will, I hope, be more lasting than an opera programme.

It is very easy to go to an 'entertainment' and to have a good time. I don't subscribe to the theory that you have to know a lot about background and technique to enjoy it. I believe that all art is a form of giving people pleasure, or entertainment.

'To entertain: to amuse, divert.' Perhaps diversion is a better word. 'Diversion: relief from work or absorption, amusement.' Do we really go to the opera to be educated? To be uplifted? Surely not, whatever our teachers may say; and I say 'teachers' guardedly, for our critics and writers on these subjects and any other matters of art are much too inclined to treat us all as children.

I am sure we all have one thing in common: the memory of being taught in school how important, how beautiful or (dreaded expression) how 'good for us' such-and-such was. Do we, as adults, not have the right now to make up our own minds? I hardly class myself as a novice in opera, but after umpteen performances of *Fidelio* I still haven't learnt its 'meaning', whatever that may be. I get pleasure, pure and simple, by going to the theatre, and if that is uplifting or educational, fair enough, but I still go because it pleases me. If it didn't, I wouldn't go. And if it doesn't please you, don't you go either! At least, don't go and see something you know is not to your liking. Always remember that opera is many things to many people.

There are some operas I dislike intensely, but musical theatre as such is a constant source of pleasure to me. Let us say that I am a gourmet for this fare and that like any other gourmet I sometimes, even often, am not served too well. That's all part of the fun of the thing. If everything in the garden were lovely, there would be no bliss in beauty. Pleasure in art and pleasure in beauty are relative things and the height of pleasure and beauty is its contrast with the ugly, the mediocre, or the average. May the day of unimpaired excellence never come in these fields, or any other. It would leave us with no great memories to cherish.

The ability to sing an aria does not qualify a singer to appear in a medium as complex as opera. And one very good singer does not make an opera, just as one swallow does not make a summer. Even if he or she were to develop into a great star after learning not only singing, but musicianship, acting, mime, movement, fencing, dancing, make-up (and all the other things which distinguish an opera singer from a concert singer who stands stiffly before an audience) — unless that singer is surrounded by the planned happening of an opera performance, his or her contribution is worthless.

From the practical, no matter how outrageous, to the impractical: let's look at the habits of Australian audiences. And let me hasten to say that we are very far from unique in our behaviour patterns. The trouble is that in a society starved since it began (through no fault of its own) of things which were daily fare in Europe, there was little scope for developing the kind of audiences that have kept opera alive in other countries.

Anybody who believes that being cultured means 'being seen' at the opera is doomed. He or she will never gain pleasure from the medium because the real purpose of the exercise is not to be seen but to see and, since it is a full-time job being seen at the opera, there is little time left to get anything out of the spectacle on stage. Until the early part of this century they kept the lights on in European theatres, so that those who came to be seen could be seen. Boxes in theatres were not designed for a good view of the stage, but for a good view of the other boxes. (I told you we were not unique in this field; in fact, we were, and are, as much amateurs in the field of social graces as in the more serious one of appreciating the art of our choice.)

If European audiences, even in living memory, and even today up to a point, can beat our phony culture vultures at their own game, they also beat us in Elysian fields. While the ancestors of those bores, stared, and were stared at, night after night, performances continued on stage and some members of the audiences did not ignore everything presented to them. Slowly the focus of attention swung from the auditorium to the stage. The point was reached when even the overture, the intermezzo and the preludes to acts, which had been invented as a kind of musical warning bell while people cast their final pieces of gossip across to their friends and enemies, began to be a part of the enjoyable whole.

Nobody knows exactly who started to turn the lights out during performances, (some say it was Mahler, others Toscanini) but it was the one step which made it almost impossible to ignore the happenings on the stage. And what was actually taking place up there in those days has, both in opera and in ballet, come down to us in a recognizable form. I don't think anybody will deny that an audience exposed regularly to *Rigoletto* or *The Marriage of Figaro* will in the end find enjoyment in the quality of the performance.

Thus were born the audiences who kept the arts alive overseas, while we in Australia were denied this privilege. When we were charged with aesthetic indifference, we could, until recently, cry poverty with justification. Elsewhere in this book I shall demonstrate that what was seen here, in the early history of Australia, was not so far removed from what was seen in Europe. The point is that it was not seen here often enough to leave a lasting impact and the accursed villains of cost and inflation ultimately caused the local article to fail to keep up with the more sophisticated presentations of Europe and America. It is the middle twentieth century which lies at the root of our trouble, not the much extolled 'good old days', which were no better in Europe than they were here. Artistically they were lousy by modern standards. Let us not forget that to start with.

What it was that audiences did or did not see in Australia is the subject of this book and again, I make no claim that it is, or attempts to be, a definitive history of opera in this country: too much mitigates against it. I once complained, in the course of a broadcast, about the huge amount of historical material on music in Australia which lies in dusty unopened boxes in libraries and museums. Immense collections of historical memorabilia have been donated to public bodies in the capital cities, including Canberra, but shortages of staff prevent the indexation of material appertaining to the arts, which are considered of low priority. What infuriates me is that, until such time as these monumental collections are indexed, they may not be touched by people engaged on major, or even minor research projects, such as this one.

I write books about subjects I love in the hope that they will bring pleasure to people. What follows will, I sincerely hope, pass the time pleasantly for anybody interested in the subject. I am not really worried that it will be mistaken for a cookbook or a thriller. As some of my Jewish American friends would say: enjoy already!

Opera in 1988.
Seen in New York, London, Milan or any major Australian Theatre, only the availability of the few great voices of our day give an edge to productions. Production and singing standards in Australia today compete on equal terms with some of the world's best, even when it comes to being adventurous or outrageous. (Australian Opera's 1988 *L'incoronazione di Poppea* by Monteverdi designed by Carl Friedrich Oberle and produced by Göran Järvefelt.)

ACT 1

history

ACT 1: SCENE 1
OPERATIC FOSSILS
IN A BARREN LAND

Since nobody really knows how, when or where the art form loosely described as 'opera' came into being, we should not be surprised that establishing when it began in Australia is not exactly easy — unless, of course, you are willing to simply follow in the footsteps of nearly everybody else. It would be so simple to say, as I have done myself:

The first opera staged in Australia, *Clari, or The Maid of Milan* by Sir Henry Bishop, was performed in Sydney on Friday, 31 October 1834.

Nobody of any importance is going to argue with that statement and, come to that, neither will I. Some people also claim that Australia was not 'settled' or 'founded' in 1788, but at various earlier dates. But if they wish to ignore the fact that the government of the day chose to celebrate 1988 as the Bicentenary Year, I will not do so. Historians have written at length about earlier settlements. Let them. My job is to deal with Australian operatic history, which is rather like reading a detective story; there are plenty of clues, but also a very large number of red herrings, some of them imported from what Australians used to call 'Home', meaning the British Isles, including Ireland!

I cannot prove conclusively that *Clari* was the first *opera* to be presented in Australia. I can only say that it began our history in the field and deserves close inspection. At the same time, claims that other 'operas' were staged here before 1834 should be investigated; they are fascinating and wide-ranging enough to warrant closer inspection than they have received so far. One of the first candidates was exhibited as early as 1796, while the most notable, most plausible and most difficult to disprove, is a *Marriage of Figaro* on 11 May 1833!

Nothing is more dangerous than to accept the simple word 'opera' in assessing what was staged by whom in those days. The where and when can be established by referring to the early newspapers of the Australian colonies. The trouble is that they had a nasty habit of omitting all references to *what* was staged. In fact, there is a huge log of claims on behalf of operas supposedly staged before *Clari*, but I don't propose to deal at length with more than the two I have mentioned.

The most shaky claim is the earliest, inevitably. Many odd venues have been used to stage operas and in stranger places than a penal colony. The fact that *The Poor Soldier* with music by William Shield was performed on 23 July 1796 in the Sidaway Theatre in Sydney can be established. What must be doubted is whether the Sidaway Theatre was a theatre and whether *The Poor Soldier* was an opera.

Let us take the theatre first. Robert Sidaway was one of the first convicts to be transported; he arrived in the smallest ship of the First Fleet, the *Friendship*. In due course he was given a pardon and built what must have been the first theatre in Sydney, the Sidaway Theatre, which opened on 16 January 1796 in Bligh Street. Nobody knows where it was situated, but it 'held' 120, though a breakdown of seats, standing room and the customary squeeze in the one-shilling gallery were probably exaggerated to make Australia's first theatre appear bigger than it really was. Inevitably, it attracted its share of thieves and pickpockets and was closed periodically

The first Australian theatre.

A Frenchman, Le Comte de Beauvoir, in his book *Voyage autour du Monde* (*Voyage Around the World*) printed this picture with the caption: '*Une première à Sydney 1796*'. The convict Robert Sidaway built a theatre in Sydney in 1796 after arriving with the first fleet eight years earlier. *The Poor Soldier*, 'music by William Shield' was performed there in 1796. But was it an opera?

by the authorities. It is not known when it was demolished, probably in 1801. However primitive the venue, let us not hold that against the work which was performed there; after all Mozart's *Magic Flute* was first staged in a barn 28 metres long by 14 metres wide, and nobody doubts that that was a performance of an opera!

This is not the place to go into the first, or any other, of the plays produced in Australia. That field has been explored at length by many others and I am not qualified to judge the accuracy of what has been written, but Robert Sidaway, as a presumed pioneer of opera, is a suitable subject for further investigation. Though he did not stage the first play in the colony, he certainly built its first theatre and very little is known of what he presented there. Music of some sort or another was part of every theatrical attraction in those days. Pianos were among the first furniture brought to Australia by the settlers and the soldiers had military bands which for many decades provided music for public occasions of all types. Plays were frequently billed as 'Melo-Dramas', meaning that they had musical accompaniment, and the name of the regiment which provided the accompanying band was always mentioned, as was the regiment's commanding officer of course.

What was later to become the Victorian ballad was already part of the social scene. Musical *soirées* were the rule rather than the exception in wealthier homes and there is more than a little significance in the fact that actors, musicians, dancers and singers alike were always billed as 'Mrs' Smith or 'Mr' Jones or 'Miss' Jackson. Strolling players were considered vagabonds and they gained a respectability by those titles.

The history of *The Poor Soldier* can be traced comparatively easily, though one has to go far afield before it can be conclusively established that it has no right to be described as an opera. And the lessons learnt from such researches equally rule out most other prior claimants to operatic fame. Let me quickly establish a few facts which can be historically traced from the 1790s to my own younger days as a theatre-goer — the 1930s! Plays to this date commonly included music of some sort and there is evidence that this applied to plays presented in Australia as much as elsewhere in the world. Audiences demanded music. Two hundred years ago they wanted songs, sometimes sung by the actors, sometimes by singers engaged to entertain them between the acts. By the time I began to visit the theatre, such music had

shrunk to the provision of 'palm-court' style orchestras to play overtures and interval music in the pit. But a play with incidental music is not an opera, no more than a play with musical interludes or a play in which a character or characters sing a song or songs.

To give an example applicable to early Australia, Eric Irvin in *Opera*, September 1969, claims that Henry Fielding's last work for the stage, his ballad opera *An Old Man Taught Wisdom; or, The Virgin Unmasked* was staged in Sydney in 1800. This may well be true, though neither Fielding nor the full title was advertised. It is true that *The Virgin Unmasked* played at the Sidaway Theatre as a filler after *The Recruiting Officer* and was billed as 'A Musical Entertainment'. Yet Fielding never wrote music, he wrote farces and plays, some of which were turned into ballad operas by the insertion of music by various other composers. Grove makes no mention of any setting of Fielding's 'last ballad opera'; in fact Grove makes no mention of any Fielding ballad opera at all. Sidaway mentioned neither author nor composer and only half the title, which could very well have been attached to any other plot by any other author. No composer is listed even in England! And that, we are to believe, was an early Australian performance of an opera?

The Poor Soldier was a play by one John O'Keeffe, first produced in Dublin in 1777 and staged at Covent Garden in 1783—unsuccessfully—under the title *The Shamrock; or The Anniversary of St Patrick* (now you see why I made sure that Ireland was included in the term 'British Isles') and later under its original title. Unfortunately for the champions of *The Poor Soldier* as an opera, William Shield was in London, not Ireland, in 1777 and did not produce his first primitive comic opera until 1778. Futhermore, Covent Garden was not one of the two theatres in London licensed to present opera in English. No license was required to stage Italian operas, but only the King's Theatre and Drury Lane could have staged any 'opera' by Shield using the English, or Irish, play *The Poor Soldier* as a libretto. Covent Garden was not an opera house, but a playhouse from 1766 until 1789, when two operas were staged there; and then only because the King's Theatre, for which they had been scheduled, had burnt down.

Evenings at Covent Garden and all major London and European theatres at that time and until near the end of the nineteenth century were long affairs, consisting usually of one major work, some dancing or a ballet, some music or singing and a short farce to close the proceedings. Australian playbills show a similar pattern. The final farce was usually described as an 'afterpiece', and *The Poor Soldier* was such an afterpiece. This fact alone should rule against it as the first opera staged in Australia. Nobody disputes that it was produced at Covent Garden, but it was a short play! The fact that it was a play with music, as were all the other plays of that time and for 150 years thereafter, does not alter this fact. And this is where our amateur historians draw some wrong conclusions.

A learned and most excellent tome by one Roger Fiske published in 1973 is called *English Theatre Music in the Eighteenth Century*, and that title is totally accurate; the book covers every type of music played in English theatres of that period. Unfortunately, Fiske uses the words 'opera' and 'ballad opera' rather loosely, never defining either, and it may be found that many pre-*Clari* works lay claim to accreditation as operas for no better reason than Fiske's haphazard use of those words. William Shield was the musical director at Covent Garden from 1778 to 1791 and Grove's *Dictionary of Music and Musicians* lists *The Shamrock* (or *The Poor Soldier*) among the 'dramatic works for which Shield wrote the music, or part of the music'.

Yes, William Shield did write music for *The Poor Soldier*. O'Keeffe had moved to London and Shield selected, arranged and occasionally composed part of the music for many of his plays. But you cannot equate an O'Keeffe play with the libretto of an opera. However primitive, a work cannot be described as an opera unless the music, or at least the majority of the music, is written specifically for the work in question and is the work of one composer. Neither description can be applied to *The Poor Soldier* or, if it comes to that, any of the works presented at Covent Garden during those years. *The Poor Soldier* contained 18 songs, only one of which was definitely by Shield, according to Fiske, while two were 'probably' by Shield and three 'may have been' by Shield. (Fiske is the very model of a modern music scholar!) On the other hand, Shield did write an overture to the piece. Cheers! But does all that add up to what we today call an 'opera'? I think not.

To flog a dead horse, it was customary to substitute other songs at will, according to the whims of the singers, and we can be almost certain that the music heard at Covent Garden was not wholly, and possibly not even

in part the same as that used in the Sidaway Theatre in Sydney in 1796. If *The Poor Soldier* were to be accepted as an 'opera', I can make a case that the first performance of an opera, in fact, took place in Australian waters even before the landing of the First Fleet! On 2 January 1788 some actors among the convicts in that fleet 'this night made a play and sang many songs'. On 4 June 1789, George Farquhar's comedy *The Recruiting Officer* became the first theatrical entertainment in Australia. It too was interrupted by numerous songs. What is to stop us from calling that Australia's first opera? Only the fact that we do not know what songs were sung, something we don't know about *The Poor Soldier* either.

What about *The Marriage of Figaro*, which was staged in Barnett Levey's New Theatre Royal in Sydney in 1833? Why has no mention of this fact ever appeared in any book on music written in Australia? The issue is confused because in London Sir Henry Bishop (the composer of *Clari*), had arranged English versions of *Don Giovanni* as well as *The Marriage of Figaro*, in each case with additional music of his own. *Don Giovanni* was at least disguised as *The Libertine*, but *Figaro* was staged in London under the original Beaumarchais title in translation. We are told that Australia saw 'the English arrangement' in 1833 and the reports were not kind about the performance which was given by *actors*, not singers! (This is negatively proved by the fact that, according to contemporary press reports, only one member of the company, Mrs Jones, 'was well able to sing the lighter ballads of the day'.) Should we pity Mozart, if it was indeed his music which constituted the 'lighter ballads of the day'? There must be some doubt whether the term 'the English arrangement' was, in fact, the one by Bishop. Otherwise, why else would everybody give the same composer's *Clari* priority over Mozart's *Figaro* for a hundred and fifty years?

Let me add a red herring of my own: in 1784, the year after *The Shamrock* at Covent Garden, William Shield provided music for nine plays, including — *The Marriage of Figaro* by Beaumarchais! (This was two years before Mozart wrote his opera on the same subject.) Is it not possible that Sydney in 1833 saw the Beaumarchais play with music arranged by Shield or others and not the Bishop travesty of Mozart's opera? It is inconceivable that one year later Levey staged *Clari, or the Maid of Milan*, without anyone ever commenting on the fact

Opera without music?
The accepted first performance of an opera in Australia took place on 31 October 1834 in the New Theatre Royal in Sydney. *Clari, or the Maid of Milan* by Sir Henry Bishop was billed as 'the celebrated opera'. Yet the *Sydney Herald* reported that it was 'a dramatic opera (without any music) . . .' A soprano later praised by Mendelssohn played the title rôle. *Clari* was built around *Home, Sweet Home* — without any music?

that Mozart had preceded Sir Henry Bishop.

So, when I accept *Clari* as the still-undisputed first opera staged in Australia, I must still admit having some reservations. It is not too difficult to dismiss *Clari* on grounds similar, though not identical, to those which disqualified earlier works which were not operas. There is some dispute as to whether *Clari* was an opera at all; Sir Henry Bishop had a nasty habit of putting other people's music into vaudevilles or operas of his own. I do not suggest that *Clari* belonged to the class of Bishop's *The Libertine, Artaxerxes* ('curtailed' from Arne, whatever that means) or *The Night Before the Wedding* ('from' Boieldieu). I do suggest that *Clari* belonged to those of his many works which were dramatic recitatives with interpolated songs, either serious or comic, works like *Teasing Made Easy, Exit by Mistake* or *Who Wants a Wife?*

If *Clari* was a work of this type, the pattern of presentations by its impresario, publican Barnett Levey, remains unbroken. Had he not been staging, with considerable success, various imported burlesques by less famous authors and composers than Bishop? Had he not, in fact, built his Theatre Royal and then the New Theatre Royal on concerts of popular music, rather than fully staged performances? A quick look at Levey's background makes the staging of any kind of serious work that could be called an opera most unlikely.

Barnett Levey ought to be a lot more famous than he is, since he was an early cousin of another upsidedown planner, Joern Utzon (*see* pages 92−6). A shopkeeper and auctioneer by profession, Levey decided to go into the theatre business and formed a company with 200 shareholders on 19 November 1827. Newspaper reports give a fascinating glimpse of what then happened. By January 1828, we are told, 'canvas has been procured for the scenes and an amateur has been employed painting them'. Later that year the scenery has been made and actors have been employed and 'Mr Levey is now looking for plays'! It takes a genius to make scenery and employ actors before knowing what the play is going to be or when the theatre will open.

A year later (no performances yet!) Levey gets a licence to open his theatre, which apparently still does not exist! There follow eighteen months of concerts given in the saloon of the Royal Hotel, which was the building on which Levey had actually been engaged, not a theatre at all. After the said eighteen months, in December 1830, Levey goes bankrupt and the hotel (not theatre) is sold at a heavy loss.

An apparently prosperous interlude as a jeweller and watchmaker ensues until 24 August 1832 when Levey obtains another licence to open a theatre. Only then, on Boxing Day 1832, the first Theatre Royal of Sydney actually opened, the attractions being *Black-eyed Susan* and *Monsieur Tonton*. The theatre appears to have been a temporary annexe to the Royal Hotel and another year was to pass before Levey converted an old store behind his hotel into the New Theatre Royal.

What was it that Levey staged in his new theatre? The titles mean little to us today, but we do know that actors and actresses had to be able to sing and dance. Buckingham, Levey's resident comedian, made history within months of the opening by striking for more pay. Levey actually paid up and was severely chastised by the editor of the *Sydney Gazette* for giving in!

More to the point, Levey's first leading lady, Mrs Taylor, 'possessed a sweet voice which enabled the management to stage such operas as *Don Giovanni*'!

Behold! What have we here? A performance of *Don Giovanni* in 1834? Our poor historians do seem to have a strange set of values. It seems more than strange to bother with Bishop's *Clari* when Mozart's masterpiece was to hand. It is not recorded whether any of Mozart's music was used on this occasion, but the presentation was actually entitled *Giovanni in London*, and nobody knows precisely what this 'operatic extravaganza' contained. It is perhaps worth noting, though, that it was a popular spectacle in London for many years and that

Figaro Without Mozart. Barnett Levey's New Theatre Royal staged *The Marriage of Figaro*, 'the English arrangement', in 1833. It was almost certainly the play by Beaumarchais with music by Sir Henry Bishop as well as Mozart or — more likely — with the incidental music provided by William Shield in 1784, two years before Mozart wrote his *Figaro*.

the part of Giovanni was usually taken by actresses (not singers!) who liked to show off their legs. In Sydney the actress-singer Mrs Taylor was described as notorious, quite possibly because of the amount of leg she showed in this non-opera.

Clari however, was the vehicle which launched 'Home Sweet Home' on the world and *Clari* had an Australian leading lady. English-born Eliza Winstanley was all of sixteen years old and appeared more than once in the course of the evening's entertainment. Since one work was not enough to attract the public, there was a lengthy playbill ending with the classic line: 'The evening to conclude with *AGNES, OR THE BLEEDING NUN* — MISS WINSTANLEY'.

Our first overseas 'star', Miss Winstanley, actually did go overseas, but it is significant that she became famous (well, let us say: known) first as an actress and later as a writer. Much has been made of this fact, and it is perfectly true that Eliza was known primarily for her Shakespearean and other classic rôles in England. However, the no longer quite-so-young lady still had a good voice in London in 1846 or 1847 when she was heard by Mendelssohn, who praised her 'rich singing voice'. Also rarely mentioned is the fact that she sang extensively in concerts and oratorios in Australia between 1834 and 1846.

Further confusion has been created, by myself among others, by the fact that the *Australian* of 4 November 1834 reported about the première of *Clari*: 'Anne Winstanley sang *Kate Kearney* very prettily'. We know that Eliza was the *Bleeding Nun*. Is it possible that Anne sang the title rôle in the Bishop opera? Or was there only one singer and Anne a misprint for Eliza? I have been able to clarify this through the intervention of the Winstanley family's descendants. Anne was a sister of Eliza, seven years her junior; that is, she was nine years old and presumably *Kate Kearney* was one of the customary songs used as interpolations at the time. Anne neither sang nor acted when she grew up, marrying at sixteen.

There remains a mystery which has been used more and more frequently as an argument against *Clari*'s place in our history. It is based on a single entry in one newspaper, the *Sydney Herald* of 3 November 1834, which reads: 'On Friday evening was produced the dramatic opera (without any music) of *Clari, or the Maid of Milan*...' An opera without music? The writer actually called it an opera. Too many writers have taken the view that the libretto of the opera was performed as a play. Whatever the musical value of some of the slapdash pastiches which Sir Henry Bishop put together at the drop of a hat, the background of the work in this case precludes the possibility of such a conclusion.

Clari was an attempt by Bishop to cash in on his popular song 'Home, Sweet Home'. The work, from beginning to end, is no more than a frame built around repetitions of and variations on that song and its music. *Clari* without 'Home, Sweet Home' would be like a meat pie without meat; the whole *raison d'être* of the piece would disappear. Not only that, but the very fact that little Anne appeared in her song in the course of the evening shows that some music was sung. The only logical interpretation of the newspaper report's 'without any music' is that for some reason the usual orchestral accompaniment was missing that night. A strike by the musicians would not have been an unusual thing in the nineteenth century, when singers, actors, musicians or stage hands were always underpaid or sometimes unpaid.

There is an alternative explanation, which has not been explored. As late as the early twentieth century some singers, like John McCormack, to name but one, used music or small books of words in their concerts. If *Clari* was indeed the first opera to be performed in Australia, it appears likely that concert versions of parts or even whole operas were staged during the preceding 46 years of the colony's existence. In these, the singers probably read their music from printed scores. Not even a primitive theatrical presentation, such as Bishop's 'dramatic opera' must have been, would have dared to have its characters deliver their lines from hand-held music sheets. Is it not likely that singing from memory amazed a raw reporter enough to write that *Clari* was produced without music (being held by the singer)?

I am not prepared to go into academic arguments as to what constitutes an opera, a ballad opera or a pastiche, but *Clari*, although not the kind of thing we would accept as an opera today, does meet the requirements of a continuous story set to music by one man writing an integrated score. The very fact that all of the music was built around an early form of *Leitmotiv* confirms this work's present claim as the first opera to be staged in Australia. That is my conclusion at the time of writing, but the picture is so confused that I shall not be in the least surprised if another claim is recognized if further facts are unearthed in the future.

ACT 1: SCENE 2
WOMEN START THE
FIRST OPERA SEASONS

The history of opera in Australia really begins in 1842, not in Sydney or in Melbourne, but in Hobart! For it was that city which saw Australia's first continuous season of operas in repertory, though singers and presentation may not have been of a standard anyone would accept today. What should please modern feminists is that for more than a century women played a major rôle in acting as promoters and *impresarias* of opera in Australia. An honour roll of women in the field would be a document unequalled, I think, anywhere else in the world. Mrs Michael Clarke, Madame Maria Carandini, Fanny Simonson, Dame Nellie Melba, Contessa Nancy Filippini, Gertrude Johnson and Mrs Clarice Lorenz played a major part in popularizing an art in which women were and are rarely prominent overseas, except as singers. Offhand, I can only think of Emma Carelli in Rome, Mary Garden, who headed the Chicago Opera for exactly one year, and Lilian Baylis, the founder of the Sadler's Wells Opera, which is now the English National Opera. No doubt there were others, but for an underpopulated nation like Australia the ladies were remarkably omnipresent.

It was indeed a woman who started the first proper opera season to be staged in Australia. Mrs Michael (Anne) Clarke and an ensemble of artists brought opera to Hobart in 1842. But they also brought Shakespeare and ballet to Tasmania, they sang, acted, danced and even painted their own scenery, and they continued to do so for nearly four years, playing in a theatre built in 1837 which still exists today, beautifully restored and now called the Theatre Royal.

Good luck to the admirable people who brought culture to our colonial ancestors, but are we really to believe that their performances of Weber's *Der Freischütz*, Bellini's *La sonnambula* or Auber's *Fra Diavolo* were whàt we would consider performances of opera today? I doubt it.

The stars of Mrs Clarke's troupe were the *prima donna* Theodosia Yates Stirling and 'a successful prófessional dancer', one Gerome Carandini, said to have been the tenth Marquis of Saranzo or Sargano. (I don't propose to investigate the obscure Italian ancestry of the gentleman; his Australian life is far more interesting.) Theodosia was more than a singer, she was a talented musician who had been chorus mistress at Drury Lane in London in her youth. She was to become the mother of Nellie Stewart, whose talents prior to becoming the most famous Australian to shine in comedy until well into the twentieth century included appearances in grand opera, as well as Gilbert and Sullivan, over many years. In 1888 Nellie Stewart sang Marguerite in *Faust* for twenty-four consecutive performances! No wonder she became a comedienne, after inevitably losing much of her singing voice.

Nellie's mother was partnered by the handsome Italian count, Carandini. Dancer Carandini made his debut in Hobart as a singer! A critic describes him as a counter tenor, though there is some doubt whether the term then meant what it means today. However, vocal achievements in Mrs Clarke's company may even have included a counter tenor, as we understand the term, singing Weber or Bellini. In due course Carandini

The impresarias.
Above: Women founded and ran numerous opera companies in Australia from the earliest years until the last of the 'private' companies in the 1950s. Many started life as singers. *Left to right*: Maria Carandini, Nellie Melba, Gertrude Johnson.

Leading Man in skirts No. 1.
Right: Nellie Stewart was the greatest comedienne-cum-singer in Australian history. She started as a soprano, in 1888 singing twenty-four Marguerites in *Faust* on consecutive nights. Years as Principal Boy in pantomimes proved to be more remunerative.

Leading Man in skirts No. 2.
Above: The first 'native' Australian star, Maria Carandini, was London-born (1826) Mary Burgess, a contralto who sang most of the leading tenor rôles in opera while still in her teens during Australia's first proper opera seasons — in Hobart! Later she started opera companies of her own.

married seventeen-year-old Mary Burgess, a contralto, who promptly became a professional singer under the title of Maria Carandini. Her place in later Australian history is secure, but her initial efforts in Hobart are of curiosity rather than musical value; Maria (not her husband) sang the *tenor* leads in most of the operas presented there!

It must be clear that the twice-weekly performances presented by Mrs Clarke in Hobart in the 1840s bore little resemblance to the titles we find in history books. It is not just that Theodosia Yates Stirling sang Lucy in *Lucia di Lammermoor* (vocal and orchestral parts scored by herself from memory!) one night and played Lady Macbeth in Shakespeare's tragedy the next, but opera and ballet and drama were mixed in the one evening more often than not. To make the picture even more ludicrous to us, the orchestra consisted of the local brass band which would only play on the stage itself, where it could be seen.

We thus have a picture of Boieldieu's *Jean de Paris*, the first proper opera to be presented in Australia, with a woman playing the title role, a male dancer in a singing role, scenery painted by the artists themselves and the band on stage behind the singers. It was not exactly what we would call a real performance of an opera today, but it was a recorded work by one composer, however mutilated it may have been, and we have no idea what the staging, orchestration or even the vocal parts were like. *Jean de Paris* is as forgotten today as *Clari, or the Maid of Milan*, but *Lucia di Lammermoor*, *La sonnambula* and other works presented by Mrs Clarke's company over the next four years are still around and if anybody wants to make a case against *Clari*, the verdict should not be moved back to the early convict days, as has been suggested, but forward to Mrs Clarke's company in 1842. (Sydneysiders eat your hearts out!)

In the years which followed there were large numbers of indigenous opera companies in all the major, and many minor cities, of Australia. None had continuity and opera as an art was still treated as part of the repertoire of theatre companies which were not primarily opera companies. As in England, plays were presented with musical interludes, including songs, and if enough actors were around to get through an opera with box office appeal, why not? Operas became the highlights of seasons all over the country, though for quite a few years only Hobart had a continuity of new

The Swan of Erin.
The world-famous Irish soprano Catherine Hayes came to Australia several times and is direct proof that California was way behind the Antipodes in operatic matters. She starred in San Francisco's first opera (*Norma*) in 1854, a dozen years after little Hobart's first seasons and five years after Isaac Nathan wrote and staged an Australian opera in Sydney.

works following each other, developing real singing voices which often remained in circulation until the palmy days of William Saurin Lyster in the 1860s and 1870s. Melbourne, for example, saw its first opera in 1846, but what passed for *La sonnambula* was clearly only an approximation staged by actors, for the not-exactly-expert newspapper critics condemned 'the presumption which murdered with inadequate resources... a priceless gem of the lyric drama'.

In 1855 the world-famous soprano Catherine Hayes gave concerts which produced such tumultuous applause that John Black, the owner of the brand-new Theatre Royal in Bourke Street (seating, or accommodating, 3300) quickly assembled a supporting company, including Maria Carandini, to enable Hayes to sing the title rôle in the same, previously ill-fated, *Sonnambula*. With a chorus of fifty and a good orchestra and a leading lady who could really sing, Black's success was immediate and *La sonnambula* was followed by *Lucia di Lammermoor*, *Norma*, *The Bohemian Girl* and *Lucrezia Borgia*. The quality of these performances (probably influenced by the supervision of their imported star) was such that Mrs Clarke's primitive company in Hobart

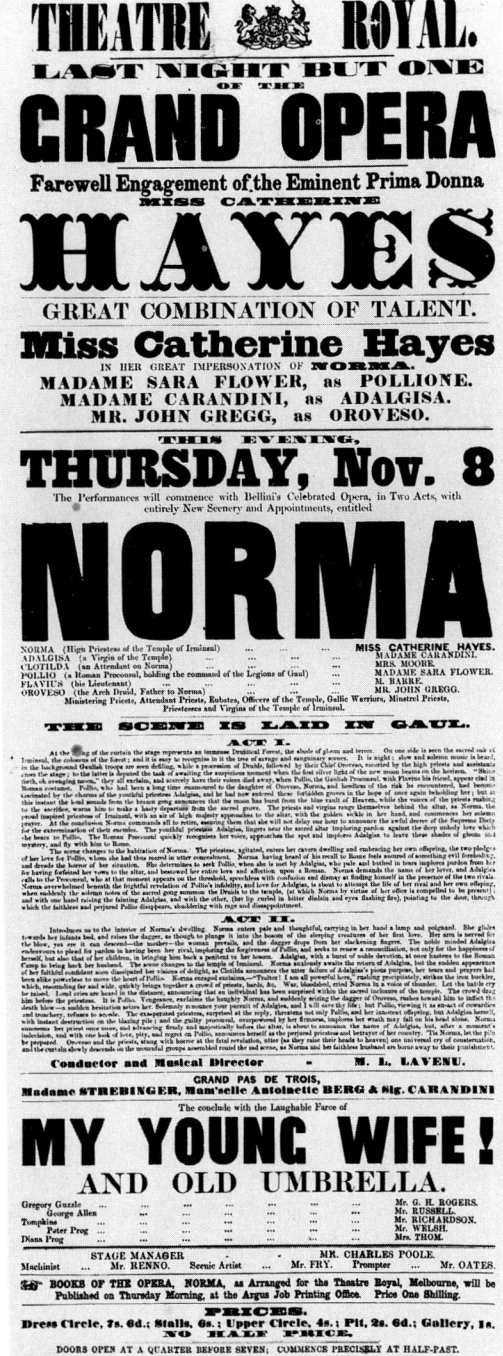

Melbourne 1855 made Sydney 1988 look small.
The Theatre Royal in Melbourne held 3300 and Maria Carandini or Catherine Hayes packed the theatre for weeks on end, while now Sutherland sings to only 1500 in the Sydney Opera House. (Note the coming attraction: the infamous Lola Montes.)

More effeminate tenors!
The tenor shortage was worse than today. Catherine Hayes' Norma was loved by contralto Sara Flower's Pollione! Note the customary ballet (starring Gerome Carandini!) and farce which followed each opera performance.

ultimately went under. In Melbourne Madame Carandini began her career as an entrepreneur, while still singing her regular parts, and soon afterwards George Coppin, the greatest showman of his time, imported Anna Bishop, a soprano who was both famous and notorious, since she was fleeing from her husband, Sir Henry Bishop, composer of the famous or infamous *Clari*: she had eloped with a French harpist, Nicolas Bochsa.

Sydney only beat Melbourne by a year or two, when it staged *The Barber of Seville* in 1843, followed by the all-pervading *Sonnambula* and Rossini's *La Cenerentola*, conducted by one Isaac Nathan. And though Nathan and others have made Sydney prominent in history books, there is no doubt that Melbourne was the opera capital of Australia for more than a hundred years. First Carandini, then Lyster and the powerful J. C. Williamson and his successors, Quinlan, Fuller and the rest, all had their headquarters in Melbourne or started their seasons there—not to mention Melba herself, of course.

1847 saw the first Australian opera, or rather, the first opera written in Australia, Isaac Nathan's *Don John of Austria*, staged at the Victoria Theatre in Sydney. (The first opera by someone *born* in Australia was probably Stephen Hale Marsh's *The Gentleman in Black*, first performed in 1861, but written in 1847 or 1848. It owed more than a little to Nathan's *Don John*). Isaac Nathan was an ancestor of one of Australia's more illustrious modern musicians, Sir Charles Mackerras. As a result we know a lot more about him than about any of his contemporaries. Equally, we know more about Nathan's music, because Mackerras, not unnaturally, has taken the trouble to unearth some of his ancestor's works. The most accessible item is the overture to *Don John of Austria*. Mackerras orchestrated the only existing score (for piano) and it has been recorded. Enjoyable as a period piece, it is ephemeral at best and it is not surprising that Nathan's descendant did not persevere with his task. Thus the first opera written in Australia (a historic milestone, if a small one) was no better and no more successful than any of those that have followed since.

Nathan published his own musical magazine, *The Southern Euphrosyne*, and consequently was his own best publicist. We have no reason to doubt Nathan's claim that it was 'the first opera written, composed and produced in Australia'. We are less likely to find in any history book, the few critiques with which the work was honoured. Not all were as damning as that of the *Port*

Philip Patriot and Melbourne Advertiser, whose correspondent wrote that it was 'the most pointless, passionless, rechauffe, unartistic production that has ever emanated from any brain'. R.I.P., *Don John*!

Since the arts rarely mix with sport in this country, there is some irony in the fact that 1861 produced not only the first visiting opera company in this country, but also the first visiting cricket team. The Irishman William Saurin Lyster and his magnificent nineteen years of presenting opera in Australia have been chronicled in great detail in Harold Love's book *The Golden Age of Australian Opera*. It is no discredit to Lyster to point out that a large part of his extensive repertoire was performed when on tour in halls without stages, scenery and sometimes even costumes. Verdi, Wagner and Meyerbeer were offered in this manner in places as far apart as Brisbane and Warrnambool. Let us praise this pioneer of opera on what must have been a grand scale for Australia in the 1860s and 1870s, but let us not delude ourselves that Lyster's *Lohengrin* or *Huguenots* were performances such as the names imply today. Lyster and the Carandinis often offered 'grand opera' performed on a stage made up of billiard tables pushed together when the occasion arose; anything to get a paying audience to hear opera, for which there was a tremendous demand. What staggers the modern mind is the selection of works thus presented. Bringing opera to the Outback is an admirable thing and, however primitive the setting, *The Barber of Seville* in English can make quite an impact on raw audiences today as much as in the 1860s. But Lyster, to quote a specific example, chose to present *William Tell* on billiard tables in the Mechanics Institute in Warrnambool in 1870. (The next Australian performance did not even attempt to stage this gigantic work, it was a concert performance by the Victoria State Opera in 1987!) In spite of this, Lyster's claim that his productions were 'on a scale which could not be bettered outside the great musical centres of the Old World' was not as far off the mark as the foregoing may imply. Still, it would be more correct to say that things were as bad overseas as they were in Australia in Lyster's time.

There are no detailed histories of opera in nineteenth century Australia, apart from the Harold Love book which concentrates only on Lyster's company, but we do know that some of the stranger happenings were only in line with things as they were in even the best opera houses overseas and I speak now of Europe and

America, not Australia. The practice of altering scores, of cutting whole acts, even of adding music from other works had not died out at that time. The haphazardness of operatic life in the 1860s, the years in which Lyster (and with him, opera) began in this country, can be read in the memoirs of Colonel J. H. Mapleson, whose career as an impresario covered London and most of the United States from 1858 to 1888.

Mapleson employed the best singers of his time, not casually picked up locals. His memoirs treat as normal what is to us extraordinary and they give a very vivid picture of what was involved in presenting opera to the most discerning public of that time. (The memoirs of Berlioz give an equally vivid picture of opera in Paris, but I choose Mapleson because his time coincided exactly with the arrival of Lyster.) Singers like Patti, Jenny Lind, Ilma de Murska, Tietjens, Trebelli, Giuglini, Nordica, Mario, Nilsson (Christine, not Birgit) and Albani sang for Mapleson. They were the Melbas and Carusos of their time. We can thus take it that his opera company was a fair example of what opera in London was like in 1861.

Mapleson's way of dealing with crises was realistic, to say the least. Barnett Levey was faced with one striking comedian and gave in. Mapleson was faced with a striking chorus in a grand opera like Meyerbeer's *Huguenots* and simply proceeded without the chorus! Indisposition hardly fazed Mapleson. When Azucena in *Trovatore* contracted influenza, he managed to get through a whole performance without the substitute, who happened to be a soprano, singing at all. The contralto's two big scenes were omitted entirely and during 'Home to Our Mountains' Azucena conveniently remained asleep, leaving Manrico to sing alone!

On another occasion the tenor, Giuglini, decided not to sing and Mapleson went off by hansom cab to cancel the performance. In the Haymarket his horse knocked down a gentleman, who turned out to be an English tenor, one Walter Bolton. Without hesitation Mapleson asked if he could sing the part of Lionel in *Martha*, which Giuglini was scheduled to sing that night. Bolton replied that he knew the part not, but had sung the aria 'M'appari' in concert at times, in English. Mapleson assembled Tietjens and Trebelli, the co-stars, and arranged for Bolton to go through the motions of Lionel without doing any singing — except for the famous aria. And so the 1862 performance of *Martha* went on that night, the tenor only opening his mouth to sing one aria in Danny Kaye-style Italian, mainly by repeating the word 'M'appari' as often as necessary. The aria was encored twice and the London Press the next morning was unanimous in their praise of the new tenor star!

Singers who had no idea of music or text, who sang parrot fashion, abounded. The tenor Giuseppe Fancelli retired after a long career to undertake an interesting hobby: to find out what the parts he had been singing were all about! 'In *Medea*', he remarked, 'I have played Jason; but what has he to do with *Medea*? Am I her father, her brother, her lover or what?' That Jason was Medea's husband seems not to have occurred to the man who portrayed the part for so many years.

It was, of course, still opera of the singer, by the singer and for the singer. Adelina Patti had the far from abnormal clause in her contract that she was not required to attend rehearsals! So much for opera in the 1860s.

Let us be clear about this: though Lyster and his successors may have presented a travesty of opera as we understand it, they did no more than follow in the footsteps of their colleagues overseas. They were impresarios in the true sense of the word, people who were out to make money from the presentation of opera and, though they all sooner or later went close to or passed the point of bankruptcy, hope sprang eternal. In the process they brought a great deal of enjoyment to the colonies, for their public was not familiar with the older operas, let alone the novelties of the day. It is hard for us to comprehend the excitement the production of a new opera created in those days, for in recent times composers have not come up with modern *Fausts* or *Lohengrins*, operas which Lyster staged as rapidly as they came out in Europe.

While history has always concentrated on singers, opera as a medium also flourished without stars in every country, more so in the nineteenth century than in the twentieth, though there are signs of a return to the old ways now. Going to see a new drama, with or without music, was a big event and we must remember that opera in Australia began at a time when the 'grand' in grand opera really was grand. We laugh today at the ridiculous plots of Verdi's *Trovatore* or *Ernani*, let alone the English ballad operas like Wallace's *Maritana* (which was *not* written in Australia) or Meyerbeer's *Les Huguenots*. Our ancestors did not; they had never heard the now immortal lines 'Never darken my doorstep again' or

Australia's first opera composer.
Isaac Nathan was famous in England for setting poetry by Lord Byron to music, but he ran foul of Prime Minister Lord Melbourne, who refused to pay him for unspecified services (probably as a spy) to William IV. Nathan fled his creditors to go to Sydney (*not* Melbourne!) and wrote *Don John of Austria*, the first opera to be composed and performed in this country.

'Dead, and never called me mother' and when they did, they were enthralled, (all the more so when the words were sung). And when Australians began to write their own operas, their plots were in line with what the public expected. The plot of Nathan's *Don John of Austria* was no worse than many a Verdi libretto; come to think of it, it includes many characters from *Don Carlos* and *Ernani*.

Like Schiller's play, on which Verdi's opera *Don Carlos* is based, *Don John* has some foundation in historical fact. Nathan's librettist, Jacob Montefiore, drew on several previous dramatizations of sixteenth-century Spanish history including Victor Hugo's *Hernani* to fabricate the plot which, had it been written well and composed by a master, should have had a success similar to the French or Italian operas of that time. It is far from easy to condense, but runs something like this: Don John is the illegitimate son of Charles V and thus the half-brother of Philip II of Spain, only he doesn't know this; he is being raised by Don Quixada (not Quixote) who wants him to enter the Church. John, however, is in love with a Jewess named Agnes (not the Bleeding Nun) who is unfortunately, also loved by King Philip. When the latter calls on her and finds John in her company, he banishes him to a monastery, the same monastery to which Charles V has retired after giving up his throne to Philip. (Remember the monk in Verdi's *Don Carlos*?) Charles, of course, is all for John and gives him his sword. In the meantime Philip, having been spurned by Agnes, sends her off to the Inquisition and confronts John, who draws Charles' sword and thus reveals his real identity. There is a big brotherly recognition scene, all is forgiven and exit poor Agnes into exile, where she is safe from both her suitors, or they from her. Finis. *Don John of Austria's* plot is an improvement on *Ernani*, though its libretto is a mess. Anyway, Isaac Nathan was not a Verdi, more's the pity for Australia.

I have spent some time in denigrating early Australian performances of opera in an attempt to shock the reader into reassessing history. The now-reversed tendency to praise the local article excessively and to gloss over failings is a common trait in all small communities. It is easy enough to admit errors in areas in which we excel. Australians can afford to be generous when dealing with cricket, pop music or beer-drinking, but the moment you enter the field of the arts the defences go up. Australia has left no lasting mark yet on the world of opera, music or other performing arts. Only self-delusion tells us otherwise.

The phenomenon of Melba was the stepping stone to the illusion that the numerous Australian singers who have gone overseas make this an operatic country. The facts were quite otherwise. During the nineteenth century opera was treated here, as it was in Europe, as a popular entertainment. The arias of Verdi and Rossini were the pop songs of their day here as elsewhere and the plots of the operas, as much as the music, were the secret of their success. If the staging was somewhat more primitive than overseas, the audiences were also less discerning.

Australia fell behind when musical and artistic standards everywhere started to rise. The public in Europe and America were beginning to see virtues in opera other than novelty and demanded ever greater musical and dramatic perfection. The Australian public was trained to applaud singing alone until long after the age of the producer had dawned. Local military bands provided the music for decades after 'proper' operatic performances became the norm. Singers capable of reading music were the exception, not the rule. Producers did not exist. Sets with any kind of unity were unknown; one garden looked like any other and few managements saw anything abnormal in presenting the Scotland of *Lucia di Lammermoor* with Greek columns as a background. There were no royalties to pay and pirated editions which had been mutilated by previous users were mutilated even further to suit local conditions.

Nowadays this matters not too much, since anyone seriously interested in any particular subject has access to specialized publications or, in the case of opera, direct

Why Melba never re-married.
Married, mother of a son and all but divorced by the age of twenty-three, Nellie Melba was no celibate when she became famous. Then she fell for the Duc d'Orleans, seven years her junior and the pretender to the French throne. Their affair lasted three years, but was doomed because the Duc could not marry a commoner. He must have been Melba's only love. There is no trace of another in her life.

contact via films, television, videos and many opera companies, which have now achieved a standard equal to that of some of the best companies overseas.

At the beginning of this century the situation was different. News from overseas was presented exclusively in the daily press which was interested in only one thing: the glorification of Australia. (Let us not forget that this was the time of the great growth of nationalism throughout the world and news everywhere was aimed at putting the homegrown article first.) In operatic terms this meant the glorification of the native-born singers who went overseas, and a totally false picture was created by the endless flow of new 'Melbas' and reports of their successes.

The time was to come (during the 1950s) when Australian singers would flood the market, in England at least, and quite a number would make it into the big time. All credit to them, though even now the percentage who are as good as we are told they are by the press is severely limited.

As recently as 1967 a major book was published about Australian singers which devoted thousands of words to the names that fled across the pages of our newspapers for the first fifty years of this century. Let us be realistic: apart from Joan Sutherland, Australia has not had a singer in the Melba class since its foundation. Among the countless 'stars' between Melba and Sutherland there were, at the most, two or possibly three who can be considered major artists, though none had the box office appeal of their greatest contemporaries.

(I do not include Frances Alda. New Zealand born, and trained by Marchesi in Paris from the age of nineteen; her years in Melbourne as a child hardly qualify her to be classed as an Australian singer.) And if you include Kiri Te Kanawa, you might just as well say that all New Zealanders are Australians. Te Kanawa's brief sojourn in Australia does not entitle us to say she is one of us.

I am not speaking of a critical assessment of their art, but purely of their box office appeal, and only Marjorie Lawrence can be said to have had that in any degree. I leave the choice of the other two to the reader, but Florence Austral, to give one example, was not among them. Austral may have been a great singer, but her career never really got off the ground — and it is no good saying that this was because she contracted multiple sclerosis: 'excuses' don't wash when you are dealing with historical fact. Austral sang with the British National Opera, a company which rates abysmally low in historical terms. She appeared occasionally at Covent Garden and she sang but once with the Berlin State Opera. No matter what critical acclaim was hers at the time, no matter how great the qualities that are apparent from her recordings, the fact remains that in her twenty years abroad her name did not rate among the stars of the time, nor did her records ever sell to any extent in England, let alone on the continent. Austral's fame, if not posthumous, came only after her retirement.

Not that this made Austral any the less newsworthy in Australia. She and Evelyn Scotney, Amy Castles, Gertrude Johnson and dozens of others were never far from the headlines. Every young singer leaving for England had her (rarely his) first appearances plastered across the front pages, not just in local papers, but in the national press. The naïvety of the press was (and still is) incredible. A concert at the Walthamstow Town Hall rated the same space as an appearance at the Albert Hall. The immense local fame of a singer like Amy Castles made news with her every appearance overseas, but it is hard or impossible to find any reference to her today. In spite of claims that she sang leading roles for two years at the Vienna State Opera, she does not rate a mention in Marcel Prawy's comprehensive book about that theatre.

If I seem to be destructive again, I beg the reader's indulgence. I seek to establish the reasons behind the decline of opera in Australia, or at least its failure to improve along with overseas trends. The constant plugging of singing as the only component worthy of mention did the art untold harm. Not only was an illusion of unrealistic vocal standards created, but any reference to musical, dramatic or scenic standards was not considered newsworthy. If Amy Castles was good

Three Sisters — without Chekhov.
Amy Castles was the most famous of three singing sisters: Amy, Eileen and Dolly (*left to right*). She was highly rated and highly fêted, since she was contracted to the Vienna State Opera as World War I broke out. Eileen had a career of sorts in America, but she and Dolly sang more often in Gilbert and Sullivan than Verdi or Puccini.

The Australian who farewelled Caruso.
Evelyn Scotney was one of the many 'discoveries' of Melba, but she went further than most, appearing during three seasons at the Metropolitan. Her debut rôle there was Eudoxia in *La Juive* with Caruso and she sang it during the last performance he ever gave, on 24 December 1920. After her marriage she gave up opera in favour of concerts.

Our most famous import.
Toti dal Monte appeared in two Melba-Williamson seasons, one of the few genuine top stars heard here in 1924 and 1928. She put opera in Australia on international front pages when she married her leading man, Enzo de Muro Lomante, in Sydney.

Our in-famous import.
Australians like to make their own stars, even if they come from overseas. Lina Scavizzi was one of the 1928 Melba-Williamson season's nonentities, but in Australia she rated as high or higher than Toti dal Monte. Unfortunately for her, nowhere else did she achieve comparable fame and she is now completely forgotten.

enough for Vienna, then Amy Castles was good enough to star in opera at home. Nobody wishes to deny this. But if Amy Castles sang *Madame Butterfly* as well in Melbourne as she did in Vienna, her conductor in Australia was Slapoffski and not Weingartner and the production facilities and staff of the Princess Theatre were not those available at the Vienna State Opera.

The public had every right to believe that the kind of opera presented in Australia from 1900 to 1950 was first class. Certainly the critics gave it no cause to believe otherwise and, lacking the ability to make comparisons, even singing standards of decidedly inferior quality were accepted. Local singers had to be praised, since they so obviously were a great success overseas, and the snob value of Italian imports seems to have played havoc with artistic values. When Melba brought Toti dal Monte to this country in 1928, the tiny singer was naturally accepted readily. Other sopranos in the same season included the great Giannina Arangi-Lombardi and Hina Spani. Yet the success of the season — for reasons which remain a mystery — was the inferior Lina Scavizzi and to this day I am asked for her recordings. Many years ago I did actually hear one of these. History is right and we were wrong. It is not just that dal Monte, Arangi-Lombardi and Spani were better than Scavizzi, but that the local public and critics could not correctly assess her qualities in line with what was then, and is now, accepted overseas.

In more recent years there was another parallel in the unaccountable popularity of Rina Malatrasi. Why she should have outpolled Gabriella Tucci in 1955 is a mystery which will remain buried in history; at no time did Malatrasi leave any impression on the world scene.

Obviously Australian audiences remained unsophisticated to a degree which is not easy to understand. Some of the greatest singers of the century had been heard in this country, yet it was only the arrival of long-playing records which brought a reaction and set new standards which have, perhaps, gone a little too far the other way. Performances like those heard on records are rarely, if ever, heard in a performance at La Scala or the Metropolitan and the fact that our singers today do not measure up to those standards does not mean that they are not the equals of the great majority of artists singing in Europe.

More important is our reluctance to discard the star syndrome which exists overseas as much as here. In Europe and America stars mean more as a tourist attraction than a genuine expression of appreciation of opera as an art. Major opera houses employ every Domingo or Pavarotti who rises to international fame and a big city with a famous theatre relies on the money-no-object tourist who will pay astronomical seat prices for such names. Opera is big business these days. But surely it is big business not solely because of the tourists or the modern equivalents of the rich aristocrats of Melba's time, but because the ordinary public has discovered that opera is an enjoyable way to spend an evening. It will never truly be a mass-medium, if only because of its enormous staging costs, but the overall excellence of an opera performance relies on more than just big stars.

There are complaints about the prominence given to producers (very briefly conductors held sway, but we have already passed that phase). The producer (or director) is also only a part of a multi-media experience and this is what the great Australian public still fails to grasp. We have a huge hole in our operatic history, roughly from the end of the Lyster period to the creation of the Australian Opera and the subsequent rise of regional companies. In colonial days we practically held our own; we even had our own stars, Lucy Escott and Armes Beaumont, to name but two. There was no way to compare what we had here with what was seen and heard overseas. There followed a hundred years of visiting companies, heavily attended and fooling the public with publicity which was often totally unrealistic. No wonder our recent ancestors had no standards and our artists had to go overseas, killing any chance of creating modern equivalents of the Carandinis or Lyster.

Today the picture has changed. Anyone who has been overseas and seen the kind of opera which is seen by the general public, not the tourist/plutocrat, must admit that much of what we can see in Australia today is as good, *or better* than the average on offer in Europe and America. There is only one area where we are failing, that of funding, and I have as yet to see a production of opera in which the leading rôle is sung by a dollar coin. Everything in life is relative and, all things considered, as you will see in a later chapter, each Australian capital city gets its share of opera no worse, and sometimes much better, than a similar city would overseas. What more can we expect?

ACT 1: SCENE 3
IMPORTED OPERA

For almost exactly one hundred years, roughly from 1850 to 1950, Australia relied almost totally on imported opera companies, though some of them remained for so long in the country that their personnel quite literally became natives. From the first, the glamour of 'imported stars' carried all before it and, if the number of singers actually imported was often small indeed, none of companies of any permanence could have come into existence or continued to operate without imported managers and artists.

The very first performances of opera in Australia were admittedly staged by Mrs Clarke, who may well have been Australian-born, though it seems unlikely. But she engaged her artists in England and her leading man was the Italian, Count Carandini. He in turn married a Tasmanian girl, Mary Burgess, who, as Maria Carandini, became a singer and, as Madame Carandini, an impresaria. Two Australian ladies started opera in this country in the 1840s, just as two others, Gertrude Johnson and Clarice Lorenz, were to do one hundred years later. The point is that the latter could and did draw solely on local talent, while the former could and did not. Madame Carandini stayed around for many decades, the *grande dame* of Australian theatre, but her activities also took her overseas and her singers there, as here, were mostly English, Irish or American. It would be pointless to list the huge number of 'stars' of those days here; their names mean nothing to us. But an Irishwoman, Catherine Hayes, was Australia's first great opera star and an Irishman, William Saurin Lyster, was the first impresario to bring some rough equivalent of European opera into existence here.

Catherine Hayes was known as 'The Swan of Erin' and her career in America prior to her tours of Australia throws an interesting light on comparative standards in opera in both countries during the 1850s. Hayes arrived in San Francisco in 1852 and was the first singer there to sing arias during concerts in costume! This was more than a decade after the Carandinis had begun regular performances of opera, however primitive, in Hobart and five years after Nathan wrote the first Australian opera. (San Francisco's first full opera was not staged until 1854 and it starred Catherine Hayes after her return from her first Australian concert tour. The opera was *Norma*.)

I think it can safely be assumed that all operas performed in Australia in those days used English translations. The practice of singing in the original language is a comparatively recent phenomenon, brought about not so much by musical purists, as by theatre managers anxious to obtain the best possible singers who can whiz into town at a day's notice and be gone after half a dozen press interviews and one performance of *Aida* or whatever the opera may be. Composers even in the early twentieth century expected their works to be translated into the language of the audience or, very strangely, into the language of the singers. New York's famous Metropolitan, for example, played all Italian or French operas, including the first Met *Aida*, in German, because it was running German opera seasons for three years and the principals would sing only in German.

Operatically-unimportant Australia holds in Melbourne's Grainger Museum a unique document. Writing in his own hand to a local correspondent on 22 October 1877, Richard Wagner himself stated: 'May you endeavour to have my works performed to you in English;

24

only then can they be understood intimately by the English-speaking public. We hope this will happen in London.' (A photograph of Wagner's original letter in German is reproduced on page 26.)

The man to whom that letter was addressed (Emil Sander) is not important. The man who produced *Lohengrin* in Melbourne only two years after London

Australia's Diaghilev.
From 1861 to 1880 William Saurin Lyster was Australia's major opera impresario, staging new operas as fast as they appeared overseas and offering standards equal to much that could be seen in

England and America. He produced *Lohengrin* in 1877, only two years after it was first seen in London, where it was played in Italian. Lyster's cast sang it in English, as Wagner wanted!

first saw the opera was the Irishman William Saurin Lyster, whose adventures as an opera impresario in Australia from 1861 to his death in 1880 laid the foundation for the long tradition of the art in this country. Sad to say, Lyster's was an imported company, yet because of that very fact he brought with him standards far higher than those accepted as the norm in the colonies.

Harold Love is quite right in describing the Lyster years as *The Golden Age of Opera in Australia*. Perhaps the Melba-Williamson seasons produced better opera than Lyster could, but nearly a century was to pass before any company, imported or local, would exist more or less uninterrupted for fully nineteen years, giving the public the opportunity to become genuinely acquainted with opera and its finer points. Presumably we can also credit Lyster with teaching Australian critics how to review the art and how to write intelligently about it — for a while at least. It was probably as well that Melba was not yet ready to join Lyster. He was staging opera to make money by selling tickets to the general public and there were simply not enough lords and ladies around to support Melba-style Galah Performances full of diamond tiaras.

Lyster brought his first company here from America and his leading stars were the American tenor Henry Squires and the English soprano Lucy Escott, who for eight years starting in 1861, sang the principal parts in almost all of the 1300 odd performances given by Lyster's company! Six performances a week was nothing unusual in those days and an unbroken fourteen consecutive stagings of *Les Huguenots* in 1862 must surely have been some kind of world record, which will never be broken now. Most of the seasons played in small theatres, but the occasional monster did by then exist and was played; Melbourne's Theatre Royal sat 3300 and singing over the mostly brass orchestra in those conditions needed a voice of some size!

While Squires was ultimately replaced by an Australian-bred, if not Australian-born tenor, Armes Beaumont, Lyster continued to rely on imported artists, ranging from half a dozen members of his own family to guests as internationally famous as Anna Bishop and Ilma de Murska. He paid rather less attention to his productions; local theatres used to carry their own selection of scenery and costumes from which the visiting artists chose whatever suited them. Lyster's original six-month tour

Geehrtester Herr!

Sie haben mich durch Ihre Nachrichten
sehr erfreut, und ich unterlasse nicht
Ihnen meinen Dank dafür zu sagen.
Mögen Sie daß ... Wasser, ... die Kleine
sich Ihnen englisch vorführen zu
lassen, ... im Nöthigen ... von einem
englisch redenden Publicum ... mich
... reden. In London hoffen
wir, dass es dazu kommt.

... ... haben mich
(Ernst und meine Familie) ... über
senden Ansichten von Melbourne.
Da Sie so freundlich sind, uns Weiteres
davon zukommen zu lassen zu wollen,
so versichere ich Sie, dass Sie damit
... uns sehr erfreuen werden.
Empfehlen Sie mich, ich bitte, Herrn
Lyster, und behalten Sie auch den
Ihren ... Mittheile eine freund-
liche Erinnerung. Ihrem

                                    sehr verbundenen,

Bayreuth,
22 Oktober 1877.   ...

English – direct from the German horse's mouth!
Opposite: The actual letter written by Wagner, old but clearly legible, in which the composer requests that in Australia all his operas should be sung in English and not German.

The importance of being Lohengrin.
The relative newsworthiness of public events in 1877 is shown by this full-page pictorial feature from *Australasian Sketches*. The discriminating editor gives top-billing to *Lohengrin*, while *Aida* is rated below the Royal Poultry Show.

turned into a nineteen-year season, interrupted only once by an unsuccessful foray into the United States. It ended in 1880 with Lyster's death in Melbourne. There seems to be little doubt that any serious following for opera which existed in Australia before the turn of the century was the result of this admirable gentleman's efforts.

Lyster was followed by Martin and Fanny Simonson, German and French respectively, in 1887. Their company followed the pattern of Lyster, except that they used to go bankrupt more often. Discipline was almost non-existent, since the directors used almost entirely Italian singers, mostly unable to speak English and used to having their own way, to the point of deciding which operas they wanted to sing and with what colleagues. Whenever the tenor and soprano wanted to sing different roles they took the law into their own hands. In 1889 a performance of *Carmen* in Sydney ended in total chaos as the singers on stage abused the conductor, whose side was capably defended by the audience. Simonson cancelled the season and swore never to go back to opera. However, within a week performances were under way again with the same singers, if not the impresario. It didn't last, of course, and neither did Simonson's resolution to forget about opera in Australia.

Meanwhile, the American actor James Cassius Williamson shrewdly acquired the Australian rights to the Gilbert and Sullivan operas and found himself the richest impresario in the land. The stars, naturally enough, were Williamson and his wife, Maggie Moore, though their prominence as performers in G & S may have been exaggerated by history. JCW made his name as a comedian. He came to Australia with a play of which he was part-author, *Struck Oil*, which became the foundation of his theatrical empire. His venture into Gilbert and Sullivan was not intended to be the first step toward permanent residence in this country, but it proved to be so.

Williamson first staged *HMS Pinafore* in Sydney in November 1879, almost exactly a year before Lyster died. Maggie Moore played Josephine and at the première Williamson himself played Sir Joseph Porter. But it was a musical performance by a company of actors. In a country replete with real opera companies Williamson quickly realised that casting anything involving music demanded better singing than he and his wife could provide. Only months later, during the Melbourne season, he was not in the cast, though Maggie was still

Josephine, and a year later, when he explored his new gold mine by presenting *The Pirates of Penzance*, he played the Sergeant of Police, and his wife was demoted to poor old Ruth. To enhance the operatic status of his new acquisitions, he imported a dubious Italian, Tom Riccardi, ('First Appearance of this Famous Basso in Australia') to sing Sir Joseph Porter. It is a moot point whether any Italian would have made a convincing First Lord of the Admiralty. As nobody has heard of Riccardi before or since, he may have been a second cousin of the Pirate King, one Signor Verdi (Guillaume, not Giuseppe) who was an Italo-franchisized William Green from Lyster's company. Verdi/Green was not the only Lyster singer to find work with Williamson; Australia's first non-imported tenor star, Armes Beaumont, sang Frederic. He also starred with Maggie Moore in *Patience*.

Apart from Williamson's series of G & S operas (hardly opera 'seasons' in the conventional sense) the years 1880 to the present century consisted of a hotch-potch of imported and local opera companies which came and went so quickly that the recording of each would be futile, though mention should be made of the Montague-Turner company run by two other ex-Lyster singers. This toured so extensively that even Mackay in Northern Queensland was visited. It was there, as far as can be discovered, that Nellie Melba saw her first performance of an opera and socialized with professional singers. Her first intention to take up opera as a profession appears in a letter written during this brief visit by Annis Montague, Charles Turner and their colleagues.

George Musgrove imported a series of opera companies from Italy and Germany and things really got busy after the turn of the century when Williamson began to bring Italian groups to this country. The then new Puccini operas inevitably led up to the great event, the first of the Melba seasons in 1911. This first truly complete company to be brought to Australia consisted of 200 people including principals, chorus and a full orchestra. The opening on 2 September 1911 offered Melba and McCormack in *La traviata* and the firm founded by Williamson did not look back for half a century. An Irishman, Thomas Quinlan, followed up with another company the following year. It was more ambitious than Williamson's and included not only Wagner's *Tristan and Isolde*, but the complete *Ring of the Nibelungen* cycle. It may have been over-ambitious, but not all the fault for the losses it incurred lay with Quinlan.

THEATRE ROYAL

LESSEES .... Messrs. COPPIN, HENNINGS & GREVILLE
STAGE DIRECTOR ... ... Mr. DAMPIER

THIS EVENING,

(And every Evening until further notice.)

The Management have much pleasure in announcing the first authorised
production in Victoria of Gilbert and Sullivan's World-famous
Operatic Satire

H.M.S. PINAFORE

Which as regards Mounting, Cast, Chorus, Orchestra,
and General Excellence, will surpass any representation ever given
in the Australian Colonies.

Double Orchestra of the Leading Instrumentalists.

CONDUCTOR ... ... Mr. VAN GHELE

Josephine .... **Miss MAGGIE MOORE**
" Our Gallant Captain's Daughter. "

Sir Joseph Porter, K.C.B. ... ... Mr. RICCARDI
(First Appearance of this Famous Basso in Australia.)
" I'm the Monarch of the Sea. "

Buttercup ... ... Miss E. LEAF
(Her First Appearance in Australia.)
" I'm Sweet Little Buttercup."

Hebe ... ... Miss KATE FOLEY
" I'll soothe and Comfort your Declining Days. "

Captain Corcoran ... ... Mr. C. HARDING
(His First Appearance in Australia.)
" And a Right good captain too. "

Ralph Rackstraw ... ... Mr. L. BRAHAM
" The Suitor Lowly Born,"

Dick Deadeye ... ... Mr. T. RAINFORD
" I'm ugly too, Ain't I ? "

Bill Bobstay ... ... Mr. OLLY DEERING
" Our Boatswain, " with Hornpipe.

A Grand Chorus, Including 60 Trained Voices.

The Crew of H.M.S. PINAFORE,
by Gentlemen of the Royal Company.
Sir Joseph's Sisters, and his Cousins, and his Aunts,
by Ladies of the Royal Company.

SCENE—Quarter Deck of H.M.S. PINAFORE

OFF PORTSMOUTH.

By JOHN HENNINGS assisted by Mr. John Little.

Mechanism by Mr. W. H. Scott. Properties by Mr. W. Gardiner

ACT 1.—NOON. ACT 2.—NIGHT.

The entire Production under the immediate Supervision of Mr. J. C.
WILLIAMSON, who has purchased from Messrs. Gilbert & Sullivan
the sole right of producing H.M.S. PINAFORE in Australia.

"THE LORGNETTE"
Dress Circle Supplement
(WITH COMPLIMENTS).

Saturday June 18th 1881

OPERA HOUSE.

LESSEE .... Mr J. C. WILLIAMSON
Stage Manager .... Mr George Leopold

LATEST & GREATEST MUSICAL NOVELTY !

Mr J. C. WILLIAMSON

By special arrangement with Mr R. D'OYLY CARTE, of London,
having secured the sole right for the Colonies, begs to
announce the

FIRST PRODUCTION IN MELBOURNE

Of Messrs Gilbert and Sullivan's famous Melo-dramatic Opera, in two
acts, entitled

THE PIRATES OF PENZANCE

Or, The Slave of Duty.

The Pirate King ... ... Signor VERDI
Frederic (the Pirate Apprentice) ... Mr ARMES BEAUMONT
Major-General Stanley ... ... Mr HOWARD VERNON
Sergeant of Police ... ...Mr J. C. WILLIAMSON
Samuel (his Lieutenant) ... ... Mr JOHN M. FORDE

Pirates and Policemen.

Mabel .... Miss ELSA MAY
Edith } General Stanley's Daughters { Miss JOSEPHINE DEAKIN
Kate Miss FANNY LIDDIARD
Isabel Miss CORA GWYNNE
Ruth (a Piratical Maid of all work) ... Miss MAGGIE MOORE
General Stanley's other Daughters.

SCENE 1.—The Pirates Lair.
SCENE 2.—The Home of His Ancestors.
(By Purchase).
FINAL TABLEAU.—BRITANNIA TRIUMPHANT.

GRAND CHORUS & DOUBLE ORCHESTRA

Conductor.................................Signor GIORZA
Leader.................................Mr T. Zeplin

The Opera produced under the immediate supervision of Mr J. C.
WILLIAMSON.

The Costumes (which are of the most costly and beautiful descrip-
tion) have all been expressly imported from Europe.
The Gentlemen's Costumes by Mons. and Madame Alias, of London
and Paris.
The Ladies' Dresses by Madame Fisher, of London, from designs by
the celebrated Faustin.
Swords and Properties by Messrs L. and H. Nathan, London:
Wigs by Mr W. Clarkson, of London.

THE NEW SCENERY, illustrating Picturesque Spots in Cornwall,
BY
MR. GEORGE GORDON.

Doors open at 7·15; Overture at 8 o'clock.
Admission—Dress Circle, 5s.; Stalls, 3s.; Upper Circle, 2s.; Pit and
Gallery, 1s.
Box Office open daily at Allan and Co.'s, Collins street east.
J. P. MACDONALD, Business Manager.

Mr & Mrs J. C. Williamson, opera singers.

The actor J. C. Williamson founded the greatest theatre empire Australia has known and imported numerous great singers and great opera companies. His wife, Maggie Moore, was a contralto of sorts, JCW himself was primarily an actor. His first venture into musical theatre was in Gilbert and Sullivan. These posters show that the master showman realised that his own talents were not much help even in light opera, while his wife was demoted from leading rôles to minor ones very quickly.

Melbourne had a smallpox epidemic, and a general strike in New Zealand forced him to cancel his season there.

Then Williamson himself died unexpectedly in Paris and the First World War wrecked plans for a 1915 season. But the demand for grand opera had been created and the successors of Williamson were ready to meet it.

The importance of the many J. C. Williamson grand opera seasons over the years lies not so much in their encouragement of local talent, which was minimal to say the least, but in the interest in the art which they generated with the public. Just as Pavlova stimulated a thousand and one young girls to take up ballet, so did Melba inspire a thousand and one young girls to follow her example. The problem all of them faced (and Williamson's did nothing to help) was always that there were no local opera companies in which to gain experience; at best, there was a chance of chorus or small parts in some company yet to be imported.

The occasional company launched by independents was more generous to local talent, though need rather than any desire to be constructive was probably the motivation. The Gonsalez Italian Grand Opera Company presented by Ben J. Fuller (later Sir Benjamin Fuller) in 1916-17 brought a large contingent of Italian singers to Australia with the intention of presenting no less than twenty-one operas, most of which were actually staged. They ranged from the expected *Traviata* and *Trovatore* to Halévy's *La Juive*, Meyerbeer's *Huguenots* (as *Ebrea* and *'Gli Ugonotti*, being sung in Italian), *Ernani*, *La favorita*, *La Gioconda* and *Mignon*! They were no better and no worse than those of earlier companies, but not in the class of the Melba seasons. Young Fuller was only feeling his way, but the first Gonsalez season would have some lasting side-effects on local singers, if not audiences. No record exists of the individual reactions to Italian singers when their tour of Australia and New Zealand ended in 1917, a crucial year in World War I. It would appear that most, if not all, of the male members of the company chose to stay in Australia rather than face a dangerous sea journey with possible conscription into the Italian army at its end. The fact is that the end of the war found them at the disposal of stage director Frank Rigo who, with the help of Williamson's, organized ambitious opera seasons with whatever singers he could find. The many seasons which resulted were sporadic, but created a continuity of opera which, for the first time, brought benefits to local as well as imported singers.

O patria mia **in wartime.**
A new opera management, the Fuller brothers, brought an Italian opera company to Australia in 1916. Its Souvenir Programme was a remarkable document for the time in its patriotic colours. Even the full-length portraits of the principal singers were coloured.

An Australian 'Count'.
The baritone Count Ercole Filippini came to Australia with the Gonsalez Italian Opera Company in 1916, married an Australian girl and later started several small opera companies. His *Contessa* Filippini not only sang but conducted his operas with some success.

There were several key members of the original Gonsalez company who were of greater influence than Frank Rigo himself. Giovanni and Ernesto Gonsalez were the musical directors and there was a Signorina Gonsalez, presumably a sister since married ladies were billed as 'Signora'. More important was the baritone who variously announced himself as Signor or 'Count' Ercole Filippini. His Rigoletto may have been unintentionally funny, as contemporary reports imply, but he saved the company's bacon by sheer leadership quality in later years and many an Australian singer was grateful for that.

Rigo had a good selection of Italian male singers and imported the not-unimportant American tenor Ralph Errole, who later sang regularly at the Metropolitan. But then, as now, the native soil had a plethora of fine sopranos and contraltos. For some years Australia played all the popular operas with long-forgotten Italian male

EILEEN CASTLES,

"MADAME BUTTERFLY," AT SYDNEY OPERA HOUSE.

MISS ELSY TREWEEK.

Lieut. Pinkerton (Lois) and Butterfly (Miss Gonsalez).

PATTI RUSSELL,

Count Filippini, as Valentine in "Faust."

Italo-Australian Opera. The male remnants of the Gonsalez Italian company tried to carry on after World War I ended, with Australian leading ladies, under the management of its old stage manager, Frank Rigo.

leads while their *prime donne* were all Australians. Gertrude Johnson, Amy and Eileen Castles, Gladys Verona, Strella Wilson, Vera Bedford, Thelma Carter, Leah Myers, Elsy Treweek, Patti Russell, Nellie Leach and others sang in *Lucia, Tosca, Butterfly, Faust* and the rest. A typical cast in 1920 of *Lucia di Lammermoor* (15 March) featured Gertrude Johnson in the title rôle with the reasonably well-known Vittorio Lois as her ill-fated lover, Filippini as her brother and Browning Mummery as the second tenor whom she murders only after he has finished his part of the famous Sextet. (Johnson's place was taken at the Following Wednesday matine by another Australian soprano, Gladys Verona.) A latecomer to the ranks was always billed as 'the Contessa Filippini'. Born Nancy McParlan, şhe was a local girl who studied with Filippini, married him and proved to be a genuine life-saver when it transpired that she was not only a very good soprano, but could also conduct the orchestra in most of the repertoire in which she sang herself! Frederick Collier was the odd man out, an Australian male principal and Joseph (later Browning) Mummery appeared in minor rôles.

Rigo's company, if such an irregular ensemble can be called a company, appeared and re-appeared in various guises in the early 1920s; at least, many of the main singers sang with some regularity under various banners. (*see also* Act 4, Scene 2.) Rigo himself appears to have returned to the safety of a salaried position with Williamson's, Filippini and others taking the glory (and the losses) of ensuing years. In 1928 one or both of the Gonsalez brothers re-emerged when the Fuller-Gonsalez company toured many states with some very inferior singers, after all the best Australians had departed for overseas careers. Nevertheless, the repertoire was an ambitious one, including operas like *Un ballo in maschera*, *La favorita*, *Mignon* and even *Norma*, starring Rosita Silvestri and Nina Algozino, never to be heard of again. The curious thing about the company's Filippini incarnations in 1924, and again in 1928, was the fact that each preceded the much-lauded Melba-Williamson seasons, almost as though inviting disaster. Fuller learnt his lesson after that; he was making a packet out of commercial theatre and the next time he tried his hand at opera (in 1935) he did the job properly.

Melba herself, of course, loved to play the great patron and the three seasons she staged with Williamson's in 1911, 1924 and 1928 had their share of Australian singers. But those were all-star companies of a quality that Williamson's never had the courage to bring out on their own and competing with McCormack, Dal Monte, Borgioli or Granforte was hardly a fair test for the local singers. The occasional English-sounding name in the Melba seasons almost invariably turned out to be non-Australian, (Phyllis Archibald), unless she happened to be a Melba protégée (Stella Power).

What makes the Melba seasons historically so important is that they were so very adventurous in their repertoire. The sop to Australian music given via one solitary Fritz Hart one-acter coupled with *Pagliacci* is unimportant in relation to the fact that a Melba season was likely to present fifteen to twenty different operas in the course of a season, all sung by more than proficient artists. The 1928 season featured twenty-four works, including the Australian premières of Puccini's *Turandot, Manon Lescaut* and the three operas of the *Trittico*, Montemezzi's *L'amore dei tre re*, Cilea's *Adriana Lecouvreur*, Mascagni's *Lodoletta*, Massenet's *Thaïs* and Hart's *Deirdre in Exile*. Though perhaps only of interest to record collectors, it is as well to remember that singers selected by Melba that year included Toti dal Monte, Giannina Arangi Lombardi, Hina Spani, Francesco Merli, Enzo de Muro Lomanto, Apollo Granforte, Fernando Autori, Aurora Rettore, Ida Mannarini and a solitary Australian who had made the grade: Browning Mummery. Not a bad line up; in fact, not far behind the Italian contingent of the 1928 Covent Garden season which, admittedly, was more Wagner-orientated that year. The point is that any of the above would have been welcomed in London and probably became available because of the lack of repertoire for them there.

As for the standard of productions, we are told that over 100 people were brought from Europe, that 'scenery has been painted to the right designs and in accordance with tradition. Thousands of costumes have been purchased', etcetera, etcetera. Yet among the 245 names listed in the credits there appears not the name of even one producer or designer! One presumes that all the twenty-four operas were staged or arranged by the Stage Director, Carlo Farinetti, who must have been a genius of the highest degree.

Once again, it should be stressed that Australia was not necessarily backward. Opera seasons in England rarely mentioned producers in those days, though the trend toward improvement had already begun. Opera

Find the stars among the dross.

Bass Fernando Autori was a fine caricaturist among the singers in the Williamson-Melba 1928 Grand Opera Season. The top row of sopranos is easy: Arangi-Lombardi, Spani, Dal Monte, Scavizzi and Zinetti. In the next row at the right is Francesco Merli and in the second row from bottom (third and fifth from the right) can be found Apollo Granforte and Browning Mummery.

was no longer pure entertainment, but it still relied on the star syndrome, the imported star syndrome, and we should not be too critical of Melba for following the system which made her name and fortune. That she knew her public is only too clear, because — unlike the 1965 Sutherland-Williamson season — the non-Melba nights also were regularly sold out. In 1924 the Melbourne season of twelve weeks included sixteen operas and attracted 211 200 paying customers! That is a truly astronomical figure for a city of 885 700 inhabitants.

Of course, it *was* Melba's Farewell Season, or so the public was led to believe. And so was the 1928 season,

The first and biggest of the many Farewells.
Melbourne 13 October 1924. The picture of the stage of His Majesty's Theatre speaks for itself, but every newspaper carried an individual farewell letter from Melba as well.

which took place fully two years after her *final farewell* at Covent Garden and the *final final farewell* at the Old Vic. I am not sticking my neck out by stating which of the many authentic last appearances of Melba was really her last (presumably the one on her death bed, when she is said to have sung a few bars of Gounod's *Ave Maria*), but in 1924 she followed her Farewell Season with a Farewell Concert at His Majesty's Theatre on the 14 October which was broadcast and heard as far away as Sydney, Auckland and, the press reported, in California. Her fellow artists on that occasion consisted of the principals of the opera company and included not one Australian. The Italians, along with the audience, which had contributed $36 000 to the Fund for Limbless Soldiers, sang 'For She's a Jolly Good Fellow' and worldwide tributes poured in, as they did again, and again, and again. Every available space in the theatre was covered with flowers, festoons of gum leaves sparkled with hidden lights and huge shields with realistic paintings of Australian native birds (excluding Melba) covered the front of the dress circle and the balcony. As for what

decorated the stage, words can hardly describe it. Fortunately a photographic record exists and this speaks for itself — of the awe in which Melba was held, of the money Melba could draw, of the power Melba held over her public and of her knowledge of publicity gimmicks, though the word may not have been invented at that time.

1928 was actually the year in which Melba's name appeared among the managers and not the singers, even though she did make her final final appearance in opera that year. Thus, by accident of touring schedule, the last of Melba's endless farewells took place on 2 October 1928 in the Theatre Royal, Adelaide. Ironically, that last farewell in her own country did not include a single Australian among the supporting cast either. The few minor concerts in which she appeared after that date would hardly be noted if the singer's name had not been Melba.

Many books have been written about Melba, too many perhaps, and her contribution to keeping opera alive through these tours is all that need be said about

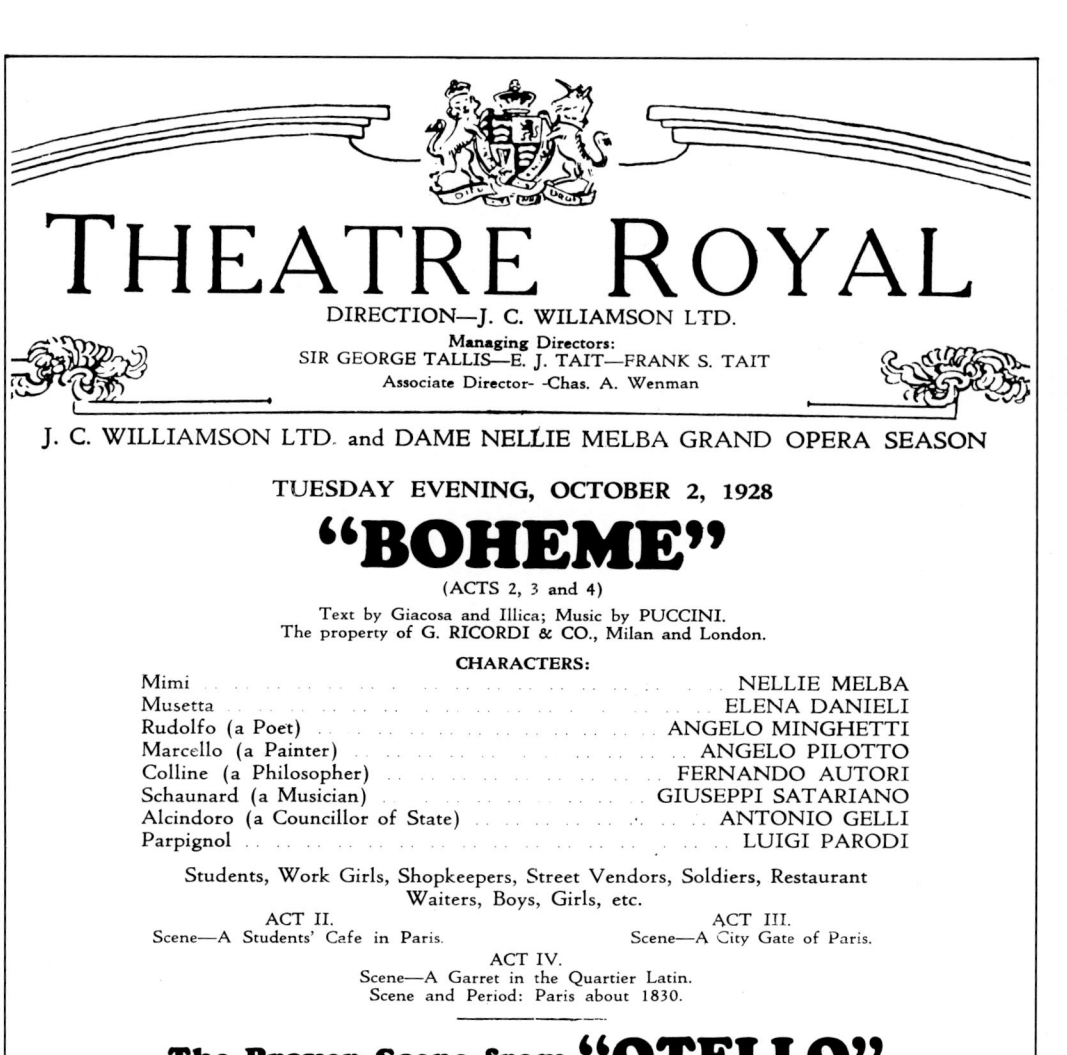

The last farewell on a stage in Adelaide. Almost exactly four years after her first great Farewell in Melbourne (where she sang again in 1928) Melba finally sang for the last time on a stage and this is the programme. She was all of sixty-seven years old. (The occasional later concerts have never been counted as Farewells.)

THEATRE ROYAL

DIRECTION—J. C. WILIAMSON LTD.

Managing Directors:
SIR GEORGE TALLIS—E. J. TAIT—FRANK S. TAIT
Associate Director- -Chas. A. Wenman

J. C. WILLIAMSON LTD. and DAME NELLIE MELBA GRAND OPERA SEASON

TUESDAY EVENING, OCTOBER 2, 1928
"BOHEME"
(ACTS 2, 3 and 4)

Text by Giacosa and Illica; Music by PUCCINI.
The property of G. RICORDI & CO., Milan and London.

CHARACTERS:

Mimi	NELLIE MELBA
Musetta	ELENA DANIELI
Rudolfo (a Poet)	ANGELO MINGHETTI
Marcello (a Painter)	ANGELO PILOTTO
Colline (a Philosopher)	FERNANDO AUTORI
Schaunard (a Musician)	GIUSEPPI SATARIANO
Alcindoro (a Councillor of State)	ANTONIO GELLI
Parpignol	LUIGI PARODI

Students, Work Girls, Shopkeepers, Street Vendors, Soldiers, Restaurant
Waiters, Boys, Girls, etc.

ACT II.
Scene—A Students' Cafe in Paris.

ACT III.
Scene—A City Gate of Paris.

ACT IV.
Scene—A Garret in the Quartier Latin.
Scene and Period: Paris about 1830.

The Prayer Scene from "OTELLO"
ACT IV.

Text by Boito. Music by VERDI.
The property of G. RICORDD & CO., Milan and London.

CHARACTERS:

DESDEMONA	NELLIE MELBA
EMILIA	CARMEN TORNARI

Scene: Desdemona's Bedroom.
A seaport in Cyprus; end of the Fifteenth Century.

Conductor ... COMMENDATORE GAETANO BAVAGNOLI
Director of the Opera Season ... Mr. NEVIN TAIT

her in these pages. She succeeded in making opera loved to a point which has not yet been equalled today — the qualities of the Australian Opera notwithstanding. Proof of this exists in a letter written to the Manager of His Majesty's Theatre during the 1924 season by an opera lover who begged him to put on a performance of *Bohème* 'without Melba'! He did so want to see Puccini's opera and all Melba nights were sold out. If only they let somebody else sing Mimì, he might get the chance to enjoy the opera of his dreams! Now, there was a true opera lover, if ever there was one, and one would assume that there were others like him in the Melbourne of 1924.

The imported companies that followed after Melba retired and finally died helped to keep the interest alive, but Williamson's without Melba did not have the gift of choosing the right artists or perhaps the peak of interest had been passed in Australia, as it had overseas. Occa-

Aida and Elsie in Egypt.
In 1928 some people still went to see *Aida* in the belief that it was a comedy also starring the other half of the radio duo Aida and Elsie. The same Aida sings the same music in ever more spectacular settings today, but Elsie is all but forgotten. Williamson's knew very well that any opera not starring Dame Nellie Melba needed that extra effort. Apart from the extras (plural) they had an internationally-renowned set of principals. (*Front from left*: Giannina Arangi-Lombardi, John Brownlee and Francesco Merli.)

sional performances were put together when a suitable combination of singers happened to be available. Williamson's had a store full of costumes and scenery which could be thrown onto any stage at a moment's notice. What resulted was not high art, but the public did not seem to mind. For example, in August 1931 the Scottish tenor Joseph Hislop was touring Australia. In Melbourne he foolishly agreed to participate in a performance of *Tosca* during a season staged at the Theatre Royal by J.C. Williamson's and the University of Melbourne; Bernard Heinze was the conductor. That Hislop was not well and had to be replaced in the last act by one Charles Nicis is of less interest than the fact that it must have been known to Heinze and the University that Hislop would sing Cavaradossi in English, the Tosca, Alice Orff-Solscher, only knew her part in German and the Scarpia, Franco Izal was an Italian who insisted on singing in his, and Puccini's, own language. It is said that Nicis (nationality unknown) sang the last act in Spanish, but I have been unable to confirm this. Minor parts and chorus were locals, who sang in English. Other operas presented during that season included *Faust* and *Carmen*, sung in English, no doubt.

After Melba's retirement the star system broke down until the arrival of Sutherland. By 1932 is was impossible

to fill the house with names alone. No doubt Gigli or Galli-Curci would still have broken all records, but Lina Pagliughi, Bruna Castagna and Apollo Granforte were simply not enough to make Willamson's last pre-war season a success. Nor would anybody have paid money to see and hear the Giovanna in *Rigoletto*, sung by a young Joan Hammond; the local 'star' was Molly de Gunst, who actually sang the title rôle in *Aida* and later starred at Sadler's Wells.

Enter the newly-knighted Sir Benjamin Fuller, who now had a whole string of theatres which were showing films, out of which he had made a fortune, because the 'talkies' had killed vaudeville. If Williamson's without Melba could not make opera work, Fuller would find another way, one which had not been tried since Quinlan's season in 1913. With tremendous fanfares Fuller announced a fully-imported company of *Grand Opera in English* for an eighteen-month tour starting in 1934 — a year in Australia and six months in New Zealand. He asked the public 'to encourage him to persevere in my endeavour to found and carry on a permanent organization, with periodical seasons in the Capital cities of each Australian State and the large centres of the Dominion of New Zealand, with headquarters in Melbourne'. He had assembled an almost identical cast and repertoire as the last of the British National Opera Company, which had closed in Covent Garden in 1924 and gone out of business. Not that Fuller acquired bad singers or works, but opera was still in the throes of the old élite dress-circle public and what failed in England had to fail in Australia. That it did not fail as badly as it might have done is a credit to the singers.

The public certainly had no cause for complaint, though in hindsight the closeness to that BNOC 1924 season did not look good for 1934. Fuller had the best Britain could provide, including most of the major Australians who had long departed these shores: Florence Austral, Browning Mummery, Frederic Collier, even old Horace Stevens. With them he brought Muriel Brunskill, Walter Widdop, Norman Allin, Ben Williams and many more. No less than eleven of the operas played in London in 1924 were in the repertoire, and the casts were as good as any English-singing cast would be today.

If only Fuller had had governmental backing, his venture might have succeeded in the end. The opening Melbourne season was a disaster only because it clashed with the Victorian State Centenary celebrations. As soon

The greatest Australian voice of all.
Fashions come and fashions go. Today Florence Austral would beat Melba hands down in opera houses if neither were known to the public. Austral had a phenomenal voice and started at the top, singing Brünnhilde at Covent Garden. She sang but one season in Australia, in 1935, before her career was cut short by multiple sclerosis.

as they were over, Fuller's houses began to resemble his name at last; they got fuller and fuller; there was even an extension of another week of operas; it was not enough. The press reported losses 'in excess of six figures'. Fuller asked the government of the day to advance some hard cash to enable the Sydney season to be completed, but using taxpayers' money to promote opera was still a concept in the very distant future. Fuller certainly spared no expense, apparently believing that more and more new operas would turn the tide. It certainly deserved to do so, for the company played six or seven performances a week for nearly four months. Only two of the sixteen planned operas failed to reach the stage: *Siegfried* and *Die Götterdämmerung*; then, and for fully forty more years, theatres used for opera were simply not big enough to cope with massive works like the Wagner *Ring*, though the demand was certainly there — and Fuller (probably unknowingly) followed Wagner's own instructions: '*Mögen Sie dafür sorgen meine Werke sich Ihnen Englisch vorführen zu lassen*'. (*See* the reproduction of the letter in Wagner's own handwriting on page 26.)

Little of Wagner's music had been heard after 1913 and the demand for it was tremendous. Even without the two cancellations, and a *Mastersingers of Nuremberg*, which was announced, but never staged, Melbourne and Sydney saw no less than five major Wagner works — in English, of course: *Lohengrin, The Valkyrie, Tannhäuser, Tristan and Isolde* and *The Flying Dutchman*. (Verdi had only three operas in the repertoire and Puccini only two!) With two of the world's best Wagner singers (Austral and Widdop) in Australia, replacing the cancelled works was not easy. To cast his Australian Isolde and Brünnhilde as Leila in Bizet's *Pearl Fishers* may sound sheer lunacy today, yet Austral was a phenomenon and took the light lyric rôle in her stride. She, as much as any of the singers, wanted the season to succeed. The results of the final Melbourne week were so good that J. C. Williamson's invited Fuller to come back to His Majesty's after the end of the Sydney season, which turned out to be a bigger success than expected. The second Melbourne season was a runaway success for another four weeks, belatedly adding two more works to the big repertoire, *Lohengrin* and, incredibly, *La Bohème*; perhaps Fuller was afraid to stage Melba's favourite opera which had been seen by most people by then. All he did was to prove that Puccini and not Melba was the real attraction. But the financial risks were too great.

Whatever Fuller may or may not have lost, he was not going to invest in opera again. Alas, Australia saw *Tristan and Isolde* only in 1935, but with Austral, Widdop and Brunskill and other goodies for which modern audiences would give their collective right arm.

After the war Williamson's tried again, twice. In 1949 they toured nine operas, popular potboilers one and all, and turned a small profit, mainly due to the unexpected popularity of Rina Malatrasi, who enchanted the Australian public. Apart from Alvino Misciano and Mario Basiola there was not a singer of even average international standard in the cast. What possessed the company to undertake the 1955 season in the manner in which it did is a mystery. No doubt Nevin Tait, getting on in years, thought he could recreate the magic of the Melba seasons — without Melba, or Dal Monte, or Borgioli, or the other popular names.

No less than thirteen operas were staged in 1955 with a huge imported cast which did not have a single box office name among them. One, Gabriella Tucci, was to go on to become a star in later years. Another, Umberto Borsò, showed immense promise in 1955, just two years after his debut, and later did manage to get into La Scala, the Metropolitan and Covent Garden, finally returning to Australia during the 1970s. Ken Neate had already made a name on the European circuit and at Covent Garden. Perhaps the aging Afro Poli had something to offer still in artistry, if not in voice. As for the rest, few if any were ever heard of again and their standards of voice and even experience were on the whole no better than that of the contingent of forty Australian singers who supported these 'stars' in the chorus and occasionally in small parts. These Australians

Pavarotti when he did *not* sell out.
The Sutherland-Williamson Grand Opera Season of 1965 lost money because people would not attend the operas in which Sutherland was not singing. *L'elisir d'amore* with Elizabeth Harwood was praised, but half-empty. Nobody had heard of the tenor Luciano Pavarotti, though he was much admired — by the few who actually saw him.

included Donald Smith, John Shaw, Clifford Grant, John Young, Kevin Mills, Rosalind Keene, Wilma Whitney and Justine Rettick. Though all the productions used existing costumes and scenery, making the venture a comparatively cheap affair, the steadily-reducing public for all but a few operas (Malatrasi still pulled them in for *Butterfly*, the critics notwithstanding) the season made a huge loss and it looked as though Williamson's had wound down the curtain on their operatic activities. But they had not reckoned on the meteoric rise of Joan Sutherland.

So, ten years later they tried to repeat the Melba success formula with the Sutherland-Williamson International Grand Opera Company. In many respects it was a good try. Apart from Sutherland, they had Pavarotti, who was certainly as good as Borgioli was in Melba's time, though not as solidly established and Elisabeth Harwood had some of the glamour of Dal Monte, though again not the name, and John Alexander did sing regularly at the Metropolitan Opera House in New York. Joseph Rouleau, Richard Cross, Alberto Remedios, Spiro Malas and Monica Sinclair also had, and have, some reputation. They were backed, with some courage on the part of Richard Bonynge, the Artistic Director, by members of the Elizabethan Trust Opera Company, which was disbanded for the duration of the season. Thus a good many local singers were given the chance to sing leading roles in the company of overseas singers and the general benefits to singers and audiences alike were probably good value for Australia, if not for Williamson's, who lost heavily.

Margreta Elkins, Joy Mammen, Robert Allman, Ronald Maconaghie, Clifford Grant and Lauris Elms were fairly billed among the company principals. It really was a pretty reasonable sort of affair with seven brand new productions, five built around Sutherland: *Lucia di Lammermoor, Traviata, Faust, Sonnambula*, and *Semiramide;* the others were *Eugene Onegin* and *Elisir d'amore*. Sutherland nights were automatically sold-out; other nights were automatically empty, Pavarotti notwithstanding! A small loss would probably have been made had all nights been sold-out. It proved to be the swan song for opera staged by the firm responsible for bringing more good opera to Australians than anybody else up to that time. It is doubtful whether Australia will ever again see a fully-imported opera company offering seasons on the scale provided by Williamson's.

FIRST INTERVAL

the national operas

Gertrude Johnson was a very determined woman, a formidable woman; the kind who is so often attracted to the arts, launches grandiose schemes and usually falls flat on her face. If 'Gertie' never actually fell flat on her face, she nevertheless reached a time when her abilities declined and with them the brain-child she brought into the world. The ambitiously named 'Australian National Theatre' very nearly became all that the name implied, though it failed to realize its creator's dream in the end. Along the way it left a lasting mark on the history of the performing arts in Australia and on opera in particular. No book on theatre in this country can ignore the National Theatre, or the tragedy that, operatically, it came to nothing in the end.

Lest it be thought that someone close to the National Theatre (the author of these lines) has lost his marbles, let me make it clear that what has arisen out of the — literal — ashes of the old National is *not* precisely what Miss Johnson would have wished, though without her it could not have come into being. I refer to it as tragic, because Miss Johnson's plan was a good one, it worked admirably up to a point and it might quite realistically have become a real national theatre, if only...

It all began in the Victoria Centenary Club in Melbourne. To be precise, it happened at 8 p.m. on 4 December 1935. Starting with a capital of £8, Miss Johnson managed to enthuse a group of leading citizens to establish 'The National Theatre Movement, Victoria'. It is ironic that the organization which ultimately became a purely Victorian body also started as one. Perhaps success came too quickly and too soon, for within five years it became the 'Australian' National Theatre, which it remains, in spite of its local character, to this day.

Miss Johnson and the National were around so long and the history of both have been written so often that it is time to bring both into perspective. The 'principal soprano at Covent Garden', who returned from London to that fateful meeting in 1935 and was inspired by Lilian Baylis and the work she had done at the Old Vic and Sadler's Wells, was not one of the great singers of Australia. Few of the 'world-famous' Australian singers were what the local press would have us believe they were or are. Miss Johnson recorded extensively in England (on the dark blue, that is, cheap, Columbia label) and her qualities as a singer are there for all to hear. She had a fine coloratura voice beset by some uncertainties and a style which was outdated even then. She was at her best in the simple art songs of Cyril Smith, which she recorded with the composer himself at the piano. In 1986 EMI in England released a two-record album, *A Treasury of English Song*, which included two of these songs. The non-alphabetical list of twenty-four singers was headed by four 'stars': Kirsten Flagstad, John McCormack, Richard Tauber and Peter Dawson. The other twenty, including famous names like Heddle Nash, Dora Labette and George Baker, were headed by Gertrude Johnson!

Miss Johnson gave up her career — some say because of a broken romance, others to realize her dream of a National Theatre — to return to Australia for good. Wealthy in her own right, though by no means rich, she was able to rally groups of prominent citizens to her

Queen of the Night and Queen of Opera.
Gertrude Johnson had a reasonable career with the British National Opera Company in England in the twenties. The Queen of the Night costume she wore in their *Magic Flute* is now preserved in the Performing Arts Museum in Melbourne. But her founding and heading of the National Theatre in Victoria brought her an OBE, not her singing.

cause and there were few, if any, in Victoria between 1940 and the mid-1950s who did not have their name on one of her ventures at some time or the other. The original subscribers paid six guineas, a lot of money in those days, but within a year the National Theatre had 2000 members, though literally nothing had been produced beyond speeches full of good intentions.

The one good intention that was there from the beginning, and is all that remains of Miss Johnson's early plans, was the idea to make the National Theatre Movement 'a testing, training and proving ground for the talented enthusiast in drama, opera and ballet'. Like the Elizabethan Theatre Trust, the National's first priority was drama, though its fate was to lie in opera. The training of young artists to professional standards was to be a continuing policy which, like the parent body, had its ups and downs over the years. It is important to remember, though, that this was the first Australian venture to acknowledge that just acting, singing or dancing is not enough. The performing arts in Australia had until then always been on an amateur level, an inspired amateur level quite often, but amateur just the same. It is only in the very recent past that artists have been able to train seriously for a career in the theatre under proper tutors, instead of finding their way through practical experience in amateur or — in the case of the more talented — professional companies. Like Lilian Baylis, Miss Johnson saw the need to create a trained pool of talent out of which young performing companies could be built and she set about the task with a vengeance.

Giving money to subsidize training is not the road to OBEs and knighthoods today, let alone in 1936. The patrons of the arts clustering around Miss Johnson wanted their friends, specially their friends in viceregal circles to see something of their 'work'. The very first National Theatre production strikes us as slightly quaint for a group aiming so high. It was a '*Joyous Pageant of the Holy Nativity*' staged in December 1936 in the Princess Theatre. Six months later this was followed by Shakespear's *As You Like It* (whose five performances resulted in the company's first profit: one shilling and three pence, or threepence per performance), then *The Barretts of Wimpole Street* and in 1938, *The Flying Dutchman*. The opera was produced by one Garnett Carroll, later to become a noted impresario and the owner of the Princess Theatre in Melbourne.

The honorary director (Miss Johnson accepted no payment for her services during the thirty-eight years of her rule) lost no time in cashing in on the glory these productions brought to her sponsors. A permanent home for the planned schools was found in a charming old church hall at St Peter's, Eastern Hill, and in due course, ballet, opera and drama schools were created, while constant productions kept the name of the National Theatre Movement before the public.

The war proved to be the making of the National. Run by do-gooders (in the best sense), the cause of the war effort, troop entertainment and the like occupied the staff of the National full time and the lack of imported shows created a suddenly larger-than-ever public for its dramas, ballets and operas. A *Marriage of Figaro* in 1940 was followed by *The Beggar's Opera*, with Beatrice Oakley as Polly Peachum. Musical direction for all these productions was in the now somewhat feeble hands of eighty-three years old Gustave Slapoffski who had been brought to Australia to conduct opera in 1900! He had been in charge of the Carl Rosa Company in England before that. Still, the public was grateful for the small mercies his band of singers could provide and nobody noticed when one night the old gentleman was found to be quietly snoozing away, while orchestra and cast continued with unallayed energy.

The fifteen operas staged during the war years at Eastern Hill were an adjunct of the new National Theatre Opera School and, if the singers were young and inexperienced, the repertoire was surprisingly varied. It included four Mozart operas, potboilers like *Rigoletto* and *Martha*, and goodies such as Messager's *Monsieur Beaucaire*, and Gluck's *Iphigenia in Aulis* as well as *Orpheus and Euridice*. Year by year the productions continued and, as the war ended, the need for a permanent opera company became clear. Through the National's effort in raising funds for patriotic causes Miss Johnson had added many valuable friends to her clan and when the time came to strike, she struck with amazing swiftness.

Forty-five principal singers, a chorus of 110, no less than forty-five dancers and an unnamed and uncounted orchestra presented a season of 'Grand Opera' at the Princess Theatre in March and April 1948. The five operas were *Rigoletto, Aida, Faust, Carmen* and *The Marriage of Figaro*. If there was ever a more ambitious first-up professional opera season in Australia, I would like to hear of it. Not that the claimed title 'professional'

should be taken too seriously. It was indeed the first truly native company in that all the singers emerged from over 600 auditions held in Melbourne. There were no imports on the stage or behind the scenes, but the main lack of professionalism was in the pay packets which, in the majority of cases, were empty.

By 1948 Herman Schildberger and his National Theatre Opera School had begun to play a leading role in providing singers for these full-scale opera productions. Miss Johnson's work, not surprisingly, proved to be most effective in the field she knew best. Though ballet and drama actually anticipated opera in the scheme of things — probably for financial reasons — it was opera which brought the National its greatest recognition. That first *Rigoletto* at the Princess Theatre had Miss Johnson's star pupil, Barbara Wilson, as Gilda and Robert Simmons as Rigoletto.

The talent in the company was versatile indeed. Stefan Haag, a member of the Vienna Boys Choir stranded in Australia when World War II broke out, not only sang Monterone, but was one of the assistant conductors! (The other was Douglas Gamley, one of the best of our musical expatriate composers and conductors of the post-war years.) The administrative cast lists already read like a social and artistic Who's Who, with the Governor, Sir Winston Dugan, as Patron, Sir John Latham and Sir Thomas Nettlefold among the Trustees, Sir Robert Knox as President and Lady Angliss (later Dame Jacobena) as his deputy. Professor Bernard Heinze and John Rowell were among the Vice Presidents and an Advisory Committee included Florence Austral and Horace Stevens!

I don't propose to start listing name after name, but the fact that, at such an early point in its career, people such as these gave their practical and financial help to the National Theatre may explain its ultimate success, (if not its final decline as a producing company).

The success of that season in 1948, based soundly on purely local talent, much of it from the National Theatre Opera School, proved conclusively that a demand for opera existed at the box office and that it could be satisfied without great star imports. Throughout the coming years the National Theatre proved that native opera could indeed exist. Only the financial realities proved a stumbling block; the days of unpaid and underpaid staff and singers were numbered.

Perhaps the artistic standards of those early years

were not of the highest, but the last international opera season had been in 1935 and a new public had grown up during the war. Joseph Post was available as musical director and Post had been the most proficient of Australian opera conductors since his debut in 1931 and was to remain so for many years yet. Visually the operas, all produced by William P. Carr, did not live up to the magnificent sound produced by the massed voices, most of them young. The veteran baritone Frederick Collier was the exception, but he lent immense strength through his experience. Among the bit players, singing both Mercedes and Siebel, was Betty (later Elizabeth) Fretwell.

Plans announced for the second season were even more ambitious: *Boris Godounov, The Bartered Bride, La Bohème, Don Giovanni* and a revival of *Carmen*. Getrude Johnson was nothing if not ambitious, and the success of the first season gave her reason to be confident. How haphazard her methods and those of her staff actually were can be gauged from the fact that only one of these five announced works materialized, *The Bartered Bride*. However, the actual season of six weeks in 1949 included six works, not five! *The Tales of Hoffman, Martha, The Magic Flute, Fidelio* and *La traviata* joined Smetana's opera to produce a season possibly even more successful than the first. Yet this was only one third of the first of many 'Festivals of the Theatre Arts' to be staged by the National Theatre in the Princess Theatre. The opera season was followed by two weeks of the National Theatre Ballet Company and two weeks of Shakespeare's *Twelfth Night* and Tennessee Williams' *The Glass Menagerie*!

Within one year of starting its professional activities the National Theatre Movement had staged ten weeks of ten different operas, ballets and plays in the 1600-seat Princess Theatre in Melbourne. And the whole thing was planned and executed from its minute offices and studios in Eastern Hill and used a huge number of the students of all three schools, who obtained some excellent experience in the process. Miss Johnson's dream of building an Australian Old Vic-Sadler's Wells looked rosy indeed in 1949. Not only did the public flock to see the productions, but the Victorian Government contributed $10 000 toward the cost of the Three Arts Festival. Miss Johnson recognized the potential of the young Ronald Dowd, who made his operatic debut in *The Tales of Hoffmann* and also appeared as Florestan in *Fidelio*. It was also through the medium of *Hoffman* that Stefan Haag first tried his hand as a producer, an event which

First feathered and later tarred.
Stefan Haag started his multi-faceted career as a baritone and assistant conductor with the National Theatre Opera, turned producer and ultimately administrator during the Elizabethan Trust's darkest years—for which he was held responsible by many. (Haag as Papageno and Barbara Wilson as Pamina in the National's *Magic Flute*.)

was to have long-lasting repercussions, particularly since his musical background gave the Offenbach work a more cohesive style than the other operas, though their musical values may actually have been higher.

Having established a successful pattern, Miss Johnson saw no reason to change it. A similar festival in 1950 saw productions of *Madame Butterfly, Rigoletto, The Barber of Seville, The Flying Dutchman* and *Hänsel and Gretel*. The opera company (meaning the management of the company, for the singers were called together only for the season) had acquired a most efficient repertoire which could be repeated *ad infinitum* and on the occasion of the hundredth anniversary of the founding of Victoria in 1951 the company actually presented a full season with only one new production. All the glory that year went to the National Theatre Ballet which not only

FIVE OPERAS in this National Theatre season at the Princess. Below: Betty Fretwell, as Madam Butterfly (right), and Justine Rettick (Susuki) in "Madam Butterfly." BOTTOM LEFT: Marie Collier as Giulietta, Lance Ingram (Hoffmann), and Dorothea Deegan (Nicklaus) in "The Tales of Hoffmann." RIGHT: Mel Clifford (The Larrikin) and Gavrie McSween (the Mayor's Daughter) ("The Tales of Hoffmann" ballet).

BELOW: Marie Collier and John Shaw (Chief of the Secret Police), in "The Consul." BOTTOM RIGHT: Doris Dodd as Hansel, Nancy Rasmussen (Gretel) and Alwyn Smith (the Dew Fairy) in "Hansel and Gretel." CENTRE BELOW: Graeme Campbell, as Amahl, and the Three Kings, Clifford Grant (Balthasar), Raymond McDonald (Kaspar), and Leonard Delany (Melchior) in "Amahl and the Night Visitors."

Opera as popular entertainment.

In 1954 the *Argus* in Melbourne devoted a full-colour eight-page supplement to the National Theatre, covering its history in ballet and drama as well as opera. Little did anyone know that this was to be its last year of full-scale glory.

offered Australia the first ever four-act *Swan Lake*, but what was to be the only genuine Australian ballet for many years to come, *Corroboree*.

The highlight of this jubilee season was *Aida*, specially staged for a returning Australian of truly international fame, Marjorie Lawrence, whose remarkable autobiography, *Interrupted Melody*, had just been published. Lawrence's continuance of her career, though paralyzed from the waist down, had brought her more fame than her magnificent voice. Getting her to sing Amneris in the Melbourne *Aida* was a tremendous scoop, though for some curious reason the company failed to take advantage of it. The programme made no mention of Lawrence's infirmity and many a curious onlooker must have wondered why Amneris remained seated throughout the production, which Lennox Brewer had built

Paralyzed seductress.
Marjorie Lawrence only
appeared once in opera in
Australia, as Amneris in the
Melbourne National Theatre
production of *Aida*. Paralyzed
by polio (the subject of the
book and film *Interrupted
Melody*), she remained seated
or reclining throughout the
performance. (Betna Pontin
as Aida and Laurence Lott as
Amonasro in front; David
Bruce as the King next to
Lawrence.)

The Indestructibles.
The late Harold Rosenthal
wrote: '. . . not only London,
but most of the leading opera
houses in the world would, if
not actually forced to close
their doors, be very hard put
to perform certain operas if it
were not for the existence of
Australian singers.' Almost all
those he listed came from the
ranks of the two National
Opera Companies. He listed
twenty singers engaged in
London at the time twenty-
one years ago, fifteen years
after the National seasons, yet
some are still singing today.

Albert Lance (Lance
Ingram), 1954.

around her. Betna Pontin's *Aida* was passable and young John Shaw already sang Amonasro well, but overall vocal standards were hardly worthy of the famous visitor.

The season as a whole was, in fact, well below the standard of the first two, though the Rossini *Barber* had a sparkling trio of Rosinas in Barbara Wilson, Margaret Nisbett and Verona Cappadonna. Others from the local rosters to leave a serious impression were baritones Morris Williams and Keith Neilson, while Betty Fretwell stepped up to sing the Countess in Mozart's *Figaro*. Nevertheless, the financial success was such that a four-week supplementary season was staged, adding *Madame Butterfly* and *Rigoletto* to the repertoire.

As a sidelight on the state of music in Australia in 1951, commercial radio stations were still running their own orchestras and when the National Theatre Festivals began to take on the aspect of truly professional success, the ABC's Victorian Symphony Orchestra took turns with the 3DB Symphony Orchestra in playing for the season. The thought of an orchestra capable of playing for opera and ballet being attached to a commercial radio station seems strange nowadays. We forget that it is still possible to buy records of music with Arturo Toscanini conducting the orchestra which was created specially for him, the NBC Symphony, (NBC standing for the National Broadcasting Corporation — of New York, not Melbourne, of course).

After three professional seasons Miss Johnson's National Opera Company appeared to be soundly ensconced. Audiences and critics responded to what was being offered and standards, if still low, were not much worse than Covent Garden under the Rankl regime was

offering in post-war London. With admirable foresight plans were made for the logical next step: collaboration with another opera company which had recently been formed in Sydney.

What should have been the beginning of the Australian Opera occurred in 1952. Miss Johnson in Melbourne joined Mrs Clarice M. Lorenz and her Sydney-based National Opera to present an Australia-wide tour using the resources of both companies. In the light of subsequent history it is amazing that this one joint venture ever took place; probably the pressure of prominent citizens behind the two ladies in their respective capital cities had something to do with it.

There had been rivalry between the two groups ever since Mrs Lorenz had decided to call her company The New South Wales National Opera during the previous year. Miss Johnson rightly felt that her use of the word 'National' since 1935 gave her some kind of priority, and she had just cause to claim that she was doing a good job under the banner of The Australian National Theatre Movement, covering also ballet and drama. And here was this New South Wales upstart adopting a name which had been her trade mark for fully twelve years!

The NSW National Opera had started modestly, but with remarkable public success in an opera-starved Sydney, with *Carmen, A Masked Ball* and *Seraglio* in 1951. Clearly, the successes of Miss Johnson in Melbourne had stirred the Sydney citizens into action. Sydney, like Melbourne, had its fair share of excellent local singers, most of whom had trained in the admirable local Conservatorium directed by Eugene Goossens. The Con. had much better facilities than the National Theatre Opera

Elizabeth Fretwell as Tosca, 1953.

Robert Allman as Germont, 1954.

John Shaw as Marcello, 1953.

Neil Warren-Smith as Antonio in *Figaro*, 1955.

School in Melbourne. Thus, while Miss Johnson had a longer direct tradition and several years of 'professional' seasons as a head-start, Sydney singers had actually performed in full-size productions of works as large as Wagner's *Mastersingers of Nuremberg*. Goossens and his predecessors were far more progressive in their thoughts and professional in their approach to opera, and gave their singers a much sounder background than that available to their Melbourne counterparts. Apart from *The Mastersingers*, the Conservatorium's last season prior to the first appearance of Mrs Lorenz on the scene included Debussy's *Pelléas and Melisande* and Verdi's *Falstaff*. Goossens had long ago abandoned the standard repertoire and in 1951 he staged *Otello, Gianni Schicchi* and his own opera, *Judith*, which gave the young Joan Sutherland her first stage experience. In later years they were followed by even more ambitious productions such as *Boris Godounov* and Wagner's *Die Walküre!* (The traditions started by Goossens and his predecessors are continued to this day by the enterprising work in staging rarely-performed operas and new Australian works with students under the direction of Professor Roger Covell at the University of New South Wales. Other universities do similar valuable work, but a book of this type cannot cover them all, unfortunately.)

The more professional approach of the Sydneysiders manifested itself from the very start. They may have been late in the race, but they were not going to be stopped from being the best. The very first season of the NSW National Opera invaded enemy territory by going to Melbourne, playing in the hardly-ideal Tivoli Theatre and opening in the middle of Miss Johnson's National Theatre Arts Festival! It *was* an outrageous invasion, particularly since it actually duplicated one of the operas of the Festival, *Carmen*, and used one of Miss Johnson's conductors, Joseph Post, whose duties with the Melbourne company ended four days before the invaders opened at the Tivoli.

For the first, and possibly the last time, Melbourne had two professional opera companies playing at the same time — not counting some early companies, whose efforts were hardly comparable. In the light of operatic history in the following years it is interesting to compare the singers appearing in Melbourne in both companies in 1951. The following list should not be taken as an attempt to play off one company against the other, let alone one singer against the other.

Melbourne National Opera	Sydney National Opera
Alan Ferris	Valda Bagnall
Elizabeth Fretwell	June Bronhill
Kevin Miller	Geoffrey Chard
Keith Neilson	Ronald Dowd
Margaret Nisbett	Neil Easton
John Shaw	Alan Ferris
Robert Simmons	Alan Light
Barbara Wilson	Eric Michelson

You will see that Alan Ferris (like conductor Post) appeared in both companies, showing that an interchange of artists was already taking place. Also, Ronald Dowd had played his first roles with the Melbourne company before the Sydney one came into being.

Thus Mrs Lorenz had a very sound basic ensemble to add to Miss Johnson's company when the joint season of 1952 was planned. It was the stated ambition to make this 'the forerunner of a truly Australian National Opera'. Each company played host in its own city and productions were identical in each, though local artists were usually given preference and John Brownlee returned to his native land to sing Don Giovanni and Scarpia. There was a further joint season in Brisbane.

1952 was the high point of native opera in Australia until the present Australian Opera began to establish itself. Melburnians will claim that the 1953 and 1954 seasons by Miss Johnsons's company were better without the Sydney group and the latter will claim the same for their team in Sydney. In retrospect, even the most biased Sydneysider may have to give the later honours to Melbourne, but the best of the Melbourne company's last two seasons could not compare with the overall excellence of the joint season, which should really have been the foundation stone of the Australian Opera Company.

Six operas were staged in three cities: *Lucia di Lammermoor, Tosca, Don Giovanni, Lohengrin, A Masked Ball* and the double bill *Cavalleria rusticana* and *Pagliacci* — the first three by the Melbourne group and the last three by the Sydney company. The season opened in Melbourne on 15 March 1952 with John Brownlee as Don Giovanni, supported by Phyllis Rogers, Joyce Simmons, Verona Cappadonna, Morris Williams, John Dudley, Alan Eddy and John Shaw (who played Masetto). Understudies included John Young as the Don, Fretwell for Donna Anna and Eric Michelson for Ottavio.

The star who faded too soon.
The first soprano stars of the Melbourne National Opera were Barbara Wilson, Elizabeth Fretwell and Marie Collier, in that order. Barbara Wilson chose to abandon the stage after some years as the National's unquestioned star attraction, even after Fretwell and Collier had begun their careers. (Here she is as Lucia di Lammermoor with Eric Michelson in 1952.)

The star who fell after shining.
Marie Collier in her first rôle, as Santuzza in *Cavalleria rusticana*, was an immediate sensation in 1952. She achieved star status internationally over the next nineteen years before tragically falling to her death from a window in London.

The second performance saw the sensational debut of Marie Collier in *Cavalleria rusticana*. Collier appeared 'cold', never having sung in opera before, her only professional experience consisting of chorus work in Williamson's short revival of *Oklahoma!* in 1951. The debut of the young chemist's assistant was awaited with interest because at a party prior to the opening of the Arts Festival of 1952 (which included the usual National Theatre ballet and drama seasons) it was announced that Collier would sing in the Triumphal Scene from Verdi's *Aida* and that this would be the National Theatre's contribution to the Royal Command performance before King George VI on 22 March 1953. The king died and the performance was cancelled, but in 1952 the announcement of a completely unknown singer as Aida for that occasion was met with joy, envy, interest, enthusiasm or laughter, according to the person involved. For any country which could produce singers like Austral, Lawrence or Brownlee to field an untried newcomer before the King seemed total folly to most, but Miss Johnson's ear had not failed her. After the première of *Cavalleria Rusticana* there were no further dissenting voices. While all other rôles, no matter how small, were covered by several singers. Collier had Santuzza to herself. No other singer was listed to sing, or sang the part, during the whole of the tour!

Ronald Dowd sang his first Canio, Alan Light was Tonio and Joseph Post again conducted the Victorian Symphony Orchestra. For the first time all the operas were properly designed and if the productions did not quite equal the designing standards, the year certainly saw an approximation of what was considered reasonable operatic presentation overseas. The operas could certainly hold their own against those seen at Covent Garden in 1952, a fact easier to appreciate after looking at the names of the designers: John Rowell, William Constable, Desmonde Downing, Robin Lovejoy, Louis Kahan and Timothy Walton.

This was also Elizabeth Fretwell's debut as Tosca and Robert Allman found his operatic feet for the first time playing the small part of Sciarrone. Lance Ingram (later of international fame as Albert Lance) sang some of the Cavaradossis and Brownlee was the Scarpia.

The Sydney season that followed was as great a success as the Melbourne one, even though, by an incredible managerial blunder, it was forced to open without Brownlee, the intended star of the opening night. Nobody had bothered to check Brownlee's commitments prior to planning the season and he was scheduled to sing a concert in Melbourne on the evening of his Gala Première in Sydney. Not only the first, but the second performance of *Don Giovanni* in Sydney starred a young unknown named John Young, one day to be the administrator of the company which is now the Australian Opera.

The failure of the two 'National' companies to repeat

The tragedy of excellence. The quality of the National Opera Companies was unquestioned. Many of their singers and productions were used by the Elizabethan Trust Opera, some as late as 1968. This Melbourne *Bohème* of 1953 was one of them. (Original cast, *right to left*: Alan Eddy, Robert Simmons, Barbara Wilson, Lance Ingram, John Shaw, Joyce Simmons.)

the unquestioned success of the 1952 joint venture did not, as might be expected, result from a head-on clash between the two leading ladies, or any other great disaster. It seems to have been the individual opinion of both Miss Johnson and Mrs Lorenz that each company was carrying the other, that each could become the truly national company on its own. Perhaps it was ultimately Mrs Lorenz and her Council who made the fatal move, because after the end of the most successful joint season of 1952, the NSW National Opera changed its name to The National Opera of Australia. Since the *Australian* National Theatre's founder, Gertrude Johnson, had been awarded on OBE for her work with the *National* Theatre Opera Company, this could only be regarded as a slap in the face. There is no record of any serious planning for a joint season in 1953, but Miss Johnson went over to the attack, planning not just a foray into Sydney, but a tour covering Perth and Adelaide and even Broken Hill, with principals identical to those seen in Melbourne. Local musical societies provided chorus and orchestras and local councils gave financial backing.

It really was a bold move by a company which had aimed to be truly 'national' according to its name since its formation nearly twenty years earlier. Subsidized by the Victorian State Government and an astonishingly large number of commercial enterprises and private donors, it obviously had good friends with influence outside Victoria as well. Australian Consolidated Press, the Sydney-based newspaper empire, actually guaranteed the Melbourne company's Sydney season against loss, while Mrs Lorenz's ambitious return season to Melbourne later in 1953 was backed by neither the NSW Government nor sponsors from either city. What both ladies forgot was that opera could not continue on a semi-amateur basis, that singers and staff would ultimately have to be paid a living wage. Miss Johnson's backing was strong, but her plans — possibly as a result of the Lorenz challenge — were too ambitious and deficits began to escalate alarmingly.

The National Opera of Australia (no mention of NSW or Sydney in the title now) fared even worse. Both companies were heading rapidly toward financial disaster, yet they could not see the writing on the wall. It was war! The fact that in opposition to each other the better woman had to lose as well, was overlooked by both parties.

Not that the public had anything to worry about. It was suddenly presented with an avalanche of opera of astonishingly good quality. Part of the Elizabethan Trust Opera's problems in years to come can be traced back to the excellence of the last seasons of both the National companies.

The annual Melbourne Arts Festival staged by the National Theatre in 1953 covered nine weeks, including five of opera, during which *La Bohème, Così fan tutte, Tosca, The Barber of Seville* and Menotti's *The Consul* were staged. *The Consul* was a runaway sensational success, again because of Marie Collier. It was an enterprising move, the first truly modern opera ever staged in Australia, and succeeded beyond all expectations to become a milestone by which operatic standards were measured for years to come. *The Consul* made Stefan Haag's name as a producer. The designs by Louis Kahan were excellent, though the drabness of the subject allowed for few frills, and modern abstract design techniques were still unknown. But principally it was the superb musical content that held the whole thing together. Menotti's opera is not great music, but it is great theatre and the long background of practical performing experience which the National Theatre had offered its singers via its opera school and its semi-professional seasons was now paying off. The cast backed up Collier's truly international standard Magda Sorel to the last man. Later charges that the Elizabethan Trust Opera Company stole all the National Theatre's artists almost look to be true. In *The Consul* alone could be found Fretwell, Shaw, Allman, Robert Simmons, Joyce Simmons, Wilma Whitney, Dorothea Deegan, Justine Rettick, Stefan Haag and a very young Lauris Elms; ten singers out of the cast of fourteen ended up in the later company, not to mention the conductor, designer and producer. No wonder *The Consul* chalked up more than seventy performances in no less than seventeen cities in one year, a record which, I believe, has yet to be broken.

For its Sydney season, split between the Tivoli and the Theatre Royal, the Melbourne company added *Madame Butterfly* for additional box office appeal, but casts remained mostly as they had been in Melbourne, though John Shaw was promoted from bit parts to Scarpia, the turning point in what was to prove a very lengthy career indeed. What the (Sydney) National Opera of Australia brought to Melbourne in exchange was hardly comparable, though it looked good on paper. It was

The end of the beginning.
Opposite: The Melbourne production of Menotti's *The Consul* in 1953 was the first major modern opera to be staged in Australia and was an immense success, being seen seventy times in seventeen cities Australia-wide. (Marie Collier's sensational Magda in the closing scene of the opera.)

The girl who was Melba.
Glenda Raymond became famous nationally by playing (and singing) Melba in a radio biography of the great Australian *prima donna*. Hers was a beautifully-placed coloratura voice, but small in the tradition of Galli-Curci and dal Monte. Rosina in *The Barber of Seville* was her greatest rôle.

identical to its Sydney season: *Carmen*, *The Barber of Seville*, *Cavalleria rusticana*, *Pagliacci*, *La Bohème*, *The Flying Dutchman*, *Endymion* and *The Devil Take Her* looks like an eight-opera schedule. In fact, the last two were Australian one-acters by John Antill and Arthur Benjamin, which were presented twice in the three-week season of five programmes. Antill conducted his own youthful and rather insipid work, while Tibor Paul was the principal conductor of the (very much) scratch orchestra. The Sydney company even had to acquire a Melbourne *prima donna*, Glenda Raymond. Its other star was Ronald Dowd and the fact that he had already sung that year with the Melbourne company was, naturally enough, not acknowledged. Others in the casts included Geoffrey Chard and Marjorie Conley, Neil Easton, John Dudley, Tais Taras, Alan Light and Robert Eddie. Compared with previous years it was not a good line-up and bringing a company such as this to Melbourne did not help the balance sheet or the Sydney company's attempt to topple Miss Johnson's operatic empire. Something had to give.

The longer-established Melbourne company moved ahead steadily, its next goal clearly in sight: 1954 would see a Royal Command Performance of opera, not the original mish-mash with Collier and the *Aida* Triumphal Scene. The Sydney group had already begun to slip. What finally sealed the fate of both companies was the very thing which seemed to assure the survival of the stronger Victorian National Opera: the visit of Queen Elizabeth II and its artistic aftermath, the foundation of the Australian Elizabethan Theatre Trust.

It was not politics which caused the Royal Command Performance of Opera to be staged in Melbourne. Not only was that city the theatre capital of Australia, but in 1953 the Melbourne National Theatre had shown beyond doubt its superiority over the Sydney company that had tried to steal its name. Prior to 1952 there might have been an equal battle, if battle there had to be. Together the combatants made a formidable team; divided they fell, and Sydney fell more quickly because Sydney had neither the history nor the political influence of Melbourne. At the same time, it should be accepted that the lack of political — meaning financial — influence may very well have been responsible for the poor showing of the Sydney group in 1953. Suffice to say that Melbourne won the fight for the Royal Command Performance of Opera, while Sydney got the Royal Variety Command

Performance. (It never has been very clear why there were no Command Performances of ballet and drama. Neither may have reached the standards of opera, but it is more likely that social 'Command Performances' were so numerous that there was not time for more than a single theatrical one in each city.)

The performance itself, which took place at the Princess Theatre on Monday, 1 March 1954 was a new production of Offenbach's *The Tales of Hoffman* which, with its many leading roles, chorus and ballet, gave an opportunity to many to show their paces. Haag's production was excellent and the cast full of the same singers who have assured continuity to opera in Australia ever since. Collier got her chance at the Royal Command showing after all, though as Giulietta instead of Aida. Albert Lance sang Hoffman with excellent volume and tone, but without a trace of the poet, and John Shaw and Lorenzo Nolan played the triple rôles Coppelius-Dapertutto-Miracle and Cochenille-Pitichinaccio-Franz admirably. The three female rôles were shared by three sopranos — the idea of a single singer for three such diverse parts was as yet unthought of in Australia. Barbara Wilson and Elizabeth Fretwell were Olympia and Antonia and greatly to be preferred to their successors in these parts only three years later. Among the chorus appeared young Nancy, now Nance Grant, Cavell Armstrong, the year's Sun Aria Winner and Jean Brunning. Among the ballet could be found Geoffrey Ingram, ten years later the first Administrator of the Australian Ballet.

La traviata (Wilson-Raymond McDonald-Allman), *Butterfly* (Fretwell-Lance-Shaw), *Albert Herring* (Max Worthley-Kathleen Goodall) a revival of *The Consul* and a double bill of *Hänsel and Gretel* and *Amahl and Night Visitors* nearly completed the eight weeks devoted to opera in the 1954 Festival, built around the Royal Command Performance.

The National Theatre Drama Company was represented by a fortnight of Shaw's *Caesar and Cleopatra*, but the ballet was absent, except as the moving spirit behind three weeks of Offenbach's *La Belle Hélène*, which followed the opera season. Produced by Stefan Haag, this had the unlikely coupling of Marie Collier and musical comedy star Max Oldaker in the leads, the year's Mobil Quest Winner, Ron Austron, as the King of Salamis and Robert Allman and Clifford Grant, starting long careers, as Calchas and Hector. Everybody else in the opera company joined in to take, if not play properly the other rôles, be they great or small. As a ballet spectacle it was a fine opera performance, as appropriate as the monumental Collier was to the part of Helen.

It was a somewhat sad wind-down for the National Theatre Opera Company, though nobody knew that this was the beginning of the end. In spite of all the public acclaim, the losses were immense. Miss Johnson was forced to place her hopes in the new Elizabethan Theatre Trust which, ostensibly, was to provide her with the means to regenerate her company's fading fortunes. What actually happened was that the National Theatre went on its own independent way, hoping against hope that the new upstart, the Trust, would fail, as it nearly did.

In the meantime Moomba, Melbourne's festival for the people, was making a slow start and the National played its part by providing opera, ballet and drama in the parks, using its own students, with the occasional outsider in a leading rôle. Typically adventurous and artistically disastrous ventures were performances of *Aida* and *Norma*, played in howling winds and rain, underrehearsed, under-sung and understaged, but still using the full symphony orchestras of the ABC! The goodwill of the golden years was still present and Miss Johnson's board of directors seemed to be able to find backing for the wildest schemes, even the quite incredible 1958 production in the Olympic Swimming Pool of Coleridge Taylor's immense oratorio *Hiawatha* with a chorus of 300 and a huge ballet (all in full Indian costumes, while a few canoes failed to complete the simplest manoeuvres). It was a complete return to the unpaid amateurism with which the National Theatre started, though Neil Easton, Alwyn Smith, Victor Franklin and others coped professionally enough with the solo parts.

The Sydney National Opera succumbed to the same financial problems which had beset Miss Johnson, and in the same year. While the latter was playing before the Queen in 1954 Mrs Lorenz sent her troupe to New Zealand with disastrous results. The last of her managers proved no better than his endless predecessors and the point was reached when there was no money to pay the singers. They had actually agreed to continue without pay when Mrs Lorenz heard about it and flew to New Zealand with some ready cash. Rumour has it that she was then forced to pay the return fares with a worthless cheque. True or not, such happenings are not uncom-

Opera, and 'How!'.
The decline of the Melbourne National Opera into oblivion was rapid after the Elizabethan Trust Opera was formed. *Aida* and *Norma* were staged in howling storms in the park, *Hiawatha*'s canoedling, however, had to be under cover, in the Olympic Swimming Pool.

mon in operatic history. Unfortunately people like Mrs Lorenz are eternal optimists and she tried to recoup the company's fortunes with a season at Sydney's huge, late and unlamented Palladium Theatre. Its four-and-a-half metre apron stage presented some unusual production problems and even the best singers found themselves floundering. Things were not made any easier by a policy of playing each opera three nights in a row to save a few dollars on stage hands!

Rigoletto, Faust, Trovatore and *Madame Butterfly* were sung more than well, under the baton of English conductor Warwick Braithwaite, by Ronald Dowd, Tais Taras, Alan Light, Neil Easton, Raymond McDonald and the young Margreta Elkins. She alternated as Azucena with another novice, Heather Begg, who had followed the company from New Zealand. Alan Light had no understudy and sang three Rigolettos in a row, while alternating as Mephistopheles, De Luna and Sharpless! The venture was doomed from the start.

When it became obvious that the Trust's lofty initial aim to 'support existing organizations' proved to have unacceptable conditions attached to it, Miss Johnson followed Mrs Lorenz into limbo, if a little more slowly. The National Theatre still had its three schools, if not the finances to give students exposure in the full-sized Princess Theatre, as of old.

Miss Johnson's answer to this situation was little short of lunatic, but her backers — unaware of what the future held — fell in with her plan. If Lilian Baylis could raise the money to build Sadler's Wells, Gertrude Johnson could build a National Theatre in Melbourne. So, in 1956, a Building Appeal was launched to build or buy a theatre to become the home for the Australian National Theatre, its schools *and companies*.

The next eighteen years were unhappy ones. Though money rolled in initially ($119 000 of it), rising building and land costs swallowed up any hopes for ultimate success. A series of fires destroyed any incentive to proceed with the venture, yet the capital invested under the shrewd eyes of Miss Johnson's few remaining backers multiplied and in 1974 The National Theatre in St Kilda was actually completed and opened, though not by the National Theatre's own opera, ballet or drama companies; that honour went to the two budding 'regional' companies, Ballet Victoria and the Victorian Opera Company. Only the schools, which occupy the ground floor of the huge building remain as a lasting memorial to Gertrude Johnson; she died in 1973, as the finishing touches were being given to the reality of her dream. It was the teaching of the arts which was her primary aim and it is the teaching of the arts which is her final monument. Ironically, the Opera School alone is no longer a part of the National Theatre. The Victorian College of the Arts planned to add an opera school to its School of Music by 1985. The directors of both bodies felt that there was room for only one opera school in Melbourne and that of the National Theatre was transferred to the College. The National's last student to make an international career, Jonathan Summers, has been a principal baritone at Covent Garden for the last decade. The Ballet and Drama Schools then expanded into the Opera School's studios and both have become major forces in the Australian educational field. Through them the National Theatre continues to fulfil its destiny.

ACT 2:

the 'trust'

ACT 2:SCENE 1
ELIZABETHAN WAYS
IN OPERA

The Australian Opera sprang out of the original Australian Elizabethan Theatre Trust which was created in 1954 to commemorate the first visit of Elizabeth II, Queen of England and Australia, to the Antipodes. The Trust, in spite of a chequered career, continues in existence and must reappear periodically in any survey of the theatrical arts in Australia, but a detailed history or assessment of its present role is out of place in these pages. Let us just say that after the arrival of a new general manager, Jeffry Joynton-Smith, in 1970 it proceeded carefully on a strictly prescribed course, governed by the one thing it never had in its more turbulent years: sound business management. Whether its existence beside the Australia Council is an anachronism or not, whether it should be disbanded, amalgamated with the Council or whether it should expand in new directions are matters which concern only the functionaries of the immense bureaucracy which has grown up around the arts since the creation of the original Australian Council for the Arts, (now the Australia Council).

After some years in which its very existence was seriously questioned, the Trust changed its character completely. In 1988 the only theatrical producing company remaining under its control was the Theatre of the Deaf — a valid part of theatre life, but a long way from opera, in fact its very antithesis. What started as an entrepreneurial body to help existing companies in 1954 can now act for major, often imported companies which have trouble raising local funds. Its charter is so broad that it can participate in practically anything, and is just as likely to find itself in partnership with Michael Edgley International as selling half-price tickets to failing shows in Sydney's Martin Place. Unfortunately, all that glitters is not Edgley and in 1986 the Trust's entrepreneurial activities lost nearly two million dollars, a sum large enough to place its future in jeopardy.

The only remaining link to Australian opera history was the Sydney Elizabethan Orchestra, which the Trust created to serve both opera and ballet in 1967, reminding us that what makes the Trust important to our history is that the Australian Opera and the Australian Ballet were originally part and parcel of the its activities. The opera was actually the Elizabethan Trust Opera Company, while the ballet was under the direction of the Trust, though it was an independent body which could have broken away had it wished to do so. In 1988 the Trust itself tried to divest itself of the orchestra, its last link with its operatic past. It seems likely that it will succeed, leaving as the sole major purpose of its continued existence the fact that many decades ago government decreed that it should be the only channel through which all taxdeductible donations to the performing arts can be made. It is an enviable, but hardly profitable activity. Only time will reveal the future of this once mighty organization.

The Australian Elizabethan Theatre Trust was born out of the desire to procreate drama, not opera or ballet!

Even more surprisingly, it was the procreation of *Shakespearean* drama which was the starting point, yet of all the performing arts, Elizabethan theatre has been least promoted by the body which actually bears its name, (though, as explained earlier, the 'Elizabethan' in the Trust's title was not derived from the Elizabeth of Shakespeare's day).

Yes, it all began with straight drama, even though in time, as the Trust grew, the complaint was universal (and justified) that it treated drama as the Cinderella of the arts. It was an odd description, because the two Ugly Sisters, opera and ballet, turned out to be beauties who ran off with two Prince Charmings, Fame and Fortune, while Cinders remained for too many years grovelling in the ashes. It is a long story, and at least the beginning must be told.

It was in the fateful year of 1951 that a company led by John Alden, in an Australia-wide tour of Shakespeare plays, sowed the seed which resulted in the Elizabethan Theatre Trust. It was the company manager, one Elsie Beyer, who approached the Arts Committee for the Jubilee Year for a grant of $20 000 to enable the John Alden Company to continue touring in Australia. She did not succeed, but the Committee's chairman, Charles Moses, found his way through the Canberra jungle to the then most famous non-medical doctor in Australia, 'Nugget' Coombs, chairman of the Commonwealth Bank.

At this point Elsie Beyer and John Alden disappear from view. Moses, the head of the Australian Broadcasting Commission, knew the benefits that a soundly-backed artistic management can bring to the arts and Coombs fell in with his ideas. Not that Moses and Coombs were worried. There was plenty of legitimate theatre around at the time. Repertory companies, both professional and amateur, were playing to good houses and the commercial theatre was in the midst of the great post-war boom. *South Pacific* and *My Fair Lady* were following *Oklahoma!* and *Brigadoon* and it needed a Jeremiah to foresee the impact of television still to come. But there was already need for subsidy in some areas of the performing arts; opera and ballet were beginning to price themselves out of the market. Moses had seen the promised land and if he objected to the take-over of his project by Dr Coombs, he did not show it.

The arrival of the Queen in 1954 gave the Trust its initial impetus. Two hundred and forty thousand dollars was raised. $180 000 from the public and $60 000 from

the Federal Government and for the first time a body dedicated to promoting the arts was offered tax-deductibility for donations. It was a revolutionary concept and so was the policy which was outlined at a series of public meetings. The Trust would not create its own companies, but would assist existing bodies to improve their standards and to work together toward a national policy in the arts!

Dr Coombs learnt his lesson very quickly, but not until he tried to implement these initial aims, which were unrealistic to say the least. The ladies and gentlemen (mainly the former) in charge of the many theatrical bodies in Australia clung tenaciously to their hard-won privileges. The successful joint opera season of the Melbourne and Sydney 'National' companies of 1952 had proved one thing: in a joint success there is less personal glory than in separate failure. And personal glory was the name of the game!

In 1954 Dr Coombs blithely waved away any thought that Mesdames Johnson and Lorenz would not collaborate if offered assistance at Federal level. After all, they were both heavily in debt and could not fail to follow lofty ideals if they were backed with hard cash. The man known as 'Nugget' still had his head stuck in the golden sands. He believed he could create great Australian opera and ballet companies, perhaps even a national drama company. Elizabeth II would be honoured by the creation of a cultural heritage as great as that present in the day of Elizabeth I.

When the Elizabethan Trust Opera Company was brought into being it was a birth too close to the birth of a typical Australian pioneer child in the 1800s for comfort. Threatened miscarriage was as real as the possibility of abortion. Fathering the infant was easy — as always! — but bringing it into the world was another matter. A nine year gestation period, with another four years in labour, was due not to any lack of innate robustness in either mother or child, but the lack of any kind of operatic gynaecologist. A series of doctors attended the confinement, each learning his craft at the expense of the child, but the Trust in its pains to bring forth the Australian Opera stubbornly refused to call in specialists to assist it.

Great credit may be due to the various novices in opera management in charge during the opera company's formative years, particularly to John Young and Stephen Hall, but they and their predecessors learnt on the job. If they learnt well, they did so at the expense of the company they were building. It is staggering that they achieved as much as they did and their failings were the failings of the theatrical community in this country, not their own. Expecting young singers to make up for poor planning, inefficient management, artistic inexperience and a basic lack of know-how in all departments was to court disaster. One top-rank administrator at the very start would have repaid his own salary in financial returns in no time at all and the unending traumas of the first ten years would have been avoided.

The fault lay not with the ever-changing administrators, but with the Trust's board of directors, for refusing to face the reality that Australia had never yet bred its own opera managers. They hired boys to do a man's job and forgot that the boys in the backroom are more important to the success of an opera company than the best of singers. The history of opera in Australia since 1954 must be read in the light of the success or failure of its administrators.

The creation of the AETT in 1954 initially had the opposite effect to its intentions in the field of opera. One of the main considerations of the new body had been the fact that the two 'National' opera companies in Melbourne and Sydney were heavily in debt and unlikely to survive without some form of financial assistance. To put the record straight, the assistance was in fact offered and rejected, because the Trust asked for a say in the two companies' affairs in return. This was not an unexpected reaction — except perhaps to the as yet artistically-innocent Dr Coombs.

Miss Johnson in Melbourne and Mrs Lorenz in Sydney, not unreasonably, pointed to the excellent work their companies had done and feared that their life-work would be destroyed through outside interference. Less reasonably, they expected money to be handed to them regardless of results. It proved ultimately to be one of the great ironies of the Trust venture into opera that its own financial forays in the field proved to be, if anything, even less successful than those of the two ladies to whom it refused to hand its funds with no strings attached.

It was a strange impasse and one, considering the people involved, which may have been unavoidable. Coombs, the money man, felt the need for tight financial accounting, as accountants have done since time immemorial. He did not know that trying to run any kind of theatrical venture, let alone an opera company, on strict business-practice lines is an impossibility.

In 1955 Hugh Hunt, the first executive director of the Elizabethan Theatre Trust actually created a board of directors to head what was to be called 'The Australian Opera Company', with power to create an opera advisory committee, a finance committee, an itinerary committee, to hire executive staff and to do a thousand and one other things needed to start an operation many times the size of the Trust itself. At that early stage the creation of a huge bureaucracy was planned down to the last detail!

Gertrude Johnson and Mrs Lorenz were members of the original board and then of the opera advisory committee which was to do the actual planning. Their colleagues on the latter included a set of reasonably independent and responsible people from whom the two ladies had very little to fear.

Sir Charles Moses, as head of the ABC, had the power to give the ABC Symphony Orchestra in each state to the company, something he had done for past Melbourne and Sydney seasons and would do in future for the Trust operas. Frank Tait controlled the Williamson theatres in which all opera companies had to play. Sir Bernard Heinze was a senior musician whose ability in programming would have been of value (though many thought Joseph Post might have been a better choice). The only other member of the opera board was the ubiquitous Colonel Aubrey Gibson, whose efforts in the fund-raising field were to be a great asset to the future company.

All in all the proposed opera board, if the two ladies had played ball, could have been a very sound proposition for them. They were the only two members who really knew what was involved and should have got their way without too much difficulty. Unfortunately their way was not one but two ways: mine and mine. Not even the success of their 1952 joint venture had been able to iron out the fact that here were two inflexible heads, neither of which would accept second billing, let alone billing *en bloc*, which is what the opera board would have meant. It is more than likely that their ultimate refusal to sit on the board was caused in each case by the presence of the other.

There was talk of the Trust offering management services, to allow each company to remain independent, with a possible interchange of artists and eventual joint seasons, but management from outside was quite unacceptable and it is not necessary to quote the exact terms of rejection on each side; they amounted to the same thing: we did all right without the Trust and we don't need it now. Famous last words!

With the chairman of the Commonwealth Bank at its head, the Trust could hardly be expected to bow to two stubborn old ladies and it finally began to plan an initial independent season for 1956.* It was a notable year for Australia because it saw the introduction of television, and for Melbourne, because it was the year of the Olympic Games. It also happened to be the bicentenary of Mozart's birth, resulting in a rash of new Mozart recordings and immense coverage being given to his works throughout the world. Perhaps fortunately, this fact finally swung the Trust to choosing an initial season of four Mozart operas, rejecting the first over-ambitious idea to programme Wagner's *Mastersingers* and Strauss' *Rosenkavalier;* the mind boggles at tours of those two productions by a raw new company.

The decision was a wise one but it would hardly have been made by the opera company's first general manager, Robert Quentin, a man widely experienced in drama, but with no experience whatever in the field of opera. Fortunately the prospect of regular pay and exposure in all states had resulted in mass desertions from the camps of both Miss Johnson and Mrs Lorenz. Stefan Haag had been responsible for the Melbourne National Theatre's most successful productions and Joseph Post had conducted the companies in both capital cities for many years. As production manager and musical director they did an admirable job in countering Quentin's inexperience. The repertoire for the 1956 season consisted of *The Marriage of Figaro, Don Giovanni, The Magic Flute* and *Così fan tutte.* On the assumption that the Olympic Games would bring immense international audiences to Melbourne, two world famous guest stars, Sena Jurinac and Sesto Bruscantini, were engaged for the Melbourne season only, replacing local singers who sang their parts in Adelaide, Perth, Brisbane, Hobart and Sydney.

Jurinac and Bruscantini were indeed fine singers to feature in an all-Mozart season in Mozart's Year. Unfort-

unately nobody thought to inform them that the operas would be performed in English and only weeks before their arrival desperate telegrams flew back and forth begging them to at least learn the recitatives in English, but to no avail, and who could blame them? By default, the leading local singers had to learn most of the set pieces in Italian so that the ensembles at least would be sung in one language. Jurinac and Bruscantini did actually lapse into variously accented English at times, but (although married at the time) they had not sung all the operas together and there were nights when Jurinac sang in German, Bruscantini in Italian and the rest of the cast in English! Lest this be taken as a reflection on the patience of management, critics and audiences in this country, it should be stated that multi-lingual performances were then still remembered at Covent Garden from the days of the recently-retired Karl Rankl, who was to find his way to our shores soon afterwards.

In the end, the Melbourne season was the least successful. Melburnians were glued to brand new television sets, or present in person at the various sporting fixtures, and takings at the opera failed to equal the 80 per cent capacity which was reached in all other cities.

Melbourne notwithstanding, the initial season of the as-yet-unnamed opera company ('The Mozart Opera Season 1956') was unquestionably a success, a much bigger success than any season for a good many years thereafter. It gave the company a flying start, and the inevitable deficit, which must accompany any tour of opera involving roughly 14 000 kilometres, was less than $40 000. Box office takings of nearly a quarter of a million dollars were $50 000 more than the company took in 1966, ten years later!

It is not too hard to find the reasons for that first season's success. The creation of the AETT had received extensive coverage. While not only the company's general manager, but also its press officer, Betty Bateman, were ignorant of matters operatic, each in his or her own way did an excellent job, the latter not least in promoting opera as family entertainment. The grand dames in their jewels came anyway, but Bateman managed to bring in the mums and dads, and what they saw was to their taste; and this last fact — too quickly forgotten — was in the end to bring the whole venture to fruition, though more than a dozen years were to pass before the instinctive correctness of this way of promoting opera was to be exploited deliberately.

*It should be noted that the last full-scale seasons by the two older companies were those of 1954, fully two years earlier, and that the Trust did not therefore madly rush into competition without giving them the opportunity to become a part of a greater Australian company.

THE AUSTRALIAN ELIZABETHAN THEATRE TRUST
by arrangement with J. C. WILLIAMSON THEATRES LTD.

present

The Marriage of Figaro

by WOLFGANG AMADEUS MOZART

Book by Lorenzo da Ponte, after Beaumarchais, Translated by E. J. Dent

with

THE WEST AUSTRALIAN SYMPHONY ORCHESTRA
by courtesy of The Australian Broadcasting Commission.

CHARACTERS IN ORDER OF APPEARANCE

Figaro, valet to Count Almaviva .... JOHN CAMERON

Susanna, maid to the Countess,
fiancee of Figaro .... VALDA BAGNALL

Doctor Bartolo .... KEITH NEILSON

Marcellina, his housekeeper .... WILMA WHITNEY

Cherubino, a page-boy .... BETTINA BENFIELD

Barbarina, a village girl .... JAN ROSS

Count Almaviva .... JOHN SHAW

Don Basilio, a music master ... EREACH RILEY

Rosina, Countess Almaviva .... NITA MAUGHAN

Antonio, a gardener, father of
Barbarina, uncle of Susanna NEIL WARREN-SMITH

Don Curzio, Counsellor at law RAYMOND McDONALD

Servants and Villagers JEAN BRUNNING, ELAINE
SIBRETT, JANICE GOLDMAN, JOAN LEVECKE,
JOY MAMMEN, BETTY WEST, JOHN COCKERILL,
GREG DEMPSEY, NORMAN HODGKINSON, NOEL
McCABE, PHILIP SHALVEY.

Footmen .... I. DONALDSON, T. GUY, L. OWENS, C.
SMITH, C. WILSON.

Musical Director: JOSEPH POST
Associate Conductor: ERIC CLAPHAM

Production by DENNIS ARUNDELL

Scenery and Costumes designed by KENNETH ROWELL

The action takes place during one day in and about the
country residence of Count Almaviva

ACT I AN ANTICHAMBER

ACT II THE COUNTESS' BOUDOIR

ACT III THE GREAT HALL

ACT IV A SECLUDED PART OF THE GARDEN

There will be three intervals ten minutes each

General Manager for Opera — ROBERT QUENTIN

OPERA STAFF

Production Director .... STEFAN HAAG
Stage Manager .... COLLEEN GOUGH
Stage Manager .... WILL THOMPSON
Business Manager .... JOHN ROHDE
Music Assistant .... GEORGE HUMPHREY
Press Officer .... BETTY BATEMAN
Assist. Stage Manager .... JOHN COCKERILL
Assist. Stage Manager .... ANGUS KIDSTON
Opera Secretary .... JOAN LEVECKE
Electrician .... ERNIE LIETCH
Wardrobe Mistress .... MARY POXON

Scenery and properties made by Joe White and assistants in
the workshops of J. C. Williamson Theatres Ltd., and at the
Princess Theatre, Melbourne. Scenery painted by George
Kenyan, Dres Hardingham and Rupert Browne.

Costumes made under the supervision of Phyll Foulkes in the
wardrobe of the National Theatre, Melbourne.

Headwear by Marjorie Head. Wigs by Barnetts and Mei Picci,
Melbourne. Footwear by Maloney and by Imbesi, Melbourne.

Special jewellery by Lustre Jewellery Co.

Handpainted costumes by the Art School of the Melbourne
Technical College.

Electrical Equipment by Strand Electrics. Special effects for
"The Magic Flute" by Pani, Vienna.

Publicity: Ron Patton Ltd.

The Opera Company wishes to state its indebtedness and to
express special thanks to Miss Gertrude Johnson of the National
Theatre Movement, Melbourne.

The birth of the Australian Opera.

An as-yet un-named opera company gave this performance of *The Marriage of Figaro* on 21 July 1956 at the Theatre Royal, Adelaide, as 'The Mozart Opera Season 1956'. Out of it grew the Elizabethan Trust Opera Company which became the Australian Opera.

The producers of this first season were Stefan Haag and Dennis Arundell, one Australian and one English, both experienced not only in making opera work, but in making it entertaining. Haag was often accused of being unsubtle, but subtlety was the last thing the Australian public wanted in 1956. Subtlety involves the grasping of finer points which can only be appreciated after long familiarity with a work. A very small proportion of the original audiences would have been familiar with these four Mozart operas and, if Haag brought many a point home with a sledge hammer, that suited them fine. As for Arundell, his productions of *Figaro* and *Don Giovanni* bore the imprint of Sadler's Wells, the home of opera aimed at the people, rather than at the snobs. No better two producers could have been chosen to launch those particular works at that particular time.

Yet ultimately the success belonged, as always in Australia, to the singers. While many of the best had wandered off overseas while waiting for the new company to become a reality (we had lost Marie Collier, Elizabeth Fretwell, Robert Allman, Albert Lance and John Lanigan, to name but a few) the pool of singers built up in Melbourne and Sydney still held enough fish to produce standards which were vocally substantially better than those at Sadler's Wells, though histrionically they still lagged behind.

A local Giovanni, John Shaw, grasped with both hands the opportunity to out-sing Bruscantini's Leporello in *Don Giovanni* and as Count Almaviva also stole *The Marriage of Figaro* from smooth-voiced John Cameron's Figaro (or Bruscantini's, when that master was singing the title role).

Max Worthley, still in his prime, was a superb Ottavio and Tamino, while Marjorie Conley amply demonstrated what a great loss to opera her early death three years later would be. Her husband, Geoffrey Chard, already well on the way to the fine career he has had (and is still having) first in England and, in the 1980s back in Australia, was Papageno, Keith Neilson, Jenifer Eddy and Valda Bagnall more than held their own and the appearance in small parts of singers like Neil Warren-Smith, Gregory Dempsey and Raymond McDonald showed that the company was already building from strength.

Australia's forgotten tenor.
Max Worthley was one of the finest tenors Australia ever produced. He appeared at home only briefly in the first Trust Opera seasons. (Worthley as Tamino in *The Magic Flute* with Marjorie Conley, a fine soprano who died tragically young.)

Mozart all the way.
The 'Mozart Opera Season 1956' featured four works: *The Marriage of Figaro, The Magic Flute, Don Giovanni* and *Così fan tutte*. (John Shaw as Don Giovanni with Valda Bagnall as Zerlina.)

There were actually four guests during that first season. Jurinac and Bruscantini, who amply justified their presence by singing superbly, were joined by expatriate Stanley Clarkson who, unlike his fellow-guests, played Sarastro in all states and made a deep impression (pun intended). Finally, another Australian, Kevin Miller, returned for some performances of Ferrando in *Così fan tutte*.

Though scenery and costumes were meagre by modern standards, they were entrusted to experienced designers who made much out of the little at their disposal. Kenneth Rowell, for example, is still one of opera's busiest and most successful stage designers in Australia, having first proved his worth on the international scene. Not only fine singers, but decorative artists prefer the stability of the local scene, though Rowell spends months each year travelling to other states (and often overseas countries) to serve the many companies which have long ago taken the place of the young Elizabethan Trust opera infant.

Lest it be thought that the infant just grew overnight without any problems, the vagaries of travel in 1956 should be remembered. Moving a company of singers by air was financially unthinkable and the thought of flying at all as recently as thirty years ago was still anathema to many people. Theatrical companies went by train and principals were envied the 'luxury' of their claustrophobic sleeping cupboards by choristers forced to sit upright all night in the coaches.

The Theatre Royal in Adelaide saw the birth of the company on 21 July 1956, but its season there was followed not by Melbourne or Sydney, but by Perth a short four weeks later. And almost immediately management and artists were plunged into their first crisis; a crisis not of their own making. Train services in those days were no better than they are now and, almost inevitably, the Opera Special struck trouble in the middle of the Nullarbor Plain. While the train was not involved in any spectacular wreck, a twelve-hour delay played havoc with pre-planned rehearsals for the 23 August opening at Her Majesty's Theatre in Perth.

It is strange what priorities people adopt in emergencies. The final dress rehearsal was to take place on the 22nd, the day the company was stuck at Kalgoorlie.

A special aircraft was chartered and brought eight of the principals to Perth by 11.30 a.m., leaving Neil Warren-Smith, Jan Ross and Raymond McDonald to follow on with the chorus. Perhaps Antonio, Barbarina and Don Curzio are not the most important members of *The Marriage of Figaro* cast, but a full-dress rehearsal without them (or the chorus) must have been a farce. Perhaps the formidable Betty Bateman arranged the whole thing as one of her superb publicity stunts? It would have been quite in keeping and certainly made the headlines, as did her promotion ideas which worked wonders, though they may make us smile today.

'Love's Amusing Round-About' advertised *Figaro,* and *Così fan tutte* was billed as 'The humorous tale of a woman's flirtations'! Presumably Marjorie Conley's Fiordiligi was the flirt, though Eunice McGowan's Dorabella could have sued for defamation. 'The intriguing story of a Don Juan' made it clear that John Shaw in *Don Giovanni* was an operatic personification of Errol Flynn, while erudite scholars pointed out that Giovanni was Italian for Juan and that the opera was in fact about Don Juan himself. As for Stefan Haag's *Magic Flute,* complete with his daring young girls on their flying machine (the three 'Boys'), it was billed in simple pantomimic language as 'Enchantment — Fantasy — Comedy'.

It was a time of happy-go-lucky improvisation, aimed at an unsophisticated audience. There were protests at the 'cheapening' of Mozart, but musical and production standards were way ahead of those of the J. C. Williamson Italian Grand Opera Season of the year before. No doubt the growing Italian migrant population stayed away in their hundreds, but this was opera for the people starting at a level which Lilian Baylis and her Sadler's Wells Opera reached only after two decades of continuous operation. And it was the people rather than the musical snobs who came to that first season. If they came for all the wrong reasons, if they were perhaps disappointed and bored when the *Magic Flute* did not include the Great Levante, the important thing was that Quentin and Bateman put bums on seats and Haag, Arundell and Post at least offered value for money, though the $2.10 top price was considered just a little steep! At a price three times as high ten years later the company's overall takings were 20 per cent less! Let us not underestimate the worth of that first season or the value of the team that started it.

There appears to have been an idea in the minds of the Trust and/or Robert Quentin that the loss made in 1956 was somehow a disgrace. The fact that J. C. Williamson's had lost a lot more during their international season the previous year was immaterial. The day had not yet dawned when operatic deficits were accepted as inevitable. Singers were, after all, only engaged by the season. Admittedly, they were paid, which is more than could be said of most of those appearing in the pre-Trust local companies, but the expense of rehearsals was minimal; no pay or half-pay was the rule and not the exception. And with salaries in the $50 per week range for principals it should have been easy to break even on 'small' operas like those of Mozart, always remembering that orchestral costs were nil, thanks to the benevolence of Moses high on Mount ABC, or so the reasoning went.

It was determined therefore to improve the performance in 1957, to eliminate all that wastefulness, to play more popular operas, to attract a larger public, to import more principals, to limit the season and to enlarge the repertoire. It was a foolproof method of going bankrupt. By some miracle the company survived 1957 with a deficit of only $53 000 after reducing its season from twenty-seven weeks to seventeen. Not that the year did not see some excellent performances of opera, but ambition began to rear an early and ugly head; everybody wanted to have his or her genius recognized and the multi-headed artistic management was the worst offender.

Nevertheless, certain patterns emerged in 1957 which ultimately proved to have such merit that they returned in later years, just as the aiming at non-operatic audiences in the first season was forgotten, only to be resuscitated by Harry M. Miller and Tony Frewin in later years. The best of these ideas was the principle of importing singers of Australian origin who had made good overseas (and God knows there were enough of those) and to star them in rôles in which they had already proved themselves. Nothing helps a young company more than to work alongside artists who know exactly what they are doing. The brief visit of Jurinac and Bruscantini during the Melbourne Olympic Season had proved the point already, though the language problem prevented it being fully effective. Now the company concentrated on people who had sung their parts in English with success.

Much has been written about Joan Hammond's great contribution to opera in England as well as in Australia.

(Let me leave her title to her post-opera life; Joan Hammond was the *grande dame* of opera long before she was damed with great praise.) In 1957 she reigned supreme in the great *prima donna* roles wherever they were performed in English. Her Tosca was universally admired in better company than Australia could provide and it was as Tosca she was brought back to her homeland by the Trust.

This was a Tosca in the grand manner, in the grand old manner perhaps, but *Tosca* defies modernization and Tosca is, after all, a *prima donna* playing a *prima donna* and Hammond had always had that strange quality of stars known simply as 'presence'. Her first act entrance may have been corny and old-fashioned, but the moment she appeared there was unmistakably Somebody up there. If ever a singer had the ability to draw applause with an entrance, that singer was Joan Hammond and Tosca was the role to bring out that quality. The fact that she sang the part superbly throughout her career is almost incidental.

In a totally different field Elsie Morison had similar presence. Hers was more ethereal in a role like Mimì and more earthy as the country lass, Mařenka, in *The Bartered Bride*; so successful, in fact, that Stefan Haag seriously suggested that *The Bartered Bride* be run as a commercial musical eight times a week to save the company's bacon. Morison calmly pointed out that she was willing to be a bartered bride, but not 'a battered bitch'. *La Bohème*, *Tosca* and *The Bartered Bride* were built around their soprano leads and proved to be the big successes of 1957. *Otello* and *The Tales of Hoffmann* were of a lesser stature and the between-seasons *Beggar's Opera* was more notable for the appearance of John Young as Mr Peachum, Shaw's McHeath and young Jenifer Eddy's Polly, than as the popular entertainment it should have been, but wasn't.

But, Hammond and Morrison notwithstanding, local singers were still the backbone of the company. No other country has produced innately adaptable singers in such quantities. The Trust may well have gained from the previous training and experience of young singers in companies such as the competing National Operas of Melbourne and Sydney, but its producers were still dealing with raw material which had instinctive artistry rather than any degree of professionalism. They carried off their performances with tremendous panache, but also with enough improvisation to give a professional

producer heart attacks. It was just as well that people like Stefan Haag were used to working in the chaos which surrounded the Melbourne National Theatre Opera seasons; he thought little of it when his singers made wrong entries, as long as they were alert enough to make the audience believe that that was where they were supposed to start. And Australian singers are nothing if not enterprising in an emergency.

Any success the company had in 1957, apart from the contributions of Hammond and Morison, came from the sheer *joie de vivre* of the enlarged company. None of the works required the ensemble discipline of the Mozart operas, all gave opportunities for belting out their best notes for the most effect and there was ample space for high jinks, although not in the two major serious works, *Tosca* and *Otello*, both produced by the veteran baritone Arnold Matters. The former relies almost totally on its three leading singers and, apart from Hammond's imposing Tosca, both Ronald Dowd and John Shaw had sung Cavaradossi and Scarpia many times before.

With Dowd and Hammond at the peak of their form and Shaw well into his best years, though still rather young, Puccini's 'cheap little shocker' was cheap only in that the Trust's economy-packaged season used Tim Walton's old Melbourne National Theatre sets. (They were still good enough to bring applause eleven years later, when they were resurrected for the Gobbi-Collier-Smith Adelaide Festival restaging!) If anything was needed to prove the quality of Gertrude Johnson original seasons, one has only to compare Walton's set for the last act of *Tosca*, with its immense statue atop the Castel Sant'Angelo, with the feeble 1974 Australian Opera setting which would have cost many times more than its brilliant ancestor.

The 1957 *Tosca* on one fateful occasion turned into more blood than thunder. John Shaw is a powerful gentleman and a powerful Scarpia. One night, as Tosca stabbed him he grabbed her knife, which jumped from his hand and hit Joan Hammond near the eye, causing it to bleed profusely. Since Scarpia was supposed to be dead, Shaw could do nothing to help his wounded colleague who, in true old trooper fashion, determinedly completed the act while wiping the blood off her face with the table napkin she still had in her hand. Cries of 'Miss Hammond has been stabbed' echoed backstage, only to be met by the reply of her inseparable companion Lolita Marriot: 'It can't be Miss Hammond! It must be

John Shaw. It wouldn't make sense if he stabbed her!' True enough, but surely that was the only case in operatic history of Scarpia turning the tables on Tosca.

The *Bohème* sets also came from the National Theatre, (as did *The Beggar's Opera*) but here Robin Lovejoy took over his first professional opera production, apart from a trial run with the NSW National Opera. His *Bohème* was not as stereotyped and traditionally fussy as Stefan Haag's and it was largely carried by Elsie Morison and her playful colleagues. Perhaps Max Worthley was too light a Rudolfo, perhaps Joy Mammen too shrill a Musetta; with Neil Easton, Alan Light and Neil Warren-Smith they produced a suitably undisciplined lot of Bohemians among whom Morison's Mimì shone in delightful contrast. Her death produced rather more than the usual flood of tears.

The logic behind this second Trust season was hard to follow. More productions spread over a shorter season were unlikely to producer a greater return, or less of a loss. Yet ambition knew no bounds and the company actually engaged dancers, who were used indiscriminately to obtain maximum value from their services. Their contribution to *The Bartered Bride* was minimal, but at least that opera does call for dancers and some of its most familiar music would have gone by the board if the 'ballet' had not been available. Smetana's immortal opera was fortunate indeed in its execution — in fact, none of the offerings fell below a pretty substantial standard, whatever the blindness of the financial planning. Elsie Morison repeated her world-famous Mařenka with pathos, fine voice and a Czech-ness surprising in an Australian. This was no *Verkaufte Braut*, but a *Prodaná Nevěsta*. She was partnered by Max Worthley, a tenor then at his lyric best. Neil Warren-Smith reached major status as the marriage broker, Kečal, and a surprise hit was made by Raymond McDonald as the stuttering Vašek. The production by Stefan Haag was 'assisted by John Young' who also played the Ringmaster, though he still appeared in the chorus, which included names like Joy Mammen, Gregory Dempsey, John Germain and Madge Stephens.

This was the year of the infamous revolving stage (hand-operated) and its vicissitudes; not only did it enable *The Bride* to change scenes without stopping the action, but it relied rather too heavily on casual scene shifters who had some difficulty in distinguishing left from right. One wheeled Kečal off stage just as he was

Elsie Morison, the singing ambassador.
One of the first post-World War II Australians to leave a major impression overseas was Elsie Morison, a great singer and a great personality. She left Melbourne in 1944 and returned only once to sing in Australia, in 1957. (In *The Bartered Bride* with Raymond McDonald.)

supposed to start his aria. Regrettably, both noticed the mistake simultaneously, both reversed the procedure and two negatives continued to make a positive — in the wrong direction! Finally Neil Warren-Smith began his aria off stage and nonchalantly wandered back onto the set which had by then miraculously found its way into the right position. It was to be a long time before stage management and lighting were to be considered worthy of skilled or experienced staff.

That ever-present opera bogey, laryngitis, made itself felt for the first time in the company's history when it hit Ronald Dowd during the Brisbane season. Trying to sing Cavaradossi while rehearsing *Otello* proved to be too much and by the time Verdi's masterpiece opened in Sydney, Dowd was in serious trouble. At the second performance his place was taken with spectacular and unexpected success by Raymond McDonald at five hours' notice. McDonald, the brilliantly weak Vašek of *The Bartered Bride*, was neither physically nor vocally equipped to sing Otello, one of the heaviest tenor rôles in the repertoire. Cast as Cassio, he did not even get a full run-through, had to be prompted from the wings, had to appear cold, not only before a live audience, but before ABC microphones broadcasting the performance, and still gave the performance of his life. McDonald actually completed all the Sydney performances before Dowd was well enough to take over the rôle in Melbourne.

(As a result of this one indisposition Ronald Dowd was to be cruelly downgraded seventeen years later! A second-rate import played the first *Tannhäuser* in the opening season of the Sydney Opera House because it was 'too risky' to cast the by then fifty-eight year old Dowd in the première. Dowd had his revenge later by giving a world-class performance in the part for weeks on end, while his reliable overstudy retired ignominiously to European obscurity.)

When Dowd finally tackled *Otello* in full voice in Melbourne he gave an impressive performance, as did Joan Hammond and John Shaw as Desdemona and Iago. If there were failings in the performance, they were to be found in Arnold Matters' stodgy production, for which Robin Lovejoy had to assist with the crowd scenes. It was much too ambitious a project for such a young company. *Otello* needs supreme singers and, whatever its virtues, *Otello's* second coming in the 1970s proved once again that it is an opera best left to international opera houses, if only because it is unrealistic to ask any singer to appear more than half a dozen times in one season as Otello.

Staging a *Hoffmann* within three years of the National Theatre one, which had featured a vastly superior cast, a much better production (by the same producer, Stefan Haag) and the glamour of a Royal Command Performance was sheer lunacy. Even the most elementary opera buff will recognize some of the weaknesses of the 1957 cast:

	1954	1957
Hoffmann	Albert Lance	Victor Franklin
Olympia	Barbara Wilson	Florence Pong
Giulietta	Marie Collier	Joyce Simmons
Antonia	Elizabeth Fretwell	Madge Stephens
Coppelius Dapertutto Miracle	John Shaw	Alan Light

No doubt audiences enjoyed *Hoffmann* as they always will, but in artistic terms it was a gamble which should not have been taken and did little more than stir up the Trust's Melbourne enemies, who quite rightly pointed out that Miss Johnson not only could do better, but had done better. It was a bad case of 'anything you can do I can do better' backfiring without much sympathy for the Trust from any quarter, least of all artists like John Young, who one night found himself, as Spalanzani, faced with the same revolving stage, which this time refused to move at all. Young spent ten minutes ad-libbing in true Tivoli fashion and wound up leading the audience in singing *I'm walking backwards for Christmas*! In the Venetian Scene matters got even worse; Gregory Dempsey and Joyce Simmons were forced to step from their gondola into Venice's Grand Canal to push their stuck vehicle into the wings. The rumbling noise detected by some was not the stage mechanism but Offenbach turning in his grave.

Joseph Post conducted all the operas in 1957 as he had during the Mozart season. His musicianship in opera was unequalled in Australia and nobody who ever sang with him had anything but the highest praise for him. There were certainly no musical failings during his two-year tenure as musical director. Whatever the reasons, and there were many, he chose to return to the bosom of the ABC and year-round employment with a safe future. His loss was to be felt keenly, though Eric Clapham more than adequately took over the balance of his performances.

The departure of Joseph Post from the Trust Opera left the door open for Karl Rankl, who was appointed musical director, (a term which to him meant artistic director) in 1958 at the magnificent salary of $160 per week. Rankl appeared to be a major catch, because he was the man who had been in charge at Covent Garden for five years! The salary the unfortunate man was prepared to accept should have warned the Trust that it was a fish too easily caught, but its ignorance in matters operatic was abysmal. English migrants with operatic tastes threw their hands up in horror; the man who had been responsible for those dreadful nights at the Garden could not possibly do anything but wreck the new Australian company! In fact, Rankl was not the only reason for the failures to come, though he did bulldoze the administration into overspending to the extent that the season of the second year of his three-year term had to be cancelled.

Rankl's term at Covent Garden was from 1946 to 1951, a period when things in England were admittedly bad. Nevertheless, the singers at his disposal included Flagstad, Schwarzkopf, Hotter, Welitsch, Silveri and just about every major English singer you could mention, plus Australians like Joan Hammond, Sylvia Fisher and Ken Neate. Rankl himself conducted twenty-four of the thirty operas produced during his five years in London, including Wagner's *Ring, Tristan, Mastersingers, Boris Godounov* and a scandal-producing *Salome* starring Ljuba Welitsch and designed by Salvador Dali; all sung in English! Yet the best that his obituaries could say of Rankl was that he was 'building for the future', meaning that possibly the great days at Covent Garden under Kubelik and Solti would not have come as quickly as they did but for Rankl's groundwork.

Was Australia really looking for more 'groundwork'? The 1956 and 1957 seasons were musically and vocally better than much produced by Rankl in London during those years. His departure from that scene was greeted with relief and I have been unable to discover anything of any value achieved by Rankl during the intervening period 1951–58. This was the man to whom the Elizabethan Trust Opera was presented on a platter, to do with as he wished. And he did and he wished; did he ever!

During that first year he imported for his unsuspecting public the travesty of an un-attractive Mary Poppins, Constance Shacklock, as Carmen, of all rôles. He cast an inexperienced chorister, Elizabeth West, as Elsa in *Lohengrin*, and expected an experienced drama producer like John Sumner to stage his first opera, without even allowing him a say in casting!

The season was not an unmitigated disaster; there was too much talent in the company for that and, despite his tendency to act the tin-pot dictator, Rankl was an efficient conductor and the good orchestras of the ABC were still at his disposal. It would have been almost impossible to fail completely and Rankl did not fail, he only ruined the company financially. God knows why his contract was renewed on the eve of 1959 when his policies were clearly the cause of the abandonment of the next season. His contract had a get-out clause, but the Trust obviously believed that Australia must be wrong and the great Rankl must be right. The man behaved like God, so he must be God and if Moses was not his prophet, neither he nor Coombs showed any inclination to interfere in Rankl's re-appointment.

As for the Trust itself — busy as it was with looking after Hugh Hunt's abortive national drama company and entering the ballet field — its financial wizards either slept or looked the other way, even before Rankl's arrival. Four of the five operas in the 1958 season required big choruses. All demanded new sets. Singers had to be imported for several key roles and it was surely no coincidence that they included Covent Garden stock from the Rankl era. Sylvia Fisher and Raymond Nilsson were at least Australians being brought back, but the choice of Shacklock to sing Carmen was the type of thing which in years to come would drive opera lovers to distraction: 'Why import at all when better local talent is available', was the most common cry. Alternatively, if local talent is not available, why schedule an opera which demands a leading role that cannot be filled within a set budget?

Only her willingness to sing cheaply or personal favouritism can explain Shacklock's Carmen, yet this, the worst opera production up to that time, was the greatest box office success. The aiming of publicity at the masses for two years was still paying dividends and packed houses clearly were unaware that this under-sung travesty of Bizet's masterpiece was anything but what grand opera was all about. There was a magnificent orchestra conducted superbly by Rankl or most acceptably by Georg Tintner, making his first appearances here. Nilsson's José cut a dashing future in his uniform, and his voice was quite acceptable, but Shacklock was prim and unexciting. The Escamillo of Robert Simmons was a sad case of miscasting and John Sumner's production amounted to little more than stage direction. According to him, 'I was asked to come and direct some traffic on a pre-ordained journey'. Sumner has never returned to opera production. His magnificent creation of the Melbourne Theatre Company has been his life's work, and working under Rankl's thumb on this one production put him off opera for life.

Carmen succeeded in spite of herself and so did *The Barber of Seville*, aimed at the same audience. The rest of the repertoire did not. With a man like Rankl, a 'world-class' conductor, in charge, the artistic pretensions of culture began to rear their ugly heads. The fact that the public accepted Mozart served up as popular entertainment was forgotten. Too many highbrows, critics included, were clamouring for a greater degree of seriousness in programming and at this point the company fell well and truly between the traditional two stools. *Carmen* and the *Barber* were offered as a sop to popular taste. *Fidelio* and *Peter Grimes* catered for higher standards and *Lohengrin* was the bridge between the two — a curious bridge when it was presented in the dullest imitation-Bayreuth culture-down-your-throat manner. The *Carmen* public stayed away from *Peter Grimes* and the *Peter Grimes* public stayed away from *Carmen*. In the meantime Rankl was busy raising his own banner of excellence by demanding more and more rehearsals and more and more singers.

What once had been a band of happy-go-lucky talented young artists suddenly became a hard-working disciplined batch of imitation-European singers. Whatever they may have learnt from Rankl, they forgot to enjoy their work and it showed. The chorus sang out magnificently, the orchestras were better than ever, the ensembles came in exactly on the beat, but something was missing. Only Joy Mammen managed to achieve considerable success by singing Micaela's foolproof aria to herself and Ronald Dowd had a tremendous personal triumph as Peter Grimes a role he was to repeat with equal success in England and Germany. It is difficult to find much else to pick out among the dozens of major performances of the season, though more shall be said about the production of Rossini's immortal *Barber*.

Robin Lovejoy alone achieved any kind of glory as a producer with his precisely paced *Peter Grimes*. Britten's opera suited Rankl's pedantry admirably. Music and production demanded the kind of discipline Rankl was trying to instil in the company, while nobody expected vocal splendours from anybody except Dowd, who obliged magnificently. Sylvia Fisher, sadly out of voice throughout her months in Australia, was a convincing Ellen Orford and the small part of the Methodist fisherman, Bob Boles, was tailor-made for the awkwardly moving young Donald Smith. Lovejoy even provided his own designs, giving the whole thing a unity of purpose which would not be equalled by the company for many years to come. Unhappily, *Grimes* was not box office with either of the publics at whom the season was aimed. *Fidelio* and *Lohengrin* were known to the *cognoscenti*, but Britten was still beyond the pale. Excellent write-ups managed to increase audiences in most cities, but it was not enough.

There are some who actually liked Stefan Haag's *Fidelio* of 1958 which was revived five years later. And why not? Didn't the full cost of all costumes and scenery add up to no more than $1600? Wasn't this exactly the kind of economy the company needed? Actually, it is doubtful whether necessity was the father of this invention, though the management surely embraced it with open arms. Haag until then had been strictly a traditional producer and when he decided to go the other way he went, like the girl from Kansas City, just about as 'fur as fur can go'! A single square rostrum with four identically-sized squares attached to each side was used for Rocco's room, the prison, the dungeon and the Halleluia finale, which can take place anywhere except in a dungeon, prison or Rocco's room. The four side panels were raised and lowered to create different patterns, all of which had only one thing in common, the necessity for the singers to climb steep inclines and to do their singing struggling to keep a foothold. Talk about leaving things to the audience's imagination!

The triumph which failed. The first production of truly international standard of the Trust Opera was *Peter Grimes* in 1958, which played to empty houses, while a dreadful *Carmen* played to capacity. (Ronald Dowd as Grimes and Neil Easton as Balstrode.)

Haag admittedly had a model from which he took his revolutionary simplification of a traditional production. Wieland Wagner, a grandson of Wagner himself, had started the vogue of replacing the very detailed realism demanded by his grandfather's scores with wide open stages lit cunningly to make much of very simple impressionistic props. There is no harm in experimentation — unless you fail, and Haag failed. His only justification was to be found among those who considered that the simplification of the stage picture allowed greater concentration on the music; in other words they welcomed a good performance in concert form. The trouble was that even at the best of times, apart from the orchestral sounds drawn by Rankl from the various ABC orchestras, the performance failed to reach musical standards acceptable to the average listener and a poor concert performance of *Fidelio* is no replacement for a traditional production.

Sylvia Fisher, as Leonora, was a shadow of her former self. Looking ill and ungainly, she sang without control and all the sincerity in the world could not mask her inability to cope with the music. Neither Raymond McDonald nor Sergei Baigildin, arising from the chorus to take over occasional performances, could carry off the deceptively negative role of Florestan. The only strength of this *Fidelio* came from two singers who continued to be mainstays of the company for two decades, who sang the same roles again as recently as the 1970s. Neil Warren-Smith's Rocco remains one of the great performances in opera and Alan Light's Pizarro is possibly the most successful role in the repertoire of the man who has probably more parts behind him than any other singer in Australia. Between them they could hardly save the evening, nor could young Clifford Grant, vocally superb, but visually awkward, as Don Ferrando.

Lohengrin is a work of great dramatic potential with some of Wagner's most easily-assimilated music to back up what any average producer can make work with a little thought and a great deal of money. Stefan Haag again tried to copy Bayreuth, but the production looked like provincial ostentation done on a shoestring. Anybody delighting in the lushness of the music, admirably realized by Rankl in the pit, was distracted by the visual cheapness of it all. As for dramatic tension, there was none. The one redeeming feature was Dowd's dignified and well-sung Swan Knight. Neil Easton was a strong Telramund and Constance Shacklock oozed villainy and

chest tones, not always at the same time, but often enough to make a substantially better impression than she did in *Carmen*.

The failure of *Lohengrin* had to be laid squarely on Haag's self-indulgent production, designed — like *Fidelio* — by himself. Stefan Haag always was a talented producer, if not an inspired one, but as he grew in administrative stature his natural talents were to fade. It was a case of the old, old story: an artist cannot judge his own work and even producers need the discipline of collaboration, preferably from above, in making decisions. To a lesser degree Stephen Hall was to follow the same path in later years, but in 1958 it seems remarkable that the supposed dictator Rankl was satisfied to throw his considerable muscle into productions which were an eyesore. Again, a knowledge of his background explains the seemingly inexplicable: at Covent Garden Rankl worked for years with dreary pre-war sets brought out of mothballs to be stuck together with tin-tacks and sticky tape. Probably he didn't notice the stage picture anyway.

Ignoring the 'artistic success' (read: box-office flop) of *Peter Grimes*, the production which was the only link with the traditions set in the first two seasons was the

The start of Australia's idol.
Productions in 1958 were shabby beyond imagination. Singers like young Donald Smith, here seen in *The*

Barber of Seville, saved the company's bacon. After eight years in England he would return to become the most popular singer in the country.

Opera in the bush.
The demand for opera has always been there outside the capital cities. The national company tried to fill it as well as possible in miniature sets. (*The Barber of Seville* 1965. Robert Gard, Doreen Morrow, Norman Yemm and Elizabeth Allen.)

Australia's most versatile singer.
Neil Warren-Smith had a superb bass voice and was a tower of strength throughout a career which lasted from his days with the National Theatre to his early death in 1986. No bass rôle was beyond his compass, from Bartolo (seen here in 1958) to Boris Godounov or Baron Ochs.

unjustly-maligned *Barber of Seville* produced by Haag in top comic form (prior to Rankl's arrival) in Hobart, admirably conducted by Eric Clapham and with bright practical sets by John Northcote. If the Trust burnt its financial fingers in 1958, it was not the fault of this *Barber* which quite possibly prevented the whole company from going up in smoke. Not only was it launched before the rest of the season, not only did it make its unspectacular way throughout the year, but it continued unstoppably for a long country tour after the season was over, its cast the sole survivors of a company which, officially, ceased to exist at the end of 1958.

It is worth spending a little time on this 'worthless' *Barber*. Its values were those of opera as staged in Australia to that time and if they were not the values of today, they were one heck of a lot better than the pretensions of the Rankl epics.

To first state the obvious, that Rossini's *Barber of Seville* is an almost foolproof bit of stage tomfoolery, it nevertheless requires two very powerful ingredients that are too often missing: good voices and singers who can act. Donald Smith, finding his professional feet for the first time, was not the most polished Almaviva, but the beauty of his voice made up for histrionic shortcomings. On the other hand Glenda Raymond and Robert Simmons were impeccably right for their parts. The career of Glenda Raymond never quite overcame her appearance as Melba in an early endless radio biography, but there can have been few more delightful interpretations of Rosina in the history of opera, for here were looks, true comedy style and a voice which, if small, was pure and well placed. However, as Lanza was penalized for playing Caruso on film, so was Miss Raymond penalized for not being another Melba. As for Robert Simmons, this excellent artist sang flexibly and acted with immense gusto. Smith, Raymond and Simmons produced a small-voiced *Barber* in a small set which toured in small theatres and they did full justice to an old warhorse in a typically Australian way; and the term is meant as a form of praise.

It was this Australian improvisatory quality which carried early Trust operas like the *Barber*. There was none of the discipline which made *Peter Grimes* a prestige product, but there was showmanship galore and really very little to which musical purists could object. The cast was completed by Neil Warren-Smith as Bartolo and Alan Light as Basilio — with Gregory Dempsey as the Notary! He has come a long way since then.

When this *Barber* went on tour Rosalind Keene took over from Glenda Raymond and John Germain claims that for two years he sang nothing but Figaros. Georg Tintner played the piano (where was Rankl when he was needed then?) and the cast not only sang, but loaded and unloaded scenery, travelled all day by bus, sang at night, re-loaded scenery, slept briefly and enjoyed life upon the wicked stage in temperatures well over 40°C, in a 9 a.m. to 1 a.m. routine which is fondly remembered by the artists today, but must have been hell at the time. In Bairnsdale one night in 1958 Neil Warren-Smith's Bartolo blithely sang 'thank you, thank you' while Donald Smith's Don Alonso was loudly proclaiming: 'Peace and joy be yours forever, hey, the bloody joint's on fire'. And it was. Exit the singers, the audience acted as firemen, and then everybody went back to Rosina's singing lesson as though nothing had happened!

In the meantime, back on the farm, the management decided that the artistic triumphs of 1958 could not be afforded in 1959 and cancelled the next season. Apart from the few singers running around the outback with the *Barber*, the whole company suddenly found itself out of work. Some went overseas, some retired, some adopted the old wartime motto: they also fight who sit and wait. Among those who waited was Joan Sutherland back in England, promised Gilda in *Rigoletto*, and Gertrude Johnson in Melbourne, promised a joint production of *Lucia di Lammermoor*. To Sutherland, as yet undiscovered, it would have meant a lot, but the contract never materialized. (And just as well, or Sutherland might never have sung that Covent Garden *Lucia* in February 1959 which made her an overnight star.) Miss Johnson, no doubt, saw her lost *Lucia* as a sign that all her predictions were coming true, that the Trust would fold and that her National Opera would be reborn. Unlike Sutherland, she did not get a consolation prize.

ACT 2 : SCENE 2
THE R. I. P. TIDE
IS REVERSED

The creation of the Adelaide Festival in 1960 was to become a major factor in boosting the cause of opera. Not only did it create an artificial market for the art in a city not exactly lavish in its past demands, but it was to provide an artistic and financial incentive which the national company used to the full. In future years major stars were imported, major productions staged and major audiences created through the Festival. Initially there was little more than goodwill — and not too much of that. All right, so Adelaide had a bright idea that it would become the Edinburgh of Australia, but what actually did it offer to any company willing to participate? Precious little in relation to the costs involved in staging opera. Nevertheless, the Elizabethan Trust Opera Company was clutching at straws in the year after its first unwilling sabbatical and the publicity alone which the Festival could bring might kick off a revival of public interest and lift fast sinking hopes for the future. Alas, it was not to be.

During the four years 1959—62 the Trust Opera Company disbanded twice and was reassembled twice, in each case to start seasons at the Adelaide Festival. There is every reason to believe that the Festival rescued the Elizabethan Trust Opera from oblivion, if not financially, then at least by encouraging it to survive for the glory of Australia — meaning the internationally-promoted Adelaide Festival.

If it did survive, the credit does not belong to the executive director of the Trust, Hugh Hunt, the director of the opera, Robert Quentin, or its musical director, Karl Rankl. The sport of Trust-bashing was well under way and, in spite of mounting criticism, bringing in top-level experts was considered unnecessary. Who could afford good management while there was a shortage of singers? And why was there a shortage of singers? Because the annual close-down of the company caused anybody with any sense to desert the sinking ship. Fortunately a few of the best had more loyalty than sense and hung around to save the company once it started moving again.

In an attempt to replace *prime donne* with cultural pretensions plans were made for the 1960 Festival to stage a major Australian Opera, Arthur Benjamin's *A Tale of Two Cities* — without first establishing where the additional $27 000 required was to be found! Not surprisingly, the Adelaide Festival Committee, which had raised an original $2000 with difficulty, declined to help and any hope of native opera at the Festival vanished into the mists of the future — 1986 to be precise.

To save his bacon Rankl went back to Joan Hammond and Ken Neate, old friends from his days at Covent Garden. The mind boggles to think what would have happened in 1960 without Hammond. She was the be-all and end-all of the season in all states, though the lack of direction in matters artistic sadly let her down again and again. A somewhat subdued Rankl was forced to curtail his demands — unfortunately only after his management agreed to stage Richard Strauss' *Salome*. In view of the huge ABC orchestras at his disposal it seemed a good idea; Hammond had the voice for the part and Rankl knew the work well from the notorious 1949 Dali-Brook production at Covent Garden. Unfortunately (that word seems to dog most of the years of Trust Opera seasons) Stefan Haag in his new position as

Assistant Director picked this production plum for himself. With due respect to Haag, who was a respectable producer of repertoire operas, the sensuous sexuality of *Salome* simply passed him by. Unfortunately (there is that word again) the same must be said of Joan Hammond's lascivious teenager. Teenager!

I have praised Miss Hammond effusively as a true *prima donna* and she certainly sang Salome with a magnificent opulent sound. If only it had been a broadcast or recording! Nothing is less likely to convince visually than a *prima donna* Salome. Hammond in 1960 produced voice and voice alone. Rankl produced sound and sound alone. Haag produced a traditional grand opera to suit his leading lady, who worked valiantly, but in vain, to change her traditional spots — and who would want her to? Certainly not the public who came to hear another Tosca and went away bewildered, and far from scandalized. Whatever had been said about Rankl's Covent Garden *Salome*, it was no better musically than this Australian one, but its producer Peter Brook did make his public sit up; he started from the premise that *Salome* should shock, and shock it did. The only shocking thing about the Trust *Salome* was its inclusion in the repertoire when the company's fortunes and policies were near their nadir.

Lest it be thought that *Salome* was a disaster, it was not. Perhaps being simply dull is a worse condemnation, but the designs of Raymond Boyce, though badly-executed, had their virtues and the singing of Hammond and Neil Easton (later Robert Allman) was virile and commanding. On the acting side Justine Rettick and Alan Ferris made much of Herodias and Herod. The original plan to sing the opera in German was abandoned, but in vain. For all the understanding the audience got of the English text, it might just as well have been sung in the original language. Playing in theatres as large as Melbourne's Palais did not exactly help either.

Unrealistic planning (*Salome* replaced an abandoned *Traviata* which was to have starred Gabriella Tucci, Elsie Morison and Una Hale in rotation!) resulted in a very strange season. Joan Hammond practically produced *Madame Butterfly*, though company manager Tom Brown was given the programme credit. The result was vocally acceptable (Hammond, Neate, Allman) but looked what it probably was: a replica of the production toured by the Carl Rosa Company in the British provinces during the war. There was a sort of *Rigoletto* with 183 cm Ronal

Jackson as a monstrously lanky jester. Ken Neate, even taller, was at least a romantic figure and so was Glenda Raymond, still singing her best as Gilda. Robin Lovejoy produced what he could under impossible conditions, but the popularity of Verdi's music won the day, as Puccini's did for *Madame Butterfly*.

And for the first time the company brought back an existing production; Haag's *Magic Flute* from the opening season was chosen to star Ken Neate, who had been a fine Tamino in years gone by, but whose voice was darkening dangerously for Mozart. The teamwork of 1957 was missing. Ronal Jackson was again hampered by his height, which made his Papageno look like a gigantic plucked chicken in his well-worn costume. Bagnall and Warren-Smith were excellent as Pamina and Sarastro, but Glenda Raymond's voice was too fine and pure for the evil Queen of the Night.

As in the case of *Peter Grimes* two years earlier, the odd man out turned out to be the artistic sleeper of the season. Stefan Haag's believable collection of Puccini operas masquerading under the then unfamiliar *Trittico* label were a model of traditional opera with exactly the three faces which Puccini had demanded. The *grand guignol* of *Il tabarro*, the sugar-sweet *Suor Angelica* and the Rabelaisian *Gianni Schicchi* made an ideal evening for those who bothered to investigate. While they grew in numbers, they did not grow fast enough in each city before the time came to move on. Louis Kahan's utilitarian sets were suitably appropriate and the casts shone with immense vigour. Neil Easton and Robert Allman vied for honours, alternating as the unhappy Michele, and Gregory Dempsey sang his first heroic voice lead in *Il tabarro*. The much under-rated Valda Bagnall did the impossible and brought *Suor Angelica* to life both vocally and histrionically. This performance, thanks to Bagnall, Rettick's excellent Princess and Haag's underplayed staging, was a revelation to local audiences, small as they were. *Suor Angelica* is said to have been Puccini's favourite opera, an opinion which few critics share. *Gianni Schicchi* was another of the endless milestones for Neil Warren-Smith, who was in his element in Haag's expert comedy routines.

Local singers carried the main weight of the season and the occasional non-appearance of Hammond or Neate was resented, though one understudy made headlines which would have been much larger had Hammond dropped out of *Salome* ten years later. Exopera singer Maria Wolkowsky was called at a few hours' notice from her faithful typewriter to save a Sydney performance of Richard Strauss' opera from cancellation. Without ever having sung Salome before (and improvising her *Dance of the Seven Veils*), she satisfied an audience which probably welcomed some excitement in the midst of a dreary season. No reports have come down to me of the prowess on stage of the lady known as Maria Prerauer or Marietta, but I have no reason to believe that our fiercest music critic in any way disgraced herself. (Do I hear cries of 'Pity'!?) As Wolkowsky she had had quite a substantial career in Europe and England, but that Salome proved to be her last appearance as a singer.

No, 1960 could hardly be called a successful year for the Trust Opera Company. One winner out of five, and that one box-office poison! (The *Trittico* was billed without mention of Puccini or the names of the operas and by the time the good word got around, it was too late.) No wonder the company collapsed again. Rankl departed into renewed obscurity and a remarkable reason was found for not having a season in 1961: none of the ABC orchestras could fit Trust seasons into their schedules! Whatever the real reasons (apart from lack of funds), the Trust did not use the year of rest to put its administrative house in order and 1962 was to be another step on the apparently inevitable road to perdition.

During the second year in recess, the first and only attempt was made to implement the Trust's original policy of helping regional companies instead of competing with them. The failure of that solitary experiment can be laid on the doorstep of both parties. It is a sad little tale, but one which needs to be told.

In 1961 Gertrude Johnson in Melbourne gloated at the failure of the Trust Opera to equal her own earlier successes. Due to good financial management the National Theatre Movement in Melbourne had succeeded in wiping out the debts made during its last pre-Trust years, it had collected substantial funds to buy the Toorak Village Cinema and was preparing to convert it into the National Theatre which would make the company's fortune yet! But, most of all, Miss Johnson was itching to show that miserable upstart, the Trust, what a mistake it had made in leaving her out in the cold.

Negotiations began for the National Theatre to stage a season in 1961, while the Trust Opera was disbanded, with financial and other assistance from the Trust, but without any interference in artistic matters. Miss Johnson actually obtained the rights to stage Richard Strauss's *Der Rosenkavalier*, which had never been seen in Australia, at a time when the famous film starring Elisabeth Schwarzkopf was packing the public in. Staging a *Rosenkavalier* takes a lot of money, but the Victorian Symphony Orchestra (which had been unavailable for the Trust Opera!) was suddenly free again, the Victorian Government of Henry Bolte was offering a subsidy and the Trust was at last coming to the party. It all looked too good to be true — and was!

With considerable shrewdness it was decided to couple the locally-unknown *Rosenkavalier* with *La Bohème*. Less logically, and possibly without the knowledge of the Trust, it was decided to stage *The Student Prince* as a sure-fire way of raising money to pay for any possible losses on the Strauss opera. Then came the crunch: the sum offered by the Trust to the National Theatre to stage a Melbourne season of grand opera in 1961 was a princely $10 000!

Miss Johnson took the $10 000 without batting an eyelid, dropped the two operas and produced *The Student Prince* alone, realizing a cool profit of $60 000 in three months! The fact that this included the Trust's $10 000 was never forgiven and the whole exercise was held up as the example why the Trust needed artistic control over ventures it helped to finance. Dr Coombs was a very angry man!

Regrettably, the unexpected financial windfall for the National Theatre was more than offset when the theatre, being rebuilt in Toorak, burnt to the ground before it had been properly insured. In the eyes of the Trust it was poetic justice, though it is interesting to speculate what would have happened if the original plans had been implemented with proper backing. When *Der Rosenkavalier* was finally staged by the Australian Opera in 1972 (at a production cost of $100 000) it was an enormous success. Could it have saved the National in 1961? In the light of its later policies, perhaps not.

By then, of course, the Sydney Opera House loomed larger than the burnt National Theatre in Melbourne ever had, if anything not yet visible above ground level can be said to loom. On the eve of 1962 the management of the opera company still believed that the magnificent edifice would open in 1964! Planning, therefore, was aimed at presenting bigger and better seasons to lead up to the big event. The logical way to start this was to cut back! The reasoning appeared to be that the money saved by reducing the 1962 season would enable a bigger one to be staged in 1963 and that this would then convince one and all that the company was ready for the big event. What actually happened was that standards slipped even further. Fortunately the opening of the Opera House also receded into the distance.

The years leading to the abyss, out of which the Elizabethan Trust Opera might well have failed to climb, were not happy ones. There was no lack of critics inside and outside the company and backstage politics waxed fast and furious. Opportunities were given and lost through prevarication or timidity. For every opera staged, two were planned and abandoned.

The age of the inferior guest 'star' rising gloomily above eclipsed local talent was at hand and the best that can be said for the last years under Haag is that the losses, which were so severely criticized at the time, were really pretty reasonable compared with subsidies being given in other parts of the world. Against that, it had to be admitted that there was very little to show for the money. *Traviata*, *Bohème* and *Carmen* continued to attract the masses in inferior productions, but the attempts to repeat artistic credits in esoteric items like *Peter Grimes* and the *Trittico* continued to fail. Nothing seemed to go right and only the high and lowlights are chronicled here.

Among the opportunities missed were two great ones indeed. Charles Mackerras was appointed musical director and Anthony Besch almost became multi-media director for the Trust by proposing to mix drama production elsewhere with the artistic direction of the opera company. Mackerras, in his then inexperience, restricted himself to some admirable, if unspectacular, conducting, but Besch backed out hastily.

The incredible Ana Raquel Sartre, however, made enough publicity for herself to more than compensate for Mackerras busily hiding in the pit. Her Australian exploits are certainly worth a closer look. In true *prima-donna* style Sartre first kept the press waiting, then tried to prove that she was one of those fabled stars, whose temperaments are an essential part of a performance off, as well as on, stage. She capped the lot by slapping a critic's face in public — a carefully staged event which made headlines throughout Australia and (supposedly) operatic centres throughout the world.

International incident. The Brazilian bombshell, Ana Raquel Sartre, made more noise off-stage than on. She slapped the face of a critic and made headlines worldwide. (With Ronal Jackson in *La traviata*.)

Sartre was one of the best-looking singers around. She even possessed a voice of reasonable size and beauty. The great mystery, which escaped the notice of the management and most of the critics, is that Sartre, *a mezzo soprano*, was engaged to sing Violetta in *La traviata*, a great *soprano* showpiece rôle of the repertoire. By eliminating the standard high-note interpolations, Sartre actually managed to sing all the notes, though not always in the correct pitch. She looked superb and made enough appearances in the press to make the non-opera buff believe that she was indeed a star — after all, even Callas had her off days by 1962! She also had, like Callas, a wealthy husband who in turn helped to keep the presses rolling by maligning the Sydney Opera House. The fact that Martin Carr happened to be right long before the big storms broke, unfortunately did not improve his wife's singing. There is no truth in the report that a vain attempt to try for a top C one night at the Palais in St Kilda dislodged a huge beam and caused it to crash to the stage from above. Fall it did, spectacularly. If its fall was not caused by her singing, it is to her credit that Sartre's voice and composure were not affected in the slightest by the commotion it caused.

It is regrettable that reports such as this one should be the biggest contribution to Australian operatic history in 1962, but facts are facts. Peter Baillie, a handsome young tenor from New Zealand, used Sartre's *Traviata* as a useful stepping-stone to a successful career in Europe. Ronal Jackson was far more at home as the older Germont than when he had been starred and feathered in *The Magic Flute*. Jackson was never given the opportunity to show his best side in this country. The day when the repertoire would be tailored to the singers available was still in the distant future. Ambition rather than sense governed the selection of works to be presented. It was: We shall do *Ariadne auf Naxos*! And only then: Who can we find to sing it? Or produce it? Or design it? It was thus that a travesty of the Richard Strauss opera came to be the dubious highlight of the 1962 Adelaide Festival.

Ariadne is one of the most difficult operas to stage successfully — it was to prove so again in 1975 when the Australian Opera made another, more successful stab at it. It requires at least three major singers and a producer of genius, since the whole thing really doesn't hang together. The second half was originally part of a multi-media production of Molière's play, *Le Bourgeois gentilhomme*. Strauss and Hofmannsthal reworked it into a full-length opera by replacing the play with a lengthy prologue involving the supposed composer of the opera proper and the singers appearing in it. It needs a delicacy of touch rarely found among producers of opera, it needs a designer of genius and, above all, it needs a production organization which can do justice to all that is involved in such a hazardous endeavour. This was to be the *Peter Grimes* of 1962 — or did that honour belong to *Falstaff*, an equally difficult opera?

It may not matter very much today, but a passé producer of plays was imported from London to stage *Ariadne*; his first attempt at opera production, I believe. Charles Hickman was experienced enough in the theatre to have bumbled his way through the whole thing had he had a first-class team to work with, but he did not. So great was the disaster in Adelaide that for the first (and last) time (to date) a production was restaged by another producer in mid-season — by two producers actually, for Stephan Beinl had to call Stefan Haag to his aid, since he was more than fully occupied getting *Falstaff* and *Don Giovanni* on the boards. Thus the triple-headed *Ariadne* wended her unhappy way from state to state playing to empty houses. What vocal virtues there were (Una Hale's big-voiced Ariadne, Althea Bridges's touching composer, Rosalind Keene's brilliantly brittle Zerbinetta) went for nought and no attempt to blame the public for ignoring the staging of the Strauss 'masterpiece' (masterpiece?) could hide the ineptness of the programming.

Falstaff was little better, once again planned without any thought of possible casting. It was Falstaff without the fat knight! In desperation veteran retired baritone Arnold Matters was brought forth as the local hero for the Festival. Since fruity Falstaff is hardly a golden-haired youth, Matters produced a more than adequate swan song to a long career, but other states had to make do with a lightweight young man imported from America via Vienna, one Norman Foster, who was an admirable artist in every way but one — he didn't have a clue what Falstaff was about, vocally or histrionically.

In the end it was Alan Light's magnificent Ford who stole the show wherever it was seen. Nobody noticed that for the third time out of three tries the local talent outshone the imports. *Falstaff* was saved by Beinl's practical staging, the first of many such productions which were to serve the Australian company well over the years to come. Beinl was no Zeffirelli or Visconti, but he knew what was wanted and almost always brought it off — when he had the right singers at his disposal.

Beinl's practical *Don Giovanni* rounded off the season with Jackson in the title rôle, Warren-Smith as Leporello, Peter Baillie, and the two *prime donne*, Hale and Sartre, sharing the soprano honours, though the success of the evening was undoubtedly Cynthia Johnston's sparkling Zerlina.

The name Edward Downes appeared on the scene fully ten years before his appointment as musical director of the Australian Opera in 1972. Prolonged negotiations in 1962 had Downes ready, willing and able to come to Australia to plan and institute a new regime. Oh, the dreams which were spun and the glories ahead! But they came to nothing because, after six years in existence, the Trust and its opera company were still run by amateurs planning without the foresight Downes had then, and proved to still have much later. Money crises are the staple diet of opera administrators and the future may have appeared bleak in 1962. Nevertheless, the failure to grasp Downes when he was there for the asking was to have more lasting effects than Haag imagined.

In 1963 Stefan Haag was appointed executive director of the Elizabethan Theatre Trust. This should have severed his connection with the opera to some extent;

in fact, it did not. Having rejected Downes, Haag was forced, perhaps against his will, to continue as the moving force in the company, though from a higher level. Charges that he was neglecting other aspects of the Trust's activities in favour of opera were justified that first year, but circumstances caused him to make a virtue out of necessity. (An almost exact parallel occurred when Stephen Hall succeeded Haag as executive director of the Trust five years later. Both men were already committed to productions and other duties with the opera company after their elevation and both insisted on continuing the work they loved not wisely but too well.)

Basically the situation at the end of 1962 looked promising. Haag had been moved up into a position in which his penchant for opera could only help the company. Federal and state governments greatly increased their grants in the hope that the Trust would one day fill the once-more-delayed Sydney Opera House after completion. John Young, well experienced in administration by now, became production director and all that was really needed was a good musical director.

The appointment ultimately made was basically sound, though based on the same faulty premise which applied in the case of Rankl. Wilhelm Loibner was another in the German *GMD* (*Generalmusikdirektor*) tradition. He was prepared to come to Australia full time, to be present throughout the season and to take charge of all matters artistic. Unfortunately (there is that word again) he was not a top man in his field and was burdened with a soprano wife who was not in the class of a later administrator's spouse, Lone Koppel-Winther, who was to raise some controversy in the mid-1970s. Ruthilde Boesch was a somewhat mature German *prima donna* of the old school, useful enough here and there, but no 'star' to overshadow resident singers. She caused considerable trouble directly and indirectly, finally refusing to sing at all when Walter Stiasny, the conductor of *Die Fledermaus*, chose to give the première to a pretty young New Zealand soprano, Mary O'Brien. It is an indication of Loibner's ineffectiveness as a Musical Director (and/or husband) that one of his three assistant conductors was able to go against his wishes in this manner. His lack of authority was not replaced by a firm hand elsewhere and 1963 turned out to be, if anything, a greater disaster than 1962. Only the introduction of

the foolproof *Fledermaus* kept the company together during the summer of 1963-64 and managed to stave off total financial disaster.

The choice of *Die Fledermaus* was prompted by the undoubted successes in the field of a commercial management's import, the Sadler's Wells production of *Orpheus in the Underworld*, starring June Bronhill, and of the Melbourne National Theatre's *The Student Prince*, which was followed by *The Desert Song* and *Show Boat*. The American musical was dying, but the public wanted musical theatre and *Die Fledermaus* was a good choice; in fact, with one exception, it was the best production of the year, thanks to Stefan Beinl's staging and Desmond Digby's commercial designs. Unfortunately this high rating was due more to the dismal standards elsewhere than to any particular brilliance of *Die Fledermaus*. Be it recorded that Stiasny conducted stylishly, Mary O'Brien showed voice, looks and charm as Rosalinda, and Robert Gard made an excellent impression as Alfred in his first rôle with the company, straight from the National Theatre *Show Boat* tour. Beinl was also responsible for the one acceptable opera of the year, *The Marriage of Figaro*, with designs by Kenneth Rowell. The vocal standards were not as high as during the first season, in spite of Elizabeth Fretwell's return after nine years overseas. Ronal Jackson was a good Count, Cynthia Johnston superb as Susanna and Figaro marked the debut of another New Zealander, Ronald Maconaghie, who immediately caught the public's fancy and hasn't disappointed it since. *Faust*, *Fidelio* and *Bohème* completed the repertoire.

John Young produced *Faust* with some incredible back-projections, anticipating in a less erotic manner the idiocies of the 1973 *Tannhäuser*. In his own words: 'It was the worst production anybody ever staged'. Haag repeated his bare-stage *Fidelio* and New Zealand provided an imported *Bohème* designed by Raymond Boyce. It was quite a year for New Zealand/Australia operatic trading. Mary O'Brien, Peter Baillie, Ronald Maconaghie and *La Bohème* proved a pretty good exchange for the Trust's *Magic Flute* which had toured New Zealand the previous year.

Vocal standards were generally poor. Another 'star' import, Edward Byles, had a notably large voice, but also a notable lack of musical and dramatic abilities. His Rodolfo was acceptable in a full-throated Italian provincial style, but his Faust was an abomination. Later Byles was to have a long career in England as a small-part character tenor. Fretwell starred as Fidelio, Light and Warren-Smith repeated their fine Pizarro and Rocco, and Raymond Myers made an early debut as a resonant Ferrando. Light also stole the *Faust* honours as Mephisto, Mary O'Brien was overtaxed as Marguerite.

Attendances in 1963 fell to an all-time low, principally because the general public was beginning to wake up to the fact that popular operas also need to be sung well. Neither *Bohème* nor *Faust* packed them in. The company itself was in disarray with internal faction fighting and an almost total loss of team spirit — and it showed.

Incredibly, worse was to come.

Opera and ballet don't mix — or do they? Many German opera houses, La Scala in Milan, and Covent Garden in England run opera and ballet companies simultaneously. The economics are fearful, but there are certain advantages which cannot be ignored, mainly the fact that opera principals cannot sing on consecutive nights without endangering their voices; it is much easier to train muscles for continued exertion than vocal cords. In fact, muscles must be exercised constantly, while excessive strain on the fine membranes of the throat is positively dangerous to their continued well-being. Thus the ability to alternate ballet with opera reduces a company's needs in the star-singer field, and that can be of vital concern to the artistic, if not the financial success of a season. The monetary counter-productiveness lies in the fact that the ensemble must be paid by the week, whether singers are used nightly or not, and the same applies to the ballet company, which usually ends up as a very secondary step-child when it comes to numbers of performances scheduled.

Nobody has yet invented a 'ballet house' in opposition, or parallel, to the opera house which can be found throughout the world. The exceptions which prove the rule, Covent Garden or Stuttgart, to name but two, are rare indeed. More commonly the ballet company is used as a filler to take the pressure off the singers and fillers rarely are blessed with generous budgets. In its early days at Sadler's Wells the Vic-Wells Ballet played only two out of each week's seven performances and one of those was the Saturday matinee! To what extent the arrangement held back the company's emergence as a major force cannot be established at this late stage. It could even be argued that it was a good thing because it prevented a limited amount of talent from being over-extended.

The continued drubbing which the Trust received from all quarters in 1963 was far from encouraging, but the policies implemented by it under the leadership of Stefan Haag became almost masochistic in nature. There seemed to be a death wish in the air. Lack of money was the universal complaint at the door of which all blame was laid, but the real villain was ambition. Too much too soon was the motto and when too much failed, the logical (?) thing was to try something even bigger. Thus the concept of the joint opera/ballet season of 1964 was created. If there was thought in the planning, it defies identification. When original ideas were aborted through outside influences, through unexpected disasters or through the inevitable cash shortages, the management was not prepared. Only one thing is certain: the season began with the Adelaide Festival and proceeded from there according to schedule. No changes were made beyond what would normally occur in the course of any theatrical tour; in other words, plans were laid and executed regardless of the consequences. The best that can be said is that the year enabled the opera company to stay together a little longer. Ironically, or perhaps consequentially, there was to be no season in 1965!

It is easy to be wise after the event, but all sensible indications pointed to a pulling in of horns in 1964. The undiscriminating public had ceased following the standard box office works like *Bohème* and the discriminating public had long ago lost interest. Only a drastic raising of standards could pull the company out of the doldrums. Operatically, the sum total of 1964 proved to be an acceptable esoteric showpiece for the Adelaide Festival in Walton's *Troilus and Cressida*, an experimental staging of Verdi's *Macbeth* (hardly box office at the best of times), an un-Mozartean *Così fan tutte*, another shockingly bad *Carmen*, a revival of *Die Fledermaus* of the previous year and the Carl Orff double bill *The Wise Woman/Catulli Carmina*, which was the only literal collaboration between the opera and ballet companies. All of this was staged throughout Australia alternating with performances of ballet which, perhaps in silent protest, proved to be dispirited and uninspired, though on a higher level than the opera since the Australian ballet was a continuing body which had created its own standards.

A side effect of the season, which was to have lasting results, was the howls of protests from the players of the ABC orchestras. The reluctance of ABC musicians to exchange their white tie and tails image for obscurity in

Only fit for festivals!
Walton's *Troilus and Cressida*
was only staged at the
Adelaide Festival in 1964.
After the flop of the excellent
Peter Grimes the company was
not game to try it on its
regular subscribers. (Marie
Collier and Richard Lewis.)

the pits of Her Majesty's in Adelaide, the Palais Theatre in Melbourne or the despised Tivoli in Sydney was understandable. Doubling their duties by adding ballet to their chores in 1964 made matters worse and also cut into planned concert schedules. It speaks highly for the ABC that it agreed to the ambitious new schedules. If anything precipitated the creation of the first Trust orchestra it was the experience of this year.

The third of the Adelaide Festivals began to attract international attention. Britain's grand old man of music, Sir William Walton, was the star attraction and the Australian première of his only opera, *Troilus and Cressida*, was a logical centrepiece, though it is hardly a popular work. The idea to extend *Troilus* to form the nucleus of an all-Shakespeare Festival was put forward and prompted the addition of Verdi's *Macbeth*. When it was found that the scheme was unworkable, and *Carmen* was added to cater for the masses, *Macbeth* unaccountably was retained. Probably John Shaw had been engaged to sing the title role before the impracticability of the scheme had been discovered: it was the kind of thing which happened regularly in those days, as was the non-appearance or late appearance of overseas artists. Raymond Boyce's new production of *Carmen*, using his own designs, was rehearsed in Sydney and also in Adelaide without a Carmen. Jean Madeira graciously turned up for the final dress rehearsal! Marie Collier was more generous, putting in an appearance fully five days before *Troilus and Cressida* was premièred!

The performances of Walton's opera were probably the last, as well as the first, to be staged in Australia. It is a static work at the best of times and really suitable only for festivals. No attempt was made to tour *Troilus*, though the Adelaide production by Robin Lovejoy (with designs by Frank Hinder) with two imported leads, Richard Lewis and Marie Collier, was more than acceptable. Peter Baillie, Alan Light, Ronald Maconaghie and Norman Yemm (not yet of TV 'Homicide' and 'The Sullivans' fame) carried the local banner very much to Sir William's satisfaction and Joseph Post miraculously resurfaced to conduct later performances.

The company had no musical director, only conductors. John Hopkins and Walter Stiasny did their best with the South Australian Symphony Orchestra to save *Carmen* and *Macbeth*, but to no avail; the goings-on (or lack of) on stage and backstage proved an insuperable barrier. It is ironical that throughout those early years of

the Trust Opera Company its strength lay always in its orchestras and conductors, who were unable to make up for the lack of artistic standards, while in later years, when the ABC orchestras were replaced by the Trust's own musicians, the stage action improved to the point that critics throughout Australia were firing off at the pit. The protesting ABC musicians in 1964 certainly had a point: their excellent efforts to save poor productions went for nought, yet the good productions of later years received their full due, in spite of poor orchestral playing.

Macbeth, the other part of the ill-conceived Shakespearean season, was entrusted to designer Stan Ostoja-Kotkowski. This Polish-born lighting genius had carved quite a groove for himself in Australian arts, but *Macbeth* was more a grave than a groove. Resident producer Stefan Beinl, who carried the major burden of Trust productions until his untimely death in 1970, tried to build a brooding modern shadow-play around his imported expatriate protagonist, John Shaw. Ostoja-Kotkowski provided a multi-purpose set which served as both battle field and banquet hall. What an enormous steel bridge had to do with either was never clear and the monstrous structure was sold for scrap at the end of the season on the sound principle that $24 in hand is worth many hundreds in storage costs. With it went any hope of ever restaging one of Beinl's few outright failures. Ukrainian-born migrant Tais Taras was a sweet-voiced Lady Macbeth, making nonsense of Verdi's desire that her voice should be hard, stifled and dark, 'the voice of a devil'. Serge Baigildin sang Macduff's aria very well.

Macbeth was sung in Italian and *Carmen* in French, the latter presumably because Jean Madeira was a reasonably well-known exponent of the rôle in French. The fact that she was born in Illinois was neither here nor there. Why *Macbeth* was produced in Italian is not clear either, unless there was a sudden thought that international visitors to the Adelaide Festival should hear opera as they would hear it overseas. It is not known what they thought of a French *Carmen* sung by American, Italian and Australian singers or an Italian *Macbeth* with Australian, Ukrainian and Russian soloists. It was certainly not the start of an original language policy, but just another of the haphazardly-made decisions of a company without an artistic policy.

Nicola Filacuridi was the Don José to Madeira's *Carmen*. Boyce's production was so bad that it followed *Ariadne*, in that it had to be doctored by another, production

The other Dame Joan.
Joan Hammond's last part
was Salome and she sang it
during her last Australian
season in 1960. Health
reasons forced her retirement
soon afterwards while she
was still in her prime. Here
she is seen with Stefan Haag,
the man in charge of the
early years of the Australian
Opera.

director John Young, who (quite rightly) makes no claim to having improved it. Madeira left after Adelaide to have her place taken by Gloria Lane, a much better singer if not as realistically earthy as Madeira. Miss Lane, best-known previously as the excellent Secretary in the original production of Menotti's *Consul*, arrived in Australia primly respectable until greeted by Edward Downes (here to inspect his supposedly-imminent new realm) with: 'What are you doing here, Tits?' Thereafter Miss Lane did her best to live up to her nickname, in the process somewhat distracting public and critics alike from her undoubted vocal abilities. That she had a magnificent voice, apart from a magnificent figure, was considered of less import than that she 'cheapened' *Carmen* by showing too much of both ends of her anatomy. (And at a critics' convention it was claimed that opera critics are music critics!)

Robert Allman took over Macbeth from John Shaw and also sang Escamillo, both with great verve and volume, though his voice then was on the rough side.

The Australian Ballet staged the world première of Helpmann's *The Display* for the Adelaide Festival and a gigantic tent production of Shakespeare's *Henry V* starred John Bell, later to appear with the Australian Opera as a producer. Less noticed was a young actor playing the Earl of Cambridge and the Duke of Orleans. Dennis Olsen did not dream that within a few years he would sing the lead in five operas for the national company — Gilbert and Sullivan comic leads, but leads just the same — and any success they had was certainly Olsen's.

The fact that both the ballet and the opera played simultaneously at the Adelaide Festival was not of tremendous significance. Each played on its own nights and few people, apart from the harassed stage staff, thought any more about it. Despite the fact that the two companies were brought together, curiously their only joint production was not staged for the Festival. And yet the coupling of Carl Orff's opera *Die Kluge* (under the title *The Wise Woman*) with the ballet-pantomime-oratorio *Catulli Carmina* would have been an ideal presentation for any Festival, while having small audience potential elsewhere.

Oddly enough, the opera came off best in this double bill when seen in non-Festival cities. *The Wise Woman* was played for laughs by producer Stefan Beinl. The political and humanistic purposes of Orff's morality play were lost in slapstick, just as in Haag's *Così fan tutte*

Mozart's satire on love and marriage disappeared. Nevertheless, *The Wise Woman* was well sung and brilliantly acted by its three Rogues, Robert Gard, Ronald Maconaghie and Alan Light, while Cynthia Johnston sang beautifully in the title role and the miniature set of Ronald Sinclair served its purpose admirably.

Catulli Carmina, in total contrast, was a disaster. Orff used an antique Latin text to tell some ribald tales, which would have created a sensation in 1964 had they been staged in their true colours. Producer-choreographer Joanne Priest either was a prude or assumed (perhaps rightly) that the time for sexual liberation was not yet at hand. It is a mystery how a production based on a major erotic work was allowed to proceed in a Sunday School atmosphere of delicate posturing by the ballet, while the opera chorus lustily sang about the pleasures of the flesh — in Latin! The academics attending might have got some kicks out of the lyrics. The general public did not.

Haag's *Così fan tutte* met some degree of success as a musical farce, but his production in modernistic period style built around a single bandstand-like set (by Desmond Digby), with young Patrick Thomas conducting, failed to please most critics and Mozart lovers. The cast was more than adequate. Neil Warren-Smith as Don Alfonso and Cynthia Johnston's Despina were closest to the ideal not reached by the production.

It was also Neil Warren-Smith who produced the only worthwhile contribution to the Gala Performance staged at the Elizabethan Theatre in Sydney on 29 September 1964 to celebrate the tenth anniversary of the foundation of the Elizabethan Theatre Trust. Warren-Smith conducted and sang Cimarosa's delightful one-man opera *Il Maestro di Capella*, with the Sydney Symphony Orchestra fully dressed in period costumes, complete with wigs. As for the rest, Stravinsky's *The Soldier's Tale* represented all aspects of the Trust's activities — opera, drama and ballet. Helpmann produced and appeared as the devil with Kathleen Gorham, Norman Yemm and John Bell. The rest of the programme was made up of ballet *divertissements*. The whole thing was typical of the Trust at that time, a multitude of talent all rushing off in different directions at once.

When it was announced that J. C. Williamson's were proposing to stage an international opera season in 1965 starring Joan Sutherland everybody heaved a sigh of relief. Here was a way to continue operatic life without risk to the Trust, while the opera company could be completely overhauled. It was thought that with a full year's planning a new start could be made in 1966. The singers would be used by Williamson's in the interim.

The usual grandiose plans were afoot. Edward Downes was about to have his dreams for putting opera in Australia on its feet realized after some years of haggling. 1966 would be the turning point in the company's fortunes, as every past year had been the turning point. That the forecast happened to be true this time was not thanks to the plans made in 1964. None of those materialized, but the management structure of the Trust Opera was altered. John Young officially became its administrator and, in the course of discussions with Downes in London, was introduced to Stephen Hall. The stage was set for the hard climb to success, even though Dr Coombs never did raise enough cash to meet the artistic demands Downes made as a condition of coming to Australia.

It was back to square one in 1966, and to a most unlikely character who was to produce the impetus which would start the ball rolling.

1966 to 1969 were the years of John Young's administration, but they were also the youth of the present Australian Opera. Before dealing with John Young, the rôle of Stefan Haag must be examined. Haag was a product of Gertrude Johnson's National Theatre, a young singer of character roles who had shown an early flair for production and gone through the mill of pre-Trust opera in many states, learning his craft the amateur way, through experience. It is a pity that events were to highlight his activities during those years in which he was the subject of criticism, because Haag was to a very large extent responsible for the early successes of the Trust Opera. One dreads to think what Robert Quentin would have done in 1956 without Haag's experience to back him. Unfortunately, the very fact that he was the most experienced Trust executive — the most experienced amateur, perhaps, but the most experienced just the same — caused successive administrators of the Trust to leave matters operatic to Haag.

The Australian Ballet was always a separate entity. The drama activities of the Trust never really got off the ground and, in line with previous theatrical history in Australia, opera was the great hope for the Trust's future. The man who knew most about opera had to be a key person and Stefan Haag was that man.

With hindsight it would, of course, have been better to back up Haag with somebody who had professional experience in running an opera company. Perhaps the ubiquitous Karl Rankl was thought to be the answer, perhaps not. The point is that everybody from Dr Coombs downward knew even less than Haag about it. Nobody has suggested that Haag was not sincere, that he did not do his best, that he ruled with a hand of iron or even that he engaged in the kind of power politics which were to beset the company after his departure. He was a sincere man doing a job to the best of his ability, but as time went on it became more and more obvious that it was not within his compass to develop further. There is a close parallel between Haag and his mentor, Gertrude Johnson, who also started an opera company, brought it considerable success and then did not know how to go on from there.

It may not matter now exactly what went wrong, but Haag's complete control of the opera must be stressed in any history of the company as 1966 approaches. He was by then executive director of the whole Trust. Will Thompson was the 'manager' of the opera company and John Young was 'production director'. Theoretically Thompson and Young were in charge. In practical terms Haag ran the opera company and its artistic policies. He also continued to produce at least one opera each year. A man who loves opera doesn't let go easily, as history has shown, and Haag was no exception.

There are many parallels between the careers of Haag and Young. Both were Australians, both started as singers, went into production and ended up running the Trust Opera. In fact, it was Haag who first brought Young into the company, just as Young was to bring in his own successor, Stephen Hall. Young started with Eugene Goossens at the Sydney Conservatorium, singing in those incredible productions Goossens managed to put together. During the 1952 combined National Operas season Young went to Melbourne to understudy John Brownlee's Don Giovanni and ended up opening the Sydney season singing the part. That, I am afraid, was the high point of John Young's career as a singer, though he was to play many parts over the years, curiously enough many of the same parts in which Haag specialized — the *comprimario* roles in *La Bohème*, for example.

Young's adventures after that initial start to his career read like something out of a novel. One day he should write a book about his travels around Africa, of singing Faust to a bass Mephistopheles from the Paris Opéra in a nightclub in the Chad, of being stranded without petrol in the Algerian revolution and having to sell not only his truck, but his wife's harp (!) to get out. Unlike Haag, Young had no continuity in opera because he lost his voice too many times, didn't work with any one company for long and started his producing piecemeal in odd places. Among other things, he sang the Wazir in the Australian production of *Kismet* and was the compère of the floorshow at Checkers night club in Sydney. You could say that he had a checkered career. (Pun intended.) Finally, John Young sang Sparafucile in Hobart in 1959, directed *Oklahoma!* (also singing Judd) and ended up as manager of the Theatre Royal because he was the only theatre man around, a sequence of events not unnatural in the operatic history of this country.

That Young was a good artist of natural ability is unquestioned. He proved it when singing Mr Peachum in the Trust's *Beggar's Opera* back in 1957. He had his first try at producing professionals when he 'took over' the circus scene in the Trust's *Bartered Bride* in which he played the Ringmaster. Young is nothing if not realistic about his abilities and disabilities as a producer. He freely admits to having been responsible for two of the worst productions ever seen anywhere, *Hänsel and Gretel* in Perth in 1959 and the infamous Trust *Faust* in 1963. Disarming as such candour may be, it does make one wonder on what basis he was chosen to become production director of the opera company.

At the end of 1964 John Young was sent overseas to learn all about the job he had been doing since 1962, production director of an opera company. When he returned, he found himself in the midst of a lengthy game of unmusical chairs, involving yearly changes of titles, and a most convoluted power-play worthy of any soap opera on television. Rather than recount the details of these vital years, which would only confuse, let me sum them up in the pecking order in which they began in 1966. It was then Haag, Hall, Young. It became Haag, Young, Hall. Then Haag was knocked out and Hall became Young's boss as executive director of the Trust. Finally, four years later, Young departed and only Hall remained as the head of the opera company, which became the independent Australian Opera. Any attempt to clarify further would simply confuse the reader, but the background should be kept in mind when assessing the work done by Young and Hall to build a major force out of the shambles which existed following the Sutherland-Williamson's year (1965).

It would be foolish to underestimate the part John Young played in the three short years after he became the administrator of the company under Haag in 1966. The company was at its lowest point, it had just missed a full year of activities for the third time in the ten years of its existence. Young was not qualified for the job he took and he did not set the world on fire. It can even be argued that his departure came at the right moment. The fact remains that after three years in office he left a company well on the way to becoming what the Australian Opera is today, a world-class company.

There had actually never been a continuous Trust Opera Company, but only a series of seasons which drew on singers who, by luck or perseverence, had managed to remain available in Australia. Jobs between seasons were hard to get and not all were in the singing field. Some kind of continuity of employment was essential if a permanent company was to be formed, but it would take more than one year in which to make this a reality. Perhaps it was the threat of having the Sydney Opera House's large hall taken away from opera which was the final straw, but solid forward planning began in 1965, for 1967!

On paper, 1966 was a step backward compared with the season prior to the Sutherland-Williamson tour. There were only three productions compared with six in 1964 (excluding two operas produced in Perth alone) and seasons in each state were cut back severely. Yet suddenly there was quality rather than quantity. The repertoire was chosen to suit the singers available locally, except for one who returned on a permanent basis. Donald Smith, who had gone overseas some years before and had done well in England, answered the call to sing Manrico in Verdi's *Trovatore* with alacrity; this was another production which was imported, complete, from New Zealand. *Boris Godounov* was staged as a vehicle for Neil Warren-Smith and *The Barber of Seville* used the small pool of established local favourites in minimal settings by Ronald Sinclair.

The whole thing was an economy package which worked. The operas were well balanced, the singing was good enough to satisfy people who the previous year had heard Sutherland and Pavarotti, and the general climate for opera was looking up, even though the

The artistic turning point.
1966 saw a reversal in
standards and audiences,
both of which had been
declining for ten years. *Boris
Godounov*, thanks to Neil
Warren-Smith's Boris, was a
box-office success against all
odds.

double disappointments of no Sydney Opera House and
the non-arrival of Downes must have depressed the
management no end. Nothing could be done about the
Sydney Opera House which, in any case, was clearly not
going to be completed for many years yet. A replacement for Downes was found more easily.

The availability of Denis Vaughan to become musical
director of the company was a badly-needed stroke of
good fortune. Vaughan was an Australian in the news,
because he had been making waves in musical circles by
extensive research into the authenticity of published
operatic scores, principally those of Puccini. None of the
conglomerate of guest conductors used in 1964 were
available and strong musical leadership, for what was
basically a new company, was needed. Vaughan was
a pedagogue first, a conductor second and a musical
director last, but Verdi's *Trovatore* was right up his street
and John Young's conception of *Boris Godounov*, in its
original Mussorgsky version, undoubtedly challenged
Vaughan's musical taste buds. This *Boris* remained
Young's one outstanding achievement as a producer. He

had seen the opera in Russia in 1965 and came to the conclusion, well before the general overseas trend, that Mussorgsky's own scoring suits the psychological drama of the tragic Russian tsar much better than the lush re-orchestration of Rimsky-Korsakov which was, and still is, frequently used in place of the original. By adopting it for his Australian production he immediately lent an aura of adventurousness to the occasion, which went well with Vaughan's notoriety as a musicologist in revolt against the establishment. It is doubtful whether Vaughan made any revolutionary returns to original Verdi in the score of *Il trovatore* ('Di quella pira' retained its unwritten top Cs) but in terms of giving the season appeal for serious opera lovers, the Young-Vaughan enterprises succeeded admirably.

A further indication of the new serious-mindedness was the decision to announce a policy of playing operas in the original language wherever possible. In 1966 this meant compromise as practised in most European capitals, that is, standard works which are well-known to the public and do not rely on verbal drama are sung in the language of origin, while comedies and works involving spoken dialogue are produced in the language of the audience. Only one work, *Trovatore*, in 1966 was affected; not even Covent Garden was game to produce *Boris* sung in Russian at the time and *The Barber of Seville* obviously fell into the second category anyway. The point is that the Italian *Trovatore* established once and for all that Australians would accept original language productions, making the engagement of guest artists in future years easier, and generally lending a sense of international quality to the works so produced.

The thought is inescapable that the snob appeal of 'foreign' opera can make the singing sound better than it actually is. Fortunately the decision coincided with a general raising of artistic and vocal standards and it was certainly not imagination or snobbishness which caused public and critics alike to take to the new system.

The success of the 1966 season, in spite of the severely-trimmed budget, proved that sensible planning can pay. With only three operas in the repertoire, there was still something for everybody; the *Barber* for the family, *Il trovatore* for the lover of singing and *Boris* for the man seeking the unusual. Coincidentally anyone going to a work outside his own field of interest was not disappointed, though the usual charge that *The Barber of Seville* was played for slapstick was levelled. It is true

that Rossini's masterpiece can be made into a work of art, but nobody seeing the work can doubt that it is intended to be farce, and interpreting it as such is as common in the European theatre as it is in Australia. The fact remains that it was well sung and well acted by Robert Gard's highly professional Almaviva, Maconaghie's Figaro and actor-singers like Norman Yemm and Alan Light as Bartolo and Basilio. Rosalind Keene finally became an official principal as Rosina. Gerald Krug conducted.

Clearly *Boris* and *Trovatore* were the more important musical events of the season and it is hard to say which was more successful. That the public actually flocked to *Boris Godounov* is remarkable in itself and Neil Warren-Smith's powerful interpretation must be given the major credit. It was an astonishing achievement for an Australian artist without a long international career behind him and totally justified the staging of a difficult and far-from-popular work. Not only did he act with deep conviction but he coped with the music in a quite astonishing manner, cutting with ease through the large ABC orchestras, even in theatres like the cavernous Palais in Melbourne. It was an achievement which would have convinced any sensible singer to aim for a career overseas without delay. It was Australia's good fortune that Warren-Smith decided not to be sensible, and in the years which followed he produced a regular series of great performances.

The other star of *Boris* was, of course, the chorus. Russian operas are always chorus-happy and *Boris* is no exception. Not since 1958 had the Trust tackled a chorus opera with any seriousness, but Young's idea was to use the chorus as the nucleus of the future company and when *Boris* proved that such a nucleus could be as good as this one he set out to implement his plan as quickly as possible. Within a year being a chorister was the only sure way to obtain full-time employment with the Trust.

Rosina Raisbeck joined the company to sing Marina in the Polish Scene, which Young had added to his arrangement of the 'original' *Boris*. (There is no actual original, because Mussorgsky's first thoughts were never performed and what passed for a first performance in 1874 was dictated by political rather than musical considerations.) Serge Baigildin was a fine, if small-scaled Dimitri, Light a boisterous Varlaam and Donald Shanks, singing Pimen and still in his early twenties, already looked like a Boris of the future. The admirable Robert Gard left a

The popular turning point.

The first opera sung in Italian was *Il trovatore* in 1966. With Donald Smith returning to belt out Manrico in real Italian style, success was assured, though the steeply-sloping sets threatened life and limb of the singers. No limbs, only dignity sustained injury.

deep impression as the Simpleton, a very minor part which represents Mussorgsky's bridge to the political thoughts he was not supposed to have about Mother Russia's problems. I have actually seen *Boris Godounov* performed without the Simpleton and few would miss him. To create a central character out of his few lines needs artistry of a high degree and this was one of the first instances in which Gard showed what a great asset the company had acquired when he joined it. (His Almaviva may have been more important to the general public, but Rossini's high jinks are in a different class.)

Enforced economies meant basic sets for *Boris Godounov* and William Constable's painted cloths were not the most successful. Producer Young insisted on realistic costumes, however, and the distribution of funds was indeed a wise one. You cannot crown a tsar of Russia without splendour and, by concentrating attention on the central character, the background came to be of secondary importance. William Patterson created a coronation robe covered with 2208 beads, pearls and glass pendants which was worthy of the Bolshoi itself. The rest of his costumes were equally authentic. Props used throughout were solidly realistic and when, in the Clock Scene, Doreen Morrow looked, acted and sang convincingly like the boy the Tsarevitch is supposed to be, the illusion was perfectly realized. *Boris* can only be staged as a realistic opera and the staging was, within the limitations of the background, a complete success.

However successful *Boris* may have been (and it was a great success) it was *Il trovatore* which was to decide the future policies of the company. Both its virtues and its failings were to reappear again and again in the coming years and, fortunately, its virtues far outweighed its failings, which were totally scenic. Stefan Beinl produced and Raymond Boyce designed this *Trovatore* for the New Zealand Opera Company. It was imported lock, stock and barrels for De Luna's soldiers to sit on. (Customs men two years later solemnly watched as the huge sets were formally burnt. Had they remained in existence, or been broken up for future use, the company would have been up for heavy import duties!) There were those who liked the sets, there were those who did not. I count myself among the latter because I feel for singers who are forced to clamber over a continuing expanse of steep slopes reminiscent of the sails of the Sydney Opera House. How the season concluded without some broken bones is a mystery. Singers are not mountain goats (though they may on occasion sing like them) and the settings for which Verdi calls include private chambers and prison cells which look pretty ridiculous when the floor angles up *and* down at something like 45 degrees. Admittedly, there were a few spectacular effects, notably the Monastery Scene, but any multi-purpose set which remains in position through a performance must relate to all the scenes, not just a few.

Fortunately for the history of opera in Australia what was projected from the slopes of Biscay and Aragon was Italian opera at its best. The singing was close to the Standard of the Sutherland season and the orchestra was vastly superior. The language was Italian, the conventions were Italian, even the flaws were Italian, but they were small indeed. Any public with a desire for Italian opera was completely satisfied by this production and the Trust was certainly justified in repeating the formula in years to come. It was logical to stick to a good thing, faults and all, after ten years of continuous disaster.

Young's desire to add a Manrico voice to the company's roster was understandable. There has never been a dearth of lyric tenors in Australia, but the despised top C remains the audience's darling. Raymond Macdonald, who sang Manrico in the original New Zealand production, never realized the potential shown during his impromptu Otellos in 1957 and had returned to lighter roles. Ronald Dowd was enjoying a successful career overseas, which he was unlikely to break on any kind of permanent basis. For personal reasons Donald Smith wanted to return to Australia and, if the gamble paid off, the company could afford to offer him permanent employment. The gamble did come off and Smith himself played no small part in it. His success was immediate. His was no longer the lyric tenor of old. He had been singing Calaf in *Turandot* opposite Amy Shuard at Covent Garden and the voice that filled that huge theatre with ease could hardly fail in the much smaller ones in Australia.

It is no reflection on Donald Smith's Manrico to say that in the end his was not the greatest success of the production. That honour went to Lauris Elms, appearing for the first time with the Trust. Elms had gone overseas after early work with the Melbourne National Opera, had been successful in England, but returned to Australia for family reasons. Her appearances in the Sutherland-Williamson season no doubt brought her to the attention of the Australian public, but her success as Azucena was much more spectacular. The combination of Smith and Elms was exciting in the best way that opera should be exciting and it was their joint effort which was the springboard from which native opera really took off.

Their colleagues were competent enough, but not in the same class. Rosemary Gordon, a New Zealander of German birth, was the only member of the original production to come to Australia. Leonora was not really her part, but she was beautiful and sang with intelligence and musicianship, carefully avoiding the fireworks which were outside her range. It was not an exciting performance, but one which complemented the others very well. Alexander Major as De Luna was a different proposition. He was a Hungarian migrant who appeared one day as the last singer in a day-long audition and left his audience stunned.

Major had a superbly controlled high baritone of excellent quality which should have been a great asset to any company. Unfortunately it was not matched by musical or dramatic intelligence of the same standard. His bearing was stiff and unyielding and he had a notable gift of always finding the right spotlight and standing just outside it when he had to be seen. In the already-dark sets of *Trovatore* this tendency served to hide his awkward carriage and dull acting; his contribution was a largely invisible voice singing some very difficult music superbly. It was some time before the public would realize that Major was not a potentially great new star, but that he was Major at the first performance of *Trovatore* and would stay Major in exactly that manner for the rest of his stay with the company, a useful singer capable of coping with almost any role efficiently, but without creating much excitement. Although a Hungarian, Alexander Major was the very model of an Italian opera singer. It also happened that that was the kind of singer the company needed at that moment and his contribution in the years to come should not be underestimated.

Denis Vaughan's tenure as musical director was restricted to 1966. He was the last to have the ABC orchestras at his disposal. Gerald Krug, a young musician of undoubted ability was his assistant and for a few performances Romanian Robert Rosen took over all three operas with great efficiency. Why Rosen, an operatic conductor of extensive experience, did not continue with the company is one of those mysteries which will never be solved. It may have been a communication problem; his English was very far from perfect.

1966 was the turning point for opera in Australia. After ten years of steadily-declining standards, the jump in quality was quite spectacular. The spectre of the Sydney Opera House appeared to haunt Haag, Young and Hall again and again. The exterior of the building was complete, but opera had, in this first year of success, been relegated to the smaller hall. What went on in that building, which looked like turning into the whitest elephant in history, was of vital importance to the future of the opera company.

Living up to a name – or tit for tat.
Gloria Lane was affectionately nicknamed 'Tits'. Good looks and a good voice made her a fine Carmen. The mammaries did not hurt her performance at all in 1964.

SECOND INTERVAL:

australia's opera houses

Stonehenge or an opera house? (Sydney Opera House)

TV Tower or an opera house? (State Theatre, Melbourne)

The Great Australian Opera House — our answer to
La Scala and Covent Garden — is nearing completion.
What a What a pity that they built the outside in
Sydney and the inside in Melbourne!

The *Bulletin*
7 June 1983

t is nice to coin a phrase which becomes, if not a household word, something which is frequently quoted. My comments, written a year before the new State Theatre in Melbourne opened its doors, have been reprinted world-wide in many forms, only rarely mentioning the author. I don't mind this. My name would mean nothing to the readers of *The Times* in London or the *Washington Post*, two of many newspapers which headed stories about the theatre with those words. And I produced my Cheshire Cat smile when a certain rival critic could not resist using the remark, writing: 'As one of my colleagues so neatly summed it up:...'

It's all very flattering until one reads, as I recently did in the *Australian*, a respectable journal, 'I was told this joke...' That makes my little imitation of unfortunately-truthful wit become apocryphal, of doubtful authenticity. I am fortunate in having the chance — and good reason — to set the record straight. I can at last explain why this apparently jocular throw-away line is not only sustainable factually, but why its very truth causes much heartburn among those who produce opera in Australia and those who have to pay for it, meaning not only the ticket-buyer but also the people in charge of funding the various companies from your pocket and mine.

If I wrote those lines today, I could very well alter them to: 'What a pity they built the outside in Sydney and the inside in Melbourne, Adelaide and Brisbane.' All three cities now have what can loosely be called better opera houses than can be found in the Sydney building which bears that name, yet was long considered — and is still considered by some — to be a white elephant. Not only is it a unique structure, unlike any other on Earth, but it has a history which leaves its competitors standing — and they should be glad it does! If the way a building was constructed could be capitalized, no opera house in the world would take second place to the one in Sydney.

Paris has its Eiffel Tower, New York has its Empire State Building and Sydney has its Opera House. The fame of no building in history has spread more quickly than that of the monumental sculpture erected by Joern Utzon on Bennelong Point in the middle of Sydney's harbour and in the shadow of the bridge which, until 1973, was the most notable man-made landmark in Australia.

Sydney is indeed fortunate in having the Opera House. It has caused the usual surge in theatrical activity which appears in the wake of new centres of the performing arts, but it has also put Sydney and opera in Australia on the map internationally. On the face of it, all is lovely in the garden but, to coin a phrase, the flowers that bloom at Bennelong Point (tra-la) have nothing to do with the case; meaning, that the standard of opera presented in this most extraordinary building is high in spite of, not because of, its facilities.

The charge is commonly laid that the Opera Theatre of the complex is unsuitable for the presentation of opera. The resident company has often used the Concert Hall for those works that are too big for the smaller theatre and there is still talk of building a new opera house in Sydney or of converting an old cinema to provide the extra space which cannot be found at Bennelong Point. But, if faults there are in the design (and there are!), the ingenuity of the Australian Opera's technical staff has overcome them.

The theatre is as unusual as its exterior. It is not possible to move productions into it which have been designed for more conventional buildings and vice versa. Facilities backstage are cramped and artists have trouble getting to their allocated positions and even in finding their ways onto and off the sets, which must be specially designed to cope with the limitations of vertical as well as horizontal space. The opera theatre is a mess, but its tenants have overcome the difficulties to such an extent that to any but the most knowledgeable in the audience there is no visible evidence of the handicaps imposed on the performers.

How is it possible that a building costing over $100 million could fail to provide the basic necessities for the very needs implied in its name? It is a long and well-documented story and it must be told here, if in abbreviated form.

Once upon a time some long-forgotten NSW politicians decided to make sure that they would *not* be forgotten by tricking their fellow citizens into starting a monumental building which they well knew would cost far more than the seven million dollars mentioned in Parliament. The state of opera in Australia in 1956 certainly did not warrant the construction of an opera house in Sydney or any other city. On the other hand, the very name OPERA HOUSE has always loomed large in the histories of cities and there must be hundreds all over the world which sport a building so named without ever having had a resident opera company. In the nineteenth century opera was the ultimate in theatrical entertainment and any building which implied by its name that it could be used to present grand opera immediately became the focus of attention.

There are almost too many things about the creation of the Sydney Opera House which run completely counter to any kind of logic. No matter how successful the end result, the project should have collapsed and could have collapsed again and again. It was the money spent, not the money needed, which kept it alive. Building was commenced almost immediately and once hard cash had been put into concrete, nobody had the courage to see it thrown down the drain; more and more was invested to save the growing monster and, as the expenditure grew, the reasons for increasing the budget became still stronger. It was a snowball that could not be stopped. In the end, it played a major part in the 1965 elections that threw out the government which started it, but its successor could no more destroy what had been built than its creator. The Sydney Opera House was as self-perpetuating as the bureaucracy which brought it into being, and just as extravagant.

Nobody will seriously suggest today that the building should be dismantled. Human ingenuity has managed to make it work, though the costs involved in staging opera in the building are vastly greater than they would be anywhere else. The original concept was of a monument to the New South Wales 'visionaries', rather than a practical theatre complex like the ones built sensibly and without fuss in Adelaide, Melbourne and Brisbane. The monument has come into being and its problems should not concern the general public too much. But since this is a book on opera, the phenomenon must be explored. There are 102 million reasons why we are entitled to know the 'whys' and the 'wherefores' of the whole thing.

The building, which from the start was called the *Opera* House, came into being only because the late Sir Eugene Goossens demanded a better home for the Sydney Symphony Orchestra than the antiquated Town Hall. The original design specifications clearly gave concerts priority over opera.

The Sydney Opera House was intended as a home for the local symphony orchestra and facilities for presenting opera were to be made available as a secondary feature! Some opera house! Most curiously of all, the priorities remained unchanged throughout the construction of the building, though the coincidental renaissance in opera has brought public attention to that part of its operation rather than to its primary purpose as a concert hall. To this day opera only plays a minority role in the many activities which take place in this building!

In 1956 the NSW Government offered $10 000 to the winner of an international competition for the design of the Opera House. Seven hundred and thirty-three entries were received and entry fees alone more than covered the value of the prize! It was the only financially-sound deal made throughout the whole sordid mess; making the competitors pay for the competition was a stroke of genius. The fact that the whole thing was illegal was of secondary importance; the act authorizing the holding of the competition was not passed until 1960, three years after the winner had been declared and one year after work had actually commenced! It was but the first step toward the incredible bungling which was to follow.

The Danish architect Joern Utzon was declared the winner on the basis of an idealistic drawing, not the fully-detailed plans which were stipulated, reasonably expected and supplied by the other competitors. Utzon had no idea how the building he had drawn (not designed) could be built. In fact, he was a very far from experienced architect. At thirty-eight years of age he had had little practical experience; his total credits were two small housing projects and prizes in various competitions. (Later the designs for his Sydney home were rejected by the local council and Utzon never did manage to overcome the surveyor's objections; the building was left incomplete when he departed from the scene.) This was the man placed in sole charge of the whole venture!

The estimate of seven million dollars to complete the building appears to have been plucked out of the air. Any larger figure would have caused Parliament to reject the whole thing and, before anybody could query the whole idea, authority to commence building was given, though no proper plans had been drawn up, even for the foundations. Work commenced on 2 March 1959. By then budgeting of a sort had begun and within a year a 'firm' price of $9 760 000 was accepted by the NSW Parliament — 'such cost shall not under any circumstances be exceeded by more than ten percentum'. Famous last words! Five hundred and fifty piers were driven up to thirty metres into the ground until bedrock was struck, while drawings were still being prepared for the foundations which would be supported by them. In fact, throughout Utzon's period as chief architect plans were always completed after work actually started. The podium on which the building rests was begun fully three years before the design for the massive roof shells was completed. As a result, much of this costly work had to be dynamited to accommodate the final structure, which differed very substantially from the original drafts.

Utzon initially worked on the designs in Denmark, at the other end of the world. Nobody could understand why the boss of the project should hide himself so far away, but it soon became obvious that the answers to the problems Utzon had set himself were not within his capacity to solve. Instead of seeking outside help, Utzon blithely announced that he had made an ingenious discovery which would make the building better than ever. This meant changing not only the whole shape of the structure to what it is now (a remote cousin of the drawing which won the competition) but it meant starting all over again from scratch. Work then commenced on the shells — again, before the drawings were complete. When the government fell in 1965, the last of 1 055 941 roof tiles had actually been placed into position, yet no finality had been reached about the interior of the building. In other words, the shells were constructed before the use of the space they sheltered had been determined and all the later building problems and present inadequacies of the project can be traced to the limitations which Utzon had unintentionally set, by creating a building from the outside in.

The new Liberal Government, which had forced the issue of the escalating costs of the building mercilessly during the election, now had to deal with a recalcitrant Utzon, who refused to reveal his non-existent plans for the interiors and seating of the halls. Amid some cloak-and-dagger operations worthy of any James Bond thriller, Joern Utzon finally resigned from the project on 28 February 1966, because his new bosses would not allow him to continue as before, the sole master of a financially-uncontrollable monster. The case for his retention has finally died down, but at the time there were street demonstrations which treated the threat to Utzon like a threat to the environment. It was sheer emotionalism, for nobody (not even Utzon) knew what it was that was being defended, other than the magic name Utzon itself.

(The situation in 1966 bore a strong resemblance to the state of London's British National Opera House, which was rising in Whitehall nearly a century ago; and there must have been a temptation to follow the British model to the end — the London building was razed to ground level and New Scotland Yard built on its foundation.)

Dane Utzon's international team of workers, which included Scandinavians, English, Americans, South Africans and even a solitary Chinese, was disbanded. An all-Australian team led by Peter Hall (at thirty-four even younger than Utzon had been when he started work) sat down to take stock of the architectural problems, while the government took another look at the occupancy of the building, if and when it was ever to be finished.

Opera in Australia was at its lowest ebb in 1966. The Elizabethan Trust Opera Company offered only three works during one four-week season in Sydney that year and attracted less than 30 000 paying customers. How could anybody foresee that the controversial future opera house under reassessment would, within thirteen years of final completion (1973) attract opera audiences paying $7 000 000 in admission fees to see no less than 21 different operas in the course of one year, 1986? Or that such audiences would continue to multiply rapidly not only in Sydney but all over Australia in theatres, on radio and even on television?

In 1966 the original plans of a concert hall capable of being used occasionally for opera, backed by a smaller theatre for drama, were still on the drawing board, although stage machinery costing some millions of dollars had already been installed. The trouble was that Utzon had not yet solved the problem of how to seat enough people to make it a paying proposition.

At this point it not only became apparent that Utzon had to go, but that the completed work would make the large hall a doubtful proposition for what was still the primary purpose of the building, the staging of the ABC's annual concert seasons. The ABC threatened to pull out unless the large hall was completed as a proper concert hall; the concept of a multi-purpose hall, convertible into an opera theatre, had long been criticized in any case. It is easy to be wise after the event, but in 1966 the decision to transfer the opera theatre from the large to the small hall, and to move drama from the latter to the even smaller theatre in which it now finds itself, was the only sensible solution.

The way Peter Hall and his colleagues solved the various problems left by Utzon really cannot be criticized. That the end result cannot compare with a building properly planned from the beginning is inevitable. Quite apart from the impossible costs of demolishing the famous sails already dominating Sydney Harbour, nobody can deny their monumental splendour. Their retention was inevitable and credit for their creation will always lie with Utzon. But the difficulties which were engendered by their shape are the burden which opera in Sydney will have to continue to bear, unless a second and real opera house is built in that city.

The ingenuity with which the Australian Opera has managed to stage truly grand operas in the Concert Hall during the off-season has made up for some of the shortcomings of the Opera Theatre. From the time the Sydney Opera House opened its doors to opera, on 28 September 1973 with Prokofiev's *War and Peace*, the name of the building has to some extent justified itself. It is *opera* in the Sydney Opera House that makes the news, no matter how much else may be going on in that complex monument to one man's folly. Utzon's vision of this building was always external and that vision, if not in the original conformation, has become one of the seventy wonders of the world.

I could extend the sad tale of the Sydney Opera House, but too much needs to be said about the unquestioned effect the completed building has had on the rise of opera Australia-wide. In this it has been helped immensely by the three other new opera houses, none of which bear that name. The Adelaide Festival Theatre came first, the Melbourne State Theatre next and the Lyric Theatre in Brisbane last. The problem is that all three can easily accommodate anything to be found in any normal opera house. Not so Utzon's famous building. It is as unique internally as it is externally. Very few productions designed for other theatres can be done justice at Bennelong Point. And the most wonderful opera production the inventiveness of man could create for the benefit of Sydney audiences will never have the same impact anywhere else. The building is rather like a metal cake tin; you put an opera into it, but, to stay as good as it is, it must remain the same shape when transferred to another theatre. Of course, you can cut chunks off the sets or add others, but it will become a different production.

Thus the Australian Opera, which works in this landmark, is a normal touring company emerging from an abnormal building. It is not unusual today for $100 000 or even $500 000 to be invested in a new production. We have a circuit of 'arts centres' — Melbourne, Adelaide, Brisbane and Sydney. An opera staged in any of the first three can be transferred to the other two, but not to Sydney, and vice versa. Of course, improvisations take place; opera is a musical art and if the singing is good, as it usually is, people will not worry too much if the singer is not always as visible as he or she ought to be. Most ironical of all, the smallness of the Sydney stage forces the AO to instal false prosceniums on the large stages of the other theatres, whose audiences at the sides see less in the bigger theatres than in the small one in Sydney! No wonder there is talk of an alternative, or second, opera house for Sydney. The other cities don't need one; they are well supplied with facilities which are second to none in the world.

A ship-shape Opera House.

Above: The Sydney Opera House's billowing roofs were designed to look like sails in the wind. If the image was lost, during the 1988 Bicentenary of Australia's first settlement audiences in the incredible glassed-in foyers saw more sails than designer Joern Utzon could ever have envisaged.

Melbourne's Arts City.

Opposite: Note the National Gallery to left of the State Theatre and the Concert Hall to its right. The Sidney Myer Music Bowl with a huge audience is in the gardens. *Out of sight on left*: the Grant Street Theatre, the Victorian College of the Arts. Behind the spire (not seen, but now built) is the Australian Ballet Centre. The city and theatres are across the bridge.

But for Utzon's huge sculpted sails, which serve as roofs and prevent expansion, the Sydney Opera House might well be a candidate for demolition by now. Yet its fame world-wide is so great that such an action would turn the 'Greenies' as white as the tiles which cover the building. No bulldozer would be allowed within a mile of it. Nor should it. Like many an extravagent folly of the past, Sydney's Opera House is here to stay!

The Melbourne State Theatre, whose interior everybody would like to have in Sydney, has a remarkable, if less spectacular background. I am almost inclined to pun and say 'backGrounds', since the late Sir Roy Grounds designed this theatre, which is as remarkable as the Sydney one, if not as visible. And this building can be used in every way a theatre could possibly be used. It may not be an attraction for tourist buses; in fact, externally it could even be called aesthetically objectionable. The reason? Practically all of it is below ground level and the miserable assemblage of ugly white tubes which sticks like a signpost into the sky almost defies you to believe that it is only the tip of an iceberg of unimagined theatrical magnificence.

What was to have been a landmark worthy of a great city — a wonderful smooth copper-sheathed spire visible for miles by night or day — fell victim to the kind of economies which were never made in Sydney. Victorian money was needed to present operas and ballets and plays, not statues to the glories of the premiers of those days, Henry Bolte, who started it all, and Rupert Hamer who caused it to come to fruition.

Unlike Sydney, Melbourne treated the whole complex of buildings, which is by now little less than a small city of the arts covering several square kilometres, as a practical exercise to be strictly controlled and expertly supervised. The first building of all, the National Gallery, was completed within budget in 1968, two years after Sydney's lingering Opera House had passed through its greatest crisis. Unfortunately, that was also the time which saw the start of spiralling inflation and nothing thereafter was ever again 'within budget'. Nevertheless, strict quality and cost control ensured that every dollar spent went toward essentials alone. No expense was spared on any part of 'The Great Australian Opera House' and its many other auditoria, or the Concert Hall, but the costs rose astronomically for better reasons than the chaotic methods responsible for the *ad hoc* escalation in Sydney. It was discovered that the area to

Adelaide Festival Theatre.
With some of its terraces and fountains. (*Photo: Alex Makeev.*)

be excavated to hold the theatre and its workings, designed to be below ground, below the level of the River Yarra, consisted of porous silt. Work was suspended for three years, while scientific and financially-sound solutions were found for every problem; in the end the whole Concert Hall was moved to a different, basalt-based site near the river.

The end result has the State Theatre sitting in a deep concrete 'bathtub' designed to keep out water rather than contain it. The alternative was to build the theatre above ground and to ruin one of the world's great boulevards, Melbourne's St Kilda Road, at the very entrance to the city. There has not been a trace of controversy over the decision to spend the extra millions to preserve the environment in this case.

There was no competition for the design, no Joern Utzon, no brick laid, no concrete poured or nail driven which was not approved by the best possible experts in each field, who were chosen by the building committee which was formed before it all began. There was no political or other lobbying, except on the part of some acoustic engineers, whose 'science' to this day is closer to astrology than astronomy in practically-provable facts. (The opening of the Concert Hall in 1982 and the State Theatre four years later proved that neither was the predicted disaster!) The motivators who brought about this miracle of a modern theatre complex are only found with difficulty. They sought no personal glory and the absence of their names from most official publications is remarkable.

Kenneth Myer and George Fairfax got no mention in the history of the project in the lavish booklet promoting the many venues of the Victorian Arts Centre in the Bicentennial Year 1988; they are listed in a corner in microscopic print as 'Chairman' and 'General Manager' along with other directors, some of whom became such long after completion of the State Theatre. Yet Myer headed the building committee from the start and Fairfax managed the complex from the moment there was anything to manage. A whole generation of music-lovers have grown up since these two men began to create one of Australia's greatest, if least visible, assets for all our benefit.

However, neither the Melbourne State Theatre nor the Concert Hall were actually the first modern venues

Lyric Theatre and Performing Arts Complex, Brisbane.

Sydney Opera House at night. *(Photo: J Alex Langley.)*

suitable for the presentation of opera to beat the Sydney Opera House at its own game. That honour must go to the Adelaide Festival Theatre which opened more than three months *before* the Australian Opera officially launched the Sydney Opera Theatre with Prokofiev's *War and Peace*. At the same time, it must be remembered that the Festival Theatre does not, strictly speaking, qualify as an 'opera house'. It is, in fact, the very thing which the Sydney Opera House was intended to be in the first place, a multi-purpose hall suitable for use as a concert hall as well as a theatre. It was properly and economically planned, but the end result, no matter how good, is much less sophisticated than its colleagues in Melbourne or Brisbane.

Looking at the Adelaide Festival Theatre through restricting operatic glasses, it lacks very little in opera house terms. But there is no separate concert hall, as there is in the other three capitals, and its operations are indeed limited by its multi-purpose form. It has ample seating, a large stage, a fine orchestra pit and all the facilities you may wish to have, including some delightful surroundings. Its location is ideal, in the heart of the city, yet surrounded by a beautiful park overlooking a river and even a fully-fledged casino literally within a few metres of the theatre. It makes even less pretence at aesthetic exterior virtues than the Melbourne theatre; all the money has gone into the efficient working of the interior. The building can fairly be described as an eyesore, for it is little more than flat surfaces covering all the odd nooks and crannies which are needed to make a good theatre, but attractive terraces with flowers and statuary make it a sanctuary for citizens and visitors to the bi-annual Adelaide Festival alike. And there is always the hope that one day some wealthy patron will offer to enclose the whole thing in some kind of shell which will

blend into the existing landscape, just as the day may come when the scaffolding-like spire of the Melbourne State Theatre may be replaced. (Neither operation is difficult in structural terms, if the money can be found for it.)

In many respects the Adelaide theatre is the most comfortable of the existing Australian opera venues. It is certainly the most easily adapted (which is its purpose) and there is plenty of space surrounding it if a concert hall and other facilities should need to be added to what is already being enlarged almost every year. Perhaps in what was once called 'the Athens of the South' regular opera seasons may yet be looking for a permanent home larger than the tiny, though delightful, Opera Theatre a couple of kilometres up the road.

The Lyric Theatre in Brisbane is at the core of the Queensland Performing Arts Complex. It adjoins the newly developed area which occupied the Expo '88 site, both overlooking the Brisbane River. The theatre is the most monumental, if not exactly the most spectacular or beautiful of the four major opera centres in Australia, being completely above ground and covering an enormous area. Its facilities also are as large and as good as any in Australia. As the newest of the four buildings, opened on 8 August 1985 with a huge production of *Aida*, it has not yet built for itself an aura of theatrical atmosphere. By its very grandness a visit to the Lyric Theatre and its vast, as yet bare interior makes going to the opera almost a sporting event — the feeling is one of size rather than style. But as a venue for the presentation of opera it is hard to beat on either side of the footlights, although a little warmth in décor or decoration would not come amiss.

May no singer or opera-lover ever have a bigger complaint than that!

ACT 3:

out of small
acorns

ACT 3 : SCENE 1
THE AUSTRALIAN OPERA
IS BORN

The total staff of the Elizabethan Theatre Trust Opera Company at the end of 1966 was three! John Young, administrator, his secretary, Evelyn Klopfer and the newly appointed Stephen Hall, who bore by then the ambiguous title 'co-ordinator'. The total complement of principal singers was two: Neil Warren-Smith and John Germain, key people who had sung with the company since its inception and had been suitably rewarded with full-time contracts. Nevertheless, an opera company consisting solely of one bass and one baritone with an administration of three was hardly an auspicious start for 1967. The Sydney Opera House being rebuilt as a concert hall and a smaller opera theatre, was still in the dim distance, well outside any planning programme. But appearances were deceptive. 1966 had been a year of very active planning and the enormous leap forward of the following year proved that the planning was sound.

Nobody knows how John Young and his board talked the NSW Government into coming to the party at this particular moment, but in 1967 it began a series of annual grants to the company to prepare it for the glories of the new Opera House, if and when it would be finished. The first grant was used to place a nucleus of chorus singers under permanent contract and 1967 thus saw the beginning of a *continuous* company, as opposed to one which was reassembled every year, or every second year. The basis of starting with the chorus was sound; it was felt that principals had a better chance of finding casual work between seasons. As it turned out, 1967 was successful enough to enable some principals to continue under holding contracts, but it was the chorus which began the long, and happily steep,

climb to the company's present position. At the same time the Trust created its first orchestra, to be used by both opera and ballet companies, and there was thus an immediate continuity both on and below stage.

One part of the planning of Young and Haag (who was still very much involved, though in 1966 he had risen to greater aloofness as the Trust's own structure grew) was the engagement of that extraordinary showman Harry M. Miller as 'commercial and promotion consultant'. One wonders whether there was somebody just busy thinking up new titles for the staff in those days, but whatever the nomenclature, Harry Miller was worth his weight in gold and so was the new publicity director, Tony Frewin. Between them, Miller and Frewin completely revolutionized the whole principle of ticket selling in Australia. The 'subscription series' arrived belatedly, but most successfully. Not only did the purchase of tickets *en bloc* for the whole season become common practice, but the old forgotten promotion of opera as a pop-culture thing was suddenly revived and — surprise! — it still worked. The wording may have been a little more up-to-date, but basically the billing of Wagner's *Flying Dutchman* as 'A tempest-tossed romance of wild and sombre beauty' was no better and no worse than the old 'Love's amusing roundabout' which sold *The Marriage of Figaro* during the first season eleven years previously. The introduction of Youth Nights on the normally dead Mondays of the season not only filled the theatre, but created new audiences who greeted opera with open arms. Nobody worried very much if the under twenty-six youths often had some rather thirtyish bags under their eyes, the important thing was to create audiences and — full credit to Harry M —

audiences *were* created in that historic year. The repertoire jumped from three to five operas, plus a revival of the successful *Trovatore*. Seasons were played in Sydney, Brisbane, Melbourne, Canberra and Adelaide and, miracle of miracles, capacity audiences were the rule rather than the exception. For the first time in the company's history there were even overnight queues, though admittedly only for the Youth Nights. Six operas for $5.00 was too good a chance to pass up and a full house at 82 cents a seat produced a fair return in cash, quite apart from invaluable mouth-to-mouth advertising; it was mouth-to-mouth resuscitation for an art close to death in this country.

The fact that Harry Miller's revolutionary promotion schemes filled the theatres in 1967 can be explained in many ways, not least by the age-old theory that people want to be fooled by good packaging. You can dress up an opera season just as you can make a cake of soap attractive through the right kind of wrapping. Yet ultimately the proof of the pudding is in the eating, or rather the hearing and seeing. Had 1967 not seen reasonably good presentations, audiences would not have returned in 1968 and the years that followed. The fact that they did is interesting in more ways than one, because 1967 was not really an artistically-outstanding year. In many ways it resembled the very first season of the company. There were gaucheries, mistakes, even disasters, but a completely new spirit surrounded artists and audiences. 'Nothing succeeds like success' is one of the great truisms of this world and people who sat in packed houses enjoyed even an inferior opera more than a better one amid the echoes of empty seats. As for the singers, the response spurred them on to give their best and their best was often very good indeed.

The most notable advance was the improvement in the visual aspects of productions. The most negative aspect was the new Trust orchestra, which was a far cry from the excellence of the ABC orchestras of years gone by. There was actually nothing as good as the previous year's *Boris Godounov* and *Trovatore* except the latter itself, which was staged outside the subscription series to full houses. 1967 must be judged as the first year which was fully planned, and executed as planned, without financial waste to speak of. What artistic waste there was occurred in a good cause and added to the history on which the future of the company was built. It was Harry Miller who set the ball rolling and it was John Young who

produced a rollable ball.

The five completely new productions were a mixed bag, the most notable coming from Stephen Hall making a first attempt at opera production in a manner so ambitious as to be almost foolhardy. Surely no producer has ever started a career with Puccini's *Turandot*, but Hall did and succeeded, in spite of all odds. Not that Hall proved to be a master producer in this or any future opera he staged, but he had come recently from Covent Garden where he had worked (as one of many stage managers) with producers like Visconti, Zeffirelli and Hartmann. He had absorbed the then-current trend of the new realism, which was diametrically opposed to the blank stage represented in Australia by Haag's *Fidelio*, for example. That a fine stage picture can smooth over musical deficiencies is a reality, however unpalatable it may be to purists, and the impressive set by Friedrich Bliem and costumes by Mel Clifford and Robert Potter looked (and were) fantastically expensive. They were certainly the most ambitious venture in visual splendour of the company to date. With Donald Smith to sing Puccini's music, a superb chorus and a fine ensemble for the minor roles the opera only needed a strong central singer to be a runaway success.

I do not regret having described Morag Beaton's *Turandot* as 'the mouse that roared', because I have always had an immense respect for her as one of the greatest voices I have heard in my time. She was roundly condemned by many critics, but the criticism was only partly justified. 1967 was the year in which the local ensemble was created and expensive guest artists were an impossible extravagance. Perhaps it was unwise to put a small, unimpressive Scotswoman without any experience to speak of straight into *Turandot*. If so, the same criticism should be made of Stephen Hall for tackling an opera of such size first time up. In his case the gamble came off completely, in her case only partially. Morag Beaton's *Turandot* was definitely not a failure, because she coped magnificently with the music and it is a rôle which not many sopranos can encompass with ease. She was indeed a mouse that roared and her roaring was in perfect pitch and rolled across the admittedly undermanned orchestra with the greatest of ease. Rosemary Gordon was a sympathetic Liu and Donald Shanks a far too powerful old Timor. Robin Gordon, on the other hand, was an admirably feeble Emperor. An American, Robert Feist, acted as though he was musical

The mice that roared.
Tiny Morag Beaton roared mightily as Turandot, burdened down by her huge peacock train, while Stephen Hall's first stage production was also a roaring success. *Front left*: (Umberto Borsò as Calaf, *At back*: The Emperor, sung by the present administrator of the San Diego Opera, Ian Campbell.)

director of the company, which he was not, yet his conducting of *Turandot* and *Rigoletto* was highly professional; probably better than the word implies, for he was working with a completely new ensemble whose weaknesses had yet to be discovered and weeded out.

For all its failings, the orchestra from the first year was to work in much closer harmony with the company than the full symphony orchestras the ABC had supplied in years gone by. The magnificent sound the latter had provided may have been an asset, but in retrospect it is quite clear that there was a degree of competition between stage and pit which disappeared as soon as the first Trust Orchestra was formed. This was an ensemble

that knew its place and many years were to pass before it was to tackle operas in which the orchestra had to carry a burden as important as that of the singers. When the time came it was up to it. In 1967 it was still playing second fiddle, but from the start it was but rarely out of tune. (There was a grave shortage of second fiddlers that year, anyway!)

The Flying Dutchman, in its own way, equalled the success of *Turandot*. Oddly enough, it had the same principal failing, a leading lady short of perfection, but in this case there was less excuse. It may have been asking for trouble to stage two operas needing Turandot/ Senta voices, but a first-class Dutchman was available in Raymond Myers, returning with renewed vigour and some very necessary experience to these shores. Neil Warren-Smith was a world-class Daland and the chorus both here and in *Turandot* amply justified its being made first choice when continuity became a financial reality. Kurt Hommel produced traditionally, but well, and Wendy Dickson's costumes and sets, including some spectacular projections of the Dutchman's ship, worked well. The fly in the ointment was another American, Marcella Reale, accepted without audition on the recommendation of Robert Feist. Miss Reale was a good-looking singer, but the voice, while beautiful in itself and of suitable power, developed a disturbing wobble under pressure. Ultimately Reale was to make some contribution to the company's musical fortunes, but in the *Dutchman* she failed to justify importation at great expense.

It is easier to forgive the shortcomings of local singers who place smaller financial strain on the management. The practice of importing second-raters proved to be the only serious flaw in the policies of those years. Inevitably, they acted like prima donnas (male as well as female), inevitably, they got all the publicity that Tony Frewin could throw their way and, inevitably, they failed to live up to the false image which was created. It would have been better to have them absorbed quietly into the ensemble, as happened in later years with singers like Umberto Borsò or Elizabeth Vaughan.

One new production was so bad as to be almost good; good for all the wrong reasons. Putting a producer of pop musicals, aged twenty-one, in charge of *Don Giovanni* was a risk and John Young took it with his eyes open. He claims that the exercise was worthwhile and I will go along with him to the point of admitting that almost anything can be tried. I make only one proviso: that the end result must work. Jim Sharman's attempt to stage *Don Giovanni* as a game of chess on a bare stage of black and white squares did not succeed, in fact, could not succeed, if only because Mozart's opera does not contain the right combination of characters to produce any kind of chess situation. You can have Donna Anna as the White Queen and Elvira as the Black (or vice versa) but what do you do with Zerlina? And if Giovanni is the Black King (or the White) who is the White King (or the Black)? Sharman actually attempted to make his 'pieces' move according to the rules of chess, but it was a half-hearted attempt and the singers ignored their squares of operation almost from the first performance.

Never has there been a production in which so many tried so much to do so little to improve the original. What was a badly-conceived mistake rapidly became a shambles, and singers, who had attended rehearsals and enthusiastically backed this bold experiment, suddenly complained at the impossible things they had to do and

how they affected their voices. As it happened, there were few, if any complaints about the singing, which was generally of high standard. It was probably this which saved the production because – like Haag's *Fidelio* – sooner or later somebody spoke up in defence of the indefensible and controversy is the lifeblood of the theatre. Youth Nights in particular split into noisy factions and it can be said quite truthfully that demonstrations against productions also serve a useful purpose in raising interest in audiences and self-criticism in management.

Sharman's *Don Giovanni* will remain a memorable production, however much it may have failed, while others of really quite substantial excellence have already been forgotten. In the context of creating a new image to go with full houses and lively debate about the future of the company, this *Giovanni* may even have been a good thing. Complaints there were many, but they queued up for their seats in the following year just the same. This is the stuff that opera is made of.

Musically *Don Giovanni* lacked support in the pit, where Thomas Mayer had trouble getting Mozartian precision from the new orchestra. On stage Robert Gard's Ottavio was the only one of the singers to retain the style of the music completely. Neil Warren-Smith, with the task of trying to hold the whole thing together dramatically, gave up a little too easily, but sang with his usual assurance. Marcella Reale (Anna) might have been singing Puccini, while Maureen Howard was an admirable Zerlina. Rosemary Gordon sang Elvira and Maconaghie a lightweight Leporello.

With a new *Don Pasquale*, Stefan Haag once again proved how good (or backward) he remained in staging comic opera as slapstick. His team of singers supported him to the hilt and though George Molnar's witty sets were not as beautifully executed as a bigger budget might have allowed, the ensemble built around June Bronhill, for once an ideally-suited guest star, ensured a happy evening for all.

Two productions were staged 'on the cheap'. The first of these proved to be an unexpected hit. *Rigoletto*, as restaged by Stefan Beinl in cramped sets and costumes by Ron Reid, was sung so excellently that there was no room left for criticism. Following on the excellent *Trovatore*, this modest production raised operatic temperatures to such a level that future seasons seemed assured. After all, when you can stage two Verdi operas with com-

Checkmate 1967.
Twenty-one-year-old Jim Sharman tried to stage *Don Giovanni* as a game of chess, using only a bare checkered stage as a setting. It checkmated him before he began, for chess has only two queens, while Mozart provided him with three! (Rosemary Gordon as Elvira, Marcella Reale as Anna, Robert Gard as Ottavio.)

Checkmate 1974.
Another producer from the straight theatre, John Bell, tried his hand at *Don Giovanni* and also failed. Was designer Peter Corrigan's finger a warning or an opinion? (Warren-Smith as Leporello, John Pringle as Giovanni and Grant Dickson as Commendatore.)

pletely local casts of such quality in one year, then one has to be onto a winner. Audiences, state governments and the Trust certainly believed it and they were right.

Raymond Myers sang his first Rigoletto brilliantly, Donald Smith was dead right as the Duke and any criticism of Janice Taylor's Gilda was purely academic. It may be fashionable to say that Verdi wanted a bigger voice for the role. The fact remains that the likes of Galli-Curci and Dal Monte had been the most popular Gildas of the century and Taylor was completely in their spirit. Her efforts five years later to sing the role with her 'new' heavier voice were unsatisfactory, but in 1967 she made a perfect foil for her two partners. The Sparafucile of Donald Shanks was an imposing figure and poor Morag Beaton was forced to sing the contralto Maddalena during the same weeks as her Turandots.

It may be as well to examine for a moment the problems of any opera company to find voices of the rarer type and none is rarer than a true contralto. Many contraltos push themselves up into the mezzo-soprano field under the impression that being a mezzo is more glamorous. Perhaps so, but the tendency to push voices up has resulted in a range of rôles which it is very difficult to cast effectively and a company like the then Trust Opera had nothing beyond Lauris Elms in the field. Elms was and is world-class, but she either could not or would not sing Maddalena, a bit part, but an important one. The freak range of Morag Beaton's voice encompassed a strong lower register, but no singer can sing Turandot one night and Maddalena or Ulrica (A Masked Ball) the next, without developing vocal problems. Her downfall began in that first season, with those Turandots alternating with Maddalenas. I doubt whether any singer in history was ever asked to cover both roles, let alone sing them at the same time for months on end. No doubt John Young will claim that it was a necessary evil at the time. He should have known that it would end in disaster, as it unfortunately did.

Once again Die Fledermaus returned for an extended run to bridge the gap between seasons and Tosca was given a dry run for the 1968 revival with Gobbi and Collier. Maureen Howard sang Tosca and started her path down the road to heavier roles for which her voice was ill-equipped. Reginald Byers made his company debut as Cavaradossi and Alexander Major was a sonorous Scarpia. The delightful Johann Strauss Fledermaus was titivated up to include a Gala Performance in the Ball Scene, featuring stars like Donald Smith belting out

the old favourites and June Bronhill played second fiddle as a maid from Broken Hill, rather than the Austrian provinces, to Maureen Howard's excellent Rosalinda and Gard's admirable Eisenstein. The revival marked John Pringle's first appearance with the company as Falke. Pringle's ill-conceived attempts to become a bass had at last given way to better counsel and this was the beginning of his real career as a baritone. From the first, his ability as a natural actor marked him as outstanding raw material.

The third of John Young's years as administrator of the Trust Opera was a further step in the right direction. Having missed the 1966 Adelaide Festival, the company returned in 1968 in a glory which could not have been anticipated. For the first time in years there was a major figure, Carlo Felice Cillario, as principal conductor. For the first time there were some real star imports: Tito Gobbi, Marie Collier, the latter having risen very considerably on the international horizon since her visit in 1964, and also Antonietta Stella, who took Collier's place in Sydney. Marcella Reale returned again (to better effect), as did Ken Neate for the last time. With three productions scheduled for the Festival, a spectacle to surpass all previous spectacles was clearly the aim. The fact that Gobbi and Collier had to star in the old Melbourne National Theatre Tim Walton sets of Tosca once more was mitigated by the undoubted fact that they still looked mighty good — from a distance; they went to the tip after this, their last tour. Compensation was offered by a new Tannhäuser and Don Carlos, none of the three operas being sung in English.

Tito Gobbi's association with the company was to prove fruitful until two years later the tax man ended the goodwill he found out here. Stefan Haag restaged Tosca with Gobbi as Scarpia, Collier as Tosca and Donald Smith as Cavaradossi. The combination of three major singers, each a personality as well, was irresistible. Donald Smith proved once and for all, for the benefit of his own countrymen, that he was indeed capable of holding his own in the best company. Gobbi's presence on stage also showed up the fact that singers in the local company have a degree of professionalism which is not shamed by a master craftsman like Gobbi. It is all very well to hear of these things at second hand, but when it is shown that the best in his field, Gobbi, is not that far ahead of our own boys, then that really is something to crow about.

Tannhäuser and Don Carlos repeated the pattern of

**First echoes of
international standards.**
The 1968 *Tosca* at the
Adelaide Festival starred Tito
Gobbi and Marie Collier with
Donald Smith (Cavaradossi)
singing as well as either and
Cillario conducting.

Turandot of the year before, presenting a scenic spectacle with professionalism and imperfections. Nevertheless, there was progress, not only in steadily increasing attendances caused by the value for money visible in these productions, but actual improvement in quality of presentation and, more importantly, musical standards. Critics necessarily must pick out negative as well as positive qualities when reviewing a performance. As far as the general public is concerned, it is the overall enjoyment to be gained which counts and that was an undoubted advancement over 1967, though the plum of the year's productions was not staged at the Festival; once again it was a 'sleeper' that stole the honours, Puccini's *Girl of the Golden West*.

The traditional production of *Tannbäuser* (Beinl) with quite magnificent designs by Kenneth Rowell was an almost unqualified success, largely due to the conducting of Cillario. He gyrated with such verve and energy that on the opening night he knocked his score to the ground, and nearly lost his trousers when his braces gave way while he was trying to recover it. (The brand-new Head of Music Staff, conductor William Reid, who stood by as prompter, was observed backstage, via closed circuit television, attempting to hold up Cillario's vital garment and was promptly dubbed 'the Perv'.) All action on stage froze and the cast waited immobile in the midst of the most complicated Songfest ensemble wondering what had happened. Unperturbed (in spite of Reid's continuing first-aid) Cillario, orchestra and cast restarted after a long pause, a model of the team work which had taken hold of the whole company since the change of direction two years ago.

Marcella Reale had blessedly lost the *tremolo* in her voice and was an appealing Elisabeth. Unfortunately Ken Neate, looking absolutely splendid and acting with great conviction, had imported a *tremolo* of his own which marred his performance. Raymond Myers was a strong Wolfram and Morag Beaton a full-voiced Venus, but the mirrors of the Venusberg and the improvised ballet rather let the side down. On the whole it was a *Tannbäuser* worthy of a festival such as Adelaide's and by far the most impressive production, overall, that the company had staged to date.

John Young himself produced the first performance of Verdi's *Don Carlos* in Australia. Desmond Digby's costumes were admirable, but Raymond Boyce's multi-purpose set, consisting of prison-like bars surrounding the stage at all times, regardless of the scene being set indoors or outdoors, became monotonous. *Don Carlos* is a French grand opera (though sung here in Italian) and the spectacle of a whole *auto-da-fé* on stage was simply beyond the capacity of the company at the time. Yes, it was a 'grand' production, which kept faith with the new policy and whether the public liked it or not, it was not disappointed. Musically the performance conducted by Robert Feist was not in the Cillario class, nor were the singers on the whole up to their task. The notable exception was Neil Warren-Smith as King Philip, a nobly-sung-and-acted interpretation. Rosemary Gordon was a sympathetic Elisabetta and Alexander Major a well-sung dull-stick Rodrigo. For once Lauris Elms, wearing an historically accurate, but unnecessarily unflattering eye-patch, was out of her depth quite literally, the high *tessitura* of Eboli lay, possibly temporarily, out of her range, and John Young's production made her character completely unsympathetic. It was not one of Elms' best parts. Reginald Byers Sang Don Carlos, a rôle at the time right out of his reach, though the potential of the voice was already present.

The 1968 Festival was also the first occasion on which the company trotted out major singers in *comprimario* rôles for special occasions. Maureen Howard's Page in *Don Carlos* and Janice Taylor's Shepherd's Voice in *Tosca* were very worthwhile contributions to the overall effect and a welcome change from the usual dreary small part players who can be found in even the best company. Furthermore the existing one-singer-one-part policy, which had resulted in occasional spectacular last-minute appearances of understudies, went by the board. Suddenly there was advance planning for 'covers', singers who were scheduled to play parts after the original cast had had its run. Audiences will always grumble at this kind of thing, but it is standard practice in all countries and abused much more overseas than in Australia. International opera seasons begin their premières with several major stars, who then drop off one by one after the first few performances − after the critics have had their say. If Plácido Domingo sang all the performances of all the operas in which he sings the first night, he would be faced with singing just about every night of the year!

From 1968 onwards, double casts became the rule wherever possible. On many an occasion it even happened that the major singer sang the role after a minor one had premièred it, a customary practice when programming demands, it. Clearly Raymond Myers could not sing both Wolfram in *Tannhäuser* and Rodrigo in *Don Carlos*. The parts were shared by Myers and Major, with John Pringle covering both and singing his first major rôle in Sydney not as an understudy, but as a principal. Ronald Maconaghie did the same for Wolfram and outshone both his forerunners with the most pure Fischer-Dieskau-like lyricism. Rosemary Gordon and Marcella Reale shared Elisabeth, and Tosca was farmed out between Collier, the specially-imported replacement, Antonietta Stella, and the already-tried Maureen Howard. Smith and Byers shared Cavaradossi and Myers replaced Gobbi when the time came.

The new policy came not a day too late, but the best laid plans of mice and men don't always work out and disaster struck on opening night in Sydney. The audience for the Gala Première *Tosca* was ready to assemble. Donald Smith was indisposed, but Byers was ready to step in. Then, in the car on the way to the theatre, Antonietta Stella collapsed. Though Howard could have gone on, John Young decided that a special gala could not proceed with two understudies out of three and the audience was forced to go home, or rather to surrounding restaurants which had not done such a roaring trade or seen a better-dressed clientele in their history. Under the subscription system the gala audience got its *Tosca* some weeks later and, though they went home in good spirits on 11 June, they returned in a murderous mood. There is no evidence that that performance was any worse than the première would have been, but the audience wouldn't admit it.

The hit of the season came from an unexpected quarter, and was created largely by yet another of the new policies of the Young regime; *The Girl of the Golden West*, Puccini's ridiculous horse opera, became a sound success, through being sung in Italian. In spite of its American Wild West setting, it was as well that audiences could not understand the text of Belasco's outdated play. Minnie, the not-so-tough bar-owner in a Californian gold field, was made-to-measure for the American Marcella Reale. She sang and acted the part well and to say that she looked too young for a tough bar-room boss is not a valid criticism, since we are told by Puccini that she is a girl who has never been kissed. Donald Smith also was completely at home. There was just no difference between the ten-gallon hat worn by

The Man from the Golden North.
The Girl of the Golden West made Australia's best-loved tenor, Queenslander Donald Smith, feel most at home. Stephen Hall's production was too good, however, to allow the beer to come from a can.

Smith's bandit, Dick Johnson, and the traditional digger's hat; somehow the hat managed to turn up at one side without any help from anyone. More to the point, Smith's voice slipped around the Puccini melodies with the greatest of ease.

The Girl was to be Stephen Hall's best work as a producer, though it was only his second effort. The designs by Friedrich Bliem were most appropriate and worked to perfection. The ensemble of singers after nearly two years of continuous work was perfect. This Puccini opera is really an ensemble opera rather than a star vehicle, though it did have Caruso in its first production in 1910. Alan Light's villainous Sheriff was vocally and dramatically the black-hearted and black-voiced villain supreme and apart from the fine contributions from expected quarters (Gard, Maconaghie, Major, Germain) a whole row of choristers turned in excellent cameo rôles. Joseph Powell, John Heffernan, Paul Rutenis, Joseph Grunfelder, Diane Holmes and others have taken their place in the chorus before and since, while sometimes stepping into the limelight as they did in this Puccini opera in 1968. Their occasional appearances in minor rôles have been vastly better than those of any Italian or American opera chorus members. Much has been written about their collective brilliance in operas like *Tannhäuser* or *Boris Godounov*, too little about their playing of parts, though it must be admitted that responsible casting, as in *The Girl of the Golden West*, has shown them to greater effect than their occasional emergence as understudies in the really big rôles.

The one economy of the season proved to be a minor

success — against all odds. Stefan Haag reproduced his 1960 *Magic Flute*, craftily hiding the old sets in deepest shadows. Deliberately, or accidentally, this forced a playing down of the comic aspects of Schikaneder's idiotic plot and the result was an admirable exercise in straight Mozart; quite a change after the comic excesses of years gone by. Gard was the strong Tamino, backed by Maconaghie's sympathetic Papageno and Rosemary Gordon's idiomatic Pamina. Warren-Smith and John Pringle did well in the weightier rôles and only the poor Queen of the Night provided the stumbling block to overall excellence. Helen Kerby was a young American soprano about whom even Harry M. Miller could find nothing more startling to say than: 'She was offered the opportunity to audition for the Detmold Opera House but decided instead to accompany her husband to Australia.'

In the meantime it looked as though John Young's undoubted success in his third year as administrator of the Opera Company of the Trust would lead to even better things in 1969. In 1968, 160 800 seats had been sold and box office receipts exceeded half a million dollars, a 150 percent increase over the previous year. Harry Miller had produced no less than 33 000 subscribers, all of whom were potential customers for the next season and few would have argued with the fare which had been provided for them. The financial picture for the next year is not clear because the records overlap, offering a 1969/70 eighteen months to compare with the preceding twelve months. The season was planned to provide a five-month tour to the usual centres and this was followed by the first of the Gilbert and Sullivan seasons. Figures conveniently link the two, making an accurate financial assessment of the 1969 *grand* opera season difficult. On the other hand the growing number of subscribers and the generally high standard of the five productions — only slightly below those of the previous year, possibly because there was no Adelaide Festival — indicated a satisfactory state of affairs.

John Young's last year was historically a further step in the right direction, though another palace revolution should have been a warning of changes to come. The end of 1968 finally saw the departure of both Dr Coombs as chairman of the Trust and of his protégé, Stefan Haag, as its executive director. Stephen Hall leap-frogged from being John Young's assistant in the opera company to the post of 'secretary and co-ordinator' of the Trust.

In plain language he took the place of Haag and became Young's boss. Sir Ian Potter replaced Dr Coombs. Of the three men who brought about the turn in the company's fortunes, the youngest, Stephen Hall, was to steer the company into the Sydney Opera House, ultimately becoming the founder and director of the annual Festival of Sydney. Young and Haag were less fortunate. Young oversaw the creation of the Seymour Centre in Sydney, which had little bearing on the future of opera in this country, and faded from the scene. Stefan Haag became a somewhat tragic figure. Honoured for his work in building opera as a major art form, he lingered as the producer of occasional spectacles, to die unsung and largely uncredited in 1987. He had his critics, myself included, but he worked against impossible odds purely on instinct, the first victim of a malaise which Australians are only now beginning to diagnose: that the arts need not only artists, but managers. Haag tried to manage without skills. If he failed in the end, it was the system which failed him more than he failed himself.

In 1969 Tito Gobbi returned to star only in Melbourne in Stefan Beinl's *Falstaff*. It was a distinct improvement on his earlier production using the same sets and costumes, but really no more than a vehicle for Gobbi. The public still did not take to Verdi's last opera, in spite of Carlo Felice Cillario's admirable musical direction. As it happened, it was a subdued Gobbi who returned — perhaps his tax worries affected his performance. Even so, Ronald Maconaghie's assumption of the title rôle in Sydney was not in the same class and the rest of the singers did not distinguish themselves greatly. Pringle was a fine Ford and Elizabeth (formerly Betty) Fretwell returned to sing Alice. The usual lack of mezzos resulted in the promotion of chorister Diane Holmes to principal status; her Mistress Page was acceptable, if on the light side. Justine Rettick's Quickly showed the onset of a decline only too rapid, a great pity in view of the excellent work she had done over the years. Only the young lovers, Robert Gard and Janice Taylor, were in top form, but youth does not a *Falstaff* make.

The most remarkable event of this production was the sudden appearance of veteran Adelio Zagonara, a 152 cm Bardolph to the 198 cm Pistol of Donald Shanks. Zagonara, in his sixties, brought out of retirement in Australia, proved to be a joy and his clowning at no time interfered with proper reverence for the music which his voice encompassed with surprising ease.

Anticipating the Sydney Opera House.
The famous theatre, ten years a-building already, had to be ready soon. In 1969 the Trust produced Verdi's *A Masked* *Ball*, the first production designed to fit the stage of the Opera House. (Oscar, Glenys Fowles, bends over the dying Gustav, Donald Smith, while Rosemary Gordon looks on.)

Zagonara was one of the great *comprimarii* of all time. Though bit parts were his lot because of his diminutive size, he belonged to the old tradition and he added immensely to the production.

The new *Masked Ball*, again led by principal-conductor Cillario, was a roaring success, though it was based solidly on local singers and not on any imported star. Money was beginning to come in from sources other than the public; $193 000 from the new Australian Council for the Arts and $175 000 from various other subsidies. A *Masked Ball* was the first production designed for the new Sydney Opera House stage, the dimensions of which were now known, though the completion date was still in the dim future. It was indeed a splendid affair and one worthy of any opera company. Desmond Digby's designs were brilliant and so was their execution.

(They were commissioned by the Australian Elizabethan Theatre Trust's Ladies Committee, one of the earliest examples of such sponsorship in Australia. Until then we had completely missed out on one of the main-stays of overseas opera companies, obtaining private donations for productions, or parts of productions.) The producer was Tom Brown, another ex-executive of the company and he made a thoroughly professional job of it in a traditional manner which was welcomed by the public with open arms.

Donald Smith was the undoubted star as the ill-fated King of Sweden, or Governor of Boston, as Verdi had it. Smith was by now at the very peak of his form and that was truly international in quality. He moved easily and with assurance, overcoming a far-from-romantic presence with considerable dignity, completely in keeping with the character of the unfortunate monarch. His queen was Rosemary Gordon at her not-inconsiderable best and Robert Allman rejoined the company on a permanent basis, making his debut as a strong, if rough, Anckerstrom-cum-Renato. An unexpected hit came from Glenys Fowles, a young Western Australian soprano making her debut as the transvestite page, Oscar. Fowles was to become a star very quickly and perhaps too readily left us for greater glories abroad, though credit must be given that she returned, when possible, to the company that helped her to make the grade so quickly. Casting from strength to make maximum impact, the initial production had no less than Neil Warren-Smith and Donald Shanks as the two conspirators, surely the best singers the parts have ever had anywhere in the world!

For all the money which suddenly appeared to be available, the 1969 repertoire was not really so very lavish. The revival of *Boris Godounov* was indeed welcome, specially since the scenery had quietly been replaced with a new set by Friedrich Bliem, and what a difference it made! Warren-Smith was better than ever, as was his partner, Donald Shanks as Pimen. The rest was much as before, the Polish Scene still being the weakest in spite of a change of protagonists. Marina and Dimitri liked Fretwell and Byers no better than they did Raisbeck and Baigildin in 1966. Harry Miller, who had departed along with Stefan Haag, had built an entirely new audience and, with the new scenery, they found *Boris* an imposing spectacle indeed. The chorus, under its newly-acquired chorus master, Geoffrey Arnold (imported from England at the same time as resident conductor William Reid), carried all before it. The planning did not seem to be good, but it worked, and that, after all, is all that matters.

The other two new productions of 1969 are less happily remembered. There was still that tendency to unearth the esoteric. Every year there were rumours of Menotti's *The Saint of Bleecker Street* or Pizetti's *Murder in the Cathedral*. Happily these came to nothing. (Asked the reason for planning such a dismally unsuccessful work as the former at one point, John Young replied that it contained an excellent role for Nicola Filacuridi, a tenor who happened to be available. Designs were actually prepared before better sense prevailed! Menotti as a vehicle for a tenor is unheard of, even in Australia.)

The choice of Wolf-Ferrari's *School for Fathers* seemed almost as contrary, except that the work is a nice enough lark, a modern Donizetti-cum-Rossini bit of pottiness. It is tuneful and everlastingly cheerful and few would have been offended by its inclusion in the repertoire, though it could be, and was, argued that the money spent on Beinl's production could have been better used elsewhere. Perhaps so, but Bliem and Digby produced pleasant sets

and costumes, William Reid made the most of the music and the resident singers sang well – unfortunately swallowing the fine Dent translation so that hardly a word could be understood. The heroes musically, and villains philologically, were led by Donald Shanks, Maureen Howard and the two Gordons, Rosemary and Robin. (The last-named being a notable exception as far as the bad diction went.)

And then there was *Madame Butterfly*, a long way from the kind of production seen in 1960. This time the Japanese opera from the pen of Puccini was going to be authentic; it was designed by one Yoshi Tosa, produced by one Yoshie Fujiwara assisted by one Hidetaka Kiyomya, and in Sydney Cio-Cio San was sung by one Michiko Sunahara, Japanese one and all. It was authentic Japanese all right, down to the standards prevailing in opera in Japan, which were bright, clean and decidedly old-fashioned, no matter how authentic Butterfly's ugly wedding hat may have been. Fujiwara had not up to that time set any operatic world on fire and he did not do so here. There was more justification for liking the new Butterfly than the old one and it lost no audiences for the company, but it was hardly a world-beater. David Parker made a good company debut as Pinkerton. Outside Sydney Maureen Howard took over from the vocally-indifferent Japanese leading lady, only to prove again that Puccini is too heavy for her voice. Cillario in the pit at least assured everyone that Nagasaki was not worthy of the fate which befell it thirty-five years after Butterfly's act of hara-kiri.

The retitling of the company as The Australian Opera was announced during 1969 and at the end of the season John Young presided over its inauguration – two weeks before being given the sack by the newly-independent body's chairman of directors, Claude Alcorso. An official announcement that Young had become the director of orchestras for the Trust was actually made before he was asked to accept it. Young, not unnaturally, took offence and resigned on the spot. Whether it was time for him to go or not, it was one of the less glorious moments in the history of the company. Young had been a popular administrator, too popular perhaps in that he was too ready to make promises he could not always fulfil. The fact remains that he took over an abysmal failure and he left a healthy singing infant. For that alone the company should have thanked him. His place was taken by the duo which had run the

Trust after the departure of Stefan Haag. Stephen Hall became administrator and Donald McDonald director of finance and, later, general manager of the new Australian Opera. The reign of Hall was not to be entirely smooth, and in the case of McDonald it was also to be short.

Stephen Hall is the model of a self-made man. In America he would no doubt have made his financial as well as artistic fortune, if given the opportunities he was in Australia. To him belongs the credit of bringing the Australian Opera to full maturity, ready to move into the Sydney Opera House, and it was during his reign that overseas magazines began to take note of the company's activities as a valid contribution to the international scene. It is not easy to see why he failed to hold his position, unless it be the fact that Hall overestimated his capacity for work and tried to do too many things at once.

Like his predecessors, he learnt on the job, starting with six years in London during which he turned from his early acting career to stage management, including a spell at Covent Garden. He returned in 1965 to act in the same capacity for the New Zealand production of Gershwin's *Porgy and Bess* when it toured Australia. It was an enormous success, the huge Maori cast led by the late Inia Te Wiata as Porgy convincingly replacing the usual Negro cast. Hall's management of the complex production impressed the Trust and Hall became the assistant of Stefan Haag, whom he was ultimately to replace.

The appointment was made just before Christmas 1966 at a time when planning for the next year was well under way and while John Young happened to be away ill. As a result Hall was catapulted into becoming acting administrator of the opera company at a time when it was just beginning its upward climb. The first Elizabethan Trust Orchestra was being formed to cater for both the opera and ballet companies and John Young's plans for grand operas like *Trovatore* and *Boris Godounov* were being implemented. And the need for someone like Hall was great.

In line with the practice established over the years, the new member of the administration immediately began to double as a producer of opera and Stephen Hall's first-up effort (*Turandot*) certainly made people sit up. Futhermore, his contacts overseas were a great deal of help in assembling Young's fast-increasing staff. Moffatt Oxenbould, then a stage manager at Sadlers

Wells, returned, and Douglas Abbot, company manager for the London Festival Ballet, arrived. Hall, as a key man in the Trust, certainly helped John Young to build the opera company and in due course he transferred from the Trust administration to become 'co-ordinator' for the opera company under Young.

Stefan Haag was the architect of the opera company who failed to realize his ambitions through inexperience; he could be said to be the Utzon of the venture. John Young pulled the baby out of the fire for Haag and put it firmly on its two feet. Stephen Hall acted as graduating professor, bringing it to the point of professionalism. All three had one thing in common, they learnt their trade as they went along and were found wanting in the end by people who were not exactly the greatest professionals themselves.

From 1970, Hall, McDonald and the new chairman of the board, Claude Alcorso, ruled the new Australian Opera between them. During the next years, first McDonald and then Hall departed in Young's footsteps and finally an imported general manager, John Winther, was engaged for the rapidly growing company. Regardless of the rights and the wrongs of the administrative juggles, Stephen Hall oversaw the artistic growth of the company from 1970 to 1973 and he cannot be denied the credit for the quality of production offered to the public, whatever may have been going wrong behind the scenes.

Negotiations recommenced for the services of Edward Downes and this time they did not fall through; he was to succeed Carlo Felice Cillario in 1972. Resident producers and resident designers became the norm and gradually the Australian Opera changed from a part-time company working six to seven months of the year to something resembling the permanent companies of Europe, though touring still remained the major activity. Though Sydney remained its home, it was financed federally and, theoretically at least, it was obliged to service at least the capital cities. The problems of moving major productions over the huge distances separating theatres big enough to accommodate them have not been solved to this day, and 'country tours' fell by the wayside as soon as the demand for opera in major cities exceeded the available time, services, staff and singers. And that was closer than would have been believed at that time.

As late as 1972 the Australian Opera's Sydney season

totalled no more than three months, apart from a short season of *The Merry Widow*. This last was an attempt to vary John Young's original plan to close the gaps between seasons in 1969 and again in 1971 by presenting Gilbert and Sullivan operas using most of the company's principals and chorus. It worked too, although it might have been wise to drop the idea of having Stephen Hall produce all the operas after he was appointed administrator of the company. Not that there was anything wrong with his productions which succeeded only too well through a freshness in presentation that was a delightful change from fossilized tradition. But they took up much time which Hall needed for more important administrative matters. It may be argued that Hall's ultimate departure from the scene was due to his ego-tripping as a producer instead of concentrating full-time on what is most certainly a full-time job — managing a large opera company.

Gilbert and Sullivan productions form a permanent part of the repertoire of the English National Opera at the Coliseum in London. The Australian Opera presented them as separate seasons, hoping to catch new audiences for grand opera. The misleading 1969/1970 attendance figures of 451 363, (covering eighteen months against all previous twelve-monthly figures) indicate an enormous rise over 1968, and a large part of this was due to the addition of the four G. & S. operas presented. Three, *HMS Pinafore*, *Iolanthe* and *The Pirates of Penzance*, were built round a local discovery, Dennis Olsen, a prominent actor at the time under contract to John Sumner's Melbourne Theatre Company. He had wanted to play those rôles all his life. Hall must be given the credit for ideal casting, but Olsen did the work and proved his worth a thousand-fold. Good as Ronald Maconaghie is as a singer and artist, the comparative failure of *The Yeomen of the Guard*, in which he played Jack Point, only served to prove the essential need for Olsen to hold the productions together. Two years later *The Mikado* and *The Gondoliers* were added to the repertoire and once again the success was immense, in this case abetted by Tom Lingwood's superb designs.

The balance of the casting of the Sullivan operas and their universally fine designs by Quentin Hole, Friedrich Bliem and Vicki Feitscher made Hall's productions an automatic success wherever they played. The company had a lot of natural talent and voices unspoilt by experience in the J. C. Williamson Theatres' G & S seasons

The man who brought G & S back into fashion.
The Savoy operas have never lost their popular appeal, but Stephen Hall's productions between 1968 and 1972 gave them a gigantic boost, thanks largely to the inspired antics of Dennis Olsen. (In *The Pirates of Penzance*.)

which (as in England) were more concerned with tradition than excellence; a perfect example of Mahler's dictum that 'tradition is sloppiness'. Robert Gard, Janice Taylor, John Pringle, Glenys Fowles, Maureen Howard, Alan Light and Neil Warren-Smith offered both youth and experience to bring enjoyment to their audiences.

The accent on productions of quality became even more obvious from 1970 onwards, for the importation of producers began in that year. But for the misconceived Japanese *Madame Butterfly* of the previous year, there had not been a professional imported producer since the inaugural year of 1956. The company had not perhaps gone back to the good (?) old days when singers invented their own movements, but producers had been recruited at the cheapest possible price, more often than not from the ranks of the resident staff, which meant that they came cheaply indeed, usually free! Four of 1970's five productions were staged by overseas producers and if only one of them proved to be a major acquisition in the long run, all improved substantially on their predecessors. It is not clear whether it was the producers' professionalism or intuition on Stephen Hall's part that caused fine collaboration with designers as well, but the end results spoke for themselves, though the most lasting example was governed by fate.

Stephan Beinl's sudden death caused the importation

of John Copley to stage the new *Fidelio* on which Beinl had worked with designer Allan Lees. Copley in England was forced to accept his work, if not unseen, at least without being able to influence it, as he would have wished to. Copley is one of the world's great producers and Australia has been fortunate in obtaining his services repeatedly since that first *Fidelio*. The results he has produced have been world-class, as is to be expected from an overseas producer. No doubt Hall, by allowing Lees a generous budget, had a share in making the immense sets a success, but it needs a producer and a conductor to direct a first-class cast in even the best sets to make Beethoven's imperfect opera a success. Copley and Warwick Braithwaite met the requirements, though Braithwaite, already mortally ill, did not equal Copley's *tour de force*. Rosemary Gordon, singing and speaking in her native German with complete authority, looked and acted Leonora to a tee, while Alan Light was a superbly villainous Pizarro, the peak of a long and remarkably well-balanced career.

An even more astonishing case of mind over matter occurred with the new staging of *La Bohème*. This stand-by of all run-of-the-mill opera companies was produced by an Italian, Renzo Frusca. Designs were by Tom Lingwood who, like Copley, was to have a long association with the company, proving himself a great asset. Frusca was little more than a hack, certainly basically no better than the kind of producer Australia had had until then. The cast he was given was deliberately low-key; this was to be a 'young' *Bohème*, a small *Bohème*; the company could not afford the stars to give Puccini his full due, could not even equal local casts of years gone by, when singers like Albert Lance or Marie Collier could ring the rafters. They therefore threw everything behind the designer (as in *Fidelio*) and the producer. Why Frusca was inspired to produce something quite so extraordinary will always remain a mystery; his following productions certainly showed no great genius at work. (What is an even greater mystery is why Stephen Hall three years later chose to 'recreate' the production, deliberately destroying the delicate texture of Frusca's original.)

The *Bohème* of 1970 must remain a milestone in the company's history and, happily, Tom Lingwood's designs remain the same to this day, saving at least the visual charms of the original. John Serge (Sydney-born, but then Italy-based), Glenys Fowles, Ronald Maconaghie,

They wanted to set the world on fire, and did! Umberto Borsò, Rosemary Gordon and John Shaw generated sparks of enthusiasm during their performance of *Otello* on the night of 30 July 1970. By the following morning Her Majesty's Theatre, Sydney, and most of the season's productions were just that, sparks among the ashes of the burnt-out building.

Robert Eddie, Donald Shanks and Maureen Howard led the cast. Later alternatives, Anson Austin and John Pringle, as Rodolfo and Marcello, also fitted the picture of the young, under-voiced, but most authentic bohemians. It was indeed a memorable production, one which has survived some brutal mutilations, which were at least in part corrected by David Neal for the 1976 performances presented as a vehicle for New Zealand soprano Kiri Te Kanawa to make her Australian debut, after conquering the world's stages.

In the backwash of Tito Gobbi's difficulties in getting his fees out of Australia, the company acquired a resident producer in the person of Bernd Benthaak from Hamburg. Gobbi was supposed to produce Verdi's *Otello* and to sing Iago in 1970. He had chosen his own Otello, Umberto Borsò, an Italian with an Australian wife. He had been immensely successful here during the 1955 Williamson Opera Season, when he was at the beginning of his career. Suddenly Stephen Hall was faced with an Otello without an Iago, and the need to find a new producer. Ronald Dowd, a fine Otello in his own right, suggested Bernd Benthaak and Hall engaged him on the spot, not just for *Otello*, but as resident producer. John Shaw was talked into returning to Australia to play Iago and Douglas Smith produced some bold, if not exactly inspired, designs.

Otello was a success because, like *Bohème*, it was prepared and conducted by Carlo Felice Cillario, the company's musical director. It is hard to go wrong with Verdi's masterpiece if you have the right conductor and the right singers. While Borsò was no Martinelli, he had an excellent voice and was no mean actor. Similarly Shaw was vocally and physically imposing as Iago. The problem was that Borsò and Gobbi would have been matched much better vocally as well as physically. Shaw's towering figure dwarfed Borsò and the drama suffered accordingly. Rosemary Gordon was a most touching Desdemona.

While the production did not set the world on fire, it did manage to leave more than a spark of interest in Sydney's Her Majesty's Theatre, which burnt down during the night following the performance on 30 July 1970, destroying the sets and costumes for all of the season's productions except *Fidelio*. With eight of the season's performances still to go, all completely sold out on subscription, alternative arrangements had to be made in a hurry. Not only were subscribers not disappointed, though they saw only concert versions for their money, but the presentations in the huge Capitol Theatre were so successful that the last night of Verdi's *The Force of Destiny* was attended by an extra 1400 casual opera-goers, doubling the capacity of the burnt theatre.

The success of that concert *Force of Destiny* was somewhat surprising, since the original production had been the one weak link of the season. Produced in a pedestrian manner by Frusca in sets hardly worthy of Tom Lingwood's usual standards, it featured an imported guest 'star' as inept as any which the company had ever had. The reasons why Franca Como was considered worthy of being imported from Italy are obscure. Her only noteworthy appearance on the international scene since then occurred at the opening of the San Carlo in Naples in 1972 when she took over the part of Turandot from Amy Shuard in the last act, whereupon the artistic director of the theatre resigned because the company held him responsible 'for what was happening'. Any success in *The Force of Destiny* belonged to Cillario and to Donald Smith, who was simply superb in one of Verdi's most difficult roles. Robert Allman was the strong Carlo, a role which was later sung by John Pringle, who was highly praised, but wisely retired to lighter rôles in later years; the kind of controlled belting this rôle demands would not have done his excellent voice much good in the long run.

The rakes failed to progress.
Stravinsky's *The Rake's Progress* did not take advantage of the new liberalism of 1972; Hogarth's explicit orgy took place with every trouser button firmly in place. The ladies were less fastidious.

The last opera of the year was the usual experiment considered so necessary to the public's 'education' at the time, Stravinsky's *The Rake's Progress*. Beautifully designed by Francesca Crespi (her first designs for the theatre) after Hogarth's original engravings, this was notable mainly for the fine work of Robert Gard (the Rake), John Pringle (Nick Shadow) and Janice Taylor (Anne). John Tasker's production suffered inhibitions for which he is not usually noted; the realistic orgy scene featured simulated sex scenes in which the gentlemen kept their trousers not only on, but carefully buttoned up!

The years leading up to the opening of the Sydney Opera House were artistically the most productive of the company and the public response was suitably enthusiastic. The imbalance created by seasons aimed at recruiting audiences for the new Sydney venue's opening left other states complaining that New South Wales was being favoured, and so it was. It was an inevitable pattern dictated by history and Australia would not have the place in the annals of opera that it has today if Hall and his very active Chairman, Claude Alcorso, had not proceeded as they did.

Listing the operas of recent years in detail would produce a book on its own. I have devoted most space to the years during which records were not kept by the many companies which have risen and, too often, fallen over the years. That the Australian Opera is and will remain the main trunk of our operatic family tree must be accepted by everybody now. It has had its ups and downs and the very nature of the beast will ensure that its future will not be smooth sailing. This book will necessarily be a step toward completing a picture which can have no completion. It will, however, be read (I hope) by people who are at least familiar with the Australian Opera and some of the more recent companies. Not only that, but careful records are being kept now of precisely what the national companies have done and will do. The need for a detailed history becomes less urgent as we talk about the immediate past. Let me thus assume that much of what occurred in the 1970s and 1980s will still be fresh in the minds of most readers. Others will one day fill the gaps I may leave. One man's evaluation of recent events must necessarily be biased and I do not apologise for that.

What I would describe as the opera explosion began in 1971 when the Australian Opera staged no less than ten operas, of which only three were revivals. (I do not count the *Otello* which was rebuilt after the previous year's fire and staged only in cities which had not previously seen it.) *Bohème, Turandot* and *A Masked Ball* were restaged, some with the assistance of other than their original producers, but almost entirely with similar casts as before. The fact that the public flocked to hear the same again, reflects the enjoyment it received from them. The exception was Amy Shuard, a great international Turandot, who shared the performances with Morag Beaton. (Shuard died tragically young in 1975.)

The great success of 1971 was John Copley's first production which he completely planned and executed for the company (with sets by Henry Bardon and costumes by Michael Stennett), Mozart's *The Marriage of Figaro*. This, more than anything that had been seen during the past fifteen years, pointed up the immense changes which had taken place since the first Trust Opera season. The first *Figaro*, which started the ball rolling in 1956, belonged to a different era, good as it was at the time. Copley showed Australia what opera in the 1970s was really about. Realism without excess, characters able to survive as dramatic entities regardless of the music and, finally, complete integration of what was happening on stage with the music itself. The *Bohème* of 1970 could have been a fortunate accident, the *Figaro* of 1971 was planned excellence, which worked exactly as its creators intended. This production has been the yardstick by which all subsequent productions have been judged and it is to the immense credit of Stephen Hall that so many in the following years equalled its success, though none surpassed it.

The singers in *The Marriage of Figaro* entered the spirit of Copley and Mozart most admirably and the decision to revert to English to point up the comedy worked, since Copley managed to obtain a much greater clarity of diction from Ronald Maconaghie, John Pringle, Rosemary Gordon, Glenys Fowles and the rest, than others had done before him. Copley also staged a fine *Rigoletto* which the public loved, and some critics hated for its realistic court orgy in Act 1.

Nabucco by Verdi was an unknown quantity in Australia, but Verdi's first great success has the needed tunes to appeal to the masses and the production by Renzo Frusca with Tom Lingwood's designs was spectacular indeed, though the Sydney opening was almost ruined by the indisposition of the apparently indestructible Donald Shanks who, after years of rock-like steadiness,

Shrink-proof splendour.
Tom Lingwood's designs for *Nabucco* were first seen in the Elizabethan Theatre in Newtown in 1972. They have proved to be just as effective in the many huge modern theatres in which they are still being used.

Wrestling with a musical conscience.
Director John Copley has done more than anyone to raise production standards in Australia. Yet in his first year (1971), he was violently attacked for introducing wrestling as a spectator sport at the sixteenth-century court at Mantua in *Rigoletto*.

The first $100 000 production.
There were protests when the cost of Tom Lingwood's sets for Australia's first *Der Rosenkavalier* was revealed in 1972. Yet spectacles like this have paid for themselves many times over by inspiring singers and audiences alike. (Yvonne Minton as Octavian and Glenys Fowles as Sophie.)

succumbed to laryngitis. No understudy was available and Shanks went on, miming the important role of Zaccaria, while a chorister sight-read the music in the pit! The inability to provide an alternative singer was greatly and justly criticized, but the occurrence is not unusual even in more important houses. Elizabeth Vaughan, a rather prim and un-evil English soprano, was imported for the key role of Abigaille and acquitted herself well vocally, if not dramatically. Robert Allman was a fine Nabucco.

Apart from two successors to the Gilbert and Sullivan series, *The Gondoliers* (excellent) and *The Mikado* (not quite up to scratch), the balance of the new productions paled into insignificance next to the high standards now being set by the company. A new *Faust* produced by Bernd Benthaak was mediocre, except for the most promising debut of Joan Carden as Marguerite and Shank's larger-than-life Mephisto. Reginald Byers continued to improve as Faust, but the whole thing did not jell. Moffatt Oxenbould's debut as a producer for Benjamin Britten's *The Rape of Lucretia* was even less successful, in spite of Lauris Elms' Lucretia and Pringle's excellent Tarquinius. It was an economy package and showed it, but presumably was intended to mollify the artier elements in the Australia Council, which was by now pouring hundreds of thousands a year into the company's coffers. The revival of *Otello* was as good or as bad as the burnt original had been; good enough to show what Verdi intended, bad enough to prove that it needs either a better producer than Benthaak or world-class singers to make up for his deficiencies.

There were immense cries of outrage when it was revealed in 1972 that $100 000 had been spent on a new production of Richard Strauss' *Der Rosenkavalier*. It seemed an astronomical figure at the time, but the end result more than justified this apparent extravagance to launch the company's new musical director, Edward Downes. *Der Rosenkavalier* was to producer Benthaak what *Bohème* had been to Frusca, one great achievement from an average craftsman and, like Frusca, he was backed by the superlative designs of Tom Lingwood, which really looked $100 000 − or more. With Downes conducting a specially-enlarged Trust Orchestra in each state, the effect of this *Rosenkavalier* − its first performance in Australia! − was simply stunning. Copley's *Figaro* may have been just as good, but here was spectacle as well as a brilliant result of operatic team-work.

Much of the effect was due to the cast, only one of whom was imported! Neil Warren-Smith's Baron Ochs was as good as any to be seen overseas. Yvonne Minton, an Australian who had achieved international acceptance, returned to repeat the Octavian she had already recorded for Decca three years earlier. Minton was probably the best imported artist the Australian Opera has ever had in this context, Sutherland not excepted. Rosemary Gordon was a beautiful Marschallin. Glenys Fowles completed the top cast with a Sophie so good that it foreshadowed her quick departure overseas. It was a quartet worthy of being heard anywhere in the world.

A new staging of *Cavalleria rusticana* and *Pagliacci* was the only other novelty in a year devoted to preparing for the big event of 1973 − the opening of the Sydney Opera House. Produced by Stephen Hall, both operas were sturdy, standard productions which served their purpose well. Donald Smith and Umberto Borsò alternated in the leads of the two operas and Suzanne Steele, recruited from the operetta stage, proved that she could make a strong point in opera when she sang Santuzza. Maureen Howard was equally good as Nedda in *Pagliacci* and Robert Allman was a fine Tonio. Revivals of *Figaro*, *Bohème*, *Fidelio* and *The Force of Destiny* completed the season.

Talent underused.
The late Suzanne Steele was Australia's operetta superstar, but largely ignored by the Australian Opera, though she proved her worth when singing in company with other singers with small voices. She will be remembered with affection by more people than most of her fellow singers. (In *Cavalleria rusticana*, 1972.)

In the meantime, palace revolutions continued to make headlines. Stephen Hall had, on succeeding John Young in 1969, promoted his young financial wizard. Donald McDonald, to general manager. The curious billing at the time always listed Hall first, Downes (as musical director) second and McDonald last; a strange position for anyone with the title general manager. McDonald became the most popular key person in the administration, but this did not stop the management from accepting his resignation in 1972, when it was offered for reasons which appeared dubious then and appear dubious now. It was a traumatic experience for the company and brought credit to nobody. McDonald quickly moved to Musica Viva and then to the Sydney Theatre Company, proving his abilities as general manager beyond question. In time (1987) the Australian Opera was to beg him to resume his position with more authority than it gave him originally. In the meantime Chairman Alcorso personally took over McDonald's work, pending the appointment of a new 'general manager'. The position was advertised internationally and finally filled by (echoes of Joern Utzon, if only in terms of nationality) another Dane, John Winther. Winther's idea of what constitutes a general manager were more in line with the generally understood interpretation of the title, not the third-in-line which had been accepted by the inexperienced McDonald. The acceptance of Winther meant the ultimate departure not only of Stephen Hall, but also of Claude Alcorso. But those two gentlemen still had their hands full to launch the first season at the Sydney Opera House and, whatever John Winther's organizational work, the glory of that opening season belongs first to Hall and second to Alcorso.

The Sydney Opera House finally opened on 28 September 1973 with a new production of Prokofiev's *War and Peace*. The bridge from the preceding year had been a dreadful *Merry Widow*, capitalizing cheaply on the presence of Suzanne Steele in the company, and a Melbourne season which included a new production of Puccini's three-opera evening, the *Trittico*. But the big news was *War and Peace* and how the Opera House could cope with such a production. The American Sam Wanamaker was imported to produce, Tom Lingwood designed and Edward Downes not only conducted, but provided the English translation. It was a venture almost too large in conception, but it succeeded brilliantly.

War and Peace.
No more apt title can describe the process of building the Sydney Opera House, which opened with Prokofiev's opera for no better reason than that it was ostensibly too big for the cramped facilities of the new theatre. Its problems were solved ingeniously, but it is unlikely that it will ever be seen there again. (Neil Warren-Smith as Marshall Kutuzov.)

Unfortunately the work itself is hardly world-shattering and it seems unlikely that it will ever be revived. To show off the new building it was, however, an ideal choice.

The stage of the Opera Theatre is a curious thing, duplicated nowhere else in the world, having been designed to obtain maximum acting area in a space not only limited, but shaped by the strange roof shell which surmounts it. Wanamaker used the enormous revolving stage to create, quite literally, a round production which, unlike the conventional theatre-in-the-round, had an audience fronting one third of the circle only, instead of surrounding it. The enormous crowds, demanded by Prokofiev and provided by the Australian Opera, entered and exited in circles converging toward the back. The whole thing was stylized to a degree and the twelve scenes followed each other without a single curtain or blackout, an effect similar to what is known as *montage* in films. The star of the show here, as before and again in following years, was Tom Lingwood and his scenic designs, which worked so well, though they aroused comparatively little comment, because the building itself inevitably overshadowed the spectacle of the production.

Nevertheless, what took place on the stage of the Opera Theatre in *War and Peace* is unlikely to be repeated there, because the company (meaning Lingwood) in 1975 found ways of using the Concert Hall for truly grand opera, which is what *War and Peace* is in effect. Downes and the orchestra outdid themselves, naturally enough, though few in the audience had a great deal of time for what they were playing. The enormous cast was dominated by Neil Warren-Smith as Field Marshall Kutuzov. While Warren-Smith never ceased to amaze, his Boris should have prepared audiences for his performance. The leading lady, Natasha, was, surprisingly

WAR AND PEACE

Opera in 12 Scenes by Sergei Prokofiev
(by arrangement with Boosey & Hawkes Music Publishers Ltd.)

Libretto: Sergei Prokofiev and Myra Mendelssohn-Prokofieva after the novel by Leo Tolstoy
English text: Edward Downes

Conductor: Edward Downes; Producer: Sam Wanamaker; Designer: Tom Lingwood; Lighting Design: Robert Ornbo

Choreographer: Boris Romanoff; Production Assistant: Warner Whiteford; Stage Manager: Freda Chapple

THE ELIZABETHAN TRUST SYDNEY ORCHESTRA
Concertmaster: Robert Ingram

THE AUSTRALIAN OPERA CHORUS
Chorusmaster: Geoffrey Arnold

Characters in order of appearance:

Prince Andrei Bolkonsky	*Tom McDonnell*	Tikhon Shcherbaty	*John Durham*
Countess Natasha Rostova	*Eilene Hannan*	1st German General	*John Germain*
Sonya	*Jennifer Bermingham*	2nd German General	*Robert Simmons*
An elderly nobleman, the host	*John Germain*	An orderly from Prince Andrei's regiment	*Lamberto Furlan*
Footman	*Trevor Brown*	Field Marshall Michael Ilarionovich Kutuzov	*Neil Warren-Smith*
Count Ilya Rostov	*Grant Dickson*	Aide de Camp to Kutuzov	*Trevor Brown*
Maria Dmitryevna Akhrossimova	*Rosina Raisbeck*	1st Staff Officer	*Graeme Ewer*
Madame Peronskaya	*Mary Hayman*	2nd Staff Officer	*John Germain*
Countess Hélène Bezukhova	*Suzanne Steele*	Napoleon	*Raymond Myers*
Count Pierre Bezukhov	*Ronald Dowd*	Aide de Camp to General Compans	*Anson Austin*
Prince Anatole Kuragin	*Robert Gard*	Aide de Camp to Murat	*Virginia Lloyd-Owen*
Dolokhov	*John Shaw*	Marshall Berthier	*Alan Light*
Chambermaid — Servants to	*Dolores Cambridge*	Marshall Caulincourt	*Gregory Marinos*
Old footman — Prince Nicholas	*John McKenna*	Monsieur de Beausset	*Robert Gard*
Valet — Bolkonsky	*Donald Solomon*	General Belliard	*Robert Simmons*
Princess Marie Bolkonskaya	*Elizabeth Connell*	Aide de Camp to Prince Eugene	*Ian Campbell*
Old Prince Nicholas Bolkonsky	*Alan Light*	Aide de Camp to Napoleon	*Wallace Carroll*
Balaga, Dolokhov's coachman	*Joseph Grunfelder*	General Barclay de Tolly	*Graeme Ewer*
Joseph, Dolokhov's footman	*Gregory Marinos*	General Bennigsen	*John Germain*
Matryosha, a gypsy girl	*Jacqueline Kensett-Smith*	General Rayevsky	*Robert Eddie*
Dunyasha, young maid to the Rostov family	*Beryl Furlan*	General Yermolov	*Joseph Grunfelder*
Gavrila, footman to Akhrossimova	*John Durham*	General Konovnitsyn	*William Bamford*
Denisov	*Ronald Maconaghie*	Chorus leader	*John Durham*
Fyodor	*Barry Culhane*		

There will be one interval of approximately 30 minutes after Scene 6.

First Performance (first 8 scenes only): June 12, 1946—Maly Theatre, Leningrad. First complete performance (in Italian): Florence Maggic Musicale, 1953.
First complete performance in Russia: Bolshoi Theatre, Moscow, 1959. First performance by The Australian Opera: Sydney Opera House, September 28, 1973.
The Australian Opera is indebted to Benson and Hedges for its sponsorship of War and Peace. It gratefully acknowledges this as a major contribution to the development of opera in Australia.

They sang at the opening!
The cast list of *War and Peace* at the opening of the Sydney Opera House 28 September 1973 shows what an immense undertaking it was to stage this huge work in the confines of this monumental sculpture. The impossible interior makes every production a major headache.

enough, the most recent graduate of the company's soprano ranks, Eilene Hannan. She acquitted herself more than well and continued to justify the faith placed in her in the years which followed. Practically the whole of the company made up the rest of the forty-seven roles with individual lines to sing.

Since statistics are the most impressive thing about *War and Peace*, this may be the moment to produce a roll-call of the company which only seven years earlier had consisted of two singers and a staff of three. In September 1973 the Australian Opera consisted of fifty principals, fifty chorus, twenty-nine administrative staff, twenty-five production staff, plus Winther, Downes and Hall (in that order) and a Board of Directors of twenty-two. The Elizabethan Trust Sydney Orchestra had seventy members, not all of whom could fit into the tiny orchestra pit of the Sydney Opera House at the same time. A grand total of 246 people being gainfully employed by one Australian opera company!

Stephen Hall's plans for the rest of that first season included a fair proportion of successes in line with recent standards, but also one major dud which, unfortunately, followed the opening attraction. Apart from its novelty value, it was hardly a notable event. Bernd Benthaak's *Tannhäuser* in its initial staging was something of a *fiasco de scandale*. Musically just acceptable (only Downes' conducting was up to scratch), the idea of replacing the ballet Wagner unwillingly added for the Venusberg with colour slides of the intimate female anatomy was unerotic and totally boring. The rest of Ralph Koltai's sets looked nice, but his costumes left a lot to be desired. To top the lot, Hall had imported a Finnish tenor of total mediocrity, never heard of again, to sing the title role, Rosemary Gordon looked fine, but found Elisabeth's music a little rich, expatriate Australian Tom McDonnell was a rough Wolfram and only Elizabeth Connell's Venus, made up to look hideous instead of seductive, sang brilliantly. Matters improved musically later when Ronald Dowd sang Tannhäuser to Nance Grant's Elisabeth. Dowd proved in a long series of performances that he could outsing the imported tenor by a mile. He later proved to be one of the most consistently good performers the company has ever had.

On the credit side, John Copley equalled his *Figaro* success with a magnificent *Magic Flute* using just his resident singers (Maconaghie, Carden, Austin, Shanks, etc.) and John Stoddart's sets worked magnificently in the Opera House with all its lifts, if not so well on tour in other states. The *Trittico* produced by Moffatt Oxenbould in Melbourne was on a level with Hall's *Cav. and Pag.* routine Italian opera, handsomely mounted and well sung. Donald Smith and Elizabeth Fretwell appeared in *Il Tabarro*, Nance Grant in *Suor Angelica* and Raymond Myers sang the title role in *Gianni Schicchi*. Rosina Raisbeck brilliantly appeared in all three works.

The Australian opera which had been commissioned from Peter Sculthorpe for the opening of the Sydney Opera House did not materialize until 1974. His *Rites of Passage* and two of the seven one-act operas commissioned by the Australian Opera two years earlier from other Australian composers — Werder's *The Affair* and Sitsky's *Lenz* — were performed in the same year. Sculthorpe's *Rites* was really a ballet-cum-chorus oratorio. It had no soloists and used dancers of the Australian Dance Theatre from Adelaide under the direction of Jaap Flier and Geoffrey Arnold's well-trained Australian Opera Chorus. The Werder-Sitsky double bill had its share of soloists, who could do little with the Werder opus, but Ron Stevens was an effective Lenz, a difficult tenor rôle which needed an actor with a strong voice. American-born Stevens does not have a beautiful voice, but he has plenty of power, a good presence and considerable acting ability.

By some strange magic each year had produced at least one outstanding production since the tide of the company's fortunes turned in the late sixties. The highlight of 1974 was Janáček's *Jenůfa*, another Copley triumph in which he was greatly assisted by the decor of Allan Lees. It was an outstanding event by any standards, highlighted by an astonishing performance from Elizabeth Connell, a young South African mezzo soprano, who is among the top dramatic sopranos in the world today. A complete unknown in 1973, she was sensationally successful here during her two-year stay. Her Kostelnička was a totally absorbing study of peasant maternalism and sung quite stunningly. The title rôle fitted the company's controversial new soprano, Lone Koppel-Winther, like a glove and Robert Gard and Ron Stevens completed a superb set of principals.

When it was found that John Winther, the new general manager, had a soprano wife, hackles rose very quickly. Charges of favouritism flew fast and furious, but were hard to support during her first three years with the company. Mrs Winther was a major actress with a very fine voice, lacking only in clarity of diction, a handicap she shared with Joan Sutherland! Her initial appearance in Stephen Hall's new *Tosca* in 1974 was a major event because of her, rather than Hall, whose production was no more than acceptable on the whole and in parts ludicrous. (No dawn in Act 3!) Koppel-

Bottoms up!
The *Venusberg* ballet Wagner wrote unwillingly for the Paris produuuction of *Tannhäuser* was turned into a gynaecological slide show for the 1973 production — cheaper than paying dancers and a tasteless thrill which did not survive more than one season. (Lone Koppel-Winther as Venus.)

A star was born.
Jenůfa in 1974 was not only an outstanding achievement of the Australian Opera, but the final and best achievement of young Elizabeth Connell's two-year contract with the company. (In black, she sings Kostelnička, with Koppel-Winther as Jenůfa.) Today she is a major international figure.

Winther's performance as Jenůfa should have set all minds at ease; it also was outstanding. After that she took her turn with other artists and her performances, like theirs, varied: not all were good. When she was good she was very, very good and when she was bad she was not horrid. What more could anyone ask?

One of the the more surprising results of this *Jenůfa* was the fact that it resulted in the long association of Joan Sutherland with the company. The work has no rôle for a high soprano and Richard Bonynge had no ambitions to conduct Janáček's opera. They had patriotically returned to honour her home-town's new opera house by appearing in *The Tales of Hoffmann*, just another engagement in their world-wide heavily-booked schedules. Throughout its rehearsals they saw little of the company, though they admired its professionalism. *Jenůfa* was a production which, exactly as it stood, could have held its own in any opera house in the world. For the first time the Bonynges realised that their excellent *Hoffmann* was not the outstanding exception in the repertoire of a semi-colonial operatic outpost, but a fine addition to a major company's general excellence. Like most Australians, they were under the impression that no company with a background as chequered as this one's could possibly be world-class. Standards such as those achieved in *Jenůfa* are rare even today, no matter where they may be produced. In 1974 they opened Bonynge's eyes to the fact that here was a company in a city full of old friends which could provide a regular and worthy frame for his famous wife. It was *Jenůfa*, a most unlikely vehicle, which caused the start of serious negotiations for regular appearances by Sutherland here and the ultimate appointment of Bonynge as musical director. (Ironically, some years later, when the arrangement went sour, one of the bones of contention was the suggestion that Sutherland should tackle another Janáček score, *The Makropoulos Case*. Not exactly a bright idea for someone of Sutherland's looks and age — Emilia Marty turns into a three-hundred-year-old woman in the course of the opera!)

There was a new *Barber of Seville* in 1974 produced by Glyndbourne's John Cox, small-scale in design and in singing, however good. John Pringle's Figaro and Elizabeth Connell's Rosina stood out. A new *Don Giovanni* produced by John Bell (again starring Pringle) was not as revolutionary as Jim Sharman's in 1967, but failed to please the public.

Giulietta

Olympia

Stella

Cheap at any price!
Much controversy surrounded the many performances by Dame Joan Sutherland because of her high fees. Whatever they were — $10 000 per performance in 1974 — she brought not only glory but subscribers to the company, starting with her assumption of all four heroines in *The Tales of Hoffmann*.

Antonia

Opera in the Concert Hall.
Tom Lingwood was the
genius who showed that
opera could be staged in the
larger Concert Hall of the
Sydney Opera, which was
supposed to have been its
home originally. The 1975
Aida set used the architecture
of this modern hall as part of
ancient Egypt, a remarkable
achievement not equalled
since then.

What could not fail to please anyone was the return of Joan Sutherland to Australia when she sang the four leading rôles in Offenbach's *The Tales of Hoffmann* in Sydney with Richard Bonynge conducting. The production was by the Argentinian producer-designer team of Tito Capobianco and José Varona. The budgets of productions were carefully played down after the controversy about the 1972 *Rosenkavalier*, but the cost of this *Hoffmann* must have been astronomical. And, once again, it fully justified itself. The Sydney performances with Sutherland and Henri Wilden (Hoffmann), Raymond Myers (as all three of the villains) and Graeme Ewer (in the three far-from-small minor rôles) were outstanding in every respect. Mezzo-soprano Huguette Tourangeau, who had sung in the same opera with Sutherland under Bonynge in New York at the Metropolitan earlier in the year, was brought out to play Nicklausse again. As someone who saw both productions, I can only state that the Sydney article won hands-down on every count. Later performances in other states, with Joan Carden singing exceptionally well in the

Sutherland rôles, failed to keep up the standard because the sets were not half as effective in theatres for which they were not designed and Bonynge's guidance in the pit was sorely missed. Full credit, though, to Jennifer Bermingham for taking over Nicklausse with distinction.

The Tales of Hoffmann also played its (or their) part in the success of a remarkable experiment which began in January 1975. The institution of a Summer Season in Sydney brought a completely new dimension to the activities of the Australian Opera. After many successful years of subscription seasons during the colder months in theatres which were not air-conditioned, the gamble that people would go to the Sydney Opera House in mid-summer succeeded brilliantly, not least because operas like *The Tales of Hoffmann* and *The Magic Flute* were suitable for family audiences. Not only that, but the availability of the Concert Hall of the Opera House enabled the company to experiment with a box-office opera which was too large to be staged in the Opera Theatre — Verdi's *Aida*.

Once again the credit belonged almost entirely to that

remarkable Englishman, now Australian, Tom Lingwood. Though Stephen Hall and Tom Lingwood were credited with the production of *Aida* in the Concert Hall, Lingwood was responsible for little more than the scenic designs of *Aida* and for solving the problems of staging opera in a venue which was not designed for the purpose. The difficulties the Opera Theatre presents to productions are as nothing to those Lingwood had to overcome in the Concert Hall. There was no fly tower, no proscenium, no orchestra pit, no lighting, no dressing rooms; almost nothing. On the other hand there was an immensely decorative *modern* ceiling, which could hardly be hidden, right over the proposed acting area. Lingwood cleverly incorporated the hall's own features in his designs and built a huge Egyptian Temple of incredible versatility. The effect was somewhat like staging an open-air opera in a modern Baths of Caracalla under cover, if such a thing can be imagined.

The success of the *Aida* was instantaneous and all performances in 1975 (and again in 1976) were instantly sold out. Musically, the opera was under the direction of Carlo Felice Cillario, who returned to Australia for the purpose. Donald Smith, Marilyn Richardson, John Shaw and Elizabeth Connell made a fine singing team, though the human drama in such a huge space was somewhat lost. Much to everybody's surprise, a second cast of Reginald Byers, Elizabeth Fretwell, Raymond Myers and Lauris Elms sang as well, or, in the case of Elms, even better. A somewhat tame production of the Weill-Brecht *Rise and Fall of the City of Mahagonny* completed the programme for the first Summer Season.

The other 1975 seasons in Sydney and elsewhere began to show weaknesses in repertoire, since operas suitable to local conditions were running out. The economy of the country was in recession, costs were climbing astronomically and smaller works were sought

and produced, whether resources were suitable or not. Only penny-pinching could justify the return of Stefan Haag to produce Donizetti's *L'elisir d'amore* in sets by Tim Walton, not the kind of *déjà vu* to be welcomed by more sophisticated audiences. Few will want to remember this backlash to the bad old days of the Trust.

Tito Capobianco and John Copley, not unexpectedly, did better than Haag. The former staged a spectacular *Simon Boccanegra* by Verdi, which suffered more from Verdi than the performance; it is an opera which needs superlative stars to come to life, not just a fine ensemble such as the Australian Opera provided. Robert Allman was a most impressive Doge, alternating with John Shaw. Joan Carden, Reginald Byers and Shanks, alternating with Warren-Smith, made up the rest of the cast, with Cillario in the pit. In Sydney illness struck again, necessitating the importation at a moment's notice of Joseph Rouleau to cover the part of Fiesco. A similar mishap occurred when Myers dropped out of *Rigoletto* and Peter Glossop was brought from London to sing the

Not wrestling with a musical conscience.
Opposite: The critics squawked at the supposed anachronism of wrestlers in *Rigoletto*, but found bathing belles in *Ariadne auf Naxos* quite acceptable four years later.

Pretty outdated.
Stefan Haag's *L'elisir d'amore* looks attractive here, but it was a throw-back to the bad old days of the Trust. This was 1975, not 1960! (Donald Shanks as Dulcamara.)

jester at a few days' notice. The fact that singers of this calibre were considered necessary to replace local artists is an indication of how standards in the company had risen.

Richard Strauss's *Ariadne auf Naxos* returned under Copley's direction in 1975 in a 'mod' interpretation, with John Stoddart's designs transposing it into the 1920s. It worked up to a point, though seeing the *commedia dell'arte* characters as the Marx Brothers, Rogers and Astaire and Marlene Dietrich was a bit startling. Nance Grant was a truly outstanding Ariadne, Ron Stevens a good-looking Bacchus, while Lone Koppel-Winther again proved her value as the Composer. A newcomer to the company, Rhonda Bruce sang a good Zerbinetta.

The year saw other innovations in repertoire, though the total number of performances given (194) was actually less than in previous years. Partly this was due to an increase of touring commitments, partly to various experiments which, no matter how worthy, required staff and singers to devote themselves to activities which could have been replaced with additional performances. The almost quarter-million dollar surplus of 1974 was turned into a comparatively modest loss of $22 743, an interesting figure in the light of a single line in the year's report: 'Mounting costs of productions which did not proceed, $32 581'.

Though the experimental *Aida* in the Concert Hall of the Sydney Opera House was all but sold out with 97.1 per cent paid attendances, other novelties were not as well received. Janáček's *Diary of a Man Who Vanished* was staged at the Seymour Centre in conjunction with the old Dance Company (NSW) — since revitalized as the Sydney Dance Company. This was supposed to lead to the latter company becoming the 'resident' provider of dance and/or ballet for the Australian Opera, a venture doomed to failure. The Janáček work (hardly an opera) was coupled with two Glen Tetley ballets, *Pierrot Lunaire* and *Circles*. They went well enough with the semi-abstract *Diary*, but dancers and choreographers specializing in Schoenberg and Berio were not suitable, or willing, contributors to the almost entirely romantic repertoire of a professional opera company. The scheme came to nothing.

Another more worthy venture of 1975 was the creation of an 'Opera Studio' to give young singers with potential a chance to perform major rôles outside the

Beauty from squalor.
Performances of Alban Berg's twentieth-century masterpiece *Wozzeck* were truly excellent, but only seen at the 1976 Adelaide Festival. The depressing subject was relieved by the occasional beauty of the setting, but even at the Festival less than 60 per cent of the seats were sold.

Unheroic Hero.
The first Australian opera staged by the Australian Opera was also its greatest flop, the only production ever to be cancelled before the end of its run for lack of audiences. The Seymour Centre was not the Sydney Opera House and Craig McGregor's rock-opera *Hero* did not even attract teenage audiences in 1976.

full-scale productions of the company. It failed in the end, probably because sustaining such a tertiary opera-training programme without proper facilities or funding proved to be impossible.

The most lasting new venture of 1975 was the first concert given at the Sydney Town Hall in conjunction with the ABC. Elizabeth Fretwell, John Pringle and Lone Koppel-Winther, conducted by Edward Downes, sang the music of Mahler, Richard Strauss and Wagner. This experiment was to lead to the presentation of the major Wagner works in concert form accompanied by a larger orchestra than can ever be accommodated in the Opera Theatre of the Sydney Opera House.

The experiments of the following year saw the start of a stormy period in the company's management, throughout which the standard of performances stayed remarkably high. Singers and staff alike did not allow backstage politics to interfere with their duties to the paying public and far too little credit for this was given in the press; it is much easier to write scathing attacks on management's real or imaginary problems than to make the single quote, which I have as yet to see: 'no evidence of the company's troubles was apparent during this excellent new (or old) production'.

1976 saw the twentieth birthday of the Australian Opera, the replacement (amicably) of musical director Edward Downes by Richard Bonynge and a disastrous venture into the then popular rock-opera field, the staging of *Hero* by Craig McGregor, which was abandoned in mid-season because of lack of audiences — I don't believe its low-attendance record of 11 per cent capacity over fourteen performances in the small Seymour Centre has ever been beaten in the company's history. The other two financial lowlights of the year were probably to be expected: two Australian one-acters — Felix Werder's *The Affair* and Larry Sitsky's *Lenz* — and the second, and last, co-production with the Dance Company (NSW), Stravinsky's *Les Noces* coupled with Vecchi's *L'Amfiparnasso*.

Curiously enough, the opera with the lowest attendance figures (59.8 per cent) after *Hero* was one of the year's artistic highlights. Elijah Moshinsky directed the first Australian *Wozzeck* by Alban Berg for the Adelaide Festival and Edward Downes produced some glorious

playing from the ABC's Adelaide Symphony Orchestra. Timothy O'Brien and Tazeena Firth created some most beautiful, if controversial, designs and the cast, led by Raymond Myers and Lone Koppel-Winther, while unable to duplicate more famous singers used to Berg's twelve-tone score, were certainly not responsible for the standard of attendance at this important event in local opera history.

The second Summer Season in Sydney (1976) repeated the successful *Aida* in the Concert Hall and added a fine Lingwood production of Strauss' *Salome* with Marilyn Richardson and Lone Koppel-Winther alternating. Richardson was, and probably still is, one of the greatest Australian singers resident in this country, but it was generally agreed that Koppel-Winther made more of the part. (She headed the second cast, so what was that about favouritism now?) *The Magic Flute* was repeated and new productions of *Così fan tutte* (Copley-Barden-Stennett) and *Albert Herring* (Cox-Butlin) were added. Copley's *Così* was as good as his other ventures into Mozart. *Albert Herring* featured an excellent Graeme Ewer in the title role and Nance Grant as Lady Billows. In *Così* and *The Magic Flute* a new young Scottish soprano, Isobel Buchanan, made a deep impression.

Sydney, but no other city, was again offered Sutherland, this time in *Lakmé*, the voice showing some signs of wear (which were no longer apparent ten years later!) and the word was that Our Joan's time had come. How wrong can you get? Almost confirming the suspicion was the engagement of the newest international sensation, Kiri te Kanawa, for *Bohème*. A new *Carmen* admirably-designed and badly-produced by Lingwood starred Huguette Tourangeau, a much under-rated member of the Bonynge stable. Mozart's *Seraglio* was given a new production by George Ogilvie which, while quite acceptable, was to linger for more years than it deserved and an attempt to duplicate Jonathan Miller's Glyndebourne production of Janáček's *Cunning Little Vixen* failed miserably in a full-sized theatre, in spite of the delightful Vixen of Eilene Hannan, who only one year later was to appear at Glyndebourne itself in this rôle with immense success.

1976 also saw the departure of John Winther, the first of a series of general managers. (*See* Act 3, Scene 3.)

ACT 3 : SCENE 2
THE BONYNGE YEARS

Although both Sutherland and her husband, Richard Bonynge had appeared with the Australian Opera as guests for the past three years, Bonynge's appointment as musical director in 1976 steered the company into new paths. Bonynge's part (if any) in the managerial crises of his tenure are discussed elsewhere. The 1977 season was the first planned by him and the new general manager, Peter Hemmings. With the possible exception of introducing *Fra Diavolo*, the repertoire remained similar.

Fra Diavolo was a good choice by Bonynge to diversify into areas in which he, as musical director and principal conductor, intended to specialize. It was inoffensive, if hardly a milestone in the history of opera, and appealed to the general public. Also, it did not demand the greatest voices and there was a plentitude of fine singers in the company who could act. Robert Gard excelled himself in the title rôle and Bonynge made the most of his new discovery, Isobel Buchanan. Her first appearances in *The Magic Flute* had already made her a favourite with public and critics alike. In *Fra Diavolo* she helped to make unfamiliar music suddenly popular. The supporting cast was superlative by Australian standards: Dennis Olsen, Heather Begg, Anson Austin, Donald Shanks and Neil Warren-Smith in the Laurel and Hardy-type rôles, and Graeme Ewer. If Bonynge wanted to make an impression

with his novelties, he certainly did so in this case, whatever the highbrows may have thought of Auber's tuneful score. And it may even have been welcome to enlarge the repertoire where the funding cuts of 1976 hurt the least: the two Elizabethan Orchestras had been reduced from sixty-nine to fifty-seven players each.

Hemmings and Bonynge, whatever their later differences, must have been on one wavelength initially, yet this was the year in which the board of directors created a programme committee to tell the two experts they had engaged how to do their job. 1978 was already set by the new team, but the committee announced their choices for 1979 and 1980, including *Wozzeck*, which we have yet to see, and 'an Australian opera', which finally turned up in 1986.

Nineteen operas were performed in 1977 without producing a deficit, probably by keeping new productions to a minimum. The vocal highlight of the year turned out to be a mixed blessing. Miraculously, Sutherland had recovered all her old brilliance when she starred in George Ogilvie's *Lucrezia Borgia*, marvellously costumed by Kristian Fredrikson. What must have startled the management was the fact that Sutherland appeared to have lost some of her box-office appeal. Whatever her much-disputed fees were, even the abysmal *Lakmé* had drawn 90 per cent capacity. Now, only one year later, the excellent *Lucrezia* was down to 78.3 per cent! Producer John Copley turned up trumps twice this year, with the first Australian appearance of Leona Mitchell as Madame Butterfly — she was hailed by audiences and critics alike — and his new *Macbeth* was the only other unqualified success of the season.

The collaboration with the ABC was revived with a concert version of *Parsifal* with Ronald Dowd, Shaw, Light, Shanks and Koppel-Winther. The ever-present Cillario conducted that as well. The new Opera Studio for trainees was still going, if not with noticeable results in producing new principals. In 1977 it collaborated with the New South Wales Conservatorium Opera School to stage Ullmann's *Der Kaiser von Atlantis*, the only opera to be written in a Nazi concentration camp, a fascinating experiment even though, as so often, the purpose of the exercise was not clear. No Kaiser of singers ever emerged from the Opera Studio, which folded in the following year. With two publicly-funded existing opera schools in Sydney it had to produce better results to justify its cost to the parent company.

A major disaster befell the AO when a fire destroyed nearly half its productions stored in an Ultimo warehouse. An even-greater disaster might have befallen it if the monarch in 1977 had been Elizabeth I or Henry VIII. For some unfathomable reason a single performance of *Albert Herring* was rehearsed and staged especially for the benefit of Her Majesty Queen Elizabeth II. With nineteen other operas in that year's repertoire, why Her Majesty was served up a specialist work with little bearing on the company's standing as a major force internationally is one of those mysteries which only opera boards can produce.

1978, the year of the interim manager Kenneth Tribe, post-Hemmings and pre-Veitch, was a busy one and had to be accepted as pre-planned; singers do not write contracts months ahead, but years. Thus the avalanche of guests, which enhanced the international standing of the company (and its costs) must have been planned by Bonynge and Hemmings. What their plans were for the future of the company elsewhere at that time is anybody's guess, but the two capital city seasons in Sydney and Melbourne had already been announced. 1978 saw eleven operas staged in Sydney and five in Melbourne. Not a single imported singer appeared in the southern capital, which was, at that time, showing impatience with the offerings of a company to whose coffers Victorians had provided substantially through taxation. The excuse that Melbourne seasons had to play in the small Princess Theatre hardly washed as far as capacity was concerned, but the scenery of many productions could not be adapted

Indian Summer for Sutherland.

In 1977, at the age of fifty-one, Joan Sutherland began the Indian Summer of her career. After a temporary vocal decline in the previous year, she suddenly re-emerged with unimpaired brilliance in *Lucrezia Borgia*. The realization of this gave her a radiance not usually found in her un-photogenic features. She was still singing in 1988!

The opera which caught Bonynge.

Richard Bonynge and Joan Sutherland became interested in regular seasons in Australia after seeing a very non-Sutherland opera, Janáček's *Jenufa* in 1974. John Copley's world-class production caused the famous pair to make Sydney their professional base for a decade.

to it. *Macbeth*, *Fra Diavolo*, *The Gondoliers*, *The Flying Dutchman* and *Don Giovanni*, cast only with singers who had been seen frequently, did make quite a contrast with Sydney schedules. It was then that the Melbourne press began to refer to the Australian Opera as the 'Sydney Opera', and with some justification.

Sydney had a fully-imported Wagner production, Scottish Opera's *Mastersingers of Nuremberg*, with Hans Sachs sung by Norman Bailey, who had recorded the part with the Vienna State Opera! Sydney had Kiri Te Kanawa in *La Traviata*, which instantly sold out; a Sunday performance had to be added to accommodate planes-full of New Zealanders who came specially to see her. (She did not disappoint, though for reasons of her own she has chosen not to sing Violetta since then.) Sydney had Leona Mitchell singing both Mimì and Butterfly. Sydney had the Metropolitan Opera's James Morris to sing Don Giovanni! Sydney had Sutherland in *Norma* and also *The Merry Widow*! Sydney had *Nabucco* in the Concert Hall of the Opera House with the (supposedly) great Italian *prima donna* Orianna Santunione. Sydney had six new productions, Melbourne had none. Sydney even had the first internationally-renowned countertenor to sing in an opera − James Bowman, in the new *Midsummer Night's Dream* − and Sydney had Glenys Fowles, now resident with the New York City Opera, guesting as Susanna in *The Marriage of Figaro*. No wonder there were dangerous rumblings in Melbourne.

That not all that glittered in Sydney was gold was easy to overlook in Melbourne. Santunione demonstrated to Australians why Italian singers are often no longer famous outside their homeland; her excellent voice and presentable figure were the very model of a provincial Italian *prima donna*. Santunione had voice to spare, but little else. For all the imagined luxury being lavished on Sydney, there was no end of scandal in the Melbourne press about Australia Council dissatisfaction with the Australian Opera. Enquiries were instituted, submissions made and unmade. The most ridiculous charges were thrown around. If the current season was the best the Australian Opera could do for Melbourne in the years to come, perhaps a case could be made − and was made, if unsuccessfully − for keeping the national company out of Melbourne altogether.

Some radical changes were certainly overdue. At a time when the company was involved in a complex managerial change-over, the interim arrangements (whoever thought of them) did nobody any harm, though some time was to pass before long-standing resentments began to disappear. Late 1978 saw the beginning of an active collaboration between the rapidly expanding regional companies and the Australian Opera. Although these did not last very long, they had a profound effect on increasing opera audiences in Melbourne at least. (Adelaide and Brisbane cancelled out after one year.)

The last time we saw Kiri.
Australia last saw Kiri Te Kanawa on stage in 1978 in a series of *Traviata*. After that the world clamoured for the New Zealand girl who won the Sun Aria in Melbourne in 1965. A special Sunday performance was added to the season to enable New Zealanders to fly to Sydney to see their *Wunderkind* soprano.

The Merry Widow cashes in.
The plot of Lehár's operetta hinges around marriage for money. Sutherland's long cash-producing marriage to the Australian Opera began with *The Widow* in 1978 and was still going strong in 1988.

The first joint Melbourne season between the Victorian State Opera and the Australian Opera really belongs to 1979, though it started late in 1978. Since it involved ten productions from the national company and only two from Victoria, only a fool would deny that Melbourne benefitted immensely from this season, not least because the public at large (as opposed to the already-converted subscribers to both companies) was finally offered a chance to see Dame Joan Sutherland — provided that they would buy tickets to several other operas as well! It is a moot point how many of these were greatly enjoyed, but the repertoire offered was so large that there was surely something for everyone, and Sutherland was a major attraction.

The fact that Sutherland appeared outside Sydney does not mean that she had outstayed her welcome in the Harbour City, but Sydney had seen her frequently and by then she was a much bigger drawcard in Melbourne, Adelaide and Brisbane. Melbourne heard her as Violetta and Donna Anna, Brisbane as Norma and her *Merry Widow* was seen in Adelaide and Sydney, where her only other rôle was the two-aria villainous Electra in the Victoria State Opera's production of *Idomeneo* which the national company had taken over.

Melbourne was also being wooed energetically as a future income-producing source by being offered a brand-new production of *La fanciulla del West* (in Italian now) with another major imported star, Carol Neblett, plus the most popular Australian singer around, Donald Smith, and the kind of all-star first night normally seen only in Sydney. *The Mastersingers* (in English) had the same cast as Sydney, as did *Don Giovanni*, complete with the Met's James Morris. *Nabucco* starred Hunter and Allman, and Joan Carden was building a major career in the standard pops, *Bohème* and *Butterfly*. A routine *Cavalleria* and *Pagliacci* pleased the public, if not too many 'starry-eyed' operaphiles, in spite of Donald Smith's presence and John Pringle's rather nice Silvio. For the esoteric-minded there was *Albert Herring* and 'one of the great musical treasures of its time', Scarlatti's *The Triumph of Honour*, which turned out to be one of the great musical bores of *our* time, but every audience should see what went before what we enjoy today. After all, Bonynge having started well with *Fra Diavolo* was entitled to his occasional failure.

To its credit, the one sixth of the season provided by the Victoria State Opera provided the greatest hit, Bizet's *The Pearl Fishers*, and also Mozart's *La Clemenza di Tito*. The latter was not cast as well as the national company could have cast it (though Lauris Elms and Margaret Haggart shone brightly), but it was well produced by Anthony Besch with designs by John Stoddart executed, as all that company's work was by then, in a highly professional manner. The key to its success was, as usual, Richard Divall, who conducted not only the two VSO productions, but also the AO's Scarlatti.

It certainly must have been a hectic year for the rudderless administration, trying to arrange the various joint seasons, while recovering from its third major warehouse fire in the previous year, which had destroyed huge quantities of costumes and scenery. At the same time plans to import Renata Scotto for a season of *Madame Butterfly* at the Sydney Regent Theatre fell through, *after* its pit had been re-built at the company's expense. It was also a period of renewed demands for restrictions on imported artists by Actors' Equity — six foreigners a year only, foreigners to include backstage staff like teachers — and, to add injury to insult: the Computicket collapse.

While nobody ever doubted that Harry M. Miller, who had largely been responsible for the enormous increase of audiences during the early years of the Australian Opera, would succeed equally well with his venture to sell tickets by computer for all theatrical companies, Computicket was doomed from the start, because somebody else had come into the field first. BASS (Best Available Seating Service) was up and running by the time Miller entered the field and neither company had experience in computers which were not only new, but cumbersome by today's standards. To cut a long story short, Miller could not compete and Computicket folded, owing the Australian Opera no less than $204 000 which would clearly not be recovered. It could not have happened in a worse year, yet the season's loss, apart from the Computicket disaster, was only $94 000—a pittance compared with the huge explosion of activities which actually produced an increase in box-office income of more than a million dollars. Touring costs ate up the major part of this. Melbourne alone had ten operas compared with the previous season's five, and most of them had been staged at the Palais Theatre, which seats more than double the number of patrons, but has a quarter of the Princess Theatre's acoustic qualities!

If quality as well as quantity was the aim in Melbourne, with likely future audiences in mind, the joint seasons with the State Opera of South Australia and the Queensland Opera Company were decidedly makeshift affairs; no wonder both states declined participation in future years if that was the best the Australian Opera could produce. In Adelaide it added three productions to the home town's five. Apart from the sure-fire *Merry Widow* with Sutherland and *Madame Butterfly*, the dreadful *Queen of Spades* was a liability, not an asset. In Brisbane *Norma* was a dull affair, in spite of Sutherland and Elkins, and *Bohème* with Carden and *Seraglio* with Fowles were worthy partners of the failing local company's efforts rather than more attractive star attractions. Perhaps one joint season at a time would have been better than three in one year. Only Melbourne worked and only Melbourne survived — for one more year only; in the end, the economies of planning repertoire and artists proved to be simply unmanageable. The joint season in this one city involved no less than five separate visits in 1978 and 1979. No matter how worthy and no matter how successful in the long term, it was not a well-planned exercise.

With all this going on, the 'Sydney' Opera Company still had to serve its home town and did so, partly by a new venture, which has not been repeated since then: in January there were four performances called *Stars of the Bolshoi*, featuring seven singers and two conductors in extracts from Russian operas, as sung at the Bolshoi. They were hardly the top singers but admission prices to these wonderful imports from Russia's greatest theatre had a top of only $15.50, half the price of the by-then annual Sutherland *Merry Widow* and little more than half the price of a *Fidelio* — featuring Donald Smith singing in German for the first and last time — and other operas.

New original productions included a workmanlike *Falstaff* produced by Ogilvie and designed by Frederikson and John Cox's very funny English National Opera production of *Patience*, designed by Stoddart. The high-flying event of the year was not just high, it was the biggest turkey in living memory. Regina Resnik, one of the great singers of the recent past, was imported to direct Tchaikovsky's *Queen of Spades* and to sing the rôle of the old Countess at some performances. As a singing actress Resnik was a reasonable and respected artist at the end of a fine career. As a director she was still only a

reasonable and respected singer. Period. To make matters worse, she insisted on having the production designed by her husband, Arbit Blatas, who had no sense of perspective and constructed old-fashioned sets made to suit new-fangled production methods in an impossible theatre. They looked expensive and atrocious. Gregory Dempsey was unable to cope with the *tessitura* of Ghermann, but Marilyn Richardson saved what vocal glories could be milked from a production fit only for scrap. Whatever money was spent on returning it to Sydney after the Adelaide season was surely money down the drain.

Standards in the other fifteen operas were higher, the most notable ones being a fine *Salome* with Koppel-Winther, the new *Fanciulla* and two productions taken from other states. Nicholas Maw's *One Man Show* was the actual production of the State Opera of South Australia and used its original cast. Mozart's *Idomeneo* was the Victoria State Opera's production, but cast from strength. Sutherland was joined by Leona Mitchell, the latter continuing her regular Australian visits while rising on the international scene, and Elkins was in her usual superb form as Idamante. The title rôle was entrusted to Ron Stevens, whose voice does not suit Mozart, though he is a fine musician. Sergei Bailgildin replaced him with better vocal, if not histrionic, success later in the season.

1980 saw a turn-around in the company's fortunes under the temporary management of Kenneth Tribe. Money may have no artistic value as such, but a surplus of $259 000 was better than a deficit of $94 000, plus Mr Miller's negative contribution. Perhaps a row of first-class new productions worked better than routine touring with routine casts.

Richard Bonynge was criticized for scheduling operas for no better reason than that he wanted to record them with his wife and the charge could possibly be made to stick in the case of Verdi's *I masnadieri*, unsuccessful even in the composer's own lifetime. Nevertheless, the excellent designs of Michael Stennett and Alan Lees and the production by Peter Beauvais plus an excellent cast to support Sutherland (Donald Smith, Allmann, Grant, Bruce Martin) brought an 88.2 per cent attendance for the eleven performances. The unforeseen sensation of the season was Donald Smith's collapse after the first act of the fourth performance of *Masnadieri*. The fact that Paul Ferris, a light lyric tenor, finished the performance

for him in excellent style, with a well-deserved ovation, is unfortunately less newsworthy than that this marked the last performance with the company of its most popular tenor. No praise can be too high for the rôle Donald Smith played in the rise of opera as a popular art in Australia and it is deeply regrettable that illness should have brought it to such an inglorious end with the Australian Opera.

If a completely-unknown opera starring Sutherland could produce near-capacity houses, her appearance in 1980 in a brand-new *Lucia di Lammermoor*, the rôle which brought her international stardom twenty-one years earlier, packed the much larger Concert Hall to the rafters. Produced by John Copley and designed by the Bardon/Stennet team, it was worthy of every word of critical acclaim. Sutherland at 53 had lost none of her brilliance (and only a miniscule amount in 1986 when this production was re-programmed and televized), Richard Greager sang a strong, if not exactly sweet-voiced, Edgardo. Allmann was in superb form and Bonynge walked through the score, as he did through everything else he touched during his years with the Australian Opera. Only Carlo Felice Cillario could approach Bonynge for the number of performances he has conducted for the company since he first joined it in 1968. Together they made an admirable team, able to cope with almost any opera in the repertoire with ease.

The Triumph of Honour returned (old costumes and sets must be used up!) but now coupled with a truly delightful partner in Walton's *The Bear*, one of the funniest one-acters ever written and performed to absolute perfection by Heather Begg and Gregory Yurisich.

More important were the other two new productions of the year. A magnificent new *Boris Godounov* starring Donald Shanks was conducted by Elgar Howarth, produced by Elijah Moshinsky and designed by John Bury. Its appearance sadly coincided with the retirement at the end of the year of the company's original Boris, Neil Warren-Smith. *Kátya Kabanová* tried to cash in on the new vogue for Janáček with an excellent all-round cast led by Marilyn Richardson, but it could not hope to compete with the Victoria State Opera's *The Pearl Fishers*, brought to Sydney with its original cast; attendances for this were only one tenth of a percentage point below the capacity houses of *Lucia*!

The next joint Australian Opera/Victoria State Opera season (1979/80) was as successful as the first. The local company produced three of the thirteen operas, *Count Ory* by Rossini, Monteverdi's *The Return of Ulysses* and a revival of *The Pearl Fishers*. Apart from cast changes, the AO repertoire offered no novelties — Sutherland in *The Merry Widow* and *Lucia* and a final outing for *The Queen of Spades*.

The unbeatable three-and-a-quarter performances.
Opposite: For years Australians waited to hear their two top stars, Sutherland and Donald Smith together. The day finally dawned on 2 July 1980 in Verdi's rarely heard *I masnadieri*. During the first act of the fourth performance Donald Smith succumbed to the illness which had haunted him for years and Paul Ferris sang the other three acts. Smith never sang with the AO again.

The new economy Boris.
Fourteen years after turning the corner with *Boris Godounov*, with Neil Warren-Smith shining vocally and visually in the superlatively-luxurious costumes of his coronation, the 1980 *Boris* produced by Elijah Moshinsky was more authentic historically; Donald Shanks shone vocally rather than visually as the poorer Tsar of 1598.

The first year of Patrick Veitch's tenure as the new general manager was 1981, a year of disasters for which the new boy could hardly be blamed. It saw the last of the joint seasons in Melbourne and the least profitable one. The Australian Opera managed to average only 61 per cent capacity for its eleven operas, which included such goodies as Sutherland and Angelo Marenzi in *Otello* and Meyerbeer's 'Night of Seven Stars', *Les Huguenots*. The season's most saleable novelty for Melbourne, Puccini's *Manon Lescaut*, was announced as starring Leona Mitchell and Donald Smith. Mitchell decided to have a baby and Smith was ill. One wonders if he had a presentiment.

Finding an imported substitute for Mitchell at the last moment was not so easy, but the sight of the Roumanian soprano Gabriela Cegolea, if not her singing, will not be quickly forgotten. Comparatively unknown, she had sung at La Scala (third cast?) and came to Melbourne under the impression that it was the capital of Patagonia or Zanzibar; she is said to have actually brought her own posters advertising herself, though I never saw one. But I can quite believe it. The excellent Copley production did not suit her at all and she 'did her own thing', which mainly amounted to an eighteenth-century strip-tease which revealed a nineteenth-century corset and a twentieth-century petticoat and nothing of Miss Cegolea's figure at all! As to her singing, I seem to remember a voice of sorts, good looks and very little intelligence. She was partnered by Lamberto Furlan in place of Smith. And that was the $40-a-seat Gala Opening of the Melbourne season, which coincided with the results of the latest opera enquiry.

The Australia Council decided that the Australian Opera was, in fact, 'the national company', but recommended that it should cease visiting Melbourne after 1985! (The logic of those two contradictory conclusions is worthy of Lewis Carroll's Alice.) The Victoria State Opera would then become a full-time company. This added fuel to the political fires which had begun to die down by then. The most ridiculous exchange of insults and wild charges flew back and forth. It was Sydney versus Melbourne with a vengeance. Sydney claimed that the Victorian premier had personally ordered the Health Department to close the dress circle of the Palais Theatre to ruin the Australian Opera's box office. The fact that the order had been made four years earlier was ignored, of course. Melbourne replied that the interior

The legacy of Helpmann. Australia's most famous son of the theatre arts, Sir Robert Helpmann, proved with Handel's *Alcina* in 1981 that overall theatricality can make almost anything enjoyable. A specialist work of no great box-office value became a major attraction, with John Bury's designs eclipsing its musical virtues, though the singers never let him down. (*Left to right*: Anne-Maree McDonald, Donald Shanks and Heather Begg.)

decorator of the wife of the then Prime Minister (Malcolm Fraser) had been responsible for having the Australia Council grant to the VSO stopped! And so on. The whole issue was quashed for the most elementary reason that it would cost millions to do what was recommended and the government had better things to do than wipe certain substances off the proverbial fans. Happily the slingers of euphemistic mud have been muted since then and both companies have gone from strength to strength, apart from occasional financial hiccups.

Nevertheless, the disasters of 1981 were not restricted to Melbourne. Luis Lima, the company's first visiting tenor of international standing, was engaged for a series of Sydney *Rigolettos* and was forced to cancel. Henri Wilden was hardly a box-office substitute. Elijah Moshinsky was engaged to produce *The Bartered Bride* and withdrew. The Czech team of producers and designers, who shall be charitably unnamed, made a hash of what they should have known very well indeed. A new *Ariadne auf Naxos* was replaced by another revival of *Jenůfa* as deficits mounted. Budgets planned before Veitch's arrival overshot madly in all directions. What turned out to be one of the all-time successes of the company, Handel's *Alcina*, became a triumph of producer's will over accountant's sense. The director, the late Sir Robert Helpmann, certainly built himself a lasting monument with the help of his designer, John Pascoe. Helpmann admitted that he had expected Sutherland to sing the title rôle. Joan Carden by no means disgraced herself in the part, nor did Margreta Elkins, Angela Denning, Heather Begg, Anne-Maree McDonald or Paul Ferris, but Helpmann wanted something to replace Sutherland's star quality and the stage picture was obviously it. Nobody knows to this day how much *Alcina* cost, but it was something astronomically higher than the budget.

There was also a superb new *Tosca* (again: Copley/Stennett/Lees, starring Marilyn Zschau) and a passable *Otello*, built rather strangely around Desdemona, who happened to be sung by Sutherland. The Otello, Angelo Marenzi, was adequate enough, but seemed capable of singing only the one part. Still, *Otello* is a usable repertory piece.

This was also, unfortunately, the year in which Richard Bonynge, with Hemmings well and truly forgotten, let himself off the leash. Out came three of his pet projects, none of which helped the budget. Many opera lovers were deeply grateful to him for staging Meyerbeer's *Les*

Huguenots, but this is a major undertaking. In Sydney he had Sutherland and Zschau, in Melbourne Rhonda Bruce and Zschau. The rest were adequate staff singers. But Lofti Mansouri, an expensive producer, was out of his depth and the reliable Stoddart/Stennett team were cut back financially. It was a wonderful opportunity for Australians to see as well as hear a work unlikely to be found even at La Scala these days, but it had neither public appeal nor lasting repertory value to the company. As the Americans say: 'Strike one!'

That Bonynge should at some point want to stage his own edition of *The Beggar's Opera* was logical, but it was poorly-cast and has long ago lost appeal in opera houses. It could perhaps be staged as a star vehicle for some great actor as a commercial play with music; it is a dead loss in an opera company. ('Strike two!') The same cannot even be said about Piccini's *La buona figliuola*, a period piece which once upon a time (250 years ago) swept all Europe before it, almost as Gilbert and Sullivan did when they first arrived. I do not know whether an all-star cast with a brilliant producer could make it work, but done on the cheap with singers not used to the period it was a disaster. ('Strike three!')

Even the revivals included box-office duds like *The Rape of Lucretia*. ('Strike three and a half!')

Subscription series still relied on Sutherland for their appeal. For this year's *Traviata* Bonynge brought back local-boy-made-good at Covent Garden, Jonathan Summer, to sing Germont. Sir Charles Mackerras came and conducted *Macbeth* with Rita Hunter and Allmann. A series of wonderful concerts was organized with the ABC orchestras to prepare for a *Ring des Nibelungen* cycle to be mounted in the near future, two performances of *Die Götterdämmerung* in Sydney and two of *Die Walküre* in Melbourne. But it was no good. 1981 and its deficit of over $800 000 would have dire consequences long after surpluses made occasional, if temporary visits in the annual accounts.

With the arrival of the new American general manager, Patrick Veitch, many things were to change. The Australian Opera took giant steps after his arrival. Every year new ventures were announced. If the aim was to increase audiences and the demand for opera, Veitch certainly succeeded. That this sudden expansion would result ultimately in financial problems was inevitable and, in fairness to all the managers the company has ever had, the utterances of many ministers for the arts,

The Night of the Seven Stars.
Top: That was the name under which Meyerbeer's *Les Huguenots* was known when it was the biggest opera a company could put on. Richard Bonynge tried the impossible with a limited budget, though he had Joan Sutherland as Marguerite de Valois.

The Night of the Long Swords.
Above: *Les Huguenots* is pretty bloodthirsty and ends in a massacre. Bonynge's vocal battle was fought by every major singer at his disposal: Sutherland, Marilyn Zschau, Anson Austin, John Pringle, Clifford Grant, Bruce Martin and Anne-Maree McDonald as the Big Seven, plus Denning, Donald, Eddie, Ferris, Fretwell, Fulford, Gunn, Stender, Stevens and Yurisich! (The kitchen sink had not been invented in 1572.)

at local as well as federal level, were rarely in line with the grants without which no opera company can survive. The general attitude was holier than thou: opera is a wonderful thing, we must not let it die, we must bring it to a bigger public and the government (local or federal) will help. Far too many public enquiries implied that all problems were solvable and that the mistakes of the past, if any, would not recur. They did just the same.

The fly in the ointment is only now being publicly acknowledged by governments and their public servants: any body as complex as an opera company must plan ahead. Veitch, his colleagues and predecessors were given annual hand-outs, but never more than grand words for the years to come. The words were more important than the hand-outs, because good singers are contracted for many years ahead and plans have to be made long before the subsidies for the year of those plans are fixed. More than one season actually began before the amount available for that year itself had actually been paid and construction of sets for the following year frequently had to be started before a budget could be struck. Agitation for at least three-yearly funding has been strong since the early 1970s and at the time of writing, though within sight, it is still not yet a reality.

Under such circumstances the sudden expansion of the Australian Opera in the eighties was dangerous, though it was what the government wanted. The be-all-and-end-all of the company, Joan Sutherland, starred in its first, free, open-air opera in Sydney's Domain in *La traviata* in January 1982 before 25 000 people. The first of many live telecasts (*Die Fledermaus*), with Sutherland again as the bait, took place in the same year and more than justified itself by attracting an audience of over two millions. Mackerras conducted concert versions of *Tristan und Isolde* in Melbourne as well as Sydney with the ABC orchestras. Simulcasts of operas on radio were developed. Recordings and videotapes of AO productions went on sale. Community activities were enlarged and the year's 212 performances were spread over four cities.

Seasons independent of regional companies took place in Brisbane, Canberra and Melbourne with a truly remarkable lack of success. Choosing the disastrous *Bartered Bride* as the sole novelty for Brisbane was a mistake. More performances of *Madame Butterfly* in that city and of *La Bohème* and *Die Fledermaus* in Canberra with singers who, however good, had been seen before did not help either. Nine performances in each of these

two cities produced average audiences of less than 600 in Canberra and about 800 in Brisbane. Clearly these cities expected more.

The pattern was clearer in Melbourne which, on paper, did not do much better (nearly a thousand tickets sold for each of the forty-five performances). The unsuitable Palais was dropped and the company returned to the old Princess Theatre, which has a large upper gallery which is very hard to sell. What did produce surprise was that the first appearance in Australia of one of the world's greatest singers, Sherrill Milnes, in *Macbeth* with Rita Hunter, failed to fill the house any more than Carden's excellent *Traviata*, or revivals of *Bohème*, *Butterfly* and a truly terrible *Cav. & Pag.*, now without even the consoling presence of Donald Smith.

Being a transitory year, not much attention was paid to the financial results, which were surprising. In spite of the failure of the tours and all the yet-untried experimental expansion, Veitch produced a surplus of nearly a quarter of a million dollars! (Accumulated losses at the end of the year still exceeded a million, however.) The 149 performances in Sydney were, of course, the mainstay of the company's success and, whatever its failings elsewhere, standards here certainly did not drop, nor

Opera in the Park.
Started in Sydney in 1982 with Sutherland in *La Traviata* these open-air concert performances of opera have attracted hundreds of thousands of people to explore a new medium and have spread to other cities as well.

A star is born.
Truth and fiction mix disconcertingly at times. 1982 saw the standard Hollywood plot of an unknown catapulted to instant fame come true when Joan Carden broke her wrist and was unable to sing Ophélie in a new production of *Hamlet* by Thomas, starring the world's most famous baritone, Sherrill Milnes. Jennifer McGregor not only sang and looked, but acted a beautiful Ophelia to her famous Hamlet and became an instant star.

did the programming which avoided the routine which had been thought good enough for 'the provinces'. Milnes switched from *Macbeth* to play in the seldom-performed *Hamlet* by Thomas and was nearly eclipsed by one of those truth-is-stranger-than-fiction theatrical fairy tales. Joan Carden had been the natural choice for Ophélie, but she broke her wrist and young Jennifer McGregor found herself catapulted into the limelight, singing all the Sydney performances of Lofti Mansouri's very acceptable production, in sets by Alan Lees and costumes by Desmond Digby. At the risk of sounding corny, a star was born and for some years it looked as though McGregor would be the logical successor to Sutherland.

Wisely, in accountancy terms, *Hamlet* was the only major venture of the year. Otherwise audiences saw only the long-awaited *Manon*, which had been planned to use the same costumes and most of the scenery of Puccini's opera on the same subject. Glenys Fowles sang very well in the title rôle of an opera not seen in Australia for far too long and if the scenery-swapping was not a complete success, it was not a failure either. Bonynge, possibly voluntarily, restrained his mania for esoteric novelties. He dropped the far-from-triumphant *Triumph of Honour*, but kept the successful *Bear*, adding to it Offenbach's *Ba-ta-clan*, delightfully designed by Kenneth Rowell; and only one minor Bonynge specialty, *Rosina* by William Shield, an eighteenth-century English pastiche restored by Bonynge himself.

The financial success of 1982 was topped in the following year, in spite of some very ambitious expansion of the repertoire. The long-awaited *Ring des Nibelungen* was actually started with a production of *Die Walküre*. This has been overshadowed by the failure of the next opera in the cycle and its subsequent abandonment. No opera company worth its salt is without a *Ring* and the attempt had to be made; it was the platform on which Peter Hemmings had tried to build his aborted career in Australia. Four years later the scheme finally got off the ground, though by then Mark Elder was no longer available to undertake the gigantic conducting task with the reduced forces which can be fitted into the ridiculously small pit of the Sydney Opera House. It is easy to forget that the *Ring* does not demand huge casts and the very smallness of the Opera Theatre solved half the problems of finding big voices to ride over Wagner's big orchestra, which can not, in any case, be accommodated in this venue. The versatile Cillario proved well able to take Elder's place and, with minor reservations, enough singers were available by 1983 to cope with the music in this theatre.

Worthy though the motive, to entrust what is, even in miniature, a gigantic task to a raw young Australian producer was the major artistic error on which the venture ultimately foundered. Andrew Sinclair had had experience at Covent Garden and even at Bayreuth. He clearly had the ability to work out how to stage a *Ring* cycle; *Die Walküre* proved that. But he was too inexperienced to follow through. *Das Rheingold* was a disaster and that was the end of the Australian Opera's first stab at the *Ring*. Several singers, including Rita Hunter and Alberto Remedios, who had counted on the *Ring* to see them safely ensconced here through the next four years at least, had cause to regret placing their faith in the Australian Opera.

None of this should denigrate the very good start which was made with *Die Walküre* in 1983. Placing his faith in tradition rather than the modern 'interpretations' (to use a polite word) of Wagner's multi-faceted cycle of four operas − or, if you insist, three operas and a preliminary evening − Sinclair chose Allan Lees and Desmond Digby as his designers. Lees's sets have been criticized, unjustly I believe, because they included what looked like a drawbridge. With the restrictions of the Opera House stage to consider, it was an admirable effort. So was Sinclair's direction of his protagonists. Hunter was and is an internationally-renowned Brünnhilde, Elkins was the beautiful and vocally-secure Sieglinde, Bruce Martin an admirable Wotan and Elms an expectedly-fine Fricka. If weakness there was, it was Jon Weaving looking an ideal Siegmund, but not sounding like one. Later Robert Gard, though small of voice, at least sang well and acted superbly. Regardless of the *Ring's* fate, this *Walküre* should remain in the repertoire.

The other new productions were successful for different reasons. Sir Sidney Nolan is one of Australia's great artists; a stage designer he is not. The designs for his *Trovatore*, directed by Moshinsky, may look well on the wall of an art gallery; on the stage they did not work. On the other hand, Verdi said that this opera above all needed voice, voice and more voice and that is what Sydney got, with Sutherland, followed by Hunter, Kenneth Collins a stentorian, if rather small-statured

A dream of a singer.
Every opera company dreams
of having a tenor who can
and will sing any part
without complaint on his or
the audience's part. They are
rare indeed and never
become great 'stars'. Robert
Gard would like to be a
Heldentenor, but simply does
not have the right voice for it.
Yet when Wagner's *Ring* was
started at last the ideal Loge
also sang a convincing
Siegmund. Good companies
are built on Gards, not
Domingos.

**The opera can end, though
no fat lady sings.**
At least, the Australian
Opera's productions do.
When Gounod's *Roméo et
Juliette* was scheduled in
1982, the lovers of Verona
(Anson Austin and Glenys
Fowles) could have been
playing Shakespeare instead
of singing Gounod; nor did
the other youthful firebrands
of the plot have an ounce of
excess fat.

The new Sutherlands who aren't.
Once every new soprano was the 'new Melba', now emphasis has switched to 'new Sutherlands' in Australia. Newspapers have tried to create a new Sutherland out of Joan Carden, who is a great singer and needs no such sobriquet. Young Jennifer McGregor (here seen in *Lucia di Lammermoor*, a Sutherland rôle) shot to fame by replacing Carden. Neither needs the 'new Sutherland' label.

Pavarotti returns.
After eighteen years the now world-famous, and somewhat larger, Luciano Pavarotti returned briefly to Australia to sing *Bohème* three times in Sydney and to give two concerts; the one with Sutherland was televized to an audience of six million! (With Madelyn Renée as Mimì.)

Manrico, Elms as good an Azucena as she had been in 1966, Jonathan Summers as De Luna and Shanks as Ferrando. Even more successful, if less famous, was a new *Roméo et Juliette* by Gounod. In Melba's time this work was more popular even than Faust, but now it is largely forgotten. With a believably young-looking cast, (Fowles and Austin as the lovers, Pringle as Mercutio and Anthony Warlow as Paris) the famous story really came to life, choreographed rather than directed by Helpmann and designed by Rowell. Only a thrown-together *Norma* with Sutherland and Rachel Gettler let the side down pictorially, if not vocally.

The rest of the year was an outstanding one in every way, the only touring was to Melbourne and performances throughout were of a high standard. Among the highlights were *Lucia di Lammermoor*, cashing in on the new 'star' Jennifer McGregor, and Sutherland finally made it to *Alcina*, where she belonged in the first place; Leonie Rysanek showed great dramatic power in her declining years when she sang Tosca, Leona Mitchell tried her hand, or throat, as Desdemona, Joan Carden steadily grew in stature in all she did and a number of younger singers were feeling their way to the top. Last, but very far from least, 1983 was the year when young Stuart Challender proved himself to be the first major Australian-born conductor to excel in everything he did.

This was conceivably the most successful year artistically that the company ever had; the expansion of its activities made it bigger and better all the time. The highly-publicized short visit by Luciano Pavarotti must be recorded, though it has no bearing on the past or future of the Australian Opera. He sang in three performances of *La Bohème*, bringing his own Mimì, Madelyn Renée, and being suitably modest and un-star-like to endear himself with audiences and casts alike. His televized concert with Sutherland in Sydney attracted an audience of six million people, about half the adult population of the whole country! Another half-million saw his solo recital in Melbourne on television. *Il trovatore* was also telecast by the ABC, which also broadcast no less than ten live performances that year in 'simulcast', a primitive form of stereo broadcasting using FM and AM channels together. *Opera in the Park* quadrupled its audience to 100 000 for Sutherland in *Die Fledermaus*, while Canberra got a Sutherland-less *Bohème* under the stars, also planned for Melbourne, where it rained!

Further expansion occurred through Veitch's never-ending extensions to his empire. What the Australian Opera was doing acting as a backer for the Sydney Theatre Company's eight-hour presentation of the play *The Life and Adventures of Nicholas Nickleby* has never been explained, but the venture did show a profit. An 'Australian Opera National Council' was established under the chairmanship of Sir Zelman Cowan. Without wishing to denigrate Sir Zelman and the many worthy people who travelled from all over Australia to attend the first and later meetings for the council twice yearly, its purpose was inadvertently given away in the initial announcements: 'an invaluable resource for the company in public relations, fund raising and expertise to the Board and management'. Note the order of priorities.

So spectacular was 1983 that the following year had to be an anti-climax. A lot happened, in fact, after the total failure in June of *Das Rheingold*, the second opera in the planned *Ring des Nibelungen* cycle. No matter how good some individual performances — and, as usual, there were plenty of those — this was a production best forgotten. I do not propose to dwell on it, preferring to let sleeping gods lie. The gods of the Australian Opera were not allowed to sleep, however. The full facts of the July 1984 revolution may never emerge, but Richard Bonynge arrived in Sydney to find himself demoted from musical director to 'Chief Guest Conductor'. Moffat Oxenbould had factually, if not in name, been in charge of the artistic administration of the company for some time and now he suddenly bore Bonynge's title. Theoretically at least, the former boss had to take orders from Oxenbould now and he had not been given any warning of this. That the Bonynges accepted the situation with good grace is a credit to their past relationship with Oxenbould and his team, though walking out would probably have cost them more than the Australian Opera.

While the news made headlines (with bigger ones to come within a few months) the rest of the year reflected the universal uncertainties under which everybody worked. Veitch's empire was in trouble, though the last balance sheet said otherwise. The fact is that *Rheingold* had been only the tip of a smouldering iceberg, if ice can smoulder. The only other première had been Cilea's *Adriana Lecouvreur*. Cilea was no Puccini, but *Adriana* is the favourite opera of many a soprano and no expense was spared on the Allan Lees sets. John Copley did an admirable job of shifting the whole thing to Sarah

The self-destructing *Ring des Nibelungen*.
The easiest of the four *Ring* operas torpedoed plans for Australia's first properly-staged cycle, planned to be completed for the Bicentenary in 1988. *Das Rheingold* followed the acceptable *Walküre* in 1983 and provided an unintended funny Muppet Show visually, and surtitles which had Alberich at the bottom of the Rhine singing: 'The damp is getting up my nose'. End (temporarily, we hope) of the *Ring* cycle.

Fiddling the books.
Operettas and musicals are standard money spinners for opera companies world-wide. The Australian Opera had access to the one star it needed to make *Fiddler on the Roof* a source of supplementary income in 1984. Hayes Gordon *is* and has been Tevye, the Jewish milkman who talks to God, in Australia. A great voice and a great actor, he is living proof of the bridge between opera and the musical.

Bernhardt's time, but Sutherland was sadly miscast as a great tragedienne of the Comédie Française. Later performances in Melbourne starred Joan Carden, who was able to bring out the real beauties of a very tuneful, if superficial, score. The big news was not Sutherland's singing, but the introduction of Surtitles, projected translations over the proscenium arch, which are by now standard equipment world-wide. Monique Brynnel was a poor *Merry Widow* substitute for La Stupenda and only occasional individual performances gave temporary life to the company: Remedios as Otello and Siegmund, Rosamund Illing as a last-minute substitute Gilda, Yvonne Kenny as Pamina. The rest of the year was not inspiring. A new *Aida* was needed because Lingwood's old one went up in the 1978 fire. For once Kenneth Rowell's designs were not inspired — though he never fails disastrously, as others have done — but the production by Christopher Renshaw left a lot to be desired. Marilyn Zschau and Elkins sang well, backed by the loud Radames of Ermanno Mauro.

The only winners of that year were an unlikely couple: *Dialogues of the Carmelites* by Poulenc and *Fiddler on the Roof* by Jerry Bock. That's an opera? Well, it was good enough for Walter Felsenstein, conceivably the greatest opera producer of the century, or at least the post-war years. Most opera companies have musicals and operettas in their repertoire, if often for purely financial reasons, which was probably the case also in Australia. On the other hand, not many countries have Hayes Gordon as a resident and his Tevye is worth the price of any opera performance. The *Carmelites* is hardly popular entertainment, but Elijah Moshinsky's production with John Bury's designs and Isobel Buchanan in the lead almost turned it into a best-seller. People who went to see it for Joan Sutherland in the minor rôle of Madame Lidoine would have been more impressed by Lone Koppel's spectacular death scene as Madame de Croissy. (There was no Winther in her name by now.)

The guest artists were a mixed lot too. Nelly Miricioiu was a good Violetta, Maria Slatinaru a very loud Aida in Melbourne, while Fiorenza Cossotto's Amneris was as welcome as Rysanek's Tosca had been. Singers like these should occasionally be honoured guests, though the reasoning behind the constant succession of imported sopranos of minor importance when we have Richardsons, Cardens and many more is incomprehensible. And in the pit that year there was Kurt Herbert Adler, who

had been conducting for sixty years without ever making it to the top. Why import him for a local *Fidelio* when Australian Stuart Challender was showing world-class talent on other nights? David Agler at least was young and ambitious, but in the long run did not make out and departed gracefully, though not covered in glory. On a brighter note, we welcomed the Polish conductor Vlado Kamirski, who will always be welcome.

Crisis year was 1985. This time it was a matter of money rather than personality clashes, though press, public and even the company's singers tried to find a scapegoat. The reality was that Veitch's ambitious expansion had resulted in a substantial increase in private sponsors, but not enough to meet the rapidly escalating costs and the Australia Council, fed up with the most expensive of its national companies, announced in April 1984 that the AO's funding would be frozen at 1985 levels for three years, a factual decrease in subsidies at a time of rapidly-rising costs. The accumulated deficit was again reaching dangerous levels and the auditors were warning of looming bankruptcy unless some radical changes took place. Something, somebody (or some body) had to give, and it was not a matter of peanuts. Veitch and his team put forward twenty options for discussion which included some practical, if unpleasant, ones (liquidation) and some, perhaps deliberately, outrageously unrealistic ones (move the company to Melbourne and tour to Sydney!).

If the directors of the company were unhappy, they did not help matters by blithely announcing, rather than canvassing the intention of turning the Australian Opera into a part-time company performing only six months in each year from the start of 1987. Suddenly the livelihood of hundreds of people directly or indirectly involved in a major industry were threatened with alternatives almost worse than total dismissal. Condemnation of the plan was universal on all sides. State governments and unions were as concerned as singers who had forsaken international careers in favour of staying with the home company.

It is conceivable, though perhaps unlikely, that Veitch deliberately tipped the bucket too far to create maximum consternation. If so, he succeeded beyond all expectations. In fact the whole thing backfired, ultimately leading to votes of no-confidence by artists and staff in the management of the company. If this can be called unfair — it was not the company which reduced the subsidies — the failure to consult all parties before making announcements at annual general meetings was a blow to the morale of the performing artists which could well have proved detrimental to performing standards. That it did not is an immense credit to the sheer discipline and professionalism of the team. The State Government of NSW made an *ex-gratia* payment of $900 000 which had been the subject of some legal dispute and refunded a quarter of a million dollars in sales tax, an input of well over a million dollars in 1985, a year which otherwise showed an operational deficit for the year of $788 000. Theoretically, the company was saved, or so the laymen and singers thought. Yet the worst was still to come. (Since the story made so many headlines in very recent years, it must briefly be told here.)

Cancellation of the plan to change to part-time in 1987 was not forthcoming. Unhappy singers, worried about their future instead of their performance, are not likely to give their best. Then, with management distancing itself ever more from its many employees, trouble came from a different quarter. On 7 March 1985 the company's first Melbourne season in the new State Theatre was to open with a special Gala Benefit Performance of *The Tales of Hoffmann* with Sutherland appearing only once after an absence of four years from the capital of Victoria; she was due to leave Australia the next day. Costumes and scenery had been brought specially from Sydney for this single performance of the opera and ABC-Television had scheduled a national simulcast on a more elaborate scale than usual. That night three unions struck for a $54 increase in their weekly touring allowance. Negotiations began as the VIP audience, which had paid up to $100 a seat, sat waiting impatiently. In view of the special nature of the event two of the unions agreed to go on, but the other held out. Fifty-five minutes after the advertised start the audience was told to go home and the ABC telecast a repeat of *Die Fledermaus*. That little exercise cost the AO roughly $100 000 and brought it neither glory nor goodwill on either side of the curtain. (The unions were to try the same trick once again in July, this time in Sydney. During a routine simulcast of *Un ballo in maschera* they literally pulled the plug to terminate the telecast just as the soprano from the Metropolitan, Carol Vaness, was about to start her big aria.)

The cancelled *Hoffmann* was a symptom of deeper ills than a mere industrial dispute. Never previously had 'the show must go on' been ignored. The company had just moved into new and luxurious headquarters costing a much-publicized four million dollars, for the first time bringing all its activities under one roof. But rumour and suspicion ruled, and few weeks passed without some new story making the headlines nationally. The public must have wondered how continued high artistic standards were achieved when, according to the papers, the company was in disarray. But except for the replacement of *Huguenots* with yet another *Bohème* in Sydney, 1985 continued with existing plans and its fair share of highlights. Of the new productions only *Un ballo in maschera* proved to be outstanding, American guest Carol Vaness was ably backed by the local team of Elms, Collins, Summers and McGregor. John Cox's production and John Gunter's atmospheric sets helped a lot. *Don Pasquale* was rather antiseptic in Roger Kirk's huge marbled halls instead of a miser's home and, in *I Puritani*, enforced economy measures placed Sutherland, Austin, Shanks and Michael Lewis — a musically superb quartet — into a mélange of sets salvaged from previous productions, mainly *Lucia di Lammermoor*.

Major imported visitors were the successes of the year, though the company's usual failure to give them adequate publicity probably resulted in no extra seat sales justifying their expense. Apart from Vaness, the huge soprano of Eva Marton as Tosca made other singers and even the orchestra sound small. Pilar Lorengar also sang the same rôle. Leonie Rysanek came to Sydney instead of Melbourne for a fine Sieglinde and a superb Kostelnička opposite Lone Koppel's Jenůfa. Leona Mitchell tried her hand at the *Trovatore* Leonora, and Stella Axarlis sang Katya Kabanová. Eight imported singers and every one of them a soprano! The pattern continued in 1986 (Zschau, Mitchell, Chiara, Miricioiu) but the excellence of that year would be quite eclipsed by the culmination of the backstage political shenanigans begun two years earlier.

The big news was the world première of Richard Meale's opera *Voss* at the Adelaide Festival. It will be long remembered after the news stories which swamped it are forgotten. Government(s) provided 2.5 million dollars to pull the Australian Opera out of the fire, and Chairman Charles Berg finally resigned, several years after this had been recommended by more than one investigating committee. Veitch followed him six months later, leaving the field open to the current management of Donald McDonald and Moffat Oxenbould. It is always difficult to analyze recent history. Writing, as I do, for the man in the street, I can only try to eliminate the misconceptions which arose through the front-page news which flooded Australia in 1986. Those interested in the details may like to consult the report commissioned by the Australia Council from the respected firm of Coopers & Lybrand under the leadership of Mr Rod Cameron and Mr Kim Williams, two gentlemen who could not by the wildest stretch of imagination be said to have been partisans with any pre-conceived notions. The recommendations of that report, which were published in January 1986, categorically stated that continuation of the Australian Opera as a full-time company is the preferable option from many points of view, but that only the following financial arrangements could bring this about:

• That the company receive in 1986 a $2.5 million cash injection.
• That the current government subsidies be increased by $740 000 per annum, indexed in 1987 and thereafter.
• That the company itself reduce current expenditure levels by $750 000.

The report was accepted by all parties, though the second item was not implemented by the Australia Council. Charles Berg resigned as Chairman of the Australian Opera Board shortly after its acceptance and David S. Clarke, his successor, at the time of writing has managed to avoid the kind of problems which beset Mr Berg's years with the company.

What remains unresolved in the public's mind is the fate or purpose of the $2.5 million 'cash injection' in 1986. The impression exists that this was to pay off accumulated losses, but I have shown that thanks to the NSW Government, the year 1985 actually showed a small surplus and past accumulated losses were down to $780 000. The report recommended an indexed increase over existing annual funding of $740 000, which was delayed interminably. Accepting the $2.5 million as a necessary fighting or sinking fund to prevent future bankruptcy of the company, the failure to provide the recommended increase meant that the 2.5 million will be exhausted by 1988 when the whole cycle should repeat itself, possibly with different protagonists fighting the same battles. The

whole thing sounds like a poor opera libretto, but the public must be grateful that the part-time plan has been scrapped and that the AO has continued on its admirably-smooth artistic path. Perhaps the Yellow Brick Road to Oz has a bank somewhere along the way.

In view of the threatened part-time conversion which, fortunately, never materialized, the repertoire for 1986 was exceptionally good. This year would have been the first completely planned by Moffat Oxenbould and it contained a little to satisfy everybody and at least one highlight, *Voss*, which will be discussed in detail during the last Interval of this opera in words. There was the usual average of four new productions, but they were supplemented not only by *Voss*, but by two of the Victoria State Opera's productions: *Eugene Onegin* and *The Consul*. The popular hit was a brand-new *Mikado*, and saying that anything by Gilbert and Sullivan can be described as 'brand-new' is about as high a compliment as you can give. Christopher Renshaw's production struck an ideal compromise between the old D'Oyly Carte way and the ultra-modern 'travesties' which work so very well. He could not have done so without the absolutely stunning designs by Tim Goodchild which ensured the opera's success almost without the help of the singers. And good as the latter were *in toto*, none individually carried the show; it was team-work all the way. If anything, the all-important Ko-Ko of Graeme Ewer was the

Australia's King of the High Cs.
Anson Austin, the good-looking New Zealand tenor, was as important to the 1985 *La Fille du Régiment* as

Sutherland, for whom Donizetti's trifle was staged. Few companies have tenors who can sing nine High Cs in two minutes, as Austin must and did in this opera.

weakest in the strong ensemble. Perhaps the old traditions with one great star and poor supports have given us a false sense of priorities for G & S.

It could be argued that staging Donizetti's *La Fille du Régiment* is pandering to the lowest common denominator. Yet it was probably the last opportunity to hear the fifty-nine-year-old Sutherland in her favourite comedy rôle, which she hammed-up extravagantly, extremely well supported by Anson Austin, complete with nine solid top Cs in *Pour mon âme*, and Gregory Yurisich as Sulpice. Jennifer McGregor and Rosamund Illing may not be super stars like Sutherland, but they later turned this *Fille* into a filly more in Donizetti's image.

On a more serious note, an overdue new *Zauberflöte* was an immense success, again mostly due to the intelligent production, in this case by Göran Järvefelt and designer Carl Friedrich Oberle. They made sense out of the nonsensical story by turning the whole masonic mess into a test devised and directed by The Speaker. Håkan Hagegård and John Fulford shared the honours as Papageno, Amanda Thane was the sweet Pamina and Donald Shanks the sonorous Sarastro. A rare tenor import, Gran Wilson, was musical but not exactly sweet-voiced. *The Consul* and *Peter Grimes* are contemporaries, yet very different and they balanced well. *The Consul* was produced by the composer, Gian Carlo Menotti, in excellent settings by Shaun Gurton. Stella Axarlis (Magda) and Bernadette Cullen (Secretary) were the good principals. As so often with the Australian Opera, the whole was better than the parts. The same applied largely to the new *Peter Grimes*; Richard Greager sang the title rôle very well, but, hidden behind a beard in this otherwise-excellent John Copley production, he failed to dominate as Grimes should. Carden was a sympathetic Ellen Orford, but John Shaw was strangely anonymous as Balstrode. David Agler conducted both operas with accuracy but little care for detail.

Eugène Onegin scored over its Victorian original by having a thoroughly-convincing Onegin in John Pringle and some fine singing from Joan Carden's Tatiana. *Un ballo in maschera* had Marilyn Richardson in Sydney pitted against Maria Chiara (direct from opening the La Scala season) in Melbourne. Well as Chiara sang, she was no match dramatically or musically against Richardson, again proving the pointlessness of importing sopranos, no matter how good. On the other hand Piero Visconti, the second tenor imported in 1986, did not exactly cover himself with glory either in *Manon Lescaut* opposite Miricioiu. Zschau made an excellent Lady Macbeth in Sydney, but was a revoltingly-realistic Salome in Melbourne — Oscar Wilde would have loved her! She also sang exceptionally well. Frank Corsaro's production of *Falstaff* was perversely unfunny, though very well sung, particularly by Helen Adams and Gary Bennett as the young lovers, and Rosamund Illing's Butterfly was outstanding.

The indestructible Sutherland went back to singing *Lucia di Lammermoor* in the Sydney Opera House Concert Hall and sounded as though she were twenty-five years younger. This remarkable performance in her sixtieth year was televized and videotaped, a valuable historical document of a great singer.

At the time of writing 1987 was incomplete. It started very well indeed with an excellent neo-realistic new production of *Carmen* by John Copley with clever semi-modern sets by Robin Don. In the first cast Kathleen Kuhlmann sang very well, but was not really sexy enough for the Spanish firebrand. Nevertheless, her death was brilliantly staged by Copley. Greager was a good José, but Michael Lewis was, literally, out of his depth as Escamillo. The change to Britten's *Turn of the Screw* was

Grimes without Grimes.

Britten's *Peter Grimes* is the only modern opera (1945) which is in the regular repertoire of most companies. An ensemble work ideal for the Australian Opera, Robin Lovejoy's cheap production in 1958 outshone the expensive one of 1986 mainly because of the strong Grimes of Ronald Dowd. Richard Greager, hidden behind a beard, did not have the same impact, though Robin Don's modern scenery was more spectacular.

The miracle of Sutherland.
In her sixtieth year, Joan Sutherland sang *Lucia di Lammermoor* once again. The performance of 8 February 1986 was televized live and the videotape can be bought to this day, a remarkable document of a remarkable singer, whose singing that night was close to the best of her career.

Yet another who is not a 'new Sutherland'.
Yvonne Kenny is a young Australian soprano who has made the grade internationally, often singing operas previously identified with Sutherland. Because she sings mostly overseas, she has managed to avoid the 'new Sutherland' tag. In Australia in 1987, she brilliantly sang that most Sutherland of all parts, Handel's Alcina.

strongly contrasted and surprisingly effective, even though the producer/designer Elijah Moshinsky had to retire from the former duty after completing the latter. Drama director Neil Armfield made a fine job of working within Moshinsky's ingenious set of movable gigantic Victorian furniture; only the bright lighting of the ghosts took away from the complete success of a chamber opera performed in too large a theatre. Eilene Hannan was the perfect Governess and Margaret Haggart most effective as Mrs Grose. Anson Austin and young Lisa Gasteen were Quint and Miss Jessel.

Alcina, in a new edition by Richard Divall, who also conducted, was a surprise success; surprise in that it even surpassed the Helpmann/Bonynge original. Yvonne Kenny was outstanding in the title rôle, a perfect compromise between Sutherland and Carden, with a strong clear voice, and beautiful to boot! Her large supporting cast was universally faultless. Cherubini's *Medée* is a showpiece for a great singer, which the company had in the form of ex-member Elizabeth Connell returning, we hope, only for the first and not the last time. Only singing of this quality can make *Medée* work.

The Victoria State Opera's production of *Lohengrin* was sung in German instead of English and cast wonderfully well by the Australian Opera. Marilyn Richardson, Horst Hoffmann and Donald Shanks· had the right Wagnerian voices and temperament and Elke Neidhardt considerably improved August Everding's original production. Wagner of this calibre makes one regret the demise of the misconceived *Ring*.

ACT 3 : SCENE 3
THE MANAGERIAL
GLASS SLIPPERS

The key men in opera management, who bear a variety of titles—'general manager', 'administrator', '*Intendant*' and a good few others which have been used in this book—rarely make much of an impact outside their own cities or, in the case of Australia, their comparatively small states. But the rise of opera here as an art has been so rapid that these key people have now become the darlings of the press; they are the real *prime donne* of opera companies world-wide and it might be as well to remember that this is the reason for the many headlines in daily papers. But, no matter what may have happened among the endless succession of managers we have had in recent years, things which have been considered a 'scandal' in this country have been poor imitations of the kind of very real scandals which have been visited on opera companies overseas.

No Australian administrator of an opera company has ever gone to gaol for taking bribes from singers to ensure their engagement, as happened not so long ago in many theatres in Italy. No Australian opera season has ever been cancelled completely and re-started from scratch in mid-season, as happens to the mighty Metropolitan Opera House in New York. No manager has ever been fired, or been forced to resign before even starting his duties, as has happened frequently in Germany. I am writing of things which occurred within living memory and not the ridiculous happenings of the nineteenth century or earlier. It is still possible in the 1980s to find yourself in a world-famous opera house and to face crises of a greater magnitude than any which have delighted Australian gossip columnists, past or present. The final scene of this act is going to write itself. And it will not be an *exposé* of the kind in which the gutter press and television reporters glory. The protagonists, without exception, have made headlines reflecting only the petty-mindedness of reporters. But if, in all fairness, you cannot tell the history of opera in Australia without mentioning singers and producers and designers and conductors, you cannot omit those names who, for varying lengths of time attracted more attention than any singer who ever appeared in this country.

Our operatic managers have not been ogres of fearful mien before whom our little operatic world trembled. More often than not they have been no more than Cinderellas, denied the basic needs of life and hounded from pillar to post by the Ugly Sisters of the Australia Council and a multitude of ministers for the arts as temporary as the governments by whom they were appointed. Our managerial Cinderellas invariably went to their Balls, some to grander ones than others. But glass slippers are not only fragile, but slippery. And Princes willing to marry the nominees of some Fairy Godmother financed by the current treasurer in Canberra are hard to find.

'The Winther of our discontent' is a good quote but, in the context of the Australian Opera, it would be just as well to complete the Shakespearean quotation: 'The Winther of our discontent made glorious summer . . .' The history of opera, or theatre, or music in this country has always been the subject of controversy at managerial rather than artistic levels. The press and the critics must take their share of the blame; few artists take up journalism as a profession and even fewer editors are willing to pay outsiders to write on matters of minority interests, meaning the arts. A few critics love the art they write about, but rather more seem to take pleasure in making headlines by being destructive. Humanity being what it is, the credo 'bad news is good news' stands supreme in any country which is free of political censorship and Australia is no exception.

A big fat headline reporting a disaster or implying a disaster will sell newspapers; of that there is no possible doubt. No 'good news' newspaper has ever been a success and, God knows, there have been more than a few. Opera has frequently made the headlines in Australia and as it has grown in popularity the headlines have grown bigger every year. Unfortunately, I have as yet to see the one which concerns the quality of a performance, at least not on the front page.

I have dwelt at some length on the personalities which fought the good fight to the best of their abilities to make opera a part of our cultural life, as it has been in Europe for centuries and in America for a shorter period. If news stories about opera were any indication of quantity or quality of productions, singers or companies, those of the last decade or so would imply that Australia has the most flourishing opera in the world. The fact that the art has, in fact, bloomed in that time is not only due to the talents of the people you see on stage, but also to those who place them there. Too many of the latter have featured in the headlines which have been concerned with the troubles of opera companies. Why the editors of our national newspapers consider to be newsworthy the managerial changes and budgetary problems which rightly belong in boardrooms, has always puzzled me. Those which take place in industry (of far greater importance to the man in the street) are banished to the financial pages at the back of the paper. Those of opera make the front page here, as they do in Vienna or New York.

Since it has been on the front pages for so many years, a summary of what took place behind the scenes at the Australian Opera will be sought by any reader who has an interest in the art. Yet, to cover the past decade in detail would need a book to itself and would make very dull reading. There have been the recommendations of umpteen investigations into the opera scene at levels from the Prime Minister's Department to submissions from the unions and at least one independent one commissioned by a group of singers employed by the Australian Opera. Some were constructive, others were destructive. In sum they agree on certain basics which nobody ever queried in the first place. As for the rest, they almost completely cancel each other out and I do not propose to give publicity to those who tried to make personal capital out of them. Nevertheless, we can not ignore those who managed the many old and new companies which, I am glad to say, today do not compete for the market, but collaborate in supplying a growing demand.

Earlier, I made an oblique reference to John Winther, the first professional general manager ever engaged by the Australian Opera, no less than seventeen years after its creation! His predecessors were inspired amateurs who, rather like their critics in the press, did their best while learning on the job. Some, like Stephen Hall, went on to use the skills they had acquired; Hall's success as director of the annual Sydney Festival is unquestioned. Others, like John Young, are devoted to the theatre, having given their whole life to it, and continue to work in it administratively, if in less newsworthy places.

In 1973 John Winther came to Australia from Copenhagen, Denmark, where he had been the manager of the Royal Danish Opera for ten years. He also happened to be a first-class musician and a fine pianist, a rare combination in anyone in arts administration and something which was to serve him rather better than he would have anticipated when he arrived to take charge of the Australian Opera.

Winther laid down a maxim which has always been universally accepted, except perhaps by his many predecessors. 'There must be one person as the final arbiter in an opera company', he said. His successors have, rightly, taken the same view. Unfortunately, in an opera company the equally-valid maxim: 'The buck stops here' is beset with unforeseeable dangers and it was these which made the headlines.

There was a becoming modesty about John Winther and at first he got what he wanted without upsetting people which, in this particular company, was a rare quality indeed. He admitted that he inherited a group of executives who did a good job and simply continued as before. He defended their policies and even their financial budgets, which he was forced to take over. Winther was obviously a diplomat, because the facts added up to a different total.

John Winther was engaged for a three-year term in February 1973, six months before the Sydney Opera

House opened its doors. The Australian Opera had ended the previous year with a deficit of $150 000, something which was too-readily blamed on the departed Donald McDonald and his staff. The projected deficit to the end of the first Opera House season was an additional $300 000 but, according to Winther, that was an over-estimate made in good faith because of the anticipated costs of running a theatre in a building with a disastrous history of inefficiency. Over-estimating a deficit is better than under-estimating one. The point is that 1973 produced a deficit of only $125 000, but this had to be added to the outstanding $150 000-odd.

The first full Winther year was 1974 and it concluded with a *surplus* of $245 000, almost wiping out the deficits of the previous two years. (All these sums are, of course, book entries, not actual dollars available for spending.) The main consideration is that 1974 was also one of the best years the company had ever had artistically; that is, Winther achieved the economic miracle without lowering standards, cutting seasons or avoiding the immense increases in wages which the year imposed on the whole community in Australia. Quite possibly these spectacular results were due to Winther's ability to raise cash in many different quarters. I don't care. It was his job to be the general manager, and to produce good opera without over-spending was something quite unheard of in the previous history of the company and its executives.

Partly it was due to a hard-headedness which upset some people in the artistic community, particularly Australian composers, whose works were not performed. Winther's attitude sounds ironical in the light of his ultimate stated reasons for resigning: 'Every night we don't play *Bohème*, we lose money', he said. Australian operas are hard to find, costly to stage and a total disaster at the box office. The example of *Rites of Passage*, which Peter Sculthorpe did not finish in time for the Opera House opening, is typical. Three operas were commissioned in 1974, but only one was completed on time and that, the rock opera *Hero* by Craig McGregor, was an unmitigated disaster artistically and financially. There was too much reason in Winther's madness to offer comfort to operatic nationalists.

John Winther, his wife and children were naturalized in 1976. His contract was extended, but the battle he initially won cost him the war in the end. The Winther/Downes partnership was musically adventurous and the new Sydney Opera House made novelties such as *War*

and Peace or *Jenůfa* acceptable for some years. Perhaps Downes saw the writing on the wall, perhaps his growing international reputation or family reasons caused him to leave a company thriving under his hand after only three years. In June 1976 Richard Bonynge succeeded him as musical director of the Australian Opera.

Bonynge's arrival coincided with a major financial crisis predicted accurately enough by the shrewd planner who was still general manager. John Winther was not prepared to wait until it was too late. He blandly announced that the company would have to disband for five months in 1977 unless an extra $970 000 in funds could be obtained in that year. To continue the company's existing work the million and a half expected at the box office simply was not enough! The crisis was ultimately averted, partly through the generosity of Utah Development Company and Foundation, which gave a solid quarter of a million, but the unwillingness of Winther to sacrifice standards at any price produced the expected repercussions.

Suddenly the importance of the box office, which the Australian Ballet had long acknowledged, took on a new meaning. Filling the house became all-important and discontent with Winther's determination to mix the esoteric with the popular repertoire became an obsession with some members of the company's board. Animosity to Winther from some singers and staff members was probably no worse than in any other case of an iron hand, no matter how velvet the glove, leading a large company. There were no public demonstrations of support for him, nor was there open glee at his fate.

The strangest aspect of the Winther regime, that aspect which not only cut it short, but was to produce the departure of the next two general managers as well, was the sudden emergence of the board of directors in what its members obviously thought was a position of leadership. For years the actual management of the company had done all the work, with the board as a benevolent deity appearing at opening nights to claim the credit for every success. Claude Alcorso's chairmanship of the board from 1970 onward may well have been inspired by the same motivation (at the time further enhanced by the prospect of the surely soon-to-be-completed Sydney Opera House) except that Alcorso again actively intervened during the crisis two years later and literally took charge of the management of the company for a year, while a new chief executive — Winther — was found. It is not clear at what point the next chairman, Charles Berg, and some of the other directors began to see themselves as mini-Alcorsos, but divergences among board members over matters which were really the general administration's affair resulted in a kind of factionalism which began to make headlines. Charges and counter-charges were made by board members in the press instead of the boardroom. Winther discovered that he was not only not the final arbiter, but that more than one other final arbiter was interfering in his affairs at a time of financial crisis. An intolerable and unprecedented situation arose in the fourth year of Winther's reign, which ended in 1977.

The legacy of Winther should not be under-estimated. Unlike his successor, Winther was a practising musician who saw eye-to-eye with his musical director, Edward Downes. Whether a similar relationship could have been established between Winther and Richard Bonynge can not be judged; their association was too brief. But Winther had the confidence of his singers and his artistic staff, if not his board. He left the company on an artistic high which should, and indeed may, have encouraged Peter Hemmings to accept the post he vacated.

Peter Hemmings was in charge of the Australian Opera for less than two years. It was a godsend, or devilsend, to the press. At first, the appointment was hailed with glee, as it should have been, for Hemmings had admirable qualifications, having been almost solely responsible for building Scottish Opera into a major company in Britain. The board of the Australian Opera had (apparently) set its house in order, by removing one of the warring factions, and the press conference given by Hemmings on arrival implied that the company had given him assurances which could only result in spectacular progress under his direction. One of the flies in the ointment was noticed by one critic, John Cargher, in a long article the next day. Besides stating that my predictions became regrettably true, let me extract two sentences from that preview of things to come: 'Hemmings and Winther think alike ... and the old problems will repeat themselves unless the ideas of the directors have changed'. They had not. 'Winther built the structure which gives Hemmings a head start. There is every reason to believe he can take advantage of it — if he is allowed his way by the many people inside and outside the company who will ... stand in his way'. They did.

The other, and possibly more important fly was Winther's maxim about one final arbiter; Hemmings felt the same way and believed that his contract so stipulated. Because Richard Bonynge's wife is Dame Joan Sutherland, the board of the company considered her continued appearance with the Australian Opera to be more important than anything Hemmings might consider necessary. Both gentlemen being gentlemen, there was never a confrontation; had there been, the ecstasy of the press would have known no bounds. However, differences on casting and repertoire did arise and, rather than risk losing Sutherland, Hemmings, like Winther, found arbiters more final than himself and he departed. For the record, his career overseas since then has been a continuing and resounding success and he is probably thanking the Lord that he left Australia when he did. I shall not adjudicate whether Hemmings or Sutherland was more important to Australia in 1979. My approval of Bonynge as musical director will be found elsewhere in this book, and it may be as well to put to rest here one general misapprehension regarding the Hemmings/Bonynge relationship: the staging of a complete *Ring des Nibelungen* cycle was never a contention. The *Ring* was planned in conjunction with Bonynge and, beyond discussing the problems of casting, Bonynge was always in favour of doing it. Casting and costing killed the venture, not anything which Richard Bonynge may or may not have done.

In view of his immense contribution to musical life in Australia, let me record that Kenneth W. Tribe, AM, became the caretaker manager of the company while a replacement for Hemmings was sought. The only regret associated with his tenure is that he thought it unwise to apply for the position himself. (A matter of age, I believe.) Also, just for the record, the various opera reports which had been, were, or would be written about this time made immense profits for printers and manufacturers of pigeon holes, but not for the Australian Opera.

1981–1986: five years in charge of the Australian Opera as general manager is a record of sorts and Patrick L. Veitch was a typical American business tycoon, on the young side, but well versed in the American way of impressing people. He had a pleasant, engaging personality. He came to Australia originally to advise the Australian Opera on the best ways of fund-raising, which was his job at the Metropolitan Opera House in New York, took the board's fancy and was engaged as general manager of the company. It is not clear what, if any, qualification he had for the job; he had never, as far as I know, managed an opera company before. On the other hand he had a good business brain, was able to get on with people and clearly anxious to show that the American way is the best way. Nobody can blame him for trying to get the job and it even seems likely that in normal times he would have learnt the ropes quickly. He did, in fact, cover an immense ground in a very short time, after frankly admitting his ignorance in the early days and acting on the advice of responsible people. To a large extent Patrick Veitch was a victim of circumstance.

The Australian Opera was in deep financial trouble, largely due to funding problems and the chaotic conditions which prompted those endless and useless enquiries. To Veitch's credit it must be said that the company did not slide artistically during his five years in charge. He made some mistakes, but if you hire a manager without experience, the blame for that lies with the employer, not the employee. Veitch himself learnt from his errors. His ideas were perhaps too grandiose, but he brought some elementary business methods into operation which, one can reasonably say, Winther or Hemmings should have done before him. For example, he gave departmental heads the responsibility of handling their own budgets; he made them financially responsible for their actions. Yet opera, all opera throughout the world, is a loss-producing business. Ridiculous as it may seem, the more performances a company gives, the bigger its deficits. With the Australia Council and the Australian Opera being headline news for years in the past, the insistence on cutbacks on the one side and the threats of reduced activities on the other gave the press a field day; it was almost like a continuing soap opera, with some reporters stirring up trouble in their papers' editorial columns. Only in Vienna does opera enter the political arena as it did during Veitch's era in Australia.

We shall probably never know whether Veitch and his board were bluffing when, in 1985, they announced that the Australian Opera would become a part-time company. They miscalculated badly by making an official, apparently irrevocable, decision to this effect. The singers passed a motion of no-confidence in Veitch and in the chairman of the board, Charles Berg, who promptly resigned. Veitch stuck it out, won his bluff, got two and a half million dollars from the government to keep the company going on a full-time basis — and then got out! Opera in general and the Australian Opera in particular have become such a huge business that it is no longer possible to pinpoint where things went wrong. Of all the departing general managers of the company Veitch probably left with the least discredit or enmity. His case is too close to stand examination in history as yet, though his acceptance as chief executive by a major commercial organisation within weeks of his departure implies that his departure may have been pre-planned. (Why he then parted company with his *new* employers quite so quickly is not known, or relevant.)

His successor is Donald B. McDonald, returning to the post he vacated under an ephemeral cloud in 1972. During the intervening fifteen years he had headed first Musica Viva, the largest chamber music society in the world, and then the Sydney Theatre Company. He did not apply for the job with the Australian Opera. International advertisements produced only thirty applicants, all obviously inferior to McDonald. The directors of the Australian Opera very sensibly then asked him to apply for the position and he accepted the challenge, no doubt administratively as much as financially, on his own terms. On his record, he should be the ideal man for the job. It was unlikely that any suitable, internationally-established candidate would want to lead a company with a history like that of the Australian Opera. McDonald started with one great advantage, a company which, largely thanks to its present artistic director, Moffat Oxenbould, has not moved backward artistically.

THIRD INTERVAL:

opera goes native

Only once in two hundred years has a 100 per cent Australian opera shown signs of having a real future – in the future. No serious piece of music theatre written in the late twentieth century appears likely to ever again attain the popularity of a *Bohème* or *Rigoletto*; the resistance of the box office to a semi-pop composer like Stephen Sondheim proves that. But the full-scale production of Richard Meale's *Voss* at the Adelaide Festival in 1986, and later in Melbourne and Sydney, implies that the endless succession of modern Australian works of recent decades may yet produce operas which, in time, may result in regular revivals, as *Voss* will undoubtedly be revived. Some may even find their way overseas. Who knows?

National pride demands that Australia should have a national school of music and that this should include opera. Fair enough, but no way has yet been found of guaranteeing quality high enough to attract present or future audiences. Since the concept of subsidizing the arts became reality, there has been much greater exposure of music written by Australians than in the past, but the sheer cost of staging opera has left it trailing far behind other contemporary music.

Current controversy is being kept alive, not unnaturally, by the composers who want to see their operas performed. Music can be judged by academics from the written page. Librettos can be read. Designs can be seen. Singers can be heard. Operas must be performed. It is as simple as that! Opera is the most complicated hybrid to be found in the arts and the sum total of its components does not necessarily make a whole of equal quality. It is all very well for the Australia Council or the Australian Opera to hand out commissions to composers to write operas; they will produce scores, and have produced scores, which must then be judged by various people with a view to possible performance.

The argument has been put forward that the commissioning of an opera must include its staging. This is hardly valid. In the arts, as much as in commerce, there is a point at which one must cut one's losses and, unfortunately, in this case the factors affecting the final decision involve not only financial risk, but personal opinions. You cannot measure the viability of a stage work as you can the working of an engine, or the design of a household article.

Writing about Australian operas is not easy. The theory that any work written by anybody loosely associated with this country automatically becomes Australian is a tenuous one, even though the Broadcasting Act has laid down guidelines which are almost ludicrously open to manipulation. A man who was born in Australia, but who left it as a child and never returned, can write Australian music, and a man born in Europe, who comes to Australia in middle or even old age, has his European compositions accepted as Australian music. The whole thing is an exercise in self-deceit.

The most famous 'Australian' composer of operas this century is Malcolm Williamson, born in Sydney in 1931. He left Australia in 1953 and not one of his published works, opera or otherwise, was created in this country. His operas range from chamber works aimed at children, like *The Happy Prince*, to full-blown romantic works, like *The Violins of Saint-Jacques*. All have been performed in England, most with success, and his reputation internationally is impeccable; Williamson is one of the most successful living composers of operas. Yet what is there

Australian about them, beyond the accident of his birth? None have Australian subjects and none have been performed in Australia, unless you count the presentation of some of the chamber works staged in the course of seminars run by Williamson himself during visits to Australia.

The question whether the Australian Opera should present Australian operas is a particularly sensitive one. The principle has been the subject of lip-service by every musical director and administrator the company has had, yet before 1986 the results had been a sum total of two performances of one double bill of one-acters in 1974. (I do not include Peter Sculthorpe's *Rites of Passage*, which cannot by any stretch of the imagination be called an opera in the conventional sense, whatever its virtues; and I will grant it had many.) The reasons why promises and good intentions have not materialized into anything solid are almost exclusively financial.

The relationship between modern works (operas included) and low box office is not exclusive to Australia. Managements overseas have long ago given away contemporary works as box-office attractions. In the case of music, works can be slipped into concert programmes containing other, financially more viable titles. Opera is a different matter entirely. The change in the fortunes of opera during this century came about because the public refused to accept twentieth-century music. I know that much of the music rejected half a century ago has by now entered the repertoire but basically you cannot deny that after Puccini and Richard Strauss the public eagerly awaiting the production of new operas ceased to exist. Controversy and scandal, rather than popular musical acceptance, became the only forms of box-office attraction and neither ingredient can sustain interest in a new work for very long. The few operas written since the première of Puccini's *Turandot* in 1926 which have gained continued support represent a minute part of what has actually been written for the operatic stage in all this time.

But creativity must go on and, particularly in an age when the future of music itself, let alone opera, is uncertain, composers must be encouraged to experiment. In one respect they are, of course, perfectly right: there is no way in which progress can be made unless their operas are performed. But a fiendishly expensive exercise, which has no hope of covering its costs at the box office, should not be a part of the budget of opera companies. If funds are to be made available to encourage the writing *and production* of new Australian operas, then they must be provided as a separate project undertaken by the Australian Opera or some regional company. No organization hanging on the brink of financial disaster from year to year can be expected to budget for this kind of thing and the Australian Opera's failure to do so must be taken in the context that the company has created a large market for a product by using its resources wisely. It could not have done so if the propagation of operas with in-built losses had been a part of the programme. Artistic or nationalistic considerations simply do not come into it.

The number of Australian works that have been staged within living memory by other major or minor companies is limited indeed and it is doubtful whether any one person would have seen them all. The number that have actually been written is much larger. Were this an academic chronological record, time could be spent in assembling all the information available (which would still fall short of completeness) but that is not the purpose of this exercise.

Starting with Isaac Nathan's *Don John of Austria*, which is the first locally written work described as an opera, whether it was or not, there were composers and writers galore who tried to cash in on the magic word 'opera' in the Australia of the middle nineteenth century. The craving for entertainment was great indeed and there was no shortage of cash. Every form of theatrical entertainment flourished. If much of it was substandard, the public was not aware of it. What went on on those stages, or what passed for stages, gave pleasure to a people whose life still resembled that of the early pioneers. To write operas to compete with what passed for Weber, Wallace, Meyerbeer or Verdi seemed easy, and even was easy. Nobody will ever know how many Australian operas were written in the nineteenth century, for most only existed in manuscript and, at best, the names survive in some dusty newspaper files.

In a day when novelty was still the key word to operatic success, William Saurin Lyster made capital out of presenting 'the first original opera ever brought upon the board of an Australian theatre'. Stephen Hale Marsh, whose *The Gentleman in Black* was performed by Lyster's company in Melbourne in 1861, arrived in Sydney nineteen years earlier on the same ship as the explorer Ludwig Leichhardt and initially shared a house with him. Coincidentally, the same Ludwig Leichhardt, whose exploits inspired Patrick White to write his novel *Voss*, was to break the voodoo of failure on locally-written operas 125 years later, when Richard Meale set *Voss* to music. Voss is, of course, Leichhardt, and in his opera Meale actually uses the *Doctor Leichhardt's March* which Marsh composed for his friend! Not that this in any way gives Marsh an edge over Nathan as to who actually wrote 'the first Australian opera'. Claims for other works do exist, but *Don John* was staged fourteen years before Marsh's *Gentleman* and both used original libretti.

Earlier, concurrent and later works were almost without exception straight adaptations of plays which had been seen in Australia, to which music had been added. Those were the days when references to the classics of ancient, middle and recent ages lent an aura of learning to an author or a composer. As in America about the same time, acquiring an education the easy way, by attending plays, readings, exhibitions and the like, was considered uplifting and the more entertaining the event, the greater its success. Thus, when Isaac Nathan launched his own music magazine, an amazing venture for a city like Sydney, in the 1840s, he called it the *Southern Euphrosyne*. I am sure more Sydneysiders in 1842 knew who or what a Euphrosyne is than would today. (She was one of the three Graces, the daughters of Venus.) Similarly, when Charles Nagel bastardized Moncrieff's English burlesque, *Shakespeare Festival, or The New Comedy of Errors*, he called it, believe it or not, *Shakesperi Conglommerofunidoginammoniae*! It was as good a way as any of disguising the piece's origins, lent the needed aura of respectability and duly filled the house.

Others tried to cash in on scenes set in the new colony by transplanting English plots into local settings suitably embroidered with the author's own and, presumably, his audience's morality. Nobody today wants to remember that racial discrimination against the Aborigines extended to their inclusion in plays and operas as Australian equivalents of the American Negro as portrayed during the slavery years. Not that *Life in Sydney* or *The Currency Lass* claimed to be operas, but then I ask again: was *Don John of Austria?*

During the following years numerous original (or near-original) Australian operas were written and quite a few produced. Since they were usually staged, and written to be staged, for single performances by amateurs,

they had a great deal of improvization about them. It was spectacle rather than drama which would have needed extensive rehearsal, that provided the attraction; in 1866 Charles Horsley's *The South Sea Sisters* featured a full-scale corroboree danced by real Aborigines, which was the sensation of this — opera?

The various German communities throughout Australia, specially around Adelaide, provided regular productions of Australian operas in German. These, even when performed in proper theatres, were little more than static concerts in costume. The occasional composer who managed to have his works performed by full-size opera companies did not always have the greatest of faith in his own talents. When Luscombe Searelle went to South Africa in 1889 after having had no less than three of his operas performed by the Montague-Turner Company in Sydney, he took with him a complete prefabricated theatre to Johannesburg, where his own opera company played not his *Estrella* or *Bobadil* or *Isidore*, but Wallace's *Maritana*!

It may be as well to mention at this point that William Vincent Wallace, whose two years in Australia brought immense benefits to the musical life of this country, did not start composing operas until seven years after he left Australia. The myth that *Maritana* was wholly or partly composed here was probably started by Wallace's most influential friend, John Philip Deane, the man who kept him hidden from his creditors in an attic in Rowe Street in Sydney for weeks, and who called his house 'Waldemar', a name made up of the first syllables of Wallace, Deane and *Maritana*. Wallace left Australia owing £2000; like most musicians arriving in or departing from Australia in the early years, there was an unmusical cloud over his private life.

There is little point in trying to survey the many other Australian works produced in the second half of the last century. Even the operas written in the early 1900s, though their manuscripts are being kept with great care, offer little reward to the student, and the prospect of any revival is remote indeed. What does arise out of, for example, the life of G. W. L. Marshall Hall (George William Louis, to satisfy those who, like myself, have always wondered what the initials stand for) is that the problems facing Australian composers were as great then as they are now.

Marshall Hall was a major figure in Melbourne's musical life from 1890 until his death in 1915, though his activities were mostly restricted to the orchestral field and teaching. As for all composers of the time, opera held a fascination for him, though not even he could obtain a performance of *Aristodemus*, a twenty-five scene Greek tragedy, though a German translation was actually printed for the Melbourne *Liedertafel*. His *Romeo and Juliet* showed the continued influence of the classical-scholar syndrome which so attracted audiences, but it also failed to be performed. It was taken by the composer to Germany, to no avail. In London he fared a little better; his *Stella* was performed at the Palladium as part of a variety bill in 1914. It is claimed that this was the reason for *Stella's* failure. The fact is that London variety bills in those days presented variety indeed. Mascagni himself conducted *Cavalleria rusticana* (with Alessandro Valente as Turiddu) as part of just such a bill at the Hippodrome, just as Diaghilev's Ballet Russe played at the Coliseum. They did not fail. Do we have to ask why Marshall Hall did?

The failure of most Australian operas of the past is usually attributed to outside factors, perhaps because they were performed by students or amateurs. Arundel Orchard wrote what was for many years the only comprehensive book on music in Australia (and thereby perpetuated any number of fallacies and errors) but his

operas did not have the exposure his book received. *Coquette* (1905) was reasonably successful in spite of its amateur cast. *The Emperor* (1906) was a flop. *The Man in the Moon* failed to survive one rehearsal. His magnum opus, *Dorian Gray*, took ten years to write. Two years later one act was performed by the students of the NSW Conservatorium, who were promptly blamed for the failure of the opera, which has not been heard since.

Alfred Hill, the one composer who can be classed as major among resident Australians (who were born here and worked here) was a little more lucky with his ventures into opera, just as his symphonies stand head and shoulders above those of his contemporaries. Arguments that they belong to an earlier, romantic period are neither here nor there; Hill did produce the goods, and people are not only listening to his music still, but paying hard cash for it. His operas have not lasted so well, but at least two of them, *Tapu* and *A Moorish Maid*, obtained professional performances in 1904 and 1906 respectively. Royalties amounted to $200 and $120, sums not quite as small as they may appear to us today, but his *Giovanni* (what another one?) brought him nothing, because it was staged by a grand 'Australian Opera League' formed by himself and Fritz Hart with great hopes and the promise of Marshall Hall that all the

Australia's most productive opera composer.
Fritz Hart wrote no less than fourteen operas, though only one was ever staged professionally in Australia. He died in Hawaii in 1949 almost forgotten, having been quietly pushed out of the back door by his manipulative colleagues. His operas are our still Sleeping (operatic) Beauties — or Ugly Sisters.

expected proceeds of overseas performances of *Stella* and *Romeo and Juliet* would be made available to this new body. I suppose it can be said that Hall kept his promise, since he made nothing out of either.

The appearance of Fritz Hart, the most prolific of all opera composers in this country, brings a touch of sadness into the story. Hart, in spite of the Fritz, was an Englishman whose Cornish family tree went back as far as 1100. Unlike Hill, who had studied extensively in Germany, Hart was educated solely in England before coming to Australia in 1909. His fellow students included Vaughan Williams and Holst, but his music is closer to Debussy and the French impressionists. He wrote fourteen operas in all and seven of them have been staged at one time or the other. Only one gained the professional performance they all should have had, *Deirdre in Exile*, which appeared in the 1928 Williamson-Melba Grand Opera Season in a double bill with *Pagliacci*. Quite possibly Melba's friendship for Hart, the owner of the Melba Conservatorium, had a bearing on the choice.

The problem with Hart's operas lies less in the music than in the libretti, which he wrote himself. They are mostly concerned with Celtic legends and are inclined to be decidedly old-fashioned. Unfortunately words and music, as usually happens in the case of composer-librettists, are completely integrated and it would be impossible to separate them. The occasional Hart opera still surfaces. Melbourne heard *Even Unto Bethlehem* in 1973 with young Jonathan Summers.

There is an outside factor which has held back not only recognition, but even inspection of Hart's operas. Due to difficulties with the 'establishment' in Melbourne, Hart accepted the post of musical director of the Honolulu Symphony as a full-time position in 1937, and all his scores went with him. One result was that until fairly recently Hart was no more than a name to the Australian musical community and he often did not even appear in books in which he should have played a major rôle. His works have now been donated to the State Library in Melbourne by his widow, and some of his music, if not his operas, was recorded by the ABC. Time alone will tell whether the accessibility of the scores will produce any hidden masterpieces.

As head of the Melba Conservatorium, Fritz Hart was also responsible for the performance of Australian operas other than his own. He played perhaps the major role in staging Australian works, which need not be listed in detail, in amateur or student performances, and revived many of the operas which have been written in Australia during the present century. There are forty-six listed nineteenth-century operas, nearly all of which were produced in their own time, if with varying, and certainly not lasting, success. But then, things were a little different in those early days and no attempt has ever been made to revive even one of those period pieces to enable us to judge its worth.

I do not really feel inclined to play along with the theory that operas written by expatriates should appear in a volume subtitled *Two Hundred Years of Opera in Australia*. The ABC offered Malcolm Williamson's *Violins of Saint-Jacques* in a television production, proving only that the Australian Opera was probably right not to stage it. The music is certainly lush enough and the sensationalism of the voodoo-dominated story has some attraction, but by no stretch of the imagination can it be described as Australian and, if we are to have unknown works included in the local repertoire, there is a huge reservoir of operas of greater importance than *The Violins*. On the other hand, it can be stipulated with some justification that, if money is to be spent on the production of an Australian work under the terms of the Act as it now stands, we might as well be offered something tried and proved, like Williamson's opera, or Arthur Benjamin's *A Tale of Two Cities*.

The odd man out among expatriates is a woman, Peggy Glanville-Hicks, who has a following in *avant garde* circles which brought about a staging of her opera, *The Transposed Heads*, when she returned briefly in 1970. Nevertheless, she has been an American citizen for forty years. 1972 saw her short curtain-raiser, *The Glittering Gate*, performed at the Adelaide Festival and the acceptability of her music, electronics and all, and her logically dramatic libretti, may yet bring her greater local exposure. The success of *The Glittering Gate* prompted the Festival to revive it as a double-bill with *The Transposed Heads* in 1986. While its reception then was only mildly favourable, the *Heads* did not transpose the way they should have done. Still, Glanville-Hicks has two other major works up her sleeve, *Sappho* and *Nausicaa*, the latter to a text by Robert Graves based on Homer. With a cast of 150 and an audience of 4800 it had an enormous success at the 1961 Athens Festival, since when all has been silence.

The number of composers resident in Australia who are fighting for representation is really very limited in relation to the amount of noise they make. The most likely contender appears to have dropped out of the race already! Peter Sculthorpe was supposed to produce the great Australian epic to launch the Sydney Opera House. For whatever reason, his work was not staged until a year after the great event and *Rites of Passage* proved to be a vital piece of total theatre, but hardly an opera. Opera is music drama, *Rites of Passage* has no action, no principals and a chorus singing in several different languages.

The ABC made the same mistake as the Sydney Opera House supremos. For its fiftieth anniversary in 1982 it commissioned Sculthorpe to write another opera. With vision (the TV-type) rather than sound in mind, Sculthorpe actually produced something which qualified to be called an opera, but the solitary telecast of *Quiros* is unlikely ever to be seen on a stage. As an opera composer the man who should have been first choice as the founder of modern Australian opera does not appear to be in the running at the moment.

All of which only proves the unpredictability of the arts, artists and artistic creativity as such. Even ten years ago I would have nominated Richard Meale as the composer least likely to write an opera, certainly not one which would make not only the establishment but the general public sit up. That he proved us all wrong with *Voss* is no secret and I propose to stress the importance of that work and of Meale himself by devoting the end of this Interval to him and to it. In the meantime I must cover a multitude of other composers, for the country which has been all but barren in this field seems to take a positive delight in producing new talent which is determined to write operas. Although we are living in a different age, every budding Beethoven is still convinced, as that composer was himself, that the road to fame and riches starts in the opera house. The sentiment may not be quite as silly as it once was, if we consider the opening of major theatres suitable for opera during the last fourteen years in no less than four capital cities. The fact that the only one of those theatres which actually bears the name 'Opera House' is the least suitable for the purpose is dealt with in an earlier chapter. (I refer to my Second Interval, of course.)

Colin Brumby many years ago led the performing field with a whole series of home-grown and home-performed mini-operas which he and his wife staged in Queensland with considerable success. Most were chil-

dren's operas, but his *Seven Deadly Sins* was in a more serious vein. The break-up of his marriage, and therewith the opera company which created those works, stalled Brumby for some years in the opera field, though he composed prolifically for the concert platform. Recently he has returned to the fold. A full-length work, *Lorenzaccio*, follows the trend back toward conventional opera by taking audiences to the torture chambers of the Medici. It has been 'workshopped' in part by the Australian Opera, no doubt with a possible view to production, but its future is as yet uncertain. Not that Brumby has forgotten the youngsters and he is still the most serious contender in this field. His *The Marriage Machine* (1985) is a long way from conventional fairy tales, the title rôle (?) being taken by a computer which breaks down while engaged in a dating service.

Others have also taken up the cudgels on behalf of children's operas (or operas for schools) in which Australian composers seem to excel. Apart from the many works by the two Brumbys, Geoff Carroll's *Professor Kobolt and the Krimson Krumpet* and Peter Narroway's *Ticka-Tocka-Linga*, and other works mentioned elsewhere, have been frequently performed. The State Opera of South Australia went further than other companies in 1986 by catering for the monster vogue of the 1980s by staging Malcolm Fox's *The Iron Man*. Like Alan John's *Frankie*, staged more modestly elsewhere in Adelaide at the same time, it was stronger on story than music and strongest of all on decor; very much adult-theatre spectacle for children, whatever its musical virtues. Anne Boyd's *The Little Mermaid* has quite a large audience among adults as well and *The Snow Queen* by Grahame Dudley has been seen in more than one state. If adult Australian operas could equal the standard and originality of their junior partners, everything in the Antipodean garden would indeed be lovely.

Only four Australian operas have had major productions in full-sized theatres in recent years. Less ambitious works (with smaller casts) have been staged frequently, but the 'big ones' got the publicity and may be remembered longer, if not necessarily for the right reasons. In chronological order, they are Larry Sitsky's *Lenz* and Felix Werder's *The Affair*, staged in the Sydney Opera House by the Australian Opera in 1974; Barry Conyngham's *Fly*, produced by the Victoria State Opera in Melbourne's new State Theatre in 1984; and Meale's *Voss* (AO in the Adelaide Festival Theatre 1986).

The pecking order among Australian opera composers has changed a lot over the years. *Anno Domini* plays havoc with the human mind not only creatively, but emotionally. The angry young man of the 1970s was George Dreyfus, the angry (not so) old man was Felix Werder. Larry Sitsky wasn't angry at all and the rest were nowhere. All now appear resigned to a fate of 'no future in opera', perhaps unjustly so.

Felix Werder has about a dozen complete operas in

The strange *Affair* of the Prime Minister's picture.
The first Australian operas to be staged in the Sydney Opera House (1974) were two one-acters by Larry Sitsky and Felix Werder. The latter instructed his singers that it was not necessary to follow his written notes.

There was a story line, however, and producer Stephen Hall made capital out of featuring a controversial picture of a Prime Minister who helped the arts, including opera, but departed on unmusical grounds within a year. (Etela Piha and Robert Eddie.)

manuscript. They vary from small trifles to frankly over ambitious monster works. Now in his sixties, hope no longer springs eternal, though three of his operas have been performed publicly, *The Affair*, *Private* and *Kisses for a Quid*. He writes with incredible facility and speed, but shows a disregard for the human voice which, if it exists in his un-performed works, makes their neglect understandable. Werder is extraordinary in that he does not demand that his singers produce his notes correctly pitched. How he expects the end result to be duplicated in the event of an unexpected success is far from clear. *The Affair* was staged by the Australian Opera as a form of operatic tokenism, because the angry men at both ends of the age scale were making a lot of noise. The Werder work was almost certainly not chosen for its music, but for its libretto, which satirized politicians during Canberra's most turbulent years, during the reign of Prime Minister Gough Whitlam. The thought is inescapable that the AO chose that subject because it enabled its producer, Stephen Hall, to feature an enormous, and controversial, portrait of Whitlam centre stage.

George Dreyfus had a different theory. Though less productive than Werder in quantitative terms of operas actually put down on paper, he made more noise than all the other opera composers put together. He cast endless stones into the operatic millpond and it was probably a major opera symposium arranged by him (or rather by his wife, Kay Dreyfus) in 1973 which prompted the Australian Opera to stage its double bill of Australian works — deliberately omitting, however, the Dreyfus opera it had commissioned, *The Gilt-Edged Kid*. It was Dreyfus' contention that a commission to write an opera includes the production of the end result. (Regardless of the apparent merits of the work?) Whether *The Gilt-Edged Kid* was good, bad or indifferent is not really relevant. The AO refused to stage it, has not staged it and is unlikely to stage it in the future. (Dreyfus later produced a performance of it at his own expense, but it has not re-surfaced since.)

Fortunately, or unfortunately, Dreyfus has mellowed with age and is now philosophical about it all. I say 'unfortunately', because Dreyfus is a very successful purveyor of incidental music for films, television and plays and in at least one case, the Melbourne Theatre Company's *The Sentimental Bloke* in 1986, his contribution was long and original enough to imply that a full

opera of this Australian classic from his pen could be an outstanding success — if provided with an original libretto!

It was almost certainly also the libretto which ruined the early chances of the young Dreyfus. His first opera, *Garni Sands* (1965), had a hopeless text, yet he believed in it to the point of sending copies to all and sundry, thereby discouraging all but those who, for whatever reason, saw or heard the music he had written for it. *Garni Sands* has probably been staged by more companies than any other twentieth-century opera written in Australia. It was even seen briefly in New York and last revived in Sydney in 1985, twenty years after its creation. The fact that in spite of this few people have ever heard of the work, even though its composer is by now very famous indeed, seems to have soured him towards the

Angry young man with a sense of humour.
George Dreyfus may have stirred the operatic pot to his own disadvantage, but at least he has given a certain amount of pleasure to people by not taking life too seriously. Only Dreyfus could have sent up royalty right royally in *The Lamentable Reign of King Charles the Last* at the 1976 Adelaide Festival. (Patsy Hemingway as Charles with David Brennan and John Wood's Winston Churchill.)

'Du bist der Lenz', not from *Die Walküre*.
Larry Sitsky's *Lenz* (staged in 1974 with Werder's *The Affair*) could have been enlarged to produce a major work, if he had developed its potential further. It remained a 'short story' opera based on a novel by Büchner, the author of *Wozzeck*. (Ron Stevens as the straight-jacketed Lenz.)

medium. Dreyfus is just leaving his fifties and one can only hope that his current disillusionment with opera is not permanent. One good libretto is all he really needs. Dreyfus made a brief contribution to the 1976 Adelaide Festival; his *The Lamentable Reign of King Charles the Last* was good intimate-revue material knocked together by Tim Robertson. Staged on a shoestring and almost certainly written in haste, it had more merit than many an expensively staged serious opera.

The composer of the opera chosen to partner Werder's *Affair* was Sitsky's *Lenz*.

Larry Sitsky falls into a different class. He has written what could be described as the most successful modern Australian Opera before *Voss*, *The Fall of the House of Usher*, based solidly on the original Edgar Allan Poe story, which is an ideal vehicle for visual drama supplementing a music score of some body. *The House of Usher* has been produced in most Australian states and by ABC television. It is hardly a fad, nor have there been enough performances to say that it is a popular success; but the announcement of a performance is invariably greeted with respect in a field where groans are more commonly heard.

Sitsky's second work, *Lenz*, was a *succès d'estime* when staged by the Australian Opera. It is one of the few modern works which gets better as it goes along; most such operas start with a good idea and then peter out. Anybody not taken with *Lenz* at the start is completely committed when the final curtain comes down; no mean achievement. It is too early to know whether Sitsky can become the Tippett of Australia, but he is musically the most successful contender to date, though he has failed to progress since *Lenz*. How good his one major opera, *The Golem*, is remains to be seen. The Australian Opera commissioned it, but has to date declined to produce it. (Echoes of *The Gilt-Edged Kid*, except that Sitsky is sensibly not ruining his chances by shouting from the rooftops about it.)

James Penberthy in Perth is another composer who has a large number of unperformed works, several on Aboriginal themes. Until they are given a hearing, their worth cannot be evaluated. Only *Dalgerie*, with lyrics by Mary Durack, was performed in 1959; Gregory Dempsey sang the Aboriginal lead, Mundit.

Then there is a solitary work by the oldest-living Australian composer, Margaret Sutherland. The undoubted success of *The Young Kabbarli* (which has been recorded by HMV) in Hobart, Adelaide and Melbourne is all the more gratifying because the subject is genuinely Australian — the story of Daisy Bates, a pioneer lady whose care for Aborigines was her whole life. It is far from being a lasting masterpiece, but then there has never yet been an opera written in Australia which can be so described.

The last decade or so has seen the rise of various young composers whose actions have been prompted by the size of grants rather than idealistic hopes that a major company will stage them. Two, Barry Conyngham's *Fly* and Meale's *Voss* did achieve that desirable goal, but only after being backed by major funding bodies. The reality that one was a total failure and the other a substantial success only goes to prove that the project officers of the Australia Council are human. No artistic work can be judged until finally seen or heard; you cannot judge an opera by its score, though the dismal libretto of *Fly* should surely have alerted somebody to the dangers of staging the work as elaborately as if it were a new Puccini or Verdi opera.

Conyngham's music for *Fly* was no better and no worse than that of many a modern opera staged at Covent Garden or The Coliseum in London. Reading English reviews, however, it is very seldom that the libretti of musically-mediocre works are the subject of serious criticism. There is no way that *Fly* can be re-written without Murray Copeland's libretto and Conyngham is as much to blame for accepting it and the Victoria State Opera for staging it as Copeland is for writing it. How do you hold an audience's attention with the story of an Australian inventor, Lawrence Hargrave, the man on the back of our twenty-dollar note, who was the unsuccessful designer of an early flying machine and once explored the River Fly in New

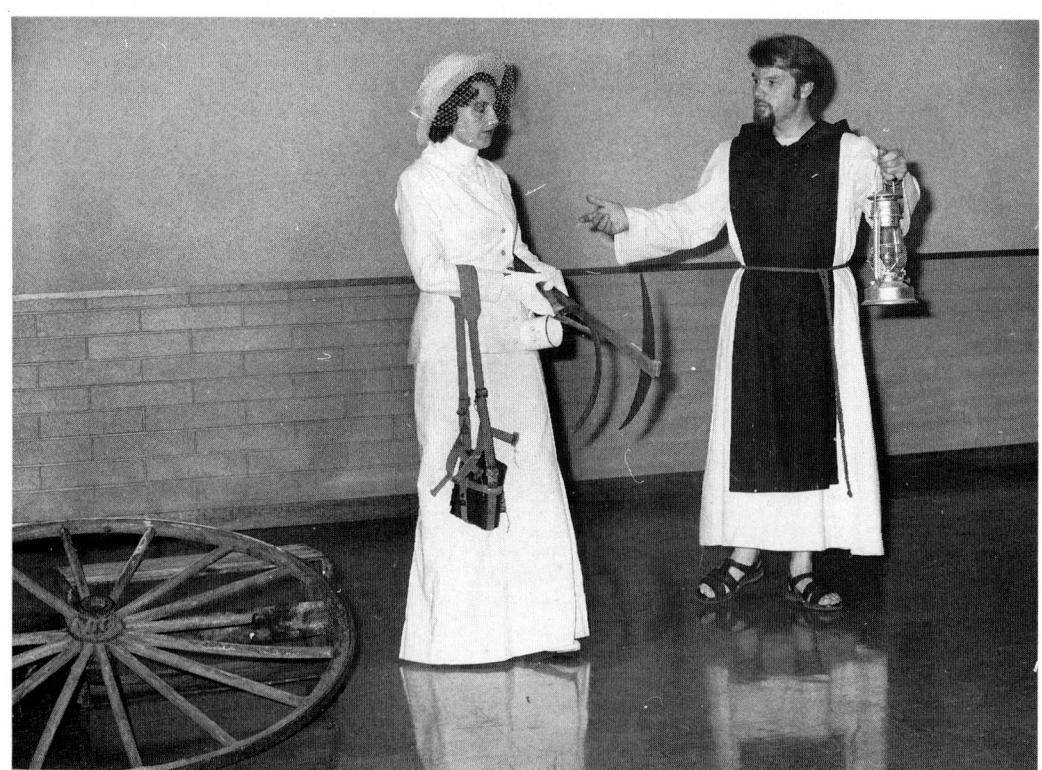

The other Sutherland.
No relation to 'Our Joan', Margaret Sutherland, the doyen of Australian composers wrote a genuine Australian opera *The Young Kabbarli* about the pioneering Daisy Bates and her care for Aborigines. It was financed, like Daisy Bates herself, on a shoestring in 1972, but was seen in three states. (Genty Stevens and John McKenzie.)

Guinea? Copeland shows no attempt at flying by Hargrave, not even a model on which he may be working. As for the flash-back to New Guinea, it can only have been inserted as a weak pun on the title of the opera: *Fly — fly* . . . On such a skeleton surely no composer could build a successful opera.

The minor works (minor purely in the dimensional sense) that are produced by mainly younger composers run very much on parallel lines with what is going on overseas. 'Music theatre', as opposed to traditional opera, can be staged on a gigantic scale, but few companies can afford to play the works of Philip Glass, for example, even though he has acquired quite a vogue since he produced *Einstein on the Beach* in 1976. I shall not attempt to define the difference between opera and music theatre;

that would be as futile as trying to explain why any record company should call itself 'Tomato'. (*Einstein* was first recorded on the Tomato label!) Nobody knows where the new medium begins or the old one ends. But in the most general, and possibly misleading, of terms: if it doesn't make sense, it is probably 'music theatre'.

It is no accident that Brian Howard's most successful theatre work to date is based on a Franz Kafka story about a man who changes into a dung beetle, or that its libretto should come from the pen of the madcap British playwright-cum-actor Steven Berkoff. *Metamorphosis* has had several productions since the Victoria State Opera produced it in St Martin's, the cheapest and most unsuitable theatre for opera in Melbourne, in 1983, with Lyndon Terracini as Gregor, the man-turned-beetle. Australian music theatre must be cheap to be produced and Howard certainly has found that no barrier. If anything, *Metamorphosis* is too operatic, in a modern sort of way; however lunatic the action, it *almost* makes sense, which is more than can be said about his earlier *Inner Voices*. This was also staged by Australia's most consistent producer of local works, the VSO, but in the acoustic graveyard called the Grant Street Theatre, four years earlier. I have been unable to trace a theatre performance

Kafka's dung beetle.
Brian Howard's innovative, modern, music theatre includes *Metamorphosis*, based on Kafka's tale of man-turned-beetle. Premièred by the Victoria State Opera in 1983, it has already been staged by the Australian Opera as well. (Lyndon Terracini as Gregor metamorphosing, with Merlyn Quaife, Ian Cousins and Fiona Maconaghie, *left to right*.)

of the most (il)logical of Howard's theatre pieces, *Fringe of Leaves*, which was inspired by the Patrick White novel of that name. Fascinated by the words, Howard was commissioned to set them to music by the Australian Chamber Orchestra, only to find that the consonants interfered with what he wanted to express. The end result was a nonsensical gabble of vowels inspired by words which were never heard, though *Fringe of Leaves* is still dedicated to Patrick White! But, remember, music theatre need not make sense.

The influence of Patrick White has been widely felt in Australian music and the reason is not hard to find. He writes neither poetry nor books, but beautiful words. His most famous work, *Voss*, was the subject of immense speculation for years in the film world. Everybody was convinced that the story about the German explorer Friedrich Leichhardt, who attempted to cross the Australian continent from east to west and was never heard from again, would make a superb film. The character Voss is clearly modelled on Leichhardt and the press had a field day discussing the immense sums which changed hands for the rights to make this great Australian movie, which somehow disappeared into the air, just like its hero. Nobody in their right mind would have imagined that Voss would end up as the lead in a very grand opera, or piece of music theatre. *Voss* is in many ways a halfway house between the two, except that Meale's previous long and hard-earned reputation as a composer should have brought him down soundly on the side of abstract music theatre, particularly since White's book was in itself an abstraction in words with only the loosest of narrative to hold the beautiful flow together. The end result has surprised not a few people on both sides of the musical fence.

Voss had a long period of incubation, being commissioned while Harry M. Miller and even Ken Russell were still making news about an always-imminent film of the novel, which has yet to materialize. The exact date of the opera's commissioning is a mystery, for all that has been written about it. It all probably started in 1969, when Stephen Hall commissioned seven Australian composers to write one-act operas for the AO. I shall not dwell on the works which failed to materialize, even though their creators had received retainers in advance, but they included Richard Meale's *Caligula*, which never got much further than the drawing board. Only Sitsky's *Lenz*, Werder's *The Affair* and *The Gilt-edged Kid* by

Delayed rights of passage. Peter Sculthorpe was commissioned to write an Australian opera for the opening of the Sydney Opera House. It was not ready for production until a year after the opening and then had no plot, no action, no solo singers, but a lot of dancers, drums, giant puppets and a chorus. His *Rites of Passage*, however good, was not an opera.

Dreyfus were ever completed. Apart from the Australian Opera's announcement in 1973 that the new Sydney Opera House would see the premières of a whole series of new Australian operas, all was very quiet on the opera front; not even the Opera Theatre's projected opening attraction, Sculthorpe's *Rites of Passage*, surfaced in time.

It must have been during those chaotic early months of John Winther's reign that the more promising of the local composers re-negotiated their contracts. Among them were two major figures, Larry Sitsky and Richard Meale. The choice of Sitsky was logical, the inclusion of Meale incomprehensible. The gestation period of *Voss* is ignored by the Australian Opera's official publications. The programme for the world première at the Adelaide Festival on 1 March 1986 starts only in 1977 with the part Peter Hemmings played in advancing the project. Presumably John Winther made the original choice, but why? Meale had written little, if anything, for the voice, had never tried his hand at opera and his reputation was based on music for which *avant garde* would have been an understatement.

Nevertheless, Meale was commissioned. A libretto was prepared by Rodney Hall for *Juliet's Memoirs*, but Meale's second try at opera was no easier than the first and he abandoned it. Yet, obviously the idea of writing an opera attracted him, and when Hemmings proposed *Voss* as a subject in 1978, with David Malouf as the librettist and Jim Sharman as the producer, Meale at last found the inspiration he needed. Malouf, one of our more intelligent music critics for many years and an author of several books, had always liked Meale's music. Sharman had produced several Patrick White plays, and so the ball started rolling, to stop in the hands of conductor Stuart Challender in 1984. A lot had happened in the intervening years in the Australian Opera, but Patrick Veitch must be given his share of the kudos for scheduling the end result for production, to the extent of arranging for *Voss* to open the Sydney season three months after the Adelaide première and the Melbourne season in 1987.

If every *Voss* performance was sold out (some *were* all but sold out) only a few thousand people could have seen it to date. It is still a largely unknown quantity, though a videotape and a recording with the original cast already exist. The big surprise and, I believe, the reason for its immediate success was the unexpected melodiousness of Meale's music. Not only did he use some genuine nineteenth-century tunes for scenes set in Old Sydney, but the second act contains a lengthy duet which can only be described as operatic in the best possible fashion; that is, originally tuneful and not reminiscent of any other composer, least of all its creator, the Australian Richard Meale. He also had at his disposal a full symphony orchestra which a talented conductor, Stuart Challender, used symphonically in a most sympathetic manner, be the scene dramatic, romantic, or corny colonial.

It is difficult for me to write coherently about the libretto which must divide the audience far more than the music ever will. The minority, which condemns Meale for leaving atonality for more conventional fields, forgets that this is a trend apparent world-wide and Meale was at least no imitator. The libretto is a work of genius. Nobody could possibly fault what Malouf did with Patrick White's basic story line, of how Voss sets out to cross Australia with a small band of men, leaving a prim spinster in Sydney whom he has promised to marry. (Love hardly comes into it.) Malouf stayed absolutely true to the text. The problem is that large proportions of the population find the book *Voss* unreadable, however much White's extravagant mastery of language may be admired. To them the opera is as incomprehensible as the book. You can equate Malouf/White with Boito/Shakespeare. You can equate Malouf/Boito. You can even equate *Othello/Voss*, if you wish. But you can not compare White with Shakespeare. Ay, there's the rub!

Enter Jim Sharman, taken from his production of *The Rocky Horror Show* in London in 1978 to participate in the years of creation of this masterpiece, flawed only in the development of the impossible, abstract plot. This is the basis of White's book and has been faithfully transferred to the opera. To give but a single example: Laura and Voss sing the love duet, to which I have already referred, while she is in Sydney and he in the Central Australian desert. On film (are you listening, Harry M.?) one can use montage and other visual tricks to bring this to life. On a stage, within sight of a live audience, it is a physical impossibility. All credit to the way Brian Thomson's set and Luciana Arrighi's costumes tried to overcome such impossible hurdles. The transformation of a dining room interior into a starry open-air plain was wonderfully well realized. But the moment the

The 'White' elephant pays off.

Patrick White's book *Voss* is considered a twentieth-century masterpiece, hard to read and aborted repeatedly as a subject for a film. That Richard Meale and his librettist, David Malouf, should have turned it into the most successful native opera to date is almost a miracle. Recorded in full by its original cast, only time will prove whether *Voss* is going to be Australia's *Peter Grimes*.

The Plan.

Above: Voss, a German explorer planning to cross the Australian continent from east to west, meets his wealthy Sydney backers. (The story is based on Leichhardt's 1844 expedition, which ended in tragedy.)

The Survivor
Opposite: Like the challenge of Australia itself, Laura Trevelyan in *Voss* is the inspiration which builds nations on the hardships of pioneers who perish along the way. (Marilyn Richardson.)

The Lovers.
Voss proposes to Laura in the garden of her home before setting out. Their 'love' is a spiritual one which is never spelled-out.

The Journey.
The last outpost before the expedition enters the desert. (*Left to right*: Irene Waugh, Steve Dodd, Robert Eddie, Geoffrey Chard.)

The Death of Voss.
Opposite: In spirit Laura communes with Voss throughout his trials and is with him as the Aboriginal Jacky (Raymond Blanco) kills him when their fate is sealed.

Geoffrey Chard as Voss

words began to be sung so beautifully, the artificiality of it all became, if not ludicrous, at least unrealistic — like Patrick White's book! One can only praise Malouf, and White's fans will hug themselves with joy. Yet, as an opera plain and simple, *Voss* has been let down by White (or Hemmings, if you like) for to the average person it simply does not make sense.

Perhaps, in all fairness, I should add: neither does many a standard eighteenth or nineteenth-century opera which is in the regular repertoire. Who are Australians that they should quibble on such a minor point while the most important part of the opera, the music and its performance, is as good as it was during the initial three seasons of *Voss*? Geoffrey Chard's Voss, Marilyn Richard-

Marilyn Richardson as Laura.

son's Laura and Robert Gard, John Pringle, Robeert Eddie, Gregory Tomlinson, Clifford Grant, Heather Begg, Anne-Maree McDonald, Lesley Stender, William Bamford, Irene Waugh and the Aborigines Steve Dodd and Raymond Blanco deserve to have their names preserved for having participated in what has been the most important event in Australian musical history to date.

Even without going into the detail which some may have expected. I have devoted considerable space to something which really does not exist, native Australian opera. It is a fragile plant with which we must persevere and which must be encouraged. At the same time it is foolish to pretend that this is not the musical field in which Australia lags furthest behind the rest of the world.

ACT 4:

great fleas have little fleas

PRELUDE

In a country as large as Australia the establishment of local groups, be they in the field of opera, ballet, drama or any other art form, is far more important than in more thickly-populated areas like Europe or the United States. Not only do these countries have literally hundreds of minor opera companies of varying importance, but their citizens are within easy reach of many major centres of the art; it is not inconceivable for a Londoner interested in opera to spend a few days in Milan or Bayreuth or, if the bug bites hard enough and the bank account permits, even in New York. Similarly, the influx of Americans into Europe each year is on a scale which enables opera buffs to see and hear the work of the majority of the world's companies almost at will.

The title of my last act comes from a book called appropriately enough *A Budget of Paradoxes*, written by a mathematician, Augustus de Morgan. The full first stanza reads: 'Great fleas have little fleas upon their backs to bite 'em, And little fleas have lesser fleas, and so *ad infinitum*'. Generally speaking, the smaller overseas opera houses are less ambitious in their attitudes than Australian ones. I have as yet to hear of a company which in all seriousness tried to replace the major national opera company of the country in which it was resident. Personal antagonisms emerge, no matter where or in what field human endeavour expresses itself, but opera is an impossibly complex flea to be seriously bothered by rivalry — except in Australia.

Distance has always been Australia's greatest enemy, and it is only in the last few decades that we have learnt to hold our own in commerce, science, the arts and everything else, thanks to the emergence of mass media like television, satellites and other methods of communication. Most Australians interested in opera have seen some telecasts from major and minor opera houses overseas, warts and all! Videotapes are usually actual performances and not the artificially perfected studio-sound recordings which have for too long made us believe that our opera is second-rate. I have no wish to start reciting chapter and verse to back my claims that we can and do compete with some of the best companies in the world, though financial limitations and the distance factor — which still frightens the better singers and the more sensible accountants in our own companies — cannot yet be ignored. But let me quote a single recent instance which may help to put the reader into a more receptive mood to the realities of operatic life in Australia.

It is no secret that England's Glyndebourne Festival Opera has a reputation for high standards in every aspect of opera production. It is even less of a secret that good tenors are rapidly acquiring a status comparable to that of the proverbial hens' teeth. Nevertheless, Glyndebourne ground rules demand good singers as much as good producers and designers. The big event of the 1985 Glyndebourne Festival was its first production of *Carmen*, directed by its own artistic director, Sir Peter Hall, a producer whose services are used by every major opera house in the world. Carmen and Don José were sung by Maria Ewing and Barry McCauley respectively.

One year later, in 1986, the Spoleto Festival in Melbourne included the controversial Ken Russell production of *Madame Butterfly* performed by the Victoria State Opera with imported soprano and tenor leads, Adriana Morelli and — Barry McCauley! I have no wish to malign

Mr McCauley, but he is not the world's greatest tenor. If the Melbourne Pinkerton was good enough for Glyndebourne's opening night only twelve months earlier, I think it is fair to conclude that Glyndebourne's tenor, who can be seen and heard in its own *Carmen* on videotapes on sale in Australia, shows that Glyndebourne is just as short of good tenors as we are in this country; we could certainly have replaced McCauley with several local tenors who would have done as well or better. (I know that comparisons are odious, but there comes a moment of truth when only concrete proof will convince our doubting Thomases and this example is recent enough to warrant inclusion here.)

Considering that Australia is immensely proud of its singers, the popularity of opera and operatic music here is not surprising. On the other hand, the snobbery element, which places anything imported above the local article, was ruinous to indigenous opera until the comparatively recent past. Even now, the true worth of the Australian Opera and several of the regional state companies is not recognized by the vast majority of audiences. Living on an illusion of excellence created through recordings of complete operas by casts which are rarely, if ever, assembled by even the best overseas houses, expectations are much too high. Unfortunately the traveller who can visit opera houses in Europe or America looks almost always for all-star casts, goes to the best available or simply does without. Anybody who has seen Domingo or Pavarotti returns to Australia starry-eyed, remembering only the greatness of each singer. Naturally, he cannot find their like in the Sydney Opera House. (It is very curious the way those who have seen inferior operas overseas conveniently forget about them very quickly.)

There is an abundance of operatic weeds which grow alongside some admittedly magnificent blooms overseas. The standards in 90 per cent of European opera houses are no better than those of Australian companies today and those of the majority are decidedly inferior. The balance includes the great showcases in the capital cities which admittedly can outclass even the best we produce in this country by sheer weight of budgets available. It is easy to forget that a small-scale production of high quality, say, the Australian Opera's *Jenůfa*, can be a lot more enjoyable than a routine *Simon Boccanegra* played at the Metropolitan with an international cast, or a scandalously inferior *Trovatore* in Munich. It so happens that I saw all three within one twelve-month span and I can assure you that the local audiences in Munich and New York on those nights would have looked with envy toward our national company. Of course, we can't equal the best the world has to offer, but we can more than hold our own against the *average* standards of opera houses overseas.

The popularity of opera as a medium of entertainment is hardly appreciated in this country, where it is considered an esoteric taste. That a family of father, mother, children and miscellaneous relatives should regularly visit the local theatre year in year out is almost inconceivable in our island nation, but it is the norm in almost any city elsewhere which has regular seasons of opera. Add to that the (unjustified) belief that what is shown here is inferior and the most expensive art form in the world becomes a luxury we cannot afford. Unfortunately, the expense of producing opera is such that its survival is dependent on the spending of some astronomical sums, while ordinary music making can exist on a much smaller budget.

Accepting that the public considers even the Australian Opera inferior in international terms, the disdain felt until fairly recently for our many amateur and semi-professional companies is understandable. Dozens of minor companies had, and some still have, their limited life-span, changing as their patrons and/or participants run out of money or into artistic crises. The introduction of subsidies at federal and state levels has changed the picture and, though the prospect of full-time opera companies in all capital cities is still a pipe dream, several *stagione*-type first-class companies already exist and will, we hope, find ways of growing as the public purse and box office returns expand. Advances made in recent years have been truly remarkable.

That the Australian Opera will one day become the Sydney Opera Company is almost inevitable, but the sheer economics involved in trying to create parallel companies for other cities staggers the imagination.

Our singers are as good as any.
While we cannot compete with the top dozen world-stars, the best Australian singers are as good or better than the vast majority of singers overseas. Joan Carden sings constantly with the Australian Opera and the various regional state companies. There is no record of an inferior performance from her since she returned to stay here in 1971. (In the VSO 1984 *Don Carlos*.)

Unrealistic attempts in the 1970s to keep the Australian Opera out of Melbourne and to turn the Victoria State Opera into a full-time opera company were doomed from the start and came to nothing. The only city which may – in the near future – support such a company on its own is Sydney. On the other hand, cities like San Francisco or Chicago have highly-respected annual opera seasons which run for a limited number of months (*stagiones* or 'seasons') and there is no reason at all why the high quality of existing state opera companies in Victoria, South Australia, Queensland and Western Australia should not develop that style of company far beyond what we have at present, God and the various funding bodies willing.

There will be hiccups, of course. The arts are full of quicksilver temperaments devoid of business sense. Like all truisms, the statement is a simple one of fact. Artists want to 'do their own thing', administrators want to run things efficiently and if the twain ever do meet, it is the exception rather than the rule; a quick look through the pages of this book will prove the point. Opera companies are invariably formed by singers and musicians, who then fine backers, who then in turn try and put in some kind of administration. The only known alternative is the company run by government decree, and that works only in countries in which the bureaucrats have been opera lovers for generations. What happens then is the lesson of Vienna, or any Italian city you may care to name; crisis follows crisis and the government foots the bill. Australia has been following the same pattern.

There is little point in trying to record the here-today-gone-tomorrow groups which have each in their own small way contributed over the years to give pleasure to audiences of varying sizes while offering valuable experience to young singers. Some, like Sydney's long-established Rockdale Opera are happy to continue on a path of semi-amateurism, occasionally producing some quite remarkable results. Others, who shall be nameless, began with the noblest of motives but faltered because of lack of administrative ability. Many a fine singer has taken part in some abysmal performances and many fine performances have been sung by abysmal singers. Australia is an opera-conscious country, but listing even the many admirable productions staged in the 1950s and 1960s in Hobart's Theatre Royal before its calamitous fire, for example, would add nothing to the history of the art in this country. It may be unfair to dismiss the conductor Walter Stiasny, who was responsible for keeping those seasons together, in a few words, but they did not lead to bigger things. Tasmania, like New Zealand, simply does not have a large enough population to support opera in a big enough way and continuity is essential to history.

Australia has celebrated the two-hundredth anniversary of the first landing of men who had actually seen the inside of an opera house. (Now, there is a concept for the Bicentenary to which no-one can object!) And today we have no less than five first-class opera companies in this country, though only one is operational full-time throughout the year. That company, the Australian Opera, and its history inevitably has formed the core of this book. But the 'competition' (horrid word) has become so strong in the last twelve years that space must be devoted to the other four; none appears to be in danger of falling apart, and some would like to become full-time competitors. Good luck to any which succeed, but opera relies on subsidies and they are as scarce as success. Many great cities have sold-out opera seasons each year without the companies being within coo-ee of full-time operation, while the vast majority of overseas state-subsidized companies which perform every week, every day – even on Sundays – are of vastly inferior standard to that which the citizens of Perth, Adelaide, Melbourne or Brisbane expect today.

Little more than a decade ago there was not one regional company capable of mounting major productions. The Victoria State Opera was close to financial collapse and the State Opera of South Australia was, after nearly twenty years of uneventful progress as an intimate opera company, capable of organizing some enterprising and original productions for the Adelaide Festivals – but not on its own! Whatever may have been happening in the other states at that time, there was one thing *all* Australian companies lacked: a foreseeable future. What was around the next corner is history now, and it makes pleasant reading, I believe.

The fact that both those state companies emerged 'victorious' – as operetta librettos would put it – is a lesson which, I very much hope, will be learnt by future generations of administrators and artistic directors. There is something about learning from your mistakes which applies as much to artists as to inventors, or politicians. Perhaps, in time, it will extend to bringing peace on Earth and goodwill (and opera) to all men. If man can put an opera company together and make it work, bringing universal peace should be easy.

Building new audiences
must start at an early age.
Most companies have special
productions designed for
schools, none more so than
the Victorian State Opera.
(*Sid, the Serpent Who Wanted to
Sing by Malcolm Fox*, 1984.)

ACT 4 : SCENE 1
OPERA IN VICTORIA

The Victorian Opera Company developed out of amateurism and its growth was gradual. For a solid twenty-five years its progress was rather like that of a butterfly, halting and sometimes not very pretty to look at, before the first signs of brilliant wings began to appear. The birth of the company can actually be pinpointed: On 13 November 1943 the Mont Albert Choral Society staged Gilbert and Sullivan's *The Pirates of Penzance*. Historically its most noteworthy personage was a seventeen-year-old schoolgirl playing Kate, one of the less important daughters of Major-General Stanley. Few would remember who was the very model of a modern major-general that night, but Kate was the first stage appearance of a soprano who was to gain world-fame: Marie Collier. The Mont Albert Choral Society became the Youth Operatic Society, the Hawthorn Operatic Society, the Victorian Light Opera Company and, finally, the Victorian Opera Company. All productions were financed by the participants, costumes were made by the singers, the board of directors elected by the artists themselves. One man, Leonard Spira, finally turned an amateurish plaything into a serious musical body when, in 1962, the constant diet of Gilbert and Sullivan grew tiresome. Playing in Melbourne venues as varied as the tiny Russell Street Theatre, the huge Palais in St Kilda or some local church hall in Toorak, Spira produced results which made both critics and the public sit up.

Spira started with excellence in a most unlikely area for an amateur company: orchestras created for each short season, whose standards were miraculous at a time when the Trust orchestras did not yet exist. (For all I know, Spira's miracle players all went into those orchestras in the end.) My first experience of the VOC was a performance of *The Merry Wives of Windsor* at Russell Street, when thirty musicians crammed underneath a microscopic stage apron produced a magical overture — and that is not an easy piece to play! On this solid foundation were placed singers in the making, who gave performances no worse than those they produced in their later professional careers. John Pringle in his early twenties may not have been a *basso profundo*, but he played parts like Osmin and Falstaff with a gusto and artistry which carried all before it. A young Janice Taylor sang with sweetness and charm. Margaret Haggart already produced that shattering top register which later was to make her a permanent member of the English National Opera at the Coliseum in London. Graeme Ewer sang and clowned with *élan* and even genuine amateurs, like tenor Ian Stapleton, gave performances of professional standards.

For six years Spira, the inspired amateur, an architect-turned-hornplayer-turned-conductor, went from strength to strength. For the first time an amateur company was treated with respect rather than condescension by the critics. Productions may not always have been of professional standards (home-made costumes and scenery) but there was little to fault on the musical side. Spira even went so far as to recruit a young and raw assistant conductor, an understudy. There always has been a good supply of singers in Melbourne, but there were, and are, no schools for conductors. In 1965 Stuart Challender began to learn his craft and was soon conducting the occasional performance. Spira naturally remained in overall charge. Then Challender became the company's musical director briefly in 1968 when Spira went overseas to study. The *Albert Herring* Challender put onto the stage was as good as any seen in Australia since then. Ian Stapleton's Albert was a joy and Margaret Haggart's Lady Billows was as subtle as her Abigaille was spectacular in the total orchestral disaster of *Nabucco* after Challender had followed Spira overseas. (Today he is the principal conductor of the Sydney Symphony Orchestra, having proved himself a major force with the Australian Opera first.)

The loss of both Spira and Challender left the VOC floundering. Standards disappeared and the debts doubled. After one short burst of renewed activity in 1969, when the season included Lauris Elms in Gluck's *Orpheus and Euridice* there was a return to amateurism of the worst kind. The new Australian Council for the Arts tried to keep the ailing infant alive, but it was a struggle until a new key man appeared on the scene in 1972 — Richard Divall, another conductor.

Divall had been a brief *enfant terrible* on the Australian music scene, doing excellent work and promptly undoing it again by an uncontrolled exuberance which sat ill with administrations trying to control him. The VOC gave him the responsibility he needed and the Council backed his plans, as did the state government. A policy of esoteric works catering for a minority audience, until then neglected, quickly brought back the packed houses of 1969.

With the company's finances in dire straights and its business management in what can only be described as a mess, Divall started his tenure with an imaginative, if risky, stroke. If theatres were too expensive, opera could be produced elsewhere: St Paul's Cathedral, for example. It was there in November 1972 that Divall made his debut with the company he still leads. The work: a fully staged production of *The Childhood of Christ* by Berlioz. The seats were hard, the acoustics abominable, but what more suitable place could there be for a semi-opera about Christ than a cathedral? Let some member of the huge cast recall the financial rewards they received in some autobiography one day. But Divall from the start showed tremendous flair for casting. His church opera was headed by Marilyn Richardson, David Parker and Brian Hansford!

In 1973 Divall went from the sublime to the sublimely ridiculous. At the Comedy Theatre the VOC presented an amateurishly-dressed and presented staging of a strange modern double bill: Poulenc's *The Breasts of Tiresias* and William Walton's very much non-opera

Façade, controversial works which might have made an impact had their staging not been quite so primitive. Poulenc's opera about child-bearing men and the lovely Tiresias who allows her breasts to escape from her bodice in the form of balloons was good fun, if incomprehensible. *Façade's* star among music lovers was Kevin McBeath who some years earlier had actually recorded the complex Sitwell text, which was spoken to Walton's strange mix of instruments playing music which has long since become popular in full orchestration as the accompaniment to a famous ballet. McBeath was, and remains, one of the best exponents of *Façade* in the world, but as a box office stunt he was made to share the work with a ludicrously notorious antique, the Melbourne hairdresser-cum-radio-personality, Stephanie Deste. There is no doubt that she sold a few tickets; it is not often that you get the chance to see a living (just) eccentric who had played leads in musicals before the First World War! It was an unforgettable evening, for all the wrong reasons and certainly did not enhance the company's reputation.

Divall returned to baroque opera, Monteverdi's *Coronation of Poppea*, starring Marilyn Richardson and Lauris Elms, played in the more economical premises of Melbourne University's Union Theatre. There were a whole series of operas in concert — works unlikely to be produced by any company. Thus an audience was created of those who simply wanted to hear the full score of musical treats they thought they would never see: *Idomeneo*, *La clemenza di Tito*, *The Trojans*, *Alcina*. Little did they know how soon genuine and good full stagings would arrive in the next decade. The company's final act for the year was Mozart's one act *Impresario*, part of a joint Opening Gala Performance (with the soon-to-be-defunct Ballet Victoria) in the newly re-built National Theatre in St Kilda. Production standards, which had been the weak point of the company even in Spira's day, began to improve. If Divall imported rather too many Sydney artists to please Victorian nationalists, at least musical standards were good and the repertoire adventurous enough to make people sit up. Lack of business management, always the weak point in young companies, made for heavy losses, but those were the days of ever-increasing subsidies.

Dame Joan Hammond became a board member and then artistic director. In 1975 the National Theatre, with a full-sized stage and large pit, was available cheaply and the VOC used it to present an ill-assorted selection of works. Purcell's *King Arthur*, with a cast of eighty or more, led by Ronald Dowd, certainly filled the stage of the new theatre, if not its auditorium. Mozart's *La finta giardiniera*, a primitive *Italian Girl in Algiers* and Gluck's *Orpheus and Euridice*, this time staged in the costumes of Gluck's own time, fared no better. Then, in a brief flourish, or flash, of grand operatic fireworks, came a production of Donizetti's *Mary Stuart* with June Bronhill, Nance Grant and David Parker, which showed promise of a future Melbourne Opera that could one day compete with the future Sydney (present Australian) Opera. Alas, over-ambition nearly killed the cat, for good opera also means money-losing opera and *Mary Stuart* was no exception. Unbelievably, the company tried to cash in on the apparent bonanza: box-office operas with box-office stars. *Hänsel and Gretel* was staged at the Comedy Theatre with two guest stars from the Australian Opera. Guest stars in *Hänsel and Gretel*? The deficit sky-rocketed. *Don Pasquale* with June Bronhill? Well, yes, but Donizetti after Donizetti? The company's new home at the National Theatre was nearly full, but three performances with expensive stars in an 800-seat theatre cannot but produce further losses. The Victorian Ministry for the Arts complained about this, that and the other. Dame Joan Hammond resigned amid a lot of publicity about changes of policy. A deficit of $84 000 was announced for 1975.

The Victorian Opera Company met a duplication of the kind of troubles which beset the best companies overseas. Financial and artistic crises while standards and audiences are rising are the norm, not the exception in opera. They were not the end of the VOC, but another step on the way up. It was only a small company as yet, but changes of repertoire or policy are a part of normal growth and the resignations of artistic directors seldom kill a company.

To be fair, Divall was not present during some of the worst crises; he has too often, and worthily, been given bursaries to study overseas. A Churchill fellowship kept him away when plans for 1976 were announced. He came back, but was then faced with the resignation of his artistic director, the sacking of the general manager, a new chairman of the board and the cancellation of the whole 1976 subscription season – including Tchaikovsky's *The Queen of Spades*; truly, there was madness in their method! Only *Don Pasquale*, which was already in rehearsal with June Bronhill, ever saw the light of day.

Instead of a 1976 subscription series the VOC was forced to accept a gift which turned out to be more valuable than many people thought at first. Ken Mackenzie-Forbes had come to the Victorian Ministry for the Arts from the Australia Council via managing the Trust orchestras. Now he was put in charge of the crumbling Victorian Opera Company, which was re-named the Victoria State Opera.

The then Victorian Premier and self-appointed Minister for the Arts, Rupert (Dick) Hamer, was a boon to the arts in the state, but had just shown suitable severity in allowing the bankrupt Ballet Victoria to go under. He stopped the VSO before it could follow the same path, little knowing that after his retirement he would become the chairman of what had by then become a major opera company which he himself, however indirectly, had really brought into being in 1976. The re-named Victoria State Opera was going to be a practical proposition, or else. Thanks to Divall and Mackenzie-Forbes 'or else' has not eventuated. Not that the funding from the Australia Council ($53 000) or from the Victorian Ministry ($191 000) was enough to justify the ambitious plans for 1977 announced by the 'new' company. Surprisingly enough, nothing was cancelled, a remarkable achievement in organization, management and bloody hard work by all the people concerned.

Credit should perhaps also be given to Robin Lovejoy, a pioneer of the old Trust Opera Company, who was approached by Mackenzie-Forbes and only reluctantly agreed to become 'artistic consultant' to the company. Artistic consultant for a long time meant little more than helping to run everything in the company other than the actual conducting. Lovejoy produced most of the best operas for years and few of the worst. Be it planning repertoire, finding staff, costumes, scenery, props, coaching, make-up or how to tie a Greek sandal, Lovejoy was there to take care of it. During the key four years of a Melbourne company this Sydney-based 'consultant' was always where he was needed most. His contribution to the early years of the VSO cannot and should not be ignored. He died in harness, so to speak, in Sydney, but not under dramatically theatrical circumstances. Australia as well as Victoria should remember his name.

The full-time singers under contract to the company at the time (an intended nucleus for the future) totalled

The successful flop.
Disaster was predicted when the Victoria State Opera decided to stage *Pelléas and Melisande* in 1977. Difficult to do well even with unlimited funds, and never good box office, it seemed a suicidal venture for a struggling regional company. Impossibly cheap but effective designs by Kenneth Rowell and Richard Divall's magic baton made it a highlight worthy of any Australian company, and the public responded. (Yvonne Kenny and Graeme Wall.)

two, Ian Cousins and Halina Nieckarz, reduced to only one when half the 'ensemble' (Nieckarz) went overseas. The company nevertheless ventured for the first time into the only real opera house Melbourne had at that time, the Princess Theatre. The two major works of the year were Offenbach's *La Belle Hélène* with the sexy Suzanne Steele in the title rôle. Later to die tragically, Steele pulled no punches, only strings; when it was pointed out that the tapes of her G-string could be seen in silhouette, she chose to appear totally nude in one scene, while Kenneth Rowell's delightfully witty designs left the Paris of Robert Gard with a mini-skirt any girl would have found to be on the brief side. Both artists produced good singing from the other end of their anatomy and the excellent supporting cast included the

Agamemnon of John Wood — looking like Winston Churchill in drag and dancing athletic ballet steps while singing complicated patter songs! The production was immediately snapped up by the Adelaide Festival Theatre and must have eased the company's financial problems considerably. Though Offenbach is not Wagner, no company has ever had a better send-off on what was a far-from-easy start.

Instant doom was predicted (by the author of these lines among others) for the other major work of 1977, Debussy's *Pelléas and Mélisande*. *Pelléas* is considered box-office poison by most opera houses, no matter how good the cast. It seemed a foolhardy choice for a company without an established regular public and with limited funds to tackle the work. Thanks to expatriate

Yvonne Kenny, who returned from London, and some brilliant casting (Graeme Wall, John Pringle, Noël Mangin, Margot Cory, Rosemary Gunn) and remarkably cheap, but very effective designs by Kenneth Rowell, the result was what must be that rarest thing of all, a sold-out season of *Pelléas*. Divall's preoccupation with baroque opera produced Monteverdi's *L'Orfeo*, an interesting contrast to the Gluck version, but quite beyond the capacities of Ian Cousins and Halina Nieckarz. Only the work of Robin Lovejoy saved some of the artistic bacon.

Bartók's *Bluebeard's Castle*, if considered as a concert version, was somewhat better, but its staging in the Great Hall of the National Gallery made it a visual and acoustic disaster, the fine singing of Lauris Elms and Noël Mangin under the direction of John Hopkins notwithstanding. The only other presentation which can be described as opera in the season took place in the Grant Street Theatre, another disaster area acoustically. A triple bill of 'contemporary music theatre' works was certainly that. Only Felix Werder's *Agamemnon* (sung straight, not *à la* John Wood) was an opera. *Mo* by George Dreyfus was a short curtain-raiser about the famous Australian comedian, but the third work deserves a place in this opera history for all the wrong reasons. *Die Puppe* by Walter Haupt of Munich was re-christened *The Sex Doll* to cash-in on the sensationalism of the subject. Suffice to say that the work's full cast consists of one single actor, who speaks but does not sing a note, and one of those inflatable sex-dolls. A piano quartet, electronic sounds, laser-type lighting, no story, only philosophizing, partly through words projected on a screen — I query whether *Die Puppe* can even be classed as contemporary music theatre, let alone opera.

The various concerts, which continue to the present day, were extensive and adventurous, ranging that year from Vivaldi's *Juditha Triumphans* to the *Triumphal Funeral Symphony* by Berlioz, which was staged in the Myer Music Bowl with 800 or so performers, probably close to the number Berlioz himself used originally. All of this was supported by a regular diet of children's operas touring schools which were a tremendous success. What child could resist *Geoffrey Goodsound Meets Dr Wrongnote and The Horrible Honky Tonks* or *The Three Lives of Penelope Paper*, all the work of Peter Narroway?

Most important of all, the new VSO reversed its anti-Australian Opera attitude and seasons were synchronized for the mutual benefit of both. 1977 was indeed a new beginning and it achieved what it set out to do in a business-like fashion. Divall built up a remarkable opera chorus of intelligent singers who to this day make themselves available for productions as needed. Doctors, dentists, lawyers and people working in professions in which they are able to take time off without losing their livelihood were enthused by Divall. Rehearsals are scheduled, where possible, for the evenings, but as D-Day arrives for each opera tighter schedules mean daytime work. Only the visible strides the company made from 1978 onward have held this ensemble together and its earning power from private sources has enabled Divall to assemble talent which would not normally be interested in full-time jobs as opera choristers.

Opera without singing.
Walter Haupt's piece of 'music theatre' *The Sex Doll* featured one actor, one inflatable sex doll, a piano quartet, but no singers. The projected texts (here in German) were translated and included the classic line 'Life wasn't meant to be easy'.

It's not the quality, just feel the price.
In 1978 the Victoria State Opera discovered that sets which look expensive can sell singing which ought to be able to do without it. John Truscott's designs for *Idomeneo* were superb, *and* looked expensive. For the first time something local looked good enough to justify purchase by the Australian Opera, which did just that.

If the new VSO had tried too much with too little in its first year as a truly professional company, it learned its lessons very quickly. 1978 saw but two new productions in the Princess Theatre, neither of which required reservations. Mozart's *Idomeneo* introduced the designs of John Truscott which were so good that they were taken over lock, stock and barrel by the Australian Opera for its next season in Sydney. The inevitable follow-up to the riotous *Belle Hélène* was *Orpheus in the Underworld*, starring Steele and Gard in Rowell designs, as before, but with a remarkable cameo by Ronald Dowd, no less, as John Styx. It was hard to believe that this was the same man who had acquitted himself so nobly in the title rôle of *Idomeneo*. In the meantime, schools tours and concert versions of unstageable operas continued. There was also an Australian triple bill at the Union Theatre, Peter Sculthorpe's *Eliza Fraser Sings*, Barry Convngham's *The Apology of Bony Anderson* and *Sin* ('An

This little piggy stayed at home – no wonder! Experimental Australian operas have been standard fare in Victoria for years. At first sensationalism, like Martin Friedl's *Sin*, with Jack Hibbert's hilarious text (1978), was needed to make Sculthorpe and Conyngham saleable in a triple bill. (*Left to right*: Evelyn Krape, Jan Friedl, John Wood.)

Immoral Fable in Seven Deadly Acts') by Martin Friedl and Jack Hibberd. The VSO has always been the most consistent promoter of Australian works and two-thirds of the programme even had Australian subjects. The humour of Jack Hibberd made the third less *Sin*ful than the audience found the earnestness of the other two works.

But all this was only the preparation for something few would have been optimistic enough to predict: the emergence of the VSO as a company with standards which could seriously compete with the Australian Opera. It was a pure accident that this coincided with its first joint-subscription series in Melbourne with the Australian Opera. Having two of its own productions sold together with the national company's *Mastersingers of Nuremberg* and Sutherland in *La traviata* was bound to increase audiences and it did. Though the VSO offered only two out of a twelve-opera series, neither was eclipsed by the five-to-one numerical superiority of the brother company from Sydney.

The production of Bizet's *The Pearl Fishers* in April 1979 was something which could be envied by almost any company in the world and the VSO has never looked back from that day. The designs, again by John Truscott, can only be described as magical and Divall's amazing knack of discovering new talent emerged with the engagement of the young New Zealander Keith Lewis to sing Nadir. Within a very short time Lewis was to be world-famous; Divall picked him when he was unknown. He was partnered by Yvonne Kenny, taking leave from Covent Garden for the second time to help the VSO. She was an ideal Leila and Noël Mangin was the High Priest. Lovejoy produced again and the whole company took their own private milestone to Sydney in the following year, where *The Pearl Fishers* shone with equal brightness as part of the Australian Opera's subscription series.

The other major production was another in Divall's 'unknown' Mozart series, *La Clemenza di Tito*, starring Lauris Elms, produced by Anthony Besch and designed by John Stoddart. Elsewhere Divall continued the schools programme and encouraged Australian composers by staging *Inner Voices*, the first opera written by the young Sydneysider Brian Howard, in the Grant Street Theatre.

In 1979 there was also a major off-stage effort by the VSO, an abortive attempt to become a full-time opera company in competition with the Australian Opera. This looks no nearer realization now than it did then, though by 1988 what was no more than a dream entertained by cockeyed optimists may well become a reality on some enchanted evening in the future.

A second, and last joint season with the Australian Opera in 1980 included Rossini's *Count Ory* with what was becoming a repertory cast: Kenny, Steele, Wood, Mangin, Besch and Rowell, plus an imported tenor, Justin Lavender, and Monteverdi's *Return of Ulysses*. Country touring for adult audiences began with a small-scale, but complete *Rigoletto* and in Sydney *The Pearl Fishers* was carrying the company's banner. From that time the VSO has stood on its own feet, though wise co-operation and collaboration with the Australian Opera and other companies has increased year by year.

Highlights of the early eighties included a *Faust* produced by Anthony Besch and transposed into the nineteenth century, with Keith Lewis in the title rôle, Joan Carden (Marguerite), Noël Mangin (Mephisto), Ian Cousins (Valentine) and Suzanne Steele (Siebel). Audiences also saw a *Don Pasquale*, with Melbourne tenor John Pickering returning for the first time from overseas and adding a long, expertly-played trumpet solo to his excellent singing. *Pelléas* and *Idomeneo* were revived and a few pedestrian productions inevitably appeared on occasion. (Was that really a *Carmen* we saw in 1982 and, we hope, never again?)

Things began to hum in 1983 in anticipation of the State Theatre opening. A booking mix-up forced the VSO to stage a revolutionary *Rigoletto* and *Eugene Onegin* in the vast spaces of the Palais Theatre. Capping the English National Opera version, which transplanted the Court of Mantua to American Mafia offices, the Melbourne *Rigoletto* adapted itself even better to Mussolini's Italy; designer Kenneth Rowell excelled himself in every way and producer Michael Beauchamp thought up some wonderful gimmicks — during the love duet the Duke looked at his watch over Gilda's shoulder! If the acoustics of the theatre robbed John Wood of real glory as Rigoletto, Amanda Thane's high soprano survived them more successfully. The point is that this was a production destined for many revivals over many years, just the kind of thing a good opera company needs. *Eugene Onegin* was the first venture into opera by ballet's Anne Woolliams and, with Anne Fraser's designs, was later borrowed by the Australian Opera. Geoffrey Chard,

Joan Carden and Keith Lewis were outstanding, over-coming the abominable acoustics of the Palais Theatre with clarity and conviction.

The year 1983 also saw Brian Howard's *Metamorphosis*, staged experimentally in the impossible (for opera) St Martin's Theatre and the list of touring operas mounted into double figures, creating a new public in country towns by offering fully-staged, if small-scale popular opera with first-class singers and a good orchestra instead of the pianos of the old Trust Touring Opera productions. The very end of the year saw the VSO sneaking into the new Melbourne Arts Centre complex ahead of the Aust-ralian Opera by staging *Samson and Delilah* in the already-completed Concert Hall. (The State Theatre was not to open until 1984.) Due tto financial limitations John Truscott's original designs for *Samson* were cancelled and Kenneth Rowell threw together a few metres off material to produce something which looked a million shekels. Nigel Triffitt added some real uninhibited nudes to the final Bacchanale to improvize an orgy of sorts and Richard Divall conducted, as he had all the other operas for years, superbly. Anthony Roden and Margreta Elkins became the first singers to star in the new complex and the fact that it was all done on a shoestring in the Concert Hall was no discredit to anyone.

The story of how such a 'shoestring' regional opera company in fact pulled itself up by its very own boot-laces, and overnight found the money to expand sensibly and practically into the Australian-Opera class, is the kind of stuff dreams or Hollywood films are made of. No doubt the VSO, thanks largely to its musical director, Richard Divall, who conducted and supervised just about everything it had done for a decade or more, had proved its worth. But it could only be as good as its Victorian Government grant and the peanuts which the Australia Council deigned to throw in its direction occasionally. Money, big money, is needed to produce top-ranking opera and the fast-growing commercial sponsors and 'Friends', who ran functions from garden parties to major balls, had little hope of providing the millions which Divall and his general manager, Ken Mackenzie-Forbes, really needed.

The unexpected realization of their dreams came in January 1984 in the Concert Hall of Melbourne's new Performing Arts Centre, but those dreams began fully two years earlier. Mackenzie-Forbes, the money manager, wanted Divall to schedule some Gilbert and Sullivan,

**Run for your life.
Here comes progress!**
The English National Opera
transferred *Rigoletto* to an
American Mafia setting.
Kenneth Rowell and the VSO
were more convincing by
putting the jester into
Mussolini's court. It worked
even better!

which can be staged comparatively cheaply and, if done as well as Divall handled anything from Monteverdi to Debussy, was bound to show a good profit. His choice was the same *Pirates of Penzance* which had launched the ancestors of the company in 1943. A foolproof box-office cast was not only assembled, but announced publicly. It was headed by the then top-ranking light operetta prima donna of Australia, Suzanne Steele and Melbourne's best-known actor, who happens to have an opera-sized baritone voice, Frederick Parslow.

In the meantime, in far-off America, the New York Shakespeare Festival, run by one Joseph Papp, had staged an immensely successful production of the same work in Central Park, from where it had transferred to a Broadway Theatre. (The fact that the same Shakespeare Festival also originated *A Chorus Line* shows that this is no joke, but the unvarnished truth. Anything is possible in the Big Apple.) Unknown to the VSO this quite-revolutionary updating of the *Pirates* was being considered by a local commercial management for an Australia-wide tour. On hearing the announcement of the VSO plans, the prospect of following a probably successful Steele-Parslow *Pirates* caused that option to be dropped and, as no director had yet been engaged for the VSO's first venture into G & S, Mackenzie-Forbes tried to get the rights of the New York production for his company. (As he had never seen this, he had no idea whether his cast would fit into it, but nobody here knew then just how different it was.)

Papp was not in favour of giving up his valuable rights to what he knew was a major money-spinner for the sake of ten performances in Melbourne in an opera-subscription series. After nearly a year of fruitless negotiation, Mackenzie-Forbes flew to New York to see for himself what earthly reason there could be for this hesitation. He soon realized that here was a Broadway show rather than a G & S opera and, undecided about details, simply signed on the dotted line. This still left him with Suzanne Steele (a most unsuitable Mabel for *The Pirates*, though she might very well have ended up as Ruth), Parslow and several other singers better fitted for a more conventional G & S production. The VSO decided to proceed with all existing plans, but scheduled *Iolanthe* in place of *The Pirates of Penzance* at the Princess Theatre in 1982. That *Iolanthe* produced no complaints about Steele, Parslow, John Wood or that scene-stealer Bev Shean, who would surely have been Gilbert's

Pirates Treasure from Broadway.
A Broadway show which started life in Central Park made literally millions for the Victoria State Opera. The jazzed-up *Pirates of Penzance* toured the nation for years, supplementing public funding.

favourite Queen of the Fairies had he still been alive.

Then the really hard work began. Mackenzie-Forbes approached several commercial managements to enter a joint venture to present a national tour of the Broadway *Pirates of Penzance* — and was knocked back. Proposals to the VSO board to do more than just use the new property as part of the 1983 season were also rejected. At that point, with money troubles right, left and centre, Mackenzie-Forbes may have been biting his nails somewhat. Then the tide turned. Dick (now Sir Rupert) Hamer was appointed Chairman of the VSO and he saw the virtues of the proposition at once. Through him the Arts Centre's George Fairfax was contacted and talked into using the new *Pirates* as a summer-holiday attraction for the Concert Hall in his new theatre complex in January 1984. The Australian Elizabethan Theatre Trust, shortly before the retirement of its long-standing, practical manager, Jeffry Joynton-Smith, joined the party to ensure follow-on seasons in other

Melbourne's new opera house — first production. Verdi's *Don Carlos* was a worthy opener of the latest Australian opera house, the State Theatre, when it opened on 1 August 1984. The sky was the limit now for the Victoria State Opera.

states. I have no idea how much money was made by the various Australian seasons of this *Pirates of Penzance*; whatever the sum, it was well-deserved. As I have seen the show on both sides of the Pacific, I can vouch for the fact that Australia's effort was as good, though perhaps not better than the original. Jon English, Simon Gallaher, John Wood, June Bronhill, twenty-year-old Marina Prior in her first stage rôle — none were in any way inferior. (Anyway, rock-singer Linda Ronstadt, who was the surprise sensation in the New York production, could not have filled the Australian theatres fuller than the capacity audiences the VSO attained — and Prior was one heck of a lot cheaper!) If the profit the VSO has made to date out of *The Pirates of Penzance* reaches two million dollars I shall not be surprised!

That the second 'opera' to be staged in Melbourne's new theatre complex was so successful and also that it was staged by the local company was to have a tremendous and unexpected effect on the future of opera in Victoria. A huge sum was suddenly at the disposal of a company which, while it had the confidence of both the Victorian government and the public by then, was still under-funded. It is interesting to speculate what form the first serious opera in the State Theatre would have taken, or whether Verdi's *Don Carlos* might not have been even more spectacular, if the ultimate results of this *Pirates* had been known at planning time.

Coincidentally, the Australian Opera also chose to present a musical as the first offering in the State Theatre, a season of *Fiddler on the Roof*. If you discount this (and you should not, for such works are played in opera houses world-wide) the VSO *Don Carlos* was the first real opera to be staged in the magnificent new theatre. It was far from bad, but over-ambitious, using every centimetre of the enormous stage when there were not enough singers to fill out the crowd scenes for which Verdi calls. John Copley's production was expectedly efficient, if not quite intimate enough in the private exchanges between characters who were made to stand twenty metres or so apart at times. Kristian Fredrikson's costumes were magnificently opulent and John Stoddart's scenery, ironically, was over-extended in the vast spaces the company insisted on using all the time. As in all Divall's work, the cast was uniformly good, without anybody outshining the theatre, which was the real star on 1 August 1984. Alphabetically, the singers were Arend Baumann (Phillip), Joan Carden (Elizabeth), Kenneth Collins (Carlos), Malcolm Donnelly (Rodrigo), Christine Ferraro (Celestial Voice), Rachel Gettler (Eboli) and Noël Mangin (Inquisitor). The opera was sung in English.

That first State Theatre season also included *Julius Caesar* with superb designs by Tom Lingwood, borrowed from the State Opera of South Australia, and starring Lauris Elms and Beverly Bergen at their considerable best; and a revival of the VSO *Faust* with John Pickering, Geoffrey Chard and Marilyn Richardson. The latter also sang Pamina to Robert Gard's Tamino in Anthony Besch's attempt to create a truly complete *Magic Flute*, which included things which might have surprised Mozart himself. Most important, though a failure, was the world première of a new Australian opera, Barry Conyngham's *Fly*. Obviously the major part of the budget had gone on *Don Carlos*, but it was an impressive season in a large and expensive venue for a company which had begun life as a continuing entity only seven years earlier.

The status of the VSO today without the windfall of the *Pirates of Penzance* profits would be somewhat different from the reality we know. No company on the verge of bankruptcy in 1975 could have staged a full-size *Lohengrin* a mere decade later and the VSO could not have done so without the money from *The Pirates* — Robert Salzer and the Wagner Society (the sponsors of *Lohengrin*) notwithstanding. Yet the most notable event of 1985 was not *Lohengrin*, but the VSO's private Spoleto Festival.

I am not convinced that the Spoleto Festival, founded with the best of motives by Gian Carlo Menotti in a tiny Italian town in 1958, needed duplication outside Italy. In 1977 he started a 'Festival of Two Worlds' by having another 'Spoleto Festival' in Charleston, a small town in North Carolina, USA. Eight years later he planned a 'Festival of Three Worlds' in Melbourne, Australia. Melbourne is a major metropolis and its city fathers could not turn the whole town over to Menotti, as the smaller cities had done. The VSO was invited to take part by staging Menotti's *The Consul* and planned accordingly and professionally. There was nothing professional about the rest of the festival. It was cancelled. The first Melbourne Spoleto Festival did not take place until the following year, 1986. But nothing was going to stop *The Consul* and nothing did. It added substantial honours to the VSO, Menotti provided his services as a producer together with a minor protégée Susan Hinshaw, no better than many local sopranos, to sing the rôle of Magda.

The most she achieved was to raise the spectre of Marie Collier's National Theatre Magda in 1953! Full marks, though, to Shaun Gurton for excellent sets, Suzanne Johnston for her fine Secretary and to the other local artists, not least Divall for his conducting. The opening night was televized.

Two popular operas earlier in the year showed signs of a sudden affluence in casting. The *Bohème* at least brought back two well-liked Australians who had made the grade overseas, Eilene Hannan from the English National Opera and John Pickering from Germany. Rosamund Illing, as Musetta, came from the Australian Opera, John Barden provided a workable set and John Copley thought up some genuinely original ideas for his Bohemians. *The Barber of Seville* caught bigger fish: Pablo Elvira was a renowned Figaro, if not in the Milnes-Bruson class, and John Brecknock is one of the best Almavivas around these days. Suzanne Johnston, rapidly approaching star status, was Rosina and Ronald Maconaghie Dr Bartolo. Margaret Haggard, surprisingly and superbly, stepped down into the minor rôle of Berta, while another Australian, Richard Curtin (Basilio) returned after nine years in Germany, France and Russia to bring his short piece of calumny to Basilio. For once Divall passed his baton to his deputy; Brian Stacy acquitted himself with honours. Anthony Besch produced and John Stoddart created the ideal designs. This really was a production equal to any previously seen in Australia and it also was televized nationally by the ABC.

The famous *Lohengrin* was a star vehicle for Kenneth Rowell, the designer, who produced beautiful images, including the occasional touch of symbolism which went over the heads of some of the dumber critics. (Where but in *Lohengrin* would you find a swan-shaped wedding bed?) The versatile Divall shone brilliantly with the ABC's Melbourne Symphony Orchestra at his disposal. The important, and probably most expensive import in this case was the producer. August Everding is as internationally famous as any producer, and he had just produced *Lohengrin* at the Metropolitan Opera House in New York. Not that this resulted in a particularly brilliant production; Everding was quite eclipsed by his local designer. Elsa was sung by the American Karen Bureau, with a huge voice and little else. (Big Karen was not a little Elsa!) Alberto Remedios was a fine Lohengrin, Nance Grant surprised with a highly dramatic

Ortrud and Noël Mangin sang a resonant King. Unhappily their big voices and the huge chorus drowned the other singers. Still, I have heard worse *Lohengrins* in Germany.

No company can sustain such excellence every year and 1986 was, almost inevitably, an anti-climax. It started badly on the basis of a single piece of miscasting so bad that the excellence of Glenys Fowles, Thomas Edmunds and Elizabeth Campbell in *Eugene Onegin* was nullified. Lenus Carlson has, we are assured, sung the title rôle at the Metropolitan: which only proves that what is good enough for the famous Met is not necessarily good enough for Victoria.

Staging *I Puritani* at all was a grave risk and accepting a production from the Australian Opera which was mostly made up of old (and easily recognizable) leftovers from *Lucia di Lammermoor* did not inspire confidence. Jenny Drivala looked pretty, and pretty is the best way to describe her singing. We had come to expect better from the VSO by then. Keith Lewis at least sang Arturo complete with top F, but it was adding insult to injury to partner two fine singers like Donald Shanks and John Wood in the duet 'Suoni la tromba'. Each sang his part admirably, but hitching a voice the size of an elephant (Shanks) to that of a fine racehorse (Wood) is doing neither a favour.

The best work of the year was a new *Don Giovanni*, for which an American guest, Louis Otey, was a welcome leading man, though Roger Howell's Leporello outsang him on the rare occasions when Howell forgot to modify his natural resonance. Gillian Sullivan (Elvira) and Suzanne Johnston (Zerlina) shone brightly and Peter Coleman-Wright (the 1986 Shell Aria Winner) made much of the normally-overlooked Masetto.

The year ended and 1987 began with operetta. Kálmán's *Countess Maritza* did not fit as well into the huge State Theatre in Melbourne as it had into the Opera Theatre in Adelaide. The VSO used the same principals, and Dennis Olsen's sprightly production lost some of its finer points in that large space. More important was the gigantic *HMS Pinafore* which tried to repeat the success of *The Pirates of Penzance* in January 1987. It was far from badly cast, (Paul Eddington, of television's 'Yes, Minister', Geraldine Turner, John O'May and Marina Prior). Henry Bardon's set was practical, spectacular, but not beautiful and the producer, Noël Pearson brought original (?) ideas from Dublin and Manchester,

Wagner beat the AO, the VSO beat Wagner.
Since there is no competition, but collaboration, winner does not take all. But the Wagner *Ring* failed in the Sydney Opera House. *Lohengrin* did not fail in the new larger Melbourne theatre in 1986. A year later the Australian Opera staged the same production.

The designer miracle.
A most ingenious paradox, as W. S. Gilbert would have said. Kenneth Rowell revolutionized *Don Giovanni* by using huge murals painted on cloth curtains, making instant scene changes brilliantly effective. (Roger Howell's Leporello sings his 'Catalogue Aria' to Gillian Sullivan's Elvira in 1986.)

The biggest test of all.
Most of the AO budget in
1987 went on a spectacular
visual failure, *Turandot*, while
the much-more-difficult
Nozze di Figaro was brought-
off brilliantly by a producer
new to opera, Jean-Pierre
Mignon, a Frenchman who
knew his Beaumarchais. (The
first-ever Papuan opera
singer, Miriam Gormley, as
Cherubino with Jonathan
Summers as the Count,
Christine Douglas as Susanna
and Christopher Dawes as
Basilio.)

two cities which are a long way behind New York in production terms. I do not doubt that this *Pinafore* played to good houses. Two million dollars it will never earn.

Happily, 1987 reversed the pattern of success, as everything in life has its ups and downs. On paper, the staging of Puccini's *Turandot* seemed far too ambitious for the VSO. It proved not to be so. The only major error was committed by costume designer Terry Ryan — Turandot is not related to Rita Hayworth, nor should she alone have been dressed in a 1950s white tulle evening dress. But what a performance musically! Perhaps Olivia Stapp had just passed her prime, but she was still ranked then among the best Turandots in the world. The Romanian Corneliu Murgu was by far the best tenor any company has imported since Pavarotti. A lack of subtlety is a small price to pay for such a powerful steady tone. And Glenys Fowles (in a monstrous dress-cum-suit) sang very sweetly as Liù. Even Ping, Pang and Pong had plenty of ping and no pong at all. The expanded chorus, plus what looked like a hundred or more extras, was truly impressive. Divall conducted superbly as usual.

Even better was *Le nozze de Figaro*, which followed. It was sung in Italian, like *Turandot* with surtitled translations. Jean-Pierre Mignon is a French drama producer and this was his first try at opera. What a debut! And the Bardon/Stennett designer partnership know their *Figaro* inside out. Peter Robinson was the excellent conductor this time and his cast was faultless vocally as well as dramatically. Everybody was so good that one cannot rank individual performances, but it is surely newsworthy that Cherubino was absolutely spot-on, performed by what must surely be the first Papuan to play a leading rôle in a major opera in a full-sized theatre. Like her colleagues, Miriam Gormley looked and acted the age specified by Beaumarchais: in her case, thirteen. Figaro (Roger Howell) *was* thirty, Susanna (Christine Douglas) nineteen, as was the Countess (Wendy Dixon), and Barbarina, who ends up with Cherubino, (Victoria Watson), was only twelve. Odd man out was the Count (Jonathan Summers, fresh from Covent Garden); his age is not stated, but he surely should be, and looked in his mid-thirties. And let us not forget that they one and all sang and acted as any opera house in the world would want to hear and see them sing and act. That was the VSO in August 1987!

ACT 4: SCENE 2
OPERA IN SOUTH
AUSTRALIA

No record of any artistic endeavour of continuing value is ever complete at the time of writing. It is impossible to judge history in the making, only retrospect can tell us whether the walls of the castle fell before or after completion. Opera or ballet as 'oncers' may ultimately lead to more lasting things, but it is opera *companies* which make the kind of history with which this book is concerned. From the start the regional companies have come and gone, some to disappear, some to reappear under new names. None avoided similar problems to those met by the Australian Opera, some in very recent years. It cannot be said with certainty that even after, say, ten years of unbroken successes any of the state opera companies may yet not collapse in disarray. But for government support over centuries, not mere decades, as in Australia, many European opera companies would not have survived financial and artistic disasters much greater than any which have made headlines in this country.

The word 'crisis' is part of the daily vocabulary of opera companies and where once upon a time the invariable blow-up was caused by clashes of temperament, in our time it is the clash of unbalanced budgets which gets unhappy administrators in every country of the world climbing one obstacle (or wall) after another in the vain hope that once this problem is solved, the next will solve itself. It never does and then the game of musical chairs begins again: this one resigns, that one is appointed and somebody or other foots the bill because: 'The same mistakes will not be made again'. There is no logic of any kind in the continuing existence of opera as a performing art. Only a lunatic argues the pros and cons with inflexible accountants and only a lunatic accountant would agree with even the best administrator of opera, because their battleground is a barren field on which neither contestant can win.

In 1975 the Australian Industries Assistance Commission was instructed by Gough Whitlam, then Prime Minister of Australia, to undertake an Inquiry into Assistance to the Performing Arts which included the following term of reference: 'Whether assistance should be accorded the performing arts in Australia and if so what should be the nature and extent of such assistance'. The chairman of the inquiry, Mr R. Boyer, took the Prime Minister's instructions literality. The question he asked for many days, of many witnesses was: 'What benefit does the public obtain from the arts?' — And answer there was none.

How does one measure enjoyment or edification, depending on whether you consider art pleasurable or educational? How do you relate this abstract astral ectoplasm which flows between performer and audience in money terms? Again and again, Boyer, saddled with an impossible task, was brought back to opera by witnesses in all walks of art, not only the opera men. This art has become so expensive to produce that seat prices would have to rise to undreamed heights to balance the budget. Would people really pay half a week's wages to spend one evening at the opera? There is no way that the existence of opera can be justified at the box office or in the accounting room. The fact that it continues to flourish in a country such as Australia can only be attributed to the existence of the most illogical animal on the face of the earth: man.

Is opera really a dinosaur nearing the natural end of its evolution, as the chairman of the IAC inquiry described it time and again? By all the rules in the book it should be, but the darn thing won't lie down; the moment it shows the slightest sign of collapse somebody manages to slip another crutch under its weakening joints, though for every surviving specimen there are three who perish, or so it would appear. The whole thing belongs in Alice's world of Wonderland; these dinosaurs are only ever seen to die, and nobody pays any attention to when or where their eggs are hatched. And the eggs must exist, for the news-making, collapsing monsters do not appear spontaneously.

From 1960 onward the Adelaide Festival played a large part in the development of opera in Australia. In 1959, the year in which the whole future of the Elizabethan Trust Opera was in doubt, Adelaide was still looking indulgently at its own little opera company, the appropriately-titled Intimate Opera Group. The capital of South Australia nursed its own baby reptile so carefully that it was to prove the critics wrong.

Let me briefly analyze the growth of what was only a baby dinosaur in 1975 and hope that in years to come it will grow into a long-lived monster capable of avoiding the suicidal tendencies of its species.

Adelaide is a city of culture, a city of comparative peace next to the fleshpots of Sydney and Melbourne. They hasten slowly in Adelaide and if I hear a murmur of 'Thank God!', my sympathy lies with the murmurer. Not for Adelaide the short-lived operatic dinosaurs that collapsed over the years in the two larger cities. It is significant that in a musically-underdeveloped country, Adelaide, meaning South Australia, was the last major state to acquire a regional professional opera company. Throughout the years of royal battles fought not *with*,

but *by* battleaxes, in Sydney and Melbourne, Adelaide was content to welcome visiting companies that fought for survival elsewhere, where the stench could not affect the delicate noses of its worthy citizens.

Melba was heard in Adelaide; J. C. Williamson's took companies to play there, first at the Theatre Royal, later at Her Majesty's. The Elizabethan Theatre Trust and the Australian Opera brought prestige productions to grace the Adelaide Festivals. Were the citizens downhearted? They were not.

In 1923 Count Ercole Filippini, ex-principal baritone of the late Gonsalez Opera Company of 1916–17, was teaching singing at Paling's studios in Adelaide. With lots of ambition and not too much sense, Filippini started a South Australian Grand Opera Company which played a two-week season at His Majesty's Theatre in August 1924, only weeks before Melba's company arrived. With no stars, and his wife, the Contessa Filippini as conductor, he staged *Trovatore*, *Rigoletto* and *Cavalleria rusticana* with *Pagliacci*, three winners in opera-starved Adelaide. A year later he added *Faust*, *Carmen* and *Bohème* to his repertoire and in 1926 blithely took a newly re-named Italo-Australian Opera Company to Perth for a very successful run. A year later his planned season in Melbourne's Princess Theatre (probably as the International Victorian Opera Company) never opened; the unions were making outrageous demands: they wanted everybody to be paid! They put paid to Filippini instead. His wife, the Contessa, however, not only conducted, but sang and was often heard in later years. She died in 1987 in Brisbane.

Why Filippini did not return to Adelaide is a mystery, but that city saw only infrequent opera seasons after that. The citizens waited their turn and when it came, it came at leisure, like everything else in Adelaide, and it came without trouble – like everything else in Adelaide? Well, perhaps that is stretching things too far, though the citizens of Sydney and Melbourne would consider if so, comparatively speaking.

The birth of New Opera South Australia was a model of how a well-behaved young dinosaur should be brought into the world. There is nothing terribly exciting about its creation and perhaps there are some budding dinosaurs elsewhere who can learn a lesson or two from their South Australian brother or sister. (What is the sex of opera?)

The amateur companies of South Australia never had the pretensions of the 'professionals' in the other states.

At best they toured operettas in the Barossa Valley before the turn of the century, or the large German community and its *Liedertafels* put on single 'operas' in costume. Occasionally 'philharmonic' groups provided the only other local attempts at opera. There were, of course, parallels to the operatic activities at the music conservatoriums in capital cities elsewhere. Clive Carey's appointment to the Adelaide Conservatorium in 1924 produced the first South-Australian opera performances recorded as 'proper' staged operas. It may well have been Carey fifty-odd years ago who set the pattern which was the reason for New Opera's success. The Conservatorium provided the only tradition of operra in Adelaide and its first work was Purcell's *Didoo and Aeneas*.

If Gluck and Mozart followed and retained their place over the years, a leavening of more popular works also crept in, including the inevitable *Maritana*.

By 1957 the continuing student productions at the Con began to pall a little. Nobody can quite say today what started the ball rolling, but the presence of Anthony Hopkins as composer-in-residence at the University of Adelaide must have been felt. He had formed the post-war Intimate Opera Company in England and it was the Intimate Opera Group in Adelaide which staged what is indeed an intimate opera, *Three's Company*, by none other than Anthony Hopkins, in that year.

This was no attempt to start an opera company. The most incredible thing in operatic terms was that for some years Intimate Opera programmes listed no administrative staff other than people who actually worked on staging the operas: stage managers, set designers, and so on. There was no manager, administrator, committee, nor even a patron; just a small group of professionals who were doing their own thing strictly within the budget of their own pockets. For some years the repertoire of the irregularly-spaced productions was restricted to small-cast operas with piano accompaniment, mainly falling back on English works like the admirable three-singer opener by Hopkins.

Three's Company has a delightful libretto by Michael Flanders (later of Flanders and Swann of *At the Drop of a Hat* fame) and could be sung easily by John Worthley, William Harrison and Jacqueline Talbot, who became the key singers of the group for some years to come. The set was designed by Stan Ostoja-Kotkowski and the producer was the chief vocal coach at the Conservator-

ium, Barbara Howard. Her name did appear on the programme, but that of Kathleen Steele Scott did not. These were the two ladies who started the stone rolling, little knowing how much moss it would gather.

What is surprising is that it was John Worthley who sang in *Three's Company*. Max Worthley, not his brother John, had been a member of the Intimate Opera Company in London and had sung in the opera there. Max Worthley has never received the credit he deserved as one of Australia's few tenors genuinely to make the grade — if not in those temples of grand opera, La Scala or the Metropolitan. Intimate opera, a long association with the Deller Consort and oratorio work alternated with long teaching spells in his native Adelaide and, later in life, in America. In 1956 he was a member of the great Mozart ensemble of the first Elizabethan Trust opera seasons and thus, when brother John showed signs of following in his footsteps, he encouraged him and his friends to start the Intimate Opera Group in Adelaide. Like Topsy, it just growed and growed, however slowly. John Worthley and William Harrison were the first members of the company and they were joined by Barbara Howard, the producer of the triple-header by Anthony Hopkins, and later, administratively, Kathleen Steele Scott. Incredibly, the ABC broadcast *Three's Company* and then even televized this obscure little opera from Adelaide.

The Intimate Opera Group continued in fits and starts over fifteen years and, incredibly for such a volatile activity, it seems to have had none of the storms and crises of similar companies elsewhere. Around the time of the 1960 Adelaide Festival, Lady Bonython became its patroness. Whether her contribution was financial or prestigious, or both, is immaterial, but her name does not appear to have been used as a fund-raising source.

The company led by Mrs Steele Scott set sights realistically. There were no *Aidas*, *Carmens* or *Maritanas*. The repertoire was solidly restricted to works that were easy to stage without making great vocal demands on its roster of local singers; Barbara Howard took turns with Rae Cocking, Marie Bates, Thomas Edmonds, Margaret McPherson and the original *Three's Company* trio.

Programmes were often shared with ballets staged by Elizabeth Dalman's ballet school which in years to come was to turn into the Australian Dance Theatre.

There is no great glamour to be found in operas like Ravel's *L' Heure espagnole*, Falla's *Master Peter's Puppet*

Show, Menotti's *The Telephone* or Mozart's *Bastien and Bastienne* and significantly, the company continued to stage English works: Hopkins' *Hands Across the Sky*, Lennox Berkeley's *A Dinner Engagement* and Arthur Benjamin's *Prima Donna*. (I know that Arthur Benjamin was born in Australia, but his music is English in every sense of the word.) Adelaide was the only Australian city to parallel the development of intimate opera in England, though the city did not produce Australian native operas in its early years. And, perhaps because Adelaide is the most English of the Australian cities, audiences accepted works which supposedly more sophisticated cosmopolitans dismissed as wishy-washy playthings.

The first steps into bigger works by the Intimate Opera Group also remained in the English sphere; in fact, it continued as an exact replica of the mother country's musical development. Benjamin Britten, unable to obtain backing for operas on the *Peter Grimes* scale, refused to leave music drama alone and wrote smaller works which could be staged more cheaply. This was exactly what Mrs Steele Scott's group needed. *Albert Herring* and *The Turn of the Screw*, small by grand opera standards, were large for intimate opera at a time when subsidies were still in the distant future at federal, much less state level.

Albert Herring was given three performances at Union Hall in October 1958 with the full orchestra demanded by Britten — all of thirteen players. Though there was no continuity of employment, no backer, no official management, the team at the core of the venture remained intact, suitably amplified for this 'major' venture. Barbara Howard played Lady Billows and Kathleen Scott, who sang Florence Pike, also produced, thinly disguised as K. Steele Scott.

In the end it was another Britten work which elicited the first official subsidy for the company. In 1960 the Elizabethan Theatre Trust handed over $1000 to pay for an orchestra for *The Turn of the Screw*, because it was the Australian première of a Britten opera. If the thinking was hazy, as it so often is with subsidies, it proved an important encouragement to the Intimate Opera Group.

The Adelaide Festivals were well under way by the early 1960s and the Intimate Opera was invariably a participant. In case this should be interpreted as a financial strengthening of this incredible self-supporting group, it should be noted that the Festival itself was struggling in those days. Companies taking part were not subsidized by it, and actually contributed to its financing by paying for inclusion in the official programme! For the Intimate Opera Group, mainly engaged in lunch-hour presentations of small-cast one-acters, this was a severe burden to carry. The Elizabethan Trust Opera and the Australian Ballet used the Festival simply as the occasion for the annual Adelaide stop in their touring programme. Local companies, without continuous existence, had to create something out of nothing for the Festival and creating a small thing where nothing exists is much harder than continuing a large and active enterprise.

Fund-raising from other sources became a necessity if the Intimate Opera Group was to continue its existence and 1970 saw the beginning of some support from the newly-created Australian Council for the Arts. Slowly but surely the company's administrative structure began to develop. The two leading ladies, who anywhere else would have insisted on being prominently displayed, discreetly withdrew into functions where they could do more good than on the stage. The late Barbara Howard, a professional singer, retreated to costume design, while Steele Scott and Powell Harrison ran the administration from their homes in Clarence Park and Lockleys.

The 1970 Festival season was a model of building up what was by then visibly a company of future potential. The temptation to aim for greater glories must have been immense after thirteen years of existence without serious problems. It was resisted. Adelaide and its visitors saw instead an example of sensible planning for a company which was in fact, as well as name, still an intimate opera group. Five evening performances of a double bill of Ravel's *L' Heure espagnole* and Menotti's *The Old Maid and the Thief* were backed by nine lunchtime stagings of each work as a single entity. With prices at 80 cents for the latter and $1.50 for the double bill at nights, both in the tiny AMP Theatre, the possibility of profit was non-existent, yet the impact on the future of the company was immense. It led to the swan song of the Intimate Opera Group two years later, a swan song which turned out to be rebirth without complications. The bird which had never been an ugly duckling turned into the most beautiful and efficient dinosaur Mr Boyer could ever have expected.

The last efforts of the group under its original management (still led by Steele Scott and still including

Barbara Howard) came at the 1972 Festival and followed the trend toward contemporary Australian opera without losing its intimate nature. An ideally-balanced trilogy of works repeated the lunchtime and evening pattern of performances of the 1970 Festival, Pergolesi's *La Serva Padrona* for the classicists; Gustav Holst's *The Wandering Scholar* to continue the English tradition which hallmarked the company's career; Peggy Glanville-Hicks' *The Glittering Gate*, to introduce an Australian work at last. Premièring an opera by an expatriate was a bold experiment. Glanville-Hicks, like Malcolm Williamson, is shunned by the establishment, which is happy to claim both as Australians, but fails to stage their works.

John Milson was the producer and the singers were Robert Dawe, Janet Lasscock, Dean Patterson, Daphne Harris, Anthony Clark and Michael Lewis, with William Harrison the sole survivor from the company's first production in 1957.

The Adelaide Festival operas of 1972 were not the most important productions of that year, nor were they the last of the Intimate Opera Group. Both honours belong to the remarkable success which grew out of two performances in The Olde King's Music Hall theatre-restaurant in November of that year. It appears an unlikely venue in which to stage an Australian opera and it says a lot for the reputation of the company in Adelaide that a modern Australian work could attract a dining public at $6.00 a person, but it did.

Nobody seems to know exactly whose idea it was, nor are the economics of the thing terribly clear, though the enthusiasm of Harry Eggington, the manager of the Olde King's Music Hall, must have helped swing the deal. The occasion was the celebration of the seventy-fifth birthday of Margaret Sutherland, the doyenne of Australian composers. The opera presented, *The Young Kabbarli*, had been premièred in Hobart in 1965. Its new look in such an inauspicious setting was to make it known Australia-wide.

The Young Kabbarli is the story of Daisy Bates, who spent fifty-two years of her life caring for Aborigines in the outback. Though it only has four singing roles, it is a difficult work to stage, involving, as it does, Aboriginal dancers, the use of a didgeridoo and a complicated score for ten players. Patrick Thomas, seconded from the ABC, conducted, and visiting Israeli guest producer Moshe Kedem was also responsible for the designs. Mezzo soprano Genty Stevens made a deep impression

as Daisy Bates and the other parts were sung by Dean Patterson, John McKenzie and Carol Kohler. Although David Gulpilil in a key rôle was described as 'guest dancer and Aborigine Singer' his excellent contribution in the latter capacity is better described as chanting; European-style singing by an Aboriginal in the most authentic-sounding primitive music sequences would have been somewhat out of place.

Plans to extend the exposure of *The Young Kabbarli* outside Adelaide were laid long before its première. Not only was the whole production transferred to Melbourne for another tribute to Margaret Sutherland in the Great Hall of the National Gallery, but EMI recorded the work in full, giving it, and the Intimate Opera Group, the honour of being the first Australian opera to be recorded. It was also the first recording in quadrophonic sound made in this country.

The fact that the Intimate Opera is given no credit on the recording of *The Young Kabbarli*, while there is a mention of 'New Opera (SA)' inconspicuously hidden after credits for financial assistance, hides the metamorphosis of the group into 'New Opera South Australia' in 1973. Once again the changeover was gradual. There was little evidence that anything radical had happened beyond a policy statement, and even that clearly stated that the new body 'Would NOT [their capitals] be a Grand Opera Company, but a Music Theatre Ensemble presenting the best works of today with a sprinkling of the classics.'

A full-time administrator, Justin McDonnel, and board of management was formed. Funds were made available by Don Dunstan, then premier of South Australia, as well as by the Australia Council. Kathleen Steele Scott became the chairman of the artistic committee which laid down policy, providing continuity. The first season was totally in keeping with all that went before — except that suddenly the money was there for a full orchestra, chorus and scope for larger works, though far from 'grand' ones. *Dido and Aeneas* and Ibert's *Angélique* started the new era and if I seem to stress development rather than change, let me remind you that this detailed dissection of what happened in Adelaide is meant to show how things should happen in opera, but so very rarely do.

The first season at the new Adelaide Festival Theatre saw productions of that old faithful *Albert Herring* and later Rossini's *Count Ory*. Guest conductors Georg Tintner and Richard Divall were brought in from other states and new singers were added to cope with the larger theatre, while regulars developed the broader style they might never have achieved without having had such long training in actual productions over the years. Eric Maddison emerged as Albert with Daphne Harris, Norene Lower, Rae Cocking and David Brennan in support. For the more difficult *Count Ory*, Norma Hunter was on loan from the ABC with Paul Ferris as the Count, Norma Knight as Isolier and Dean Patterson from the early days as Raimbaud. John Milson and Stefan Haag were the producers.

Reverting to stated policies — which the Festival Theatre productions had not really interrupted — December 1973 saw the company in Theatre 62 with smaller operas, smaller casts and a smaller orchestra. *Down the Greenwood Side* by Harrison Birtwistle and Melanie Daiken's *Mayakovsky and the Sun* both continued the tradition of modern English operas, though these belong to the *avant garde* of today instead of the yesterday of Britten and Hopkins.

In 1974 New Opera's activities positively exploded, yet artistic standards remained higher than anywhere in Australia, possibly excluding the Australian Opera. Almost overnight New Opera was on the lips of opera lovers in every state and envious glances were cast toward Adelaide. Whence suddenly came this unity of artistic and financial management? Why were the constant crises of other states not repeated in this one city alone? Perhaps the fact that management and artists were busy working hard instead of blowing their own trumpets had something to do with it. Perhaps working under ideal conditions in the Festival Theatre helped. Probably the fact that the company produced good results encouraged the subsidizing bodies to put up rather than shut up in disgust, as happened more often than not in other states.

South Australia had the only premier with a theatrical background at this time. Not that Don Dunstan was likely to take an active part in the running of New Opera, but results speak for themselves, and when the head of a government is able to judge for himself whether his financial advisers are correctly evaluating something as ephemeral as artistic standards, then the arts are likely to get all the help they need, or that the budget can stand. This happened in Adelaide and it would be as well if the rest of Australia learnt the lesson.

The emergence of Leoš Janáček as a box-office attraction in Australia did not start with the Australian Opera's *Jenůfa*, but with the far more complex and difficult *The Excursions of Mr Brouček* staged at the 1974 Adelaide Festival by New Opera. At the time Janáček was still considered too experimental for Australian audiences; none of his operas had ever been performed in this country. The logic of choosing *Brouček* rather than the much more famous *Jenůfa* or *The Cunning Little Vixen* was obscure, but it proved to substantiate the judgement of the company's directors.

What was required first and foremost was something that could be made into a major production spectacle. The fact that singers like Gregory Dempsey, Marilyn Richardson and Thomas Edmonds, were available was hardly enough to fill the immense new Festival Theatre. Something sensational was required and, whatever the opera's musical worth, it was the production which turned a respected regional body into a company worthy of national recognition.

The Excursions of Mr Brouček involves a journey to the Moon and time travel, combined with period comedy ideally suited to visual effects. Adelaide happened to be the home of Ostoja-Kotkowski, whose electronic light experiments had been prominent for years. (He had also designed the company's first production in 1957!) Dealing with the eight scenes of *Brouček*, ranging from the hidden treasury of King Wenceslaus, and various scenes of Prague in 1888 and 1420, to a very inhabited surface of the Moon, Ostoja-Kotkowski was given his head and delivered the goods. Producer John Tasker admirably used the magnificent raw materials at his disposal and Patrick Thomas took firm charge of the musical content. *Brouček* was a triumph which was only dampened by the failure of the national subsidizing bodies to make provision for this kind of success to be seen in the other states as well. Those four performances of Janáček opera will remain a legend in Australian operatic history. They were also the largest venture of New Opera, one not equalled except under Festival conditions.

Any thought that the company's worth was enlarged by presenting its work in one ideal venue alone was dissipated in the same year when its four seasons were each staged in different locations. After the major exertion of *Brouček* at the Festival Theatre, productions were staged in the three months September to December in, respectively, the Royalty Theatre, the so-called 'Space' in the Festival Theatre complex, an experimental theatre-in-the-round, and Theatre 62.

Stravinsky's *Renard* was coupled with Larry Sitsky's Australian classic *The Fall of the House of Usher* and Monteverdi's *Combattimento di Tancredi e Clorinda* with Kurt Weill's *Seven Deadly Sins*. The latter pair proved to be a near sensational coupling when presented as the opening production in the Space at the Festival Theatre.

Justin McDonnell, who had been working as administrator since before the changeover, suddenly emerged as an original designer-producer in the Monteverdi. It was an ultra-modern presentation of a very old masterpiece, played 'in-the-round' with complete success. Wal Cherry's production of the *Seven Deadly Sins* was, if anything, even more successful, capturing the Brecht style to perfection. Robin Archer and Avis Smith played the singing and dancing sides of sinful Annie, while Tessa Bremner and Roger Pahl mimed the original conceptions for the singers, David Galliver, Margaret Mac-Pherson and Eric Maddison.

The success of the Weill-Brecht *Deadly Sins* could not have influenced the choice of their *Little Mahagonny* four weeks later; the company's planning is too good to allow quite such quick substitutions. Nevertheless, it was an inspired juxtaposition. *The Little Mahagonny* is the original on which *The Rise and Fall of the City of Mahagonny* was built. The Australian Opera's production of the latter, which followed in Sydney a month after the Adelaide staging of the earlier, smaller work, lacked the bite provided by the local boys, Chris Winzar (director) and Axel Bartz (designer). It was dangerous to court direct comparison with the national company, but New Opera succeeded in upstaging it.

The year 1975, which did not have an Adelaide Festival, was a key one for New Opera. The initial two productions followed the pattern of the modest double bills which the Adelaide audiences have come to expect and appreciate. *The Soldier's Tale* of Stravinsky and Bizet's youthful four-character *Dr Miracle* were followed by Janáček's *Diary of a Man Who Vanished* and a baroque *Madrigal Show* based on Banchieri. Ronald Dowd and Gwenyth Annear appeared as guests.

The danger of a loss of individuality was there in the company's first production in Her Majesty's Theatre — the venue for really grand opera in years gone by. The choice of opera was in the true tradition of the company; Britten's *Turn of the Screw* returned to the scene of past

triumphs. Nevertheless the production's virtues lay in the three leading singers, guests Dowd, Annear and Ailene Fischer. For the first time New Opera followed the pattern of other regional companies, which are inclined to ignore the building of a local ensemble in favour of getting 'the best'. But since 'the best' can be heard anywhere else in Australia, some of the company's individualism was lost.

The next production offered a better balance. Marilyn Richardson, later resident in Adelaide after marrying James Christianson, was Fiordiligi, while Rae Cocking, Norma Knight, Christianson himself, Dennis O'Neill and John Wood backed her to create a new *Così fan tutte*, brilliantly designed by John Stoddart and produced by Anthony Besch. This opera also toured the country as part of a new scheme to keep singers employed full-time. Though it was a different cast which went outside Adelaide, the inclusion of Gwenyth Annear ensured a high standard, specially since Myer Fredman, who conducted all five 1975 productions, went on the road as well; he was one of the four full-time employees of the company by then, everybody else (specially the singers) was co-opted as required.

The history of New Opera ended with two specially-commissioned operas for the 1976 Adelaide Festival. Larry Sitsky's *Fiery Tales* and George Dreyfus's *The Lamentable Reign of King Charles the Last* had the common virtue of being excellent, if somewhat bawdy, entertainment — which is as it should be, since Sitsky's *Tales* came from Chaucer and Boccaccio and *King Charles* straight out of Canberra's most turbulent years. Perhaps the Dreyfus opera was too close to intimate revue and its subject will prevent it from gaining a permanent place in the repertoire, but it served its purpose as music entertainment pure and simple. Chris Winzar's production of *Fiery Tales* stressed the sexuality of its subjects, but Sitsky's music was good 'modern-antique' and the large cast was given music that really needed singing, instead of the usual *Sprechgesang*. An excellent cast was led by Norma Knight, Dennis O'Neill, John Wood, Patsy Hemingway and, believe it or not, a member of that first *Three's Company* cast, William Harrison!

If I have made the creation of New Opera sound like a glamorous, undramatic evolution of an opera company built upon a rock of goodwill and hard work, I have been close to the truth. Of course there were bad times and good times and things happened which should not have happened. But compare what happened in the sleepy South Australian capital with the paroxysms of operatic life anywhere else and New Opera was a Nirvana which existed for the enrichment of life in Adelaide. It had acquired an admirable permanent musical director in the form of Myer Fredman, and Mrs Kathleen Steele Scott was still on the board of management; and if that isn't a remarkable achievement, then nothing can astonish any more. One had hopes that the course of true love (for opera) would forever run smooth, and it has done so, more or less, ever since.

In 1976 New Opera South Australia ceased being 'New' and acquired the clumsy title of the State Opera of South Australia. Justin McDonnell departed for more academic pursuits at the Sydney Conservatorium and Ian Campbell became the bright new administrator, who initially maintained, or was forced to maintain, the home-based operations of the past, using almost exclusively local singers.

At first this was simple; *La Bohème* had Gwyneth Annear and Patsy Hemingway with Thomas Edmunds, James Christianson and John Wood in the main rôles. A remarkable triple bill even carried on the old programming tradition: Chabrier's *Ignorance is Bliss* had Dennis O'Neill with John Wood and Hemingway, followed by a curious *mélange* of Bertold Brecht and Rudyard Kipling called *Never the Twain*, which starred Robin Archer and was directed by Wal Cherry. *Festino* by Banchieri completed a bizarre evening.

In the following year came the last of the all, or nearly all Adelaidian operas, a *Don Giovanni* with Christianson, Richardson, Edmunds, Wood and Daphne Harris, directed by Adrian Slack and designed by Axel Bartz. Although an adequate production, it alerted Ian Campbell to the dangers of parochialism and the South Australian company finally followed the pattern of other states by importing good singers from elsewhere when locals were unavailable. *The Coronation of Poppea* starred Eilene Hannan and Gregory Dempsey, and for *HMS Pinafore* the star was none other than television's Callan, Edward Woodward — supported by Edmunds and Hemingway, two outstanding local artists ideal for their parts. 1978 featured the real *Traviata*, as well as what is known as 'The poor man's *Traviata*', Puccini's *La Rondine*, starring June Bronhill, Edmunds and Robin Donald. For the Festival that year all semblance of Intimate or New Opera disappeared with an outstanding staging of Michael

Tippett's *The Midsummer Marriage* in the Festival Theatre with Raimund Herincx (imported from London), Dempsey and Richardson.

By now Ian Campbell was being hailed as the new wonder boy of Australian opera and Adelaide was big news. The old Her Majesty's Theatre was bought by the State Government, renovated, and became the Opera Theatre in 1979, for the first time providing a permanent home for the many-named company which had begun back in 1957. *Werther, Die Fledermaus, Elisir d'amore, The Secret Marriage* and a tour to Perth of *The Marriage of Figaro* followed. (This last marked the first appearance of Angela Denning in the tiny part of Barbarina. After a very short spell in the Australian Opera she is now a major member of the Deutsche Oper in Berlin!) Last, but far from least, the novelty of Nicholas Maw's *One Man Show* (which was promptly included in the Australian Opera's Sydney season) appeared in what was not even a Festival year. Then 1980 topped all this when SOSA staged Britten's *Death in Venice* in the Festival Theatre. It starred Robert Gard, whose performance was so good that he was invited to replace Peter Pears as Aschenbach in an English film of the opera. The rest of the year's repertoire catered for every taste, from Cavalli's *L'Ormindo* to Lehár's *The Land of Smiles*.

At this point Myer Fredman departed, like McDonnell, for an academic career in Sydney and Dennis Vaughan became musical director for three years. (Smoothly as things have run in Adelaide, musical directors have always had the itch to move on, or have lost interest in local fame, unlike the stability of Krug in Perth or Divall in Melbourne.) Vaughan's repertoire ranged wide, too wide perhaps. In his first year he started with a revival of *HMS Pinafore*, ran through box office operas like *Carmen* and *Bohème*, to end gloriously with another opera written by a woman, Thea Musgrove's *A Christmas Carol*, starring James Christianson as Scrooge. The Festival of 1982 was celebrated without quite the success of the previous one — the opera this time being Janáček's *The Makropoulos Case* — though Elisabeth Söderström was the world-renowned leading lady. 1982 also marked the departure of Ian Campbell for the international opera scene; he became the first Australian administrator ever to head an international opera company, in San Diego, USA. The departure of Campbell and Fredman led to a lowering of company standards for a while.

The original *Lady Macbeth of Mtsensk* by Shostakovitch,

The Festival of Festivals. The State Opera of South Australia suddenly grew like Topsy out of primitive intimate opera, after it became a major part of the Adelaide Festivals. It cut its teeth on unusual Janáček with *The Excursions of Mr Brouček* in 1974. By 1982 it could afford a major guest star when Janáček returned with Elisabeth Söderström in *The Makropoulos Case.*

The scene which shocked Stalin.
Shostakovitch became *persona non grata* in Russia after Stalin saw his *Lady Macbeth of Mtsensk* in 1936. His objections were as much to the explicit sex and murder of the plot as to the music. In 1984 staid Adelaide took it in its stride. (Beverly Bergen as Katarina, Ron Stevens as Sergei and Gregory Dempsey as the dead Zinovy.)

starring Beverley Bergen, provided a sexational highlight for the 1984 Festival and Handel's *Julius Caesar*, superbly designed by Tom Lingwood, was taken over by the Victoria State Opera, complete with Bergen and Lauris Elms in their leading rôles. In 1985 Ian Johnston was appointed as general manager. The highlights of the year were at the extremes of the public's taste buds. They began with a fine *Capriccio* by Richard Strauss and ended with an equally fine (and more popular) *Countess Maritza* by Kálmán produced brilliantly by Dennis Olsen, re-staged by the AO in Melbourne and later Sydney and greeted with derision by the sophisticated critics of those cities. Fortunately the public paid no attention, while in Brisbane even the press applauded.

Children's operas grow like toys.
The modern child expects robots and monsters from outer space. Cinderella and Snow White are out of fashion. Malcolm Fox's *The Iron Man* in 1987 Adelaide experimented with bridging youth and adult imagery in opera.

More Australian works were produced in 1986. Again it was a female composer, Peggy Glanville-Hicks, who predominated; though her *Glittering Gate* and *Transposed Heads* were by many considered outdated musically and obscure dramatically. In a different way *Boojum*, possibly the only opera ever written by twin brothers, Peter and Martin Wesley-Smith, was no more successful. A mixture of pop theatre and pop music aimed at a young public, it was based on Lewis Carroll's *The Hunting of the Snark* and the world première was attended by Her Majesty, the Queen. (What with that and *Albert Herring* in Sydney, the old dear had a rough musical time in Australia.) Another Australian opera, Malcolm Fox's *The Iron Man* was planned, postponed and finally surfaced again in 1987. This was quite a different proposition. Though intended for a youth audience and quite short, *Iron Man* held promise of genuine operatic talent. The subject may be wild, but Graham Maclean's designs were notable. Most important of all, Fox's music is accessible to 'straight' opera audiences and that is a rare thing these days, specially in Australia. A new *Flying Dutchman*, *Macbeth* (conducted by Stuart Challender) and a frightfully-jolly-good-fun *Italian Girl of Algiers* rounded the year off nicely.

The highlights of 1987 were not all musical in nature. Nobody tried to make the ladies sing when the Prostitutes Association of Adelaide were refused permission to address the audience during the opening night of *La Traviata*. Gillian Sullivan was excellent in the title rôle, but made no attempt to side with her supposed colleagues protesting volubly outside the Opera Theatre.

A lot more attention was paid to the adventurous *Sweeney Todd*, a musical-cum-opera by Stephen Sondheim, which somehow had failed to be given an Australian professional production for eight years after it was acclaimed in New York. In 1987 the State Opera of South Australia and the Melbourne Theatre Company gave it almost simultaneous Australian premières. (Adelaide won by a matter of days.) Worthy as the far more famous MTC in Melbourne may have been, *Sweeney* found that company out of its depth for two reasons: Sondheim wrote what is, in fact, a real opera and actors simply can not cope with the music; and the MTC works in the small Playhouse of the Victorian Arts Centre and, as in so many modern musicals, the set and production of *Sweeney Todd* are as important, if in this case not more important, than the music.

Sondheim's work was certainly more difficult to stage than Adelaide's other works that year: *Traviata*, *Madame Butterfly*, Kálmán's *Czardas Princess*, Mozart's *La finta giardiniera*. This was strangely and not very well presented under the title *Sandrina's Secret* thereby ensuring that those among the public who had actually heard of Mozart's opera would also stay away. How much this added to the year's heavy deficit remains (Sandrina's) secret!

Although *Sweeney Todd* made amends to a tune which would have justified half a dozen *Sandrinas*, Sondheim continues to be unacceptable to the general public in Australia. Without doubt the remarkable Adelaide set produced by Ken Wilby and Mark Thompson would have been praised on Broadway or in London's West End as fulsomely as it was praised here. Director Gale Edwards left no stone (or bone) unturned in the gory tale and Lyndon Terracini may very well have been the best Sweeney seen on any stage. But, though Nancye Hayes, Gregory Yurisich and Fiona Maconaghie also shone among the outstanding supporting cast, the Adelaide *Sweeney Todd* was poorly attended. No blame (only praise) can be attached for choosing this work and for presenting it without falling below what we like to call 'international standards'.

The good people of Adelaide are perhaps too conservative to accept a subject which has fascinated addicts of *grand guignol* for a century, but that a city with a long history of remarkably adventurous festivals should not have crammed the Opera Theatre to the rafters for every possible performance of *Sweeney Todd* implies that some years will have to pass yet before the local population will be worthy of the kind of opera which its own company is trying so very hard to give it.

The undeserved failure of Adelaide's *Sweeney Todd* may have been an after-effect of the lacklustre earlier productions of 1987. And then the Bicentary's Adelaide Festival featured the SOSA in the usual esoteric rarity, this time Prokofiev's *The Fiery Angel*, credible and visually controversial, but not likely to build audiences lost during the previous year. The government of South Australia has announced plans for the company's future as these lines are written, but they relate to saving money, not opera. That Adelaide of all cities should step back into obscurity after decades of being envied by others is unthinkable. Unsinkable is a more suitable adjective for opera in the Athens of the South — we hope.

In Queensland (not Brisbane!) a different animal stirred. In 1948, George English may have launched a Brisbane Opera Society in true colonial fervour with the inevitable *Maritana*, which starred a young tenor named Donald Smith. Joseph Halmos may well have topped that in 1951 with his Queensland Grand Opera Society which a year later became less grand but more grandiose as the Queensland National Opera — staging opera in the Brisbane City Hall, no less. But the first local company which developed past the transitional stage of getting something, anything, staged in Australia's north-eastern state appeared not in the capital, but in country towns.

In 1968 a local couple, composer Colin Brumby and his wife Marissa, were touring country areas of Australia's north-east with operas for school children of their own devising which were astoundingly successful. Brumby had previously tried his hand in Brisbane with an 'Opera Group Workshop', singing early Haydn and Monteverdi works doomed to failure in what was — in spite of spirited local protests at the description — the artistically most-backward state of the nation. The local Arts Council commissioned Brumby to write his operas for children and their success would undoubtedly have continued had Brumby not decided to go overseas in 1972.

The five-singer group, ambitiously re-named The Queensland Opera Company, did its job so well that it gave 333 performances in 74 towns (outside Brisbane) in its first year and went from strength to strength thereafter. An 'opera company' it was not, however. What growth there was lay in occasional visits to Brisbane and the inclusion of a few one-acters from the conventional repertoire to supplement Brumby's mini-operas. In 1970 QOC gave its first performance for adults, a full-length work written on tour by Brumby himself, *The Seven Deadly Sins*, with a greatly-enlarged cast — six instead of five singers, further supplemented by the composer himself in drag as a bearded (non-singing) goddess in the Gluttony sequence!

The company ceased to be a family affair in 1971 when Richard Divall was appointed to take over as administrator and musical director, pending the departure overseas of the Brumbys. Divall prepared the first non-Brumby production, Scarlatti's *The Triumph of Honour* at the Twelfth Night Theatre in Brisbane with a twelve-piece orchestra and a guest artist, Dorothea Deegan, bringing the cast up to eight! Unfortunately the triumph of honour did not extend to that of common sense; Marissa Brumby and Divall could not agree on future policies and after a short six months Divall departed post-haste for what turned out to be a very glorious future elsewhere. No tears were shed for him then. Well may they have been in later years!

The departure of Divall coincided with that of the Brumbys overseas and, while the previously-laid plans for more country tours proceeded, the appointment of New Zealander John Thompson as administrator and artistic director in 1972 was the real start of something a little more appropriate to the company's title. The Brumby operas were replaced with Menotti's *The Medium* and *R.S.V.P.* by Offenbach. A year later the first standard repertory work, *Madame Butterfly*, was taken on tour using local choruses to supplement the twelve singers engaged, and during the ambitious 'Innisfail Centenary Opera Festival' QOC presented the immortal twins,

Cavalleria rusticana and *Pagliacci* in abridged form. What prompted the substitution of a different double bill, Menotti's *Amelia Goes to the Ball* and Ibert's *Angélique* for a two-week season in Brisbane is hard to assess; it may well have been the desire to present a 'real' opera season in 1974 without a sub-standard foretaste of more familiar works.

It should be remembered that this was the year after the opening of the Sydney Opera House with wide press coverage of opera, its future in this country, its beauties and the absolute necessity for every capital to emulate the Harbour City. (Similar moves were taking place in other states.) The Queensland Opera Company's brief eight years, which provided the bridge between the Brumbys and the foundation of the present Lyric Opera of Queensland, began in 1974 with *Madame Butterfly, La traviata* and *Così fan tutte*, staged for the first time in a proper theatre — Her Majesty's in Brisbane. It was an appropriate choice for what was basically a new public and also launched the first subscription series in that city. Bookings were substantial and guests artists were engaged for key rôles. Ailene Fischer may not have looked an ideal Butterfly, but her big voice was impressive; Kevin Mills was her Pinkerton. *Traviata* showed off the local talent, Phyllis Ball, Robin Donald and Neville Wilkie, but Dolores Cambridge was borrowed for *Così* from the Australian Opera. All the operas were produced by John Thompson and designed by Alan Lees. It was an auspicious debut for a local company with hardly any previous background as an ensemble.

The following years saw a continuation of the company's failures as well as its virtues. The bright touring programme was continued, now with operas for adults as well as children, and this kept singers employed on a year-round basis. This was something not equalled in other states on this scale. It was absolutely essential if good local talent was to be prevented from seeking its fortune elsewhere.

On the home front difficulties arose about venues. Her Majesty's Theatre was not always available, and the State Government Insurance Office Theatre was counted as a blessing in disguise because it had only 600 seats and was much cheaper to run. The fact that it is totally unsuited in every way for opera, particularly because of its dry acoustics, was played down and consequent seasons suffered accordingly. Repertoire and artists remained largely on the same level, not at all bad, but rarely improving. Strange projects, such as two performances of *Cavalleria rusticana* and *Pagliacci* suddenly appeared in Brisbane's City Hall in 1975 (and again in 1977) while the subscription series of *Die Fledermaus, Carmen* and Mozart's *Seraglio* appealed more for the familiar music than the excellence of their performances.

The strange logic of opera management discussed elsewhere in this history began to assert itself: if in trouble, don't economize, but seek greater glories. QOC was going to be a major company. It had to get bigger. It *would* get bigger. Period. That the company played in the same unsuitable small theatre, employed the same routine producers and singers, used the new (and more expensive) Queensland Theatre Orchestra and scheduled operas which everybody knew from world-famous recordings therefore making any shortcomings all the more obvious, was all ignored. 1976 saw *Rigoletto, Don Pasquale, Don Giovanni* and Rossini's *Cenerentola*. Productions increased and costs increased, but subscriptions did not. They 'fell alarmingly because of general economic difficulties', or so the board of directors concluded.

Funding for the company did not increase. Losses mounted. Thompson pulled his horns in and finally showed some enterprise by employing a well-established producer, Anthony Besch, to stage the 1977 season's highlight, *The Marriage of Figaro*, an opera less likely to suffer in the confines of a small theatre. The balance of the season repeated the 1975 experiment in the City Hall and *Il trovatore* was staged as a standard work which will find an audience, no matter how poor the cast. Not that the cast was, strictly-speaking, 'poor', but most of the praise was lavished on Peter Cooke's sets and Georg Tintner's conducting.

The years 1978 and 1979 saw Australia-wide joint seasons of the Australian Opera with the regional companies. The offer of Joan Sutherland in person (only in 1979) as part of a Brisbane subscription series should have put the company well and truly on the map, particularly since it moved for most of its productions back into the opera-sized Her Majesty's Theatre. *The Magic Flute* stayed at the SGIO, but *The Gypsy Baron, Faust* and *The Pearl Fishers* were staged in the larger venue. The failures of past seasons caught up with the company at this point. In spite of the carrot provided by the AO, its own productions failed to compete at the box office. *Faust*, in fact, was bad enough to fail in a theatre of any size.

Costs rose higher. Deficits mounted. 1980 — in spite of Sutherland, Carden and Elkins in the company sharing the season — was little better. Three Queensland Opera Company productions, *Hänsel and Gretel*, *Lucia di Lammermoor* and *Don Giovanni*, tried to fill Her Majesty's and Stravinsky's *Rake's Progress* stayed in the minor hall. The fact that a local talent like Phyllis Ball shone in *Lucia* meant little, for she and her colleagues had been seen too often by then; companies with limited seasons must cater for cast changes, an impossible goal in Queensland because few good singers were prepared to work in the bush for peanuts with only an operatic backwater like Brisbane as the icing for the cake. The absence of native-born guest stars like Donald Smith or Margreta Elkins from the Queensland Opera Company's seasons says a lot about the company's policies during what should have been formative and not degenerative years.

By then the Queensland Government, which has never been exactly generous with its grants to opera, became restless at the lack of progress. The company's roster of full-time singers in 1980 — after twelve years of existence — was four! Schools and country tours were restricted. The Brisbane season returned to the SGIO Theatre with the brilliant idea of trying to imitate the Australian Opera's *visual* rather than vocal standards; Donizetti's *Mary Stuart* featured the most expensive costumes ever seen in Brisbane. It also had first-class local artists like Phyllis Ball and Margaret Russell backed by visiting tenor Henry Howell. The designs of Michael Bridges were a sensation and much was made of the 28 000 autumn leaves which were hand-glued together for one scene. The total cost of the production was $110 000, but audiences did not even manage to fill the 600 seats of the theatre! Old-timers *Martha* (shades of *Maritana*) and *Don Pasquale* were no more successful financially, and artistically well behind *Mary Stuart*. Long before the end of the 1980 season the company should have seen the writing on the wall. It should not have been surprised, as indeed it was, when it was given forty-eight hours notice to close down. The locks on the doors were changed on 12 December 1980.

It was not the end of opera in Brisbane. Australians are inclined to look down on Queenslanders in two areas, the arts and government. Yet the Government of Queensland took an initative in the esoteric field of opera which was more practical than any made in artistically more-experienced states: at first it agitated, then pleaded and finally ordered two independent companies to overcome mutual distrust and antagonism to join in one well-managed whole. And it worked!

The history of the Queensland Opera Company has been chronicled in detail. That of the Queensland Light Opera Company is told more quickly. It was founded by a singer, David Macfarlane, in 1962, at first to stage amateur productions of Gilbert and Sullivan and later musical comedies and operettas. It was immensely successful, regularly filling Her Majesty's Theatre in Brisbane, coincidentally preventing the QOC from hiring the theatre in which the latter should have built its reputation. Not that Macfarlane used unethical methods or tried to undermine the more serious professional company. There was no conflict of interest between the two groups, one was a professional opera company and the other a group of amateurs filling the hole left by the demise of J. C. Williamson's and their once-regular ration of musicals. Brisbane wanted its light musical entertainment and the QLOC offered just that; the full houses at Her Majesty's proved it year after year.

In 1979 the proposal to join the two companies was first mooted, but no common ground for a merger could be found. At the same time, Macfarlane took a step which resulted in a short, unbloody opera war. The Queensland *Light* Opera Company decided to present a *serious* opera. In October 1980 it staged a full-scale production of *Samson and Delilah* with two major professional guest stars: Donald Smith and Margreta Elkins. The fact that it was a success is almost incidental; it was the timing which was so perfect. QOC had just burnt its last bridges in the financially disastrous 1980 season and here was this bunch of amateurs showing the government that there was a group in Brisbane which could produce better opera for less money than QOC. Renewed efforts to bring about amalgamation met no greater success than before. Only weeks after the success of *Samson* the doors closed on the Queensland Opera Company for ever.

No doubt the details of the following months will emerge in good time; at present it is difficult to see the wood for the operatic trees. Even those closest to the facts are reluctant to speak about them. Macfarlane left the Queensland Light Opera Company after *Samson and Delilah*, which he produced himself. The new Lyric Theatre in the Brisbane Cultural Centre was nearing completion and the government was determined to have an opera company in it. To cut a long story short: Macfarlane has had a say in the management of the Lyric Opera of Queensland since its first season in 1982. He has had a series of titles as varied as any ever invented by the Elizabethan Theatre Trust, but at no stage has he been called 'general manager' and he makes no claim to being its leading force. In line with Australian traditions, one general manager, imported from the English provinces via Hong Kong, departed within a year. Another from North America spoke out loudly, but left very quietly. Macfarlane continues to 'motivate' in all directions. Most important of all, in the six years of its existence – the last three in the new Lyric Theatre — the company has hardly put a foot wrong.

The company Macfarlane had left, the Queensland Light Opera Company, closed after his departure. Most of its best singers found (paid) work and a lot more glory in the new Lyric Opera. But its place was taken shortly afterwards by the Brisbane Light Opera Company, which acquired not only all the QLOC's old costumes and scenery, but also a good, but inadequate, building worth some $130 000. (This from the 'lesser' company of the two!) By 1987 it owned much better premises,

bought for a quarter of a million dollars with the help of the government and continued the previous group's work in the amateur field, giving the alternative audience the lighter music it cannot obtain from the Lyric Opera of Queensland. What will happen after the latter company's big, commercial, American-style *Student Prince* in the Lyric Theatre in 1987 remains to be seen, but one such production a year will hardly fill the current demand for light-music theatre fare in Brisbane.

LOQ's early seasons, starting in 1982, have been uneventfully successful, which is perhaps a strange way to praise sound productions with good casts which attract big audiences. Listing them in detail here would be pointless. The first two years were used to establish a public demand for opera which was to be channelled into the huge Lyric Theatre when it opened in 1985. 1984 was a year of consolidation as preparation for the big event, and it did indeed prove to be big in every way.

The Lyric Opera of Queensland took an enormous risk in opening the new theatre with an *Aida* bigger and better than any staged by the Australian Opera, and that includes the one staged in the Sydney Opera House's

Brisbane's excellent farewell to an old venue. The new Lyric Opera of Queensland started life by staging a last opera at the small SGIO Theatre. Anthony Besch's *Così fan tutte* production was borrowed from Adelaide, but the casting showed the strength to come. (Maldwyn Davies, imported from Wales, as Ferrando and Garrick Jones as Guglielmo.)

The biggest *Aida* from the youngest company.
The Lyric Opera of Queensland asserted its artistic status by creating the most impressive *Aida* seen in Australia to date as the opening attraction of Brisbane's new Lyric Theatre in 1985, though the company had only staged its first production three years earlier!

Queenslanders can hold their own.
Though opera in the Deep North has always languished, fine voices galore have never been in short supply. Donald Smith, Margreta Elkins, Donald Shanks and the like have made careers elsewhere. Now that they have a magnificent opera theatre, they and their successors can sing at home at last.
(Margreta Elkins in *Il trovatore*.)

Concert Hall. The date was 8 August 1985, and the event was remarkable in that all the principals and production staff were Australian residents available to any company in any state. The exception, conductor Thomas Schuback from Sweden, had previously been in charge of four LOQ productions and was, presumably, a potential migrant. Horst Hoffmann (Radames) and Arend Baumann (King of Egypt) were German-born. Noël Mangin (Ramphis) was a New Zealander — therefore Australasian. The rest of the cast were native Australians: Marilyn Richardson (Aida), Margreta Elkins (Amneris) and Malcolm Donnelly (Amonasro). None can be said to have outshone the other. The extensive experience of designer James Ridewood and director John Milson, some of it with QOC, proved their talents in the enormity of the venue in which they were working for the first time. The whole thing was probably a greater achievement, more difficult for being such a familiar work, than the incredible *War and Peace* which opened the Sydney Opera House.

The LOQ from the start set itself standards which make it one of the most remarkable companies in the opera history of Australia. The standard of casting and production has been close to ideal, keeping in mind that no attempt is made to keep a year-round core of salaried artists. Practically every major singer in Australia has appeared with the company and the management has not hesitated to import singers when none of a sufficiently high standard can be found locally. All have been good, or better than good. To date there have been no complaints about imported singers who are inferior to locals out of work or available, a common charge made against even the Australian Opera. Considering the lack of historical background, having sprung, so to speak, from nowhere to the top of the tree, Lyric Opera is a phenomenon, the only risk being that of complacency on the part of management or funding bodies. The danger of a hefty clanger or the in-fighting common to opera world-wide grows greater with every new season. May it never come.

If you could compare population sizes between, say, some of the smaller German towns and some Australian states, there would seem to be no earthly reason why Western Australia should not have a flourishing opera company; more people live in Perth than in Bielefeld, Freiburg and Aachen combined, yet each of the latter and any number of even smaller German towns have their own opera companies, while the capital of Western Australia only has one. I could write at length why the traditions of centuries ensure audiences in those German cities and that their proximity to other operatic centres makes casting easier. There is also the small matter of government funding which in Germany takes care of anything up to 85 per cent of all costs, while Perth is lucky if it reaches 50 per cent in some years.

Bielefeld, Freiburg and Aachen had seen a lot more than an occasional opera in 1829, the year in which the first white people settled by the Swan River. It is impossible to establish what amateur performances may have taken place in Western Australia during the nineteenth century but a Williamson touring company visited there in 1903. The only thing remotely notable in the context of this book is the fact that what was probably the only opera-cum-operetta ever written by the governor of an Australian state originated in Perth. In January 1894 Sir William Cleaver Francis Robinson, a prolific composer with many published works to his credit, wrote the music for *The Handsome Ransom, or The Brigand's Bride*, which was first performed at Government House in Perth, then in a public hall and later that year in Melbourne at the Princess Theatre, where the management of J. C. Williamson and George Musgrove quite falsely advertised it as 'the occasion being the first time an opera will have been introduced to the world through its first production in Australia'. The Brigand's Bride herself was Australia's biggest box office star of the day, Nellie Stewart.

The sole glory of Western Australia's operatic history took place in Melbourne, and so it was to remain for far too long. As late as 1969 Australia greeted with acclaim the startlingly successful debut of Glenys Fowles in the Australian Opera's *A Masked Ball*; at that time nobody believed that the new Western Australian Opera Company could last and her earlier Micaëla in their first production, *Carmen* in 1968, hardly counted. Bruce Martin, Mephisto in *Faust*, the other production of that year, had to wait another ten years before emerging as a major artist in the eastern states.

Whatever the failures of the sporadic attempts to start theatrical singing in the West, clearly Australia's production of fine voices was not related to the population of the various capital cities! Still, however good the voices, the same lack of managerial skills which held back the progress of even amateur opera elsewhere had been equally prominent in Perth in the 1940s and 1950s. Productions like Hans Briner's *Fledermaus* in 1949 actually imported the young Ronald Dowd to sing Eisenstein, but it was an amateur production, an amateurish production, if you like. And the founding of the Western Australian Opera on a professional basis in 1967 followed the pattern of the early Elizabethan Trust Opera in miniature form, and if the WAOC today is limited—more in size than in quality—compared with other modern Australian companies, the relatively small public of a city like Perth and the minimal funding of the state government are more likely to be the cause. Leadership has been continuous and practical, within the limitations of a city whose location from the nearest minor, let alone major opera centre is probably greater than that of any similar company in the world, except perhaps that of Cape Town in South Africa.

The only still-unsolved mystery about opera in Perth is the absence of major private sponsorship from the many billionaires resident in it. They are not very secretive about their sponsorships of sporting events and it seems unlikely that they are hiding behind obscure company names. The Western Australian Opera Company should by rights be the richest in the country. That it should be the poorest reflects heavily on the many whose names I dare not mention. Money may be the root of all evil; it is also the root of all opera.

The trials and tribulations of the company over the years has been paralleled by many companies worldwide. Credit must be given to the four practical people who started it on its way in 1968. James Penberthy was and is a composer, Giuseppe Bertinazzo and Alan Pearson were singers, Earl Nowotny a chorus master. Admirable though it is that all the founders were practising participants in the new art they were promoting, the absence of a sound management structure brought almost immediate trouble. The demand for opera was undoubtedly there, but ten performances of *Carmen* before audiences totalling 15 000 are pretty useless if the end result is a king-sized deficit. *Amahl And the Night Visitors* was the second opera. Verdon Williams conducted and again little fault was found by audiences not only in Perth, but when *Carmen* was taken on a country tour.

The 1969 season — built on the high hopes of the first successes — was, almost inevitably, over-ambitious. *Faust* and *Bohème* played back-to-back were fool-proof box office, as *Carmen* had been. But now most of the main rôles were taken by guest artists imported at considerable cost and the losses mounted alarmingly. Penberthy resigned as director of the company amid public outcries and predicted (wrongly) the end of the great experiment. Artists who mattered (like Williams, Fowles and Martin) had long retired before the onslaught of supposedly better imports. The free-wheeling honorary executive was decimated, a board of governors and an executive under the chairmanship of Vincent Warrener was appointed, bank loans were obtained and Georg Tintner became the musical director. What was still

missing was a general manager. His job was done by the honorary chairman for fully seven years, at which point, in 1976, he was 'demoted' to the fully, if lowly-paid position he had been doing for nothing; Chairman Warrener became General Manager Warrener, a title he holds to this day.

Warrener had held a major position in industry before devoting himself full-time to the WAOC and, starting in 1970, was a member of the Australian Opera's board of directors. He had the know-how and access to much that his predecessors did not. Tintner's abilities as a conductor, whatever his personal eccentricities, have never been in doubt. His first venture, *Traviata* in 1970, was a run-away success, as was the next year's *Fledermaus*. What should have warned Warrener of treacherous waters in Western Australia was the utter failure of the first joint production with the Australian Opera, using its most spectacular production at the time, Verdi's *A Masked Ball*. This was 'esoteric' stuff for audiences weaned on *Carmen* and *Traviata*. Back came *Madame Butterfly*, *The Barber of Seville* and even *The Gypsy Baron* in 1972, soon followed by *The Merry Widow*, what else?

The most ironical twist for a company which, due to the most minimal of funding, desperately needed box-office returns to stay alive, came in the following year. The two productions staged were a sure-fire pot-boiler, Verdi's *Trovatore*, backed by a revival of *Die Fledermaus*. The key words were 'backed by'. In 1974 the company returned to playing operas simultaneously, alternating nightly, instead of separating productions by several months. *Trovatore* with a local cast (even the tenor, Dennis Kestel, was a Perth boy, though he was brought back from overseas) was a hit all right, but the public was not ready for two operas in one week. Anyway, in a small town people have long memories and to revive even a popular work like *Die Fledermaus* after only three years was too soon. (Today the company provides gaps of seven years between revivals.)

Those were years with downs as well as ups in the administration, on stage and backstage as well. During the 1974 *Trovatore* a singer, who shall be nameless, was kidnapped by a jealous husband, putting the opening night in doubt. Fortunately, she was rescued in good time — there was no understudy. When the company staged *The Medium* in 1976, some of the singers became 'psychic' and began to believe in Menotti's spirits; one of them later committed suicide! It would, however, be stretching the imagination to associate this with the troubles which rose all around, like Menotti's spectres. Financial in-spectres should have been called in after a production of *Così fan tutte* set in the 1920s and the failure of an *Orpheus in the Underworld* staged in the large Concert Hall to raise the number of tickets available for sale. All that it raised was the deficit.

The result was an 'open revolt', a term which appears in the company's own twentieth anniversary booklet. I have been unable to discover the meaning of that provocative phrase. As for its causes, Warrener himself partly puts them down to the exclusion of local singers, though without statistical support. Factually, 1976 ended with an eight-year-old company which had never had a proper management structure, yet employed a full-time stage manager and four singers. (Which was more than made up the Victoria State Opera's full roster of singers about that time!)

Like all similar organizations, the company has members ($20 per annum) who elect the managing committee, board of directors or whatever you may like to call it. It is, oddly enough, not restricted to subscribers and the members number about 500. In 1976 only the twenty-five or so present had a vote at the 'revolting' annual general meeting. Today they vote by mail and a remarkably high percentage actively guide the company, if at a distance. Whatever happened in 1976, the internal politics (or revolt) resulted in the company's present structure which has served it well enough now for more than a decade.

The last of the Western Australian Opera Company's founders, Giuseppe Bertinazzo, was elected a member of the new board of directors in 1976 and its new chairman, Anthony van Toll, still heads the board to this day, while Vincent Warrener remains as full-time general manager; having relinquished altogether the hard paths of industry high finance. The challenge of running the low finances of an opera company must have given him more pleasure (perhaps mixed with a degree of masochism) because much has been achieved, some of permanent benefit such as the acquisition of the beautifully-restored His Majesty's Theatre as a headquarters, some ephemeral, like the money-making stagings of *The Mikado* and *The Gondoliers* with top stars like Dennis Olsen, June Bronhill and Thomas Edmunds in the huge Perth Entertainment Centre in 1977 and 1978. One of the *The Mikado* performances provided a half-hour of non-Gilbertian humour after a ten metre steel pipe crashed from the flies and stopped the performance. Bronhill and Edmunds ad-libbed a variety double-act in front of the drop curtain, while emergency repairs took place. It is recorded that only 0.001 per cent of the audience precisely (three people) preferred the bar to the entertainment, for which no extra charge was levied. (The drinks were *not* free!)

In the meantime, like Mohammed, Perth could not be expected to go to the mountain of festivals which were erupting all over Australia. So, in 1953, Perth brought its own mountain to Mohammed and started the Perth Festival. No festival is complete without at least one opera and, for once, the box office was not the primary concern. 1973's Festival of Perth saw the production of Britten's *Albert Herring*, which was so successful that parts of Mohammed finished up at the mountain in the end; *Albert* was lent to Adelaide, and Sydney as well! The lesson was not too well learnt, for it was not Britten but Albert who was the success; in 1978 another Perth Festival saw an outstanding *Rape of Lucretia* play to empty houses. Only a year later Britten was featured again, this time at second-hand, so to speak, when his version of *The Beggar's Opera* was staged in Perth and also toured the state.

The re-opening of the refurbished His Majesty's Theatre in 1980 (with the ever-popular *Traviata*) finally stabilized the company and set it on its present course as a fine regional company which does more than just give preference to Australian singers; it actively programmes its schedule to build a following for new stars of its own making, most recently Deborah Riedel and Merlyn Quaife. It uses the local autonomous Western Australian Arts Orchestra, which produces remarkable results under the man who came to dinner with the *Traviata* that year, conductor Gerald Krug. He stayed for supper, and breakfast, and lunch and dinner again — in fact, Krug has been the company's artistic centre ever since. Perth has had a series of excellent musicians in charge, but none willing to stay eight years, like Krug.

The indestructible Bertinazzo proudly produced that 1980 *Traviata* — and *The Pearl Fishers* (1982), *Carmen* (1983) and *Madame Butterfly* (1987). The designer was Graham Maclean, probably the most consistently-employed opera designer in the country; he staged his twentieth opera in eleven years for WAOC in 1987, a perfect example of the company's policy of establishing

Modern productions in old theatre.
Perth's His Majesty's Theatre was restored and modernized for the Western Australian Opera in 1980. The result has been high-quality productions, though distance forbids the importation of many major artists. (Lyndon Terracini as Don Giovanni and Cliff Arndt as the Commendatore in 1983.)

The multi-purpose tenor.
Perth has its resident tenor who sings everything from Almaviva in *The Barber of Seville* to Edgardo in *Lucia di Lammermoor*. And when the opera does not have a tenor lead, he steps down to parts like Basilio in *The Marriage of Figaro* in 1984. (Irene Waugh as Cherubino and Roger Howell as Mozart's Count Almaviva.)

continuity in production and casting. It finds new talent, or talented artists (not only singers, but designers, producers, and so on) living in Perth or willing to go there regularly and take part in the three operas a year to which the WAOC season at present restricts itself. Certain singers became household words in Perth long before the rest of Australia accepted them for their true worth. Experience can only be gained through performing. Perth gave them the opportunity, at the inevitable risk of losing them in the end. Since 1981 a previous nonentity like Merlyn Quaife has sung Pamina, Gilda, Leila, Donna Elvira, Mozart's Countess, Lucia, Rosalinda and Gretel, all in Perth! Christa Leahmann has sung the four *Hoffmann* heroines, Mimì, the Queen of the Night, Senta, Donna Anna and Butterfly.

On the other hand, some singers who do not appear interested in singing away from home are kept in constant work — heir standard must be reasonably good, or audiences would have squawked by now. How many tenors have sung Nadir, Almaviva, Ottavio, Basilio, Edgardo, Camille, Ferrando and Alfred in *Die Fledermaus*, as Graham Macfarlane has done, in an Australian city with a population as small as Perth's? Guest singers vary from the young and once completely-unknown Amanda Thane, alternating with the experienced Margaret Haggart in *La Traviata*, to one of Australia's best sopranos, Marilyn Richardson, singing Alice to her husband, James Christianson as Falstaff. Among more recent singers who will be stars of the future — says he sticking his neck out a mile — Jolanta Nagajek sang Suzuki, Fenena and the Witch in *Hänsel and Gretel*, then made a long jump to her 1987 Carmens with the Australian Opera. And Deborah Riedel got her big chance in Perth as Mignon in the same year. What does the future hold for her?

These are but a few samples of the casting policies of Warrener and what can only be described as 'his' company. He travels all over Australia looking for the best *potential* talent; the best *experienced* talent is too busy or too expensive to go to what is almost a foreign country in the eyes of Sydney or Melbourne. Joan Carden, Anson Austin, Robert Gard, Margreta Elkins and other singers familiar to us have never been seen in Perth. In the three productions staged there in 1987, *Madame Butterfly*, *Mignon* and *Traviata* (six cities in Australia saw that shady lady that year; she is box office!) only one established 'star' artist was featured, Jennifer McGregor. Obviously youngsters feeling their way can not present themselves as well as singers with ten years' experience, but while they are well-chosen and well-trained by conductors as good as Gerald Krug, Perth audiences are getting good value for their money and there is little doubt about the local support which the company commands. The United States has literally hundreds of companies like this one — 772 in 1986, of which 170 are classed as major — and so has Germany. Opera is a medium for the ordinary man as much as the connoisseur. A smaller city must have a smaller opera company. Lower standards in some ways are not necessarily worse standards in others. I enjoy operas in Perth more than many a performance at some major opera houses. And it is worth the fare just to see His Majesty's Theatre!

'Our author likes the custom of a prologue to his story', sings Tonio before curtain-rise in *Pagliacci*, while *Mefistofele* ends with an epilogue. The composers of these two operas, Leoncavallo and Boito, had but one thing in common: they were among the few who wrote not only the music but also the words for their own operas. Anyone game enough to write an *opera senza musica*, opera without music, is surely entitled to the same privilege. I thus offer you this *Epilogue*, though you will not have to suffer the indignity of having to hear me sing. Lucky you.

My book is published in 1988, the year in which Australia celebrates its Bicentenary. The title is not strictly correct, for we have not had two hundred years of opera in this country; in 1788 there was not one house in Australia, let alone an opera house! Many years were to pass before this most complex medium grew in the early colony-turned-nation. Now it is fully grown in operatic parlance. The book proves that, I think. Let me end with a confession: I have written much that the average Australian would expect to read which is, if not false, certainly misleading — my *Third Interval*, the lengthy coverage of native operas and their composers, for example.

Once upon a time it was easy enough to listen to an opera or, even better, music without words and to say: 'Ah, French!' or Italian or German or Russian. And patriotic Australians would like to be able to say: 'Ah, Australian!' If my interval dissertation gave you hope in that direction, abandon all hope. There is no such thing as 'Australian music', let alone 'Australian opera', and there never will be. Civilization — read: modern communications, records, radio, television and the rest —

has seen to that. Italian, German, French or any other kind of music or art came into being because distance caused them to develop incestuously. A learnt from B because they both lived in the same city, and later C learnt from D because they lived in the same country. Today X learns from Y because they both live on the planet Earth. Everything ever written by A, B, C, D and all the others is there to be studied, explored and found to be either desirable or not by everybody else.

The time has long passed when any nation could proudly point to its own school of music, opera, painting, sculpture, architecture, even crime! Borders are political, not artistic, and countries like Germany, to give but one example, which have had centuries of clearly-defined traditions in so many different fields, are as creative as ever. The fact that an infamous 'Wall' severs East from West Germany has divided its people, but not its art. The operas being written every year on both sides of the Wall, no matter how original, can not be distinguished from each other. There is no school of West German opera or East German opera, nor can anyone tell the difference between either of the two German arts from the works being produced in Italy or America — or Australia.

Today you can only hear the influence of individual major composers. One might say: 'Brian Howard has been influenced by Penderecki'. (Has he? I am no musicologist.) Does that make his music Polish? There are moments in Richard Meale's *Voss* which are pure Puccini. Does that make his music Italian? There is a Felix Werder String Quartet which has more than a passing resemblance to Schoenberg. Well, Werder was born in Germany, but he composed that quartet in

The power of television. One telecast of an opera can attract a larger audience than all the performances given Australia-wide in several years. Millions tuned in to *The Merry Widow* with Sutherland in 1988 and even unfamiliar works have guaranteed audiences of hundreds of thousands. The ABC has perpetuated many of its opera telecasts on videotape, and audiences have been multiplied manifold by exposure to television opera. *(Photo: Barry Gaunt.)*

Australia. I am not casting stones at our own culture. The same applies in every country in the world. We will never again have art which is identifiably of one nationality. There are no German or Italian operas being written today, only operas as such. Period.

I can go further. Not very long ago you could identify styles of singing. Dietrich Fischer-Dieskau was a German baritone, even when he was singing Italian opera in the Italian language. French singers went out of fashion, because their voice production was based on the traditions of nineteenth century grand opera. Russian singers considered an excessive vibrato a virtue. Italian singers liked to sob. To this day the best quick reference book on opera is the *Concise Oxford Dictionary of Opera* and in it you will find tenors, sopranos, baritones and basses separated by nationality, giving specific rôles as examples of what kind of voice is being described. Without exception, they come from older operas which were written at a time when the music, as well as the voice, was identifiable as belonging to a specific nationality, or at least a region of Europe. (It is easy to forget that there were German singers long before a country called Germany became a political entity — in 1871!)

Today a soprano or tenor may be at his best in certain Italian or French rôles, but there is no relationship between their place of birth and the kind of music they sing. One of the great post-World War II phenomena has been the rise of English singers, once despised as feeble bleaters. The cast lists of the best European opera houses are full of English and American names. Yet there has never been an English way of singing or an American school of opera. And there never will be an Australian one of either. Thank God!

We are blessed in having developed an operatic tradition which has assimilated the best from all countries. Every Australian singer is an individual and (provided that the casting is right) they can sing anything as well as any singer of any other nationality. Here, as anywhere else, you may get Italian sung with a foreign accent, or a German opera with no single word comprehensible. But we have it made in singing, production, design and orchestral accompaniment. If we are (apparently) behind in composition, consider how many operas are written every year overseas and then divide the successes by the population of the countries from which their composers emerged. With access to the tuition of universities which have traditions older than our country, European opera composers do have a head start. But be sure of one thing: modern operas draw no bigger houses overseas than they do here!

Australia is part of the international opera circuit. Distance alone makes us lucky in that some magnificent singers (I mention no names to do no injustice through omission) prefer to live in this country, to have a normal home-life instead of joining the jet-set. Many have shown their worth in international opera houses before returning here. Familiarity is said to breed contempt and getting the same singers, no matter how good, again and again may lessen your enjoyment. Variety may be the spice of life, but distance and the cost of importing artists must take its toll. I remember an advertisement from my youth about getting the best milk from contented cows. For milk substitute opera, for cows substitute singers (of both sexes). We've never had it so good and when it comes to opera, our life *was* meant to be easy. If only the Australia Council would remember that!

My Epilogue started with *Pagliacci*, let it end with *Mefistofele*. In the Epilogue of Boito's opera, Faust is admitted to Heaven when he exclaims: 'Hold it. That's lovely!' It is an unspoken exclamation which must be heard in many opera performances in this country these days. Does that make Australia an operatic heaven? If not, it is at least a stairway to paradise.

PICTURE CREDITS

Thanks to the following for permission to reproduce illustrations. Every effort has been made to trace all copyright holders, however advice of any omissions would be appreciated.

Adelaide Festival Centre Trust: 96–7
Australian Broadcasting Corporation: 232
Australian National Memorial Theatre: 15 (top, centre and right), 20, 21, 22 (Left, third and fourth from left), 32, 35, 42–51, 53, 172
The Australian Opera: jacket, 5, 60–87, 98 (bottom), 103–55, 169, 171, 175, 177–83
Grainger Museum Board, University of Melbourne: 26
John Cargher: 31, 34, 59
Josephine Landsberg: 30
La Trobe Collection, State Library of Victoria: 15 (bottom right), 17, 25, 27, 33
Lyric Opera of Queensland: 223–5
National Library of Australia: 8, 11, 12, 15 (top left), 16, 36
New Idea: 94
Performing Arts Collection of South Australia: 15 (bottom centre), 29, 30, 27
Performing Arts Museum, Victorian Arts Centre: 22 (second from left), 36, 40, 166
Queensland Performing Arts Trust: 98 (top)
State Opera of South Australia: 170, 216–18
Sydney Opera House Trust: 89 (top)
Victorian State Opera: 173, 187–207
Victorian Arts Centre Trust: 89 (bottom), 95
Western Australian Opera Company: 230

INDEX

References marked * indicate fuller references, *italics* indicate illustrations.

Abbreviations:

(a)	Administrator/manager
(act)	Actor
(b)	Baritone
(bs)	Bass
(c)	Contralto
(chor)	Choreographer
(comp)	Composer
(cond)	Conductor
(dan)	Dancer
(des)	Designer
(lib)	Librettist/author
(p)	Producer/director
(pl)	Play, book, newspaper
(s)	Soprano
(t)	Tenor